How to interpret the Bible

a do-it-yourself manual

by DR BENNIE WOLVAARDT

carolroberts 990 yahoo.com
615-712-7232

Carol Roberts
1320 Edmonson Circle
Nashville TN 37211

How to interpret the Bible

a do-it-yourself manual

by DR BENNIE WOLVAARDT

With Contributions by

JULIA BEKKER
MARTIN ETTER
MOIRA WOLVAARDT

Published by Veritas College and The Good Book Company

How to interpret the Bible: a do-it-yourself manual

First print January 1999
Second print August 2000
Third print May 2002
Fourth print January 2005

Published by Veritas College
P.O.Box 100
Harpenden
Hertfordshire AL5 5EU
Great Britain

Visit our website at: http://www.veritascollege.com

and The Good Book Company
37 Elm Road, New Malden
Surrey KT3 3HB
Great Britain

ISBN: 1-873166-76-1

Design by: Peter Gerrish

Contents

Bible translation abbreviations

GNB	The Good News Bible (formerly Today's English Version)
JB	The Jerusalem Bible
KJV	The King James Version (also the Authorised Version)
LB	The Living Bible
NAB	The New American Bible
NASB	The New American Standard Bible
NEB	The New English Bible
NIV	The New International Version
RSV	The Revised Standard Version
NIVSB	The NIV Study Bible

Abbreviations of Bible books

OLD TESTAMENT

Genesis	Gen	2 Chronicles	2 Chr	Daniel	Dan
Exodus	Ex	Ezra	Ezra	Hosea	Hos
Leviticus	Lev	Nehemiah	Neh	Joel	Joel
Numbers	Num	Esther	Esth	Amos	Amos
Deuteronomy	Deut	Job	Job	Obadiah	Obad
Joshua	Josh	Psalms	Ps	Jonah	Jon
Judges	Judg	Proverbs	Prov	Micah	Mic
Ruth	Ruth	Ecclesiastes	Ecc	Nahum	Nah
1 Samuel	1 Sam	Song of Songs	Song	Habbakkuk	Hab
2 Samuel	2 Sam	Isaiah	Is	Zephaniah	Zeph
1 Kings	1 Kgs	Jeremiah	Jer	Haggai	Hag
2 Kings	2 Kgs	Lamentations	Lam	Zechariah	Zech
1 Chronicles	1 Chr	Ezekiel	Ezek	Malachi	Mal

NEW TESTAMENT

Matthew	Mt	Ephesians	Eph	Hebrews	Heb
Mark	Mk	Philippians	Phil	James	Jas
Luke	Lk	Colossians	Col	1 Peter	1 Pet
John	Jn	1 Thessalonians	1 Thes	2 Peter	2 Pet
Acts	Acts	2 Thessalonians	2 Thes	1 John	1 Jn
Romans	Rom	1 Timothy	1 Tim	2 John	2 Jn
1 Corinthians	1 Cor	2 Timothy	2 Tim	3 John	3 Jn
2 Corinthians	2 Cor	Titus	Tit	Jude	Jude
Galatians	Gal	Philemon	Phlm	Revelation	Rev

Editorial conventions

Quotation marks
A quote is indicated by single quotation marks, and reference to the meaning of a word with double quotation marks, eg 'table' meaning "a piece of furniture".

Masculine and feminine forms
The masculine form is used for the sake of linguistic convenience. This means that 'he' should be understood in line with semantic principles as "a person" and not as "a man", unless the context determines differently.

ABOUT THE AUTHORS

This information on the authors was updated at the time of the publishing of this fourth print in 2005.

Bennie Wolvaardt did his first degree in classics and then read theology in which he holds an academic doctorate. He led the founding of Veritas College International and is serving as its Director since its inception in 1992. This leadership responsibility requires him to travel extensively to promote the growth of the ministry that is already working in at least 30 countries. He is currently focussing on acquiring academic accreditation for the whole training network.
In his personal capacity he is developing creative Biblical software that serves to show the relationship between the Greek text of the New Testament and English. It also provides practical tools for interpreting the Bible. Although aimed at those who do not understand Greek, it can also be put to good use by Bible translators, Greek scholars and those whose Greek has become rusty. It contains special features for home groups. More information is available on www.ScriptureDirect.com

Moira Wolvaardt holds a degree in Speech Therapy and Audiology. She has a particular ministry in teaching others how to lead Bible studies and small groups. She works as the curriculum co-ordinator of Veritas College, and also helps with the development and translation of the Veritas training materials. She is also involved in counselling. She and Bennie have four grown sons who study or work in various parts of the world.

Julia Bekker holds a degree in Biblical Studies and Education as well as a doctorate in Education from the university of Oxford. She lives with her husband Alex Flegmann and their two daughters in Bedfordshire, England. Julia is involved with Bible training in local churches.

Martin Etter trained with YWAM and Wycliffe Bible translators. He has been involved with Veritas since its inception and played a major role in helping to lay the foundation of the college. He and his wife Julia and their three daughters are missionaries of the Swiss Mission Fellowship and have been living in Malawi, central Africa for the past six years. Martin has pioneered and set up Veritas College Malawi there and has been involved in training many pastors who in turn train other pastoral leaders. This work has also expanded to Zambia and Mozambique. Martin and Julia are also involved in development work in Malawi.

PREFACE

This book has grown out of a practical ministry of teaching people how to interpret the Bible. In 1987, after moving as a family from South Africa to England, I was frequently invited to lecture at missionary and discipleship training courses particularly in European countries.

This teaching ministry led to the development of a three-month full-time residential course in England with students coming from around the world. It was at that time that the authors of this book started to work together as lecturers. The needs around the world for practical skills in biblical interpretation became clearer as we also invited students from Eastern Europe after the fall of the Iron Curtain. Even pastors left their churches and families to come for training. How could we help to meet these needs?

Wrestling with this question led to the closing down of the full-time residential training and the establishment of Veritas College. Veritas is a specialist organisation that assists churches around the world to train their own leaders. The training is based on a philosophy known as Integrated Leadership Development (ILD). ILD means that training should be integrated into the life and ministry of the church. Its purpose is to train an integrated person in skills, knowledge and character - using an integrated curriculum. More information on the work of Veritas College can be obtained from the college itself. Details, including our website address, are provided on the fourth page of this book.

This book is the fruit of many years labour in the field of Bible interpretation. Its heartbeat is the equipping of the church with practical Bible-handling skills. It has been field tested internationally with exciting results, and it forms the backbone of the Veritas curriculum.

I want to thank so many people for their input into the content and presentation of this book over so many years. Students helped to shape the teaching into a more user friendly format. Colleagues at the time of the residential training helped to think through issues. So many dear brothers and sisters in Africa, Asia, the Middle East as well as Western and Eastern Europe helped to shape the content and encouraged the publication of this book.

I am grateful to those who were willing to lend their names to recommend this book.

I want to thank the co-authors for the stimulating discussions and of course, for researching and writing their chapters. A big thank you for your friendship over many years.

Thank you to Ralf and Sonja Richter for their helpful research on wisdom literature.

A special word of thanks to my wife Moira for helping me with the overall editorial work of the book. Long hours went into editing the content, presentation and language.

The final development and publication of this book cannot be separated from the international work and ministry of Veritas College. I am greatly indebted to the board, staff, partners, friends and donors who are making the ministry of Veritas College and this publication possible.

I will always be grateful to my dear friend Johannes Louw. He has had a profound influence on my thinking and as far as this book is concerned, he has given invaluable advice.

It was a pleasure to work with Tim Thornborough of The Good Book Company as well as with Martin Cole who did the copy editing.

It is the prayer of the authors that this book will be a blessing to many.

Bennie Wolvaardt
January 1999

What's in this manual?

Objectives

1. To become familiar with the content of the book
2. To understand how the book will benefit you
3. To know how to get the most out of the book

Contents

STUDY TIP
It is important not to skip this introduction as it will help you get to grips with the material in the book.

For church members!

Many people think that there are two classes of Christian. The perception is that those who studied at a theological seminary or college are able to interpret the Bible 'properly' while the other church members will never be able to do so. The result is that many committed and active Christians go through life believing that they will always lack the ability to find out for themselves what exactly the Bible teaches. Thus the Bible continues largely to be a closed book and the average Christian has to depend on the teachings of others.

The explicit purpose of this book is to help change this. It puts forward an approach and method that can make it possible for every believer to interpret the Bible in detail and with confidence. It aims at equipping the broad spectrum of church members, including Bible-study leaders, small-group leaders, youth workers, Sunday school teachers, lay preachers, church workers, students, pastors and missionary workers.

We have written to benefit individuals in different ways. The book takes into consideration that Christians will grow throughout their lives in their ability to interpret the Scriptures and that readers will be at different levels. It therefore provides a framework for understanding, and skills for biblical interpretation that will help each reader to develop according to their own starting level. Even those who do interpretation in the original languages will benefit because the principles explained in this book could be applied to any language, including Greek and Hebrew. Also it may be useful for those who know the original languages but have to rely on a translation for their preparation because of the demands of a busy schedule.

What about the original languages?

The basic rationale behind the approach followed in this book is that a good understanding of interpretation and a good methodology can equip you for proper interpretation of a Bible translation - even better than a bad methodology applied to the original Hebrew or Greek text of the Bible! One cannot deny the value of knowing the original languages, but this knowledge is useless without understanding interpretation.

Some of the readers will know Greek and Hebrew. Others will never study the original languages. Some readers may in future decide to study one or both of the original languages. Whatever your situation, we trust that you will benefit from this book by having obtained a better understanding and methodology of Bible interpretation.

However, the results arrived at with a sound methodology applied to a translation, will in most cases produce more than adequate results for use in Christian ministry. The authors trust that the content of this book will not only show the vast possibilities of a sound methodology applied to a translation, but also show its limitations and how to draw from the knowledge of other people.

When drawing from others, one should know how to evaluate the findings of those who appeal to the original languages for their interpretations. In too many cases listeners are wrongly forced to accept an interpretation because 'the Greek means ...'. The content of this manual should at least equip you to evaluate in most cases whether it is likely that the Greek influences the meaning as a speaker may want to indicate.

The role of linguistics

In developing the approach followed in this book, extensive use is made of the insights gained from the field of linguistics during the past few decades. This makes for a method of interpretation where the context of the passage is carefully taken into consideration and the text is analysed step by step according to the principles of what is known as 'semantic discourse analysis'.

Individual and group study

This book could be used by a person studying on his own. It could also be used by a group where the individuals work through the book on their own and then meet together to discuss the content.

If a lecturer guides a class or group through the book, the students or members should first prepare at home and then discuss the content in the group. At this stage the exercises could be attempted or they could be given as home assignments together with the next passage to be read. Alternatively the lecturer could first give an overview of the content and then let the group members work through the section of the book themselves while completing the exercises.

Style of presentation

This book has been written as simply and clearly as possible. This is to make it easier for those who do not have English as their first language. Technical terms are avoided as far as possible and where used, they are first explained. For the sake of clarity extensive use of diagrams has been made.

The following headings can be found in each chapter:

Objectives

A brief summary of the objectives indicates what you should know and be able to do by the end of the chapter. Check that you have met all the objectives before you continue with the next chapter. Although the chapter contents at the beginning of the book may appear to be very straight forward, note that later chapters build on what has come before. So make certain that you do not rush through any of the chapters!

Contents

At the start of each chapter its contents are listed.

STUDY TIP
Practical tips are given that show how to approach the material. Sometimes they may even just be for encouragement! Study tips may appear anywhere in a chapter.

Exercises

These will help you in understanding and applying what you've read. After completing the exercises at the end of each chapter, you can assess yourself by checking the answers against the contents of the chapter. Where the answers are not contained in the chapter, suggested answers can be found in an appendix at the end of the book.

Overview of the contents

Part one explains the theory and purpose behind the compilation of the Bible. It also explains the processes of biblical interpretation (exegesis, hermeneutics, homiletics) and some related key issues.

Part two deals with the relationship between form and meaning and its applications for exegesis. The linguistic insights and methods explained here will be used extensively in the steps of exegesis.

Part three explains and illustrates a step by step exegesis of the literature type used in Paul's letters (exposition/exhortation).

Part four shows how to apply the steps of exegesis to the poetry found in the Bible.

Part five shows how to apply the steps of exegesis to the narrative material found in the Bible.

Part six contains a number of chapters on the specific exegesis and hermeneutics of different types of Bible books, eg the Pentateuch, Psalms, Revelation, etc.

Although the process of communication or homiletics (preaching) is explained in relationship to biblical interpretation in part one, it is not explored further, as it is considered outside the scope of this work.

What you will need

Interpretation is carried out using the NIV translation of the Bible. In addition, the Good News translation is recommended.

Required time commitment

As a general rule, the more time you invest, the more you will grow in biblical interpretation. As a guide, you should have a sufficient grasp of the chapter if you are able to complete the exercises successfully.

STUDY TIP

Always remember that your ability to interpret the Bible will grow over a period of time. Never feel discouraged if you think you are not as good as someone else.

---

part one

GOD'S COMMUNICATION THROUGH THE BIBLE

CHAPTER ONE

God wants to communicate with us

Objectives

1. To understand how and why the Bible came into being
2. To understand that God's message became clearer throughout history and that Christ is the centre of it
3. To understand the authority of the biblical message

Contents

STUDY TIP

If you understand the diagrams, you understand the contents of the whole chapter. You may like to draw the diagrams for yourself as they are explained.

The Bible came into being as a result of God's desire to communicate with human beings.

After God had created the world, he communicated with Adam and Eve:
God blessed them (Gen 1:28),
gave them their calling (Gen 1:28)
and allocated to them their sphere of authority (Gen 1:29-30).

God also communicated his command to them:

> And the LORD God commanded the man, "You are free to eat from any tree in the garden; but you must not eat from the tree of the knowledge of good and evil, for when you eat of it you will surely die." (Gen 2:16-17).

Satan challenged this by distorting what was communicated:

> He said to the woman, "Did God really say, 'You must not eat from any tree in the garden'?" (Gen 3:1).

When the woman corrected this distortion of God's words, Satan challenged its truth:

> "You will surely not die," the serpent said to the woman. "For God knows that when you eat of it your eyes will be opened, and you will be like God, knowing good and evil." (Gen 3:4-5).

Eve and also Adam chose to disobey God's command to them, but in spite of this rebellion against God, he still wanted to communicate with them in the Garden of Eden and called out to them when they were hiding:

"Where are you?" (Gen 3:9).

Even after his people had fallen into sin, God continued to communicate with them in order to heal the broken relationship. This communication addressed the people's circumstances and led to the Bible being written with Christ as the central message.

1.1 God communicated in specific circumstances

After human beings had fallen into sin, God continued his communication with them. Although never in a vacuum, it was always at a specific time to specific people with a specific message.

When Cain's offering to God was not acceptable, God spoke to him and tried to correct and warn him against the temptation of sin (Gen 4:6-7). After Cain had killed his brother, God spoke to him again with a very specific message, announcing his punishment (Gen 4 9-12).

Throughout the entire Old Testament, we find God communicating with his people

he commands;
he corrects;
he reveals more about himself and his promises;
he announces his blessing or judgment.

Each time, this communication takes place in particular circumstances to a specific person or group of people.

1.2 God's communication was written down

If God communicated with specific people in their actual circumstances, then why did he cause the communication to be written down? Was this not something merely between these individuals and God? We can illustrate this question by referring to an incident that took place after the Israelites had left Egypt, crossed the Red Sea, and were on their way to Canaan. When they came to a place with the name Rephidim, they quarrelled with Moses because they did not have any water to drink and tested the Lord by questioning whether he was with them or not. Moses appealed to God while his life was threatened and received instructions from God to strike a specific rock. When he did this, water came out of the rock. Moses called the place Massah (testing) and Meribah (quarrelling).

Why should this incident be recorded in Ex 17:1-7 to be read throughout history? The answer to this question can be found by looking at how it is used by authors in subsequent parts of the Bible. In Psalm 95:7-9 this incident at Meribah and Massah is used to warn the hearers not to harden their hearts. In 1 Cor 10:1-13 Paul refers to similar recorded incidents in the life of Israel and tells the receivers of his letter:

> These things happened to them as examples and were written down as warnings for us, on whom the fulfilment of the ages has come (1 Cor 10:11).

From these quotations we see that God wanted and caused some of his specific communication to be written down to serve as a message to his people later in history. Not only was the history of the people written down, but also the laws and decrees that God gave to them. Moses wrote them down and gave them to the priests to read to the Israelites at given times (Deut 31:9-13). It is also written of Joshua that he 'recorded these things in the Book of the Law of God.' (Josh 24:26).

God did not communicate in a vacuum but always to specific people in a specific context. The written communication was in their own language, using expressions known to them and written in a format acceptable to them. For example, God communicated with Abraham on a number of different occasions. This was recorded in the book of Genesis. Genesis was not written for Abraham, but primarily for a particular group of believers early in the history of Israel. For that reason it was written in a format acceptable to the people for whom it was originally meant. Obviously it was also meant for future generations, which is why the writer of the letter to the Hebrews could refer to Abraham as an example of someone who put his trust in God. But this does not change the fact that Genesis was written in the first place for believers in ancient Israel.

In some cases the written communication was even more specific. For example, we can think of some of the epistles, such as the one to Philemon. That was a very direct message for the receiver in his particular circumstances.

So, God's communication with specific people on specific occasions was recorded to serve as a message for all people afterwards.

1.3 God's message became clearer over time

As history continued, God communicated more with his people, and so more of these instances were recorded. This can be called 'progressive revelation'. Although, for example, Joshua was commanded by God to obey the Book of the Law (Josh 1:8), God also added to his written communication through Joshua. Even if Joshua was not the sole author of the book that bears his name (Josh 24:26), he was at least a major participant in the events that are recorded in it. Indeed we can say that from the beginning of Joshua's life to the end of it, there was growth in the knowledge of God and his ways with his people.

It is important to note that it is not growth in God's revelation in the sense of change from one message to another. But it is growth in the sense of a greater clarity and application of the content of God's message to his people and the world. This is progressive revelation.

We can graphically illustrate this progressive revelation as shown in figure 1.1. The bottom line of the figure expresses the time scale. The people are those for whom the book was originally intended. An ascending line above the word 'message' indicates that the message became clearer as time went on.

FIGURE 1.1

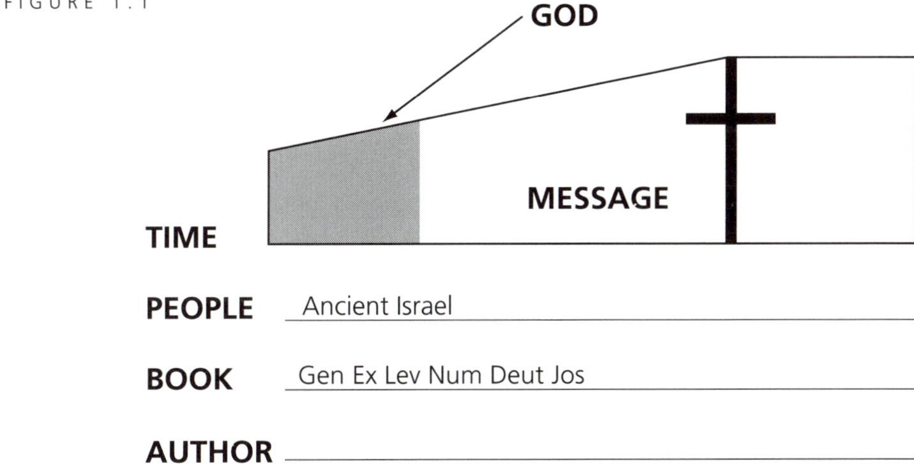

1.4 Christ is God's central message to the world

We have seen that God revealed more about himself as time went on. This does not mean that this revelation was just intended to grow and grow indefinitely, but that it was developing towards a climax to be reached in the future. This completion was already forecast in Gen 3:15:

> "...And I will put enmity between you and the woman, and between your offspring and hers; he will crush your head, and you will strike his heel."

In Heb 1:1-4 we read:

> In the past God spoke to our forefathers through the prophets at many times and in various ways, but in these last days he has spoken to us by his Son, whom he appointed heir of all things, and through whom he made the universe. The Son is the radiance of God's glory and the exact representation of his being, sustaining all things by his powerful word. After he had provided purification for sins, he sat down at the right hand of the Majesty in heaven. So he became as much superior to the angels as the name he has inherited is superior to theirs.

Figure 1.2 illustrates how Christ is the completion of God's revelation. It was a growing revelation until Christ came. Christ himself and what he did for the redemption of the world is the essence of God's communication with mankind:

> He is the image of the invisible God, the firstborn over all creation. (Col 1:15).

FIGURE 1.2

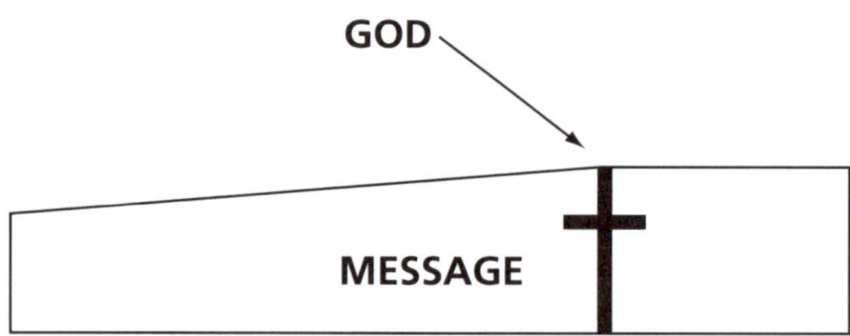

Because God communicated the essence of his message to mankind through and in his Son, Jesus Christ, there cannot be any growth in revelation after Christ. No more can be said than that which God has said through Jesus. It is true that it was necessary to have books written and included in the Bible after Christ's ascension. However these books, eg the epistles, were not written to reveal to us more than what had been revealed through the life, death, resurrection and ascension of Christ. The purpose of these books is to elaborate on the rich salvation that he achieved for us and to apply it to the life of the Christian and the church. This is illustrated in figure 1.2 where a horizontal line is drawn after the cross to show that there is no further growth in God's revelation.

1.5 God's message is consistent throughout history

Although there was growth in God's revelation of himself, it does not mean that there are inconsistencies in the message of the Bible. The centrality of Christ in God's revelation helps us to see the Old Testament in the perspective of the promises, necessity and expectation for the Messiah to come.

The New Testament is not a break with the message of the Old Testament, but rather the fulfilment of it:

> "Do not think that I have come to abolish the Law or the Prophets; I have not come to abolish them but to fulfil them. (Matt 5:17)."

Jesus refers here to the entire Old Testament and states that he came to give it its full meaning. He did this firstly by emphasising its deep underlying principles rather than the mere external knowledge and warped application by the Pharisees. Jesus illustrates this by referring to the seventh commandment:

> "You have heard that it was said, 'Do not commit adultery.' But I tell you that anyone who looks at a woman lustfully has already committed adultery with her in his heart..." (Mt 5:27-28).

Secondly, Jesus gave the Old Testament its full meaning by accomplishing all the conditions required for people's salvation, replacing the sacrifices and ritual laws of the Old Testament:

> In the same way, after the supper he took the cup, saying, "This cup is the new covenant in my blood, which is poured out for you." (Lk 22:20).

1.6 God's message carries authority

Why should the Bible be studied and obeyed? Do we not worship it by doing so? We can never study and obey the Bible enough, because it contains the message of the living God to mankind - a message of how the relationship between God and man can be restored with beneficial results for the whole of creation.

As far as God's message to people is concerned, he gave explicit commands as to the seriousness of complete commitment and obedience to it:

> Do not add to what I command you and do not subtract from it, but keep the commands of the LORD your God that I give you. (Deut 4:2).

In Prov 30:5-6 we find the following warning:

> "Every word of God is flawless; he is a shield to those who take refuge in him. Do not add to his words, or he will rebuke you and prove you a liar..."

The final word on the authority of God's message is given on the last page of the Bible:

> I warn everyone who hears the words of the prophecy of this book: If anyone adds anything to them, God will add to him the plagues described in this book. And if any one takes words away from this book of prophecy, God will take away from him his share in the tree of life and in the holy city, which are described in this book. (Rev 22:18-19).

The one who testifies to the truth of this message is Jesus himself, the one who is coming soon! (Rev 22:20).

Exercises

1. Draw a diagram to explain how the Bible came into being, showing that the message of the Bible grew in time and that Christ is the central message of it.
2. Why does the Bible have authority?

CHAPTER TWO

How God communicates through his Word today

Objectives

1. To understand why it is necessary to have three processes when interpreting the Bible
2. To be able to name and explain the three processes of interpretation
3. To be able to explain how the three processes relate to one another

Contents

STUDY TIP
If you understand the diagrams, you understand the contents of the chapter. You may draw the diagrams for yourself as they are explained.

We saw in the previous chapter that God communicated to particular people, at a particular time in history, using a particular person to write it down in a particular book of the Bible. We also saw that God wants to use this written communication as an authoritative message for people of all times. Which brings us to the question: How does God communicate through his Word today?

This question can be illustrated by the following scenario: You have been invited to speak to a youth group. In the invitation you are requested to 'bring a message from God's Word'. How should you go about it?

From the time you receive the invitation until you actually deliver the message, you will go through quite a few processes and steps - some of which are known by fairly impressive terms! Some would protest that we should not make handling the Bible too complicated. Was it not written in the first place to be understood by every Christian? This statement is certainly true but does not change the fact that everybody who uses the Bible is, knowingly or unknowingly, involved in the processes of interpretation.

2.1 The three processes of interpretation

Why does the Bible have to be interpreted? Can I not just take the passage from the Bible and read it to the youth group that I have been invited to speak to? The answer is simply that if the Bible was originally written directly addressed to them, that is, 'Paul's letter to the youth group in ...', it would have required little interpretation. As you read it to them, they understand it clearly themselves - did not the apostle Paul write it himself, in their own language, directly addressed to them and to their problems and circumstances?

The problem is that, as we observed in chapter one, such a letter or book in the Bible, directly addressed to people today, does not exist - only books and letters written many centuries ago, to and by people who lived in places and circumstances totally different from ours. For example Paul wrote his letters to specific churches located in specific towns where the members spoke a certain language and were at a certain level of spiritual growth. This is the Bible that you are going to use to bring a direct message to your youth group.

Although the different books of the Bible were originally written to communicate God's message to people very different from us, God wants to use that same message to speak to us today - to speak to 'your' youth group. The problem is that differences in culture, language, history and situation exist between the people to whom the selected passage of Scripture was originally addressed and your youth group (see figure 2.1).

FIGURE 2.1

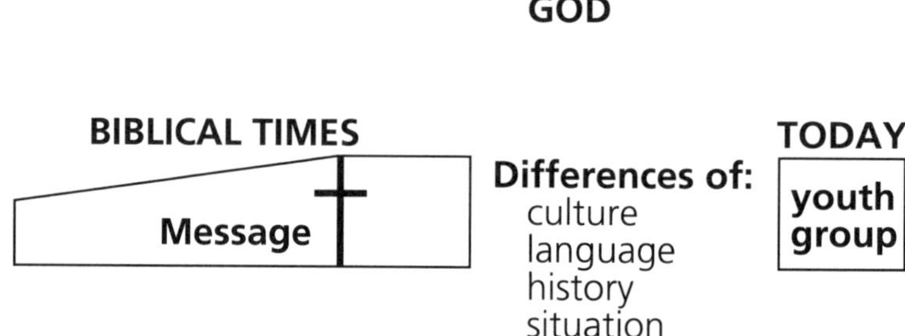

To let the Bible speak to your youth group today, you will need to bridge these differences between them and the original receivers of the Bible. To do this requires that we go through three main processes.

The fact that there are three processes involved in biblical interpretation, can be explained by looking at the nature of a passage of Scripture in relation to the whole message of the Bible. For example if you have decided to speak from Col 1:21-23 and want to know what God is saying in that passage, you make a 'cut' into God's message as illustrated in figure 2.2.

FIGURE 2.2

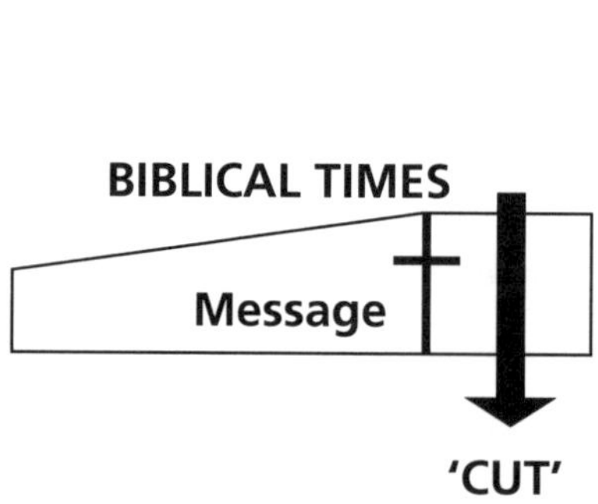

GOD

BIBLICAL TIMES

Message

'CUT'

Through a letter written by Paul at around AD60, God conveyed a particular message to a church in Colosse. The people who best understood the message of Colossians were the Christians in Colosse. If we are to understand the message to the Colossians it is necessary to place ourselves in their situation. It is like using a time machine to transfer ourselves to the situation of the original receivers of the message and to understand the 'cut' into the Bible as we should. We do this through a process called understanding or exegesis.

Once we know exactly what God communicated to the original receivers of the message, we can get back into our time machine and apply the message to ourselves and the people to whom we are ministering. You can thus move from the 'cut' in the Bible, over a period of almost twenty centuries, and apply the message to the youth group to whom you are going to speak. This process is known as application or hermeneutics. (The word hermeneutics is used by some in a broader sense to refer to the processes of both exegesis and hermeneutics.)

GOD

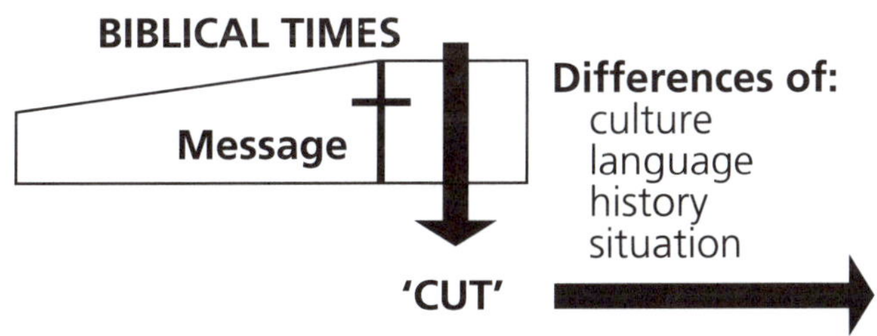

Once you have applied the message to a specific group of people, in this case your youth group, and know what it says to them, it is still necessary to communicate it to them. The process by which we communicate the applied message is called communication or homiletics in the case of preaching.

GOD

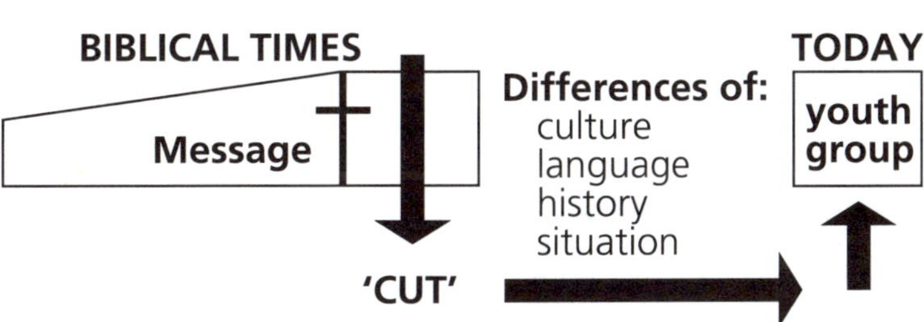

A detailed explanation of the processes of understanding, application and communication will follow under 2.2, 2.3 and 2.4. They will be illustrated by interpreting a passage. The relationship between the processes will be explained as well.

2.2 Exegesis: Understanding the message

Imagine, for a moment, a situation where you are approached with a question about the meaning of a biblical passage by a few of the new converts in a youth group. They show you Rom 16:16a: 'Greet one another with a holy kiss.' Then the question comes with all sincerity as to the reason why they do not greet one another with a kiss in the meetings of their youth group. How will you respond?

The person who would have understood this message best, is indeed the one who was a member of the church in Rome at the time that the letter was written. For us to be able to understand the passage, it is necessary to place ourselves, through exegesis, into the situation of such a church member.

To return to the question of the young converts - what did the average church member in Rome understand by the instruction that they should greet one another with a kiss? Paul gives this instruction in the context of the church in Rome, which was torn apart by tension between Gentile and Jewish believers. He wants them to greet with a kiss, not because he thought that was the 'biblical' way of greeting, but because in their culture it was a way to express love and appreciation to one another.

The end product of exegesis of Rom 16:16 is therefore that Paul instructs the church members in Rome to greet one another with a kiss so as to express their love and respect to one another.

The process of exegesis is illustrated in figure 2.3. One starts with a passage of Scripture and applies different steps to it in order to arrive at the message that the original receiver understood. The passage of Scripture is an expression of a message, consisting of words, sentences, paragraphs, etc - this is it's *form* ('form level' in figure 2.3). Through our exegesis we want to move beyond the form that we have in front of us and arrive at the meaning that was expressed by that specific form ('meaning level' in figure 2.3). This meaning is the one that the original receivers understood as the text was originally written for them.

FIGURE 2.3
Exegesis of Rom 16:16a

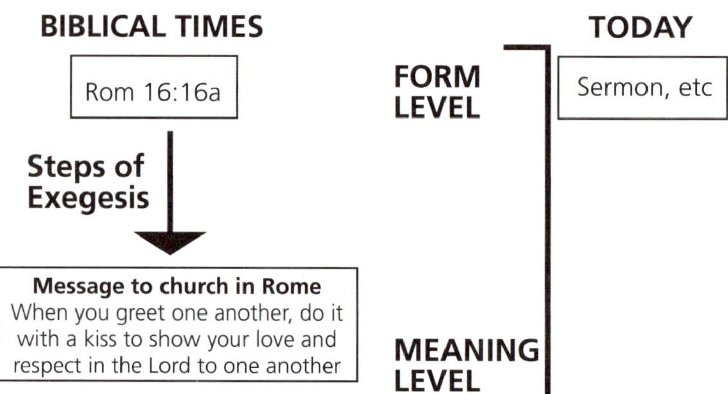

It is the task of exegesis not only to find out what a passage overtly said to the original receivers, but also what message it implicitly gives. In the case of Rom 16:16a it is necessary not only to know that the passage says they should greet one another with a kiss, but also what was expressed by that act.

Obviously there is always the risk of reading something into the text. For this reason you should make sure that exegesis is done properly. Build certain 'checks and balances' into the process. The different steps of exegesis will be explained in depth later.

2.3 Hermeneutics: Applying the message

Once you know, through your exegesis, what the meaning of Rom 16:16 was to the church member in Rome, you need to find out what its message is for the youth group to which the young converts belong. Through the process of application, or hermeneutics, you have to make the journey back through many centuries, and perhaps thousands of miles, to apply it as the message of God to a group of people today.

In hermeneutics the main question is, which part or parts of the message to the original receivers should be applied to people in our time? There are three possibilities:

1. Apply the whole message to our times.
2. Leave all of the message as only applicable to the people of biblical times.
3. Apply only some parts of the message to our times.

The whole passage has to be applied to our times when there is nothing in the message that was intended exclusively for the original receivers. This is especially true in the New Testament for many parts of Jesus' teaching and the epistles. For example, when Jesus answered the question of a Pharisee as to which is the greatest commandment, Jesus replied: ' " 'Love the Lord your God with all your heart and with all your soul and with all your mind.' This is the first and the greatest commandment. And the second is like it: 'Love your neighbour as yourself.' All the Law and the Prophets hang on these two commands." ' (Matt 22:37-39). Although this was the reply to the question from a specific person, it is still applicable to people of all times.

The whole message is only applicable to people of biblical times when it was intended as such, as in the case of very personal messages. For example when Paul wrote to Timothy (2 Tim 4:13) to bring his cloak with him when he comes to visit him, we cannot directly apply this to ourselves and go off to fetch Paul's cloak! This direct request was only for Timothy and is therefore 'relative', or non-applicable, to us. (Having said that, this does not mean that it has no value in the Bible. It serves as an example that even Paul had legitimate personal physical needs and that he had the freedom to ask a brother to help him.)

Only parts of the message are to be applied to our times when the other parts of the message were only applicable to people of that culture. Rom 16:16a is a good example of such a case. Christians from many cultures today will be very reluctant to apply that directly in their churches! What should the reason be for this?

If we look again at the end-product of our exegesis, we see that Paul instructs the Christians to greet one another in a particular way because a particular meaning is expressed by that form of greeting. In this case the form of greeting is applicable only to people of the culture of those times, while the meaning expressed by it is applicable to Christians of all times.

The first step of hermeneutics or application is to make a distinction between what was only applicable to the Romans and what is applicable to them and people of any time. We will call those parts of the message that were only applicable to the Romans, 'relatives' - they are relative as far as application is concerned because they do not apply to us today. We can indeed say that the form of greeting with a kiss is relative as far as its application to us today is concerned. Those parts of the message that were applicable not only to the original receivers, in this case the church members in Rome, but to people of any time, are called 'absolutes'.

Remember that you can only start with this after you have completed your exegesis. It is impossible to apply something from the past before I have discovered it there! The last step of exegesis will be the starting point of hermeneutics, as illustrated in figure 2.4.

FIGURE 2.4
First steps of hermeneutics of Rom 16:16a

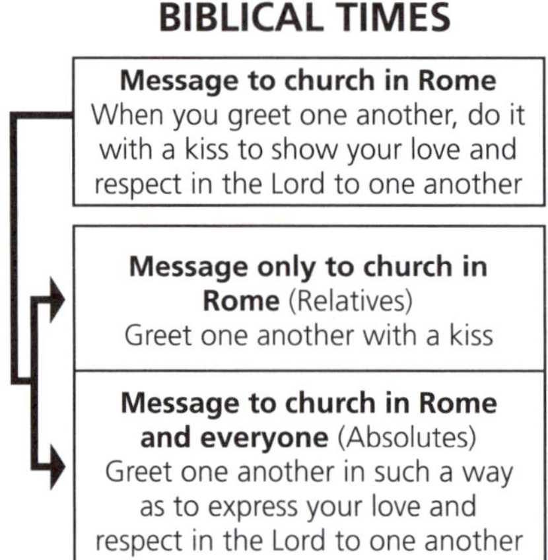

Distinguishing between the absolutes and relatives of a passage will at times require you to compare the message of the passage with other portions of Scripture. In the case of the mode of greeting, one could see whether any direct instructions like this are given in other places that could put it on the same level as an absolute. In this particular instance, the other places where we find this instruction do not add anything to our understanding.

It is important to see the 'cut' of the Bible with which one is working not only in the light of similar passages, but also in the light of the broader message of the rest of the Bible. Regarding the mode of greeting, it should be clear that an instruction that the form of kissing is an absolute for Christians of all times, does not fit into the general message of the Bible - the message of unmerited salvation and moral purity as the response to such a salvation. Obviously the better one's understanding of the broader message of the Bible, the easier it would be to make a distinction between absolutes and relatives.

At times you may find when starting with hermeneutics that the exegesis has not been done well enough. When this happens you will have to look at your exegesis again.

Only after the distinction between the relatives and absolutes has been made, can you continue with the process of hermeneutics. The next step of the process involves transfer of absolutes from the biblical time to our time. When we transfer the absolutes derived from a passage written by Paul, they will usually be exactly the same today as they were in biblical times (see figure 2.5). When absolutes derived from a passage from the Old Testament, are transferred, they will usually need to be seen in the light of the redemptive acts of Christ on the cross.

FIGURE 2.5
Further steps of hermeneutics of Rom 16:16a

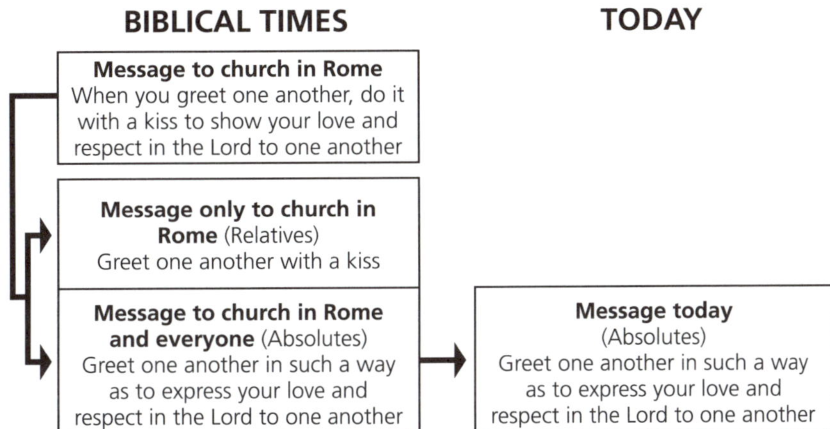

Once the absolutes have been transferred, you can apply them to the specific group that you are going to speak to (target group). In doing so you have to answer the following question: What does this absolute from the Bible say to the target group? The better you know the group, the easier it will be to apply the biblical absolutes.

The application of the absolute in our example may be that the Lord is saying to the members of your youth group that they should express their brotherly love in the Lord when they meet one another, and that they should do so by greeting one another with a friendly handshake! (see figure 2.6).

Obviously the manner of greeting will differ from culture to culture. In some cultures it will be appropriate for people from the same sex to kiss one another. In other cultures it may be appropriate for men to shake hands, women to kiss one another and also to kiss across the sexes. In some cultures it will be taboo for men and women to have any more physical contact with one another, when greeting, than shaking hands. The point is that the absolutes will be the same for all cultures, but the practical outworking (form) will differ according to the practices of the specific culture.

FIGURE 2.6
The steps of exegesis of Rom 16:16a

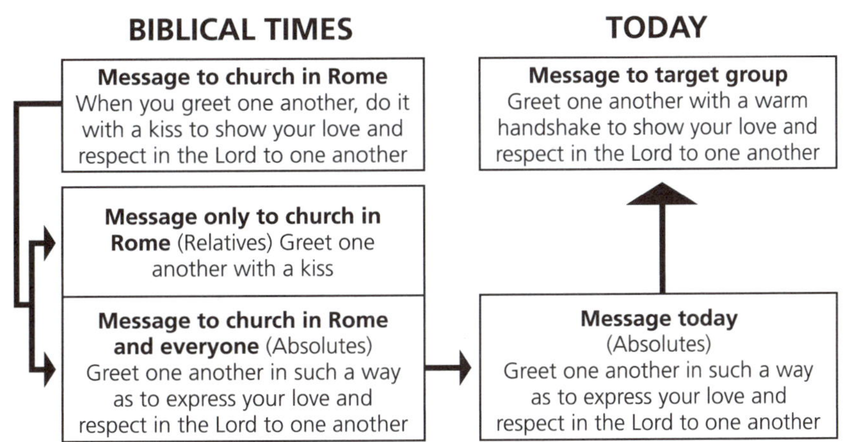

2.4 Homiletics: Communicating the message

Let us recap. You have been invited to speak to a youth group. During your preparation you first had to get into the time machine, called exegesis, transfer yourself into the situation of the original receivers of the message and 'dig in' until you found and formulated the message that those receivers understood. According to figure 2.3 you start with the visible passage of Scripture (form) and move 'down' to the level of meaning.

Starting with the second process (hermeneutics) you are still in the past. Then you first have to decide which parts of the message are only applicable to the original receivers and which parts are applicable to them and to all people. Once you have decided that, you can take a quick trip back to our time and apply the message to your target group. With that you have completed the process of application or hermeneutics and are 'back' in our time. The only problem is that you are still 'down' on the level of meaning, as you know what the message to your target group is, but have not yet expressed it in a communicable form.

The third and last process involves expressing the message in a 'sermon' and delivering it. 'Sermon' is put in inverted commas as it is not the only form that can be used to communicate the message. In addition to preaching one can also use drama, singing, writing, Bible studies, lecturing, teaching, discussion groups, etc to communicate the message arrived at through exegesis and hermeneutics. As hermeneutics starts with the end product of exegesis, so homiletics starts with the end product of hermeneutics (see figure 2.7).

FIGURE 2.7
The processes of biblical interpretation
Relationship between Exegesis, Hermeneutics and Homiletics

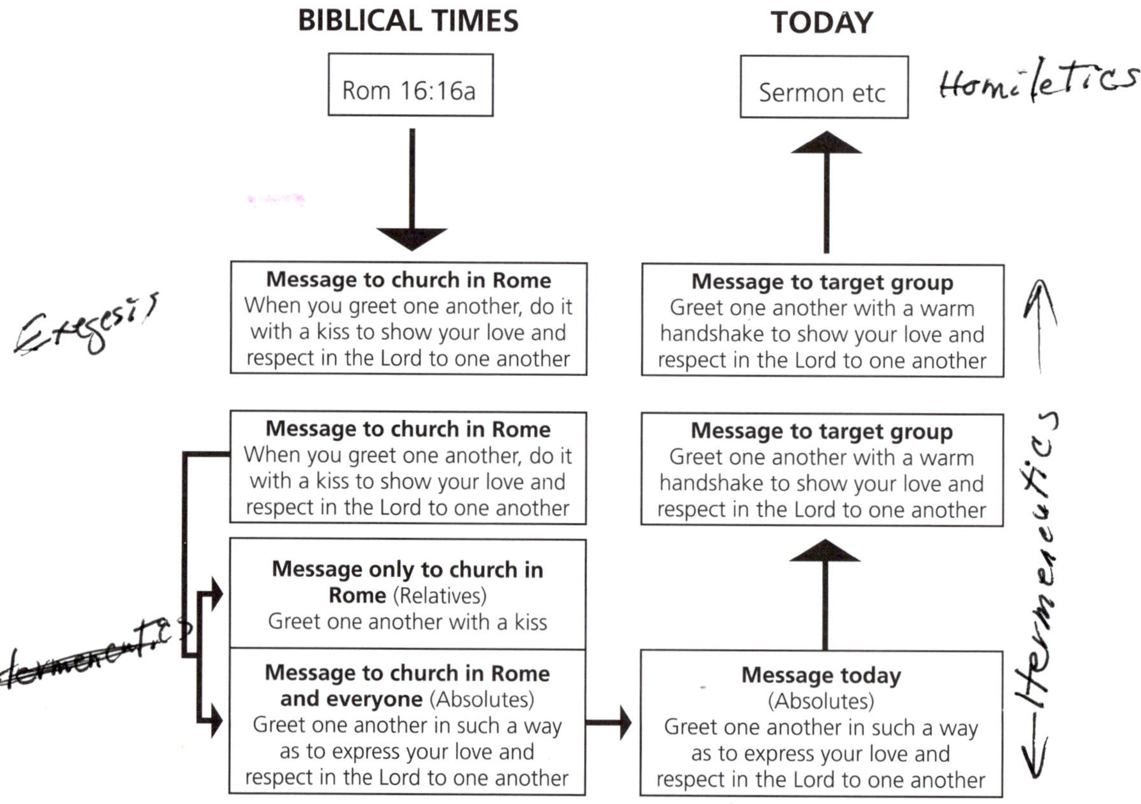

2.5 Overview of the relationship between the three processes

A graphical overview of the three processes is given in figure 2.8.

FIGURE 2.8
The processes of biblical interpretation
Relationship between Exegesis, Hermeneutics and Homiletics

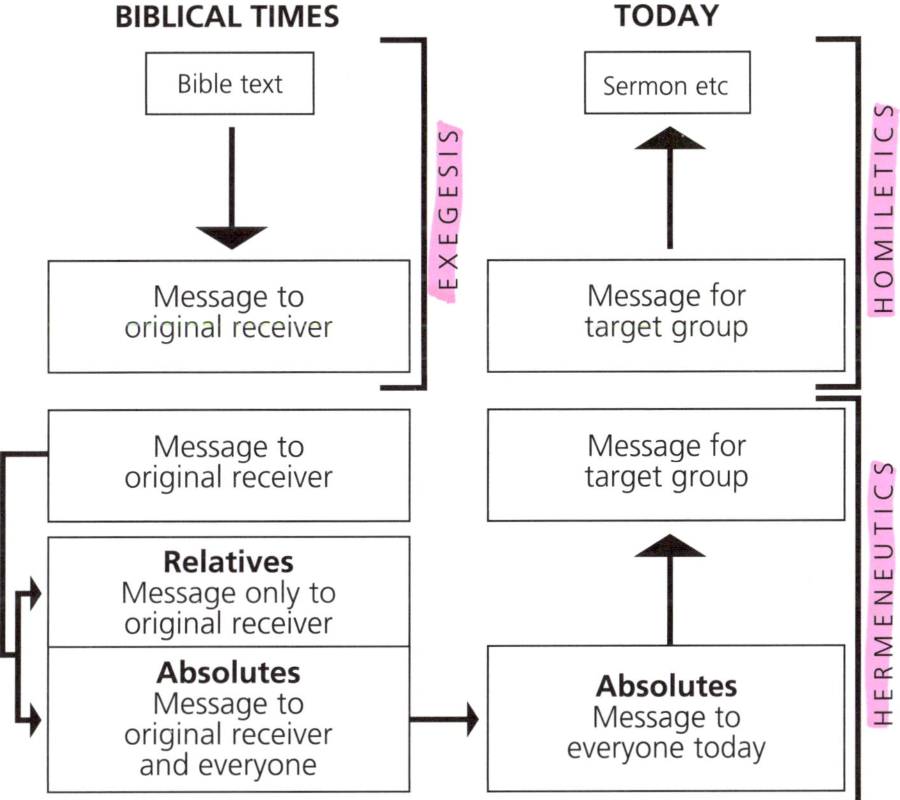

Exercises

1. There are many differences between yourself and a typical church member in Rome at the time when Paul wrote his first letter to that church, eg language. List some of the other differences that you can think of.
2. Explain briefly what exegesis, hermeneutics and homiletics are and draw a diagram to show the relationship between these processes.
3. What is the difference between an absolute and a relative?

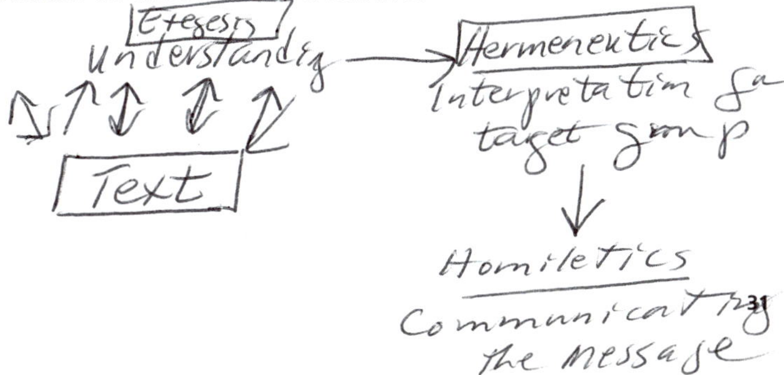

CHAPTER THREE

Key issues in Bible interpretation

Objectives

1. To understand the importance of a correct approach to Scripture and to identify extreme approaches
2. To understand the relationship between the work of the Holy Spirit and the message of the Bible
3. To grasp the relationship between understanding the Word and obeying it
4. To identify and understand liberalism and legalism
5. To comprehend the importance of sound biblical interpretation for the church

Contents

STUDY TIP

The emphasis of this chapter is very much on understanding certain issues. Even if you do not agree with all the examples used here, use this as an opportunity to think through these issues.

In chapter one we saw that the Bible carries authority because God intended it as a means through which to communicate throughout all the centuries. In chapter two we saw that man has to understand this communication, apply it to his circumstances, and communicate the contents by living it out and telling it to others. In this chapter we want to look at a few crucial issues that influence biblical interpretation.

3.1 Rationalism and false spirituality as two extreme approaches

Throughout the history of the church there has been a tendency towards dualism. That is, to divide a person into two separate parts or elements and to emphasise only one part. Although the elements of dualism may differ, it is a dualistic view of mankind that poses one of the most serious threats to the interpretation of the Bible and to Christianity.

Dualism formed the basis of the influential heresy called gnosticism. Its roots started growing in the time when the New Testament was written and it developed into the gnosticism of the second and third century with its influential teachers. It taught that spirit is entirely good and matter is entirely evil. The implication of this is that a person's body is evil, but his spirit is good. In many of the epistles of the Bible the authors addressed directly or indirectly the influence and teaching of this heresy and its outworking, as it was in direct conflict with the gospel.

Even today dualism can be at the root of some of the major departures from sound biblical interpretation. At one extreme, human reason could be seen as the authority under whose scrutiny the Bible is submitted. At the other extreme, the 'spirit' could be seen as fulfilling the same role. The first extreme can be called rationalism (not used here to refer in the narrow sense to a philosophical school of thought) and the second one false spirituality.

In rationalism, no room is left for the working of the Holy Spirit in enlightening the mind and in applying the message to specific circumstances. The mind is placed above the authority of the Bible and is used to decide what is true and what is not. The interpreter is selective in his interpretation and his reasoning is the ultimate authority. The effect of this is that doctrines basic to the faith, like the resurrection and ascension of Christ, are denied by some theologians. Churches become dead and there is no longer a living relationship with a living Christ.

False spirituality in biblical interpretation is in many cases the counter response to rationalism. The argument is that 'the letter kills but the Spirit gives life' (see 3.2 for an exposition of 2 Cor 3:6). Theology, therefore, is an unspiritual activity and the serious interpretation of the Bible is only meant for those who are spiritually dead or half alive. One should interpret the Bible with one's 'spirit' and not use one's mind too much as 'spiritual matters should be discerned spiritually' (see 3.2 for an exposition of 1 Cor 2:14). In effect the interpreter decides, through the inspiration or illumination that he claims to receive, what the message of the Bible is and the objective truths of the Bible lose their importance.

False spirituality in biblical interpretation is challenged when two equally godly Christians arrive at interpretations that are opposing and mutually exclusive. Both cannot be correct. Carson (1989:13) tells how he was in a situation where this truth dawned on someone:

> Almost twenty years ago I rode in a car with a fellow believer who relayed to me what the Lord had "told" him that morning in his quiet time. He had been reading the KJV of Matthew; and I perceived that not only had he misunderstood the archaic English, but also that the KJV at that place had unwittingly misrepresented the Greek text. I gently suggested there might be another way to understand the passage and summarised what I thought the passage was saying. The brother dismissed my view as impossible on the grounds that the Holy Spirit, who does not lie, had told him the truth on this matter. Being young and bold, I pressed on with my explanation of grammar, context, and translation, but was brushed off by a reference to 1 Cor. 2:10b-15: spiritual things must be spiritually discerned - which left little doubt about my status. Genuinely intrigued, I asked this brother what he would say if I put forward my interpretation, not on the basis of grammar and text, but on the basis that the Lord himself had given me the interpretation I was advancing. He was silent a long time, and then concluded, "I guess that would mean the Spirit says the Bible means different things to different people."

It is a real problem when such an approach, namely that the Bible says different things to different people, is accepted. This implies that truth becomes relative as it varies according to the circumstances, persons and places involved. This can even lead to Christians holding opposing and mutually exclusive views simultaneously. I once spoke to a group of Christian young people from a number of nations and was surprised about their lack of response to some controversial issues. After the lecture the course leader expressed his concern to me that the students did not think for themselves. Even when different speakers have opposing views, the students were content with what they were taught, not even trying to deal with the discrepancies.

Although rationalism and false spirituality appeal to different groupings of people, in essence these two approaches to biblical interpretation are similar in that they do not accept the Bible as God's true message. They make another source the arbiter of God's truth. The end results are also similar in that they undermine the truth of God's Word and lead to relativism. An elitist group of teachers can emerge who dominate the thinking of Christians either on the basis of their intellects or on the basis of their spirituality.

3.2 The involvement of the Holy Spirit in biblical interpretation

If you are to avoid rationalism as well as false spirituality, then what should be the approach to the role of the Holy Spirit in biblical interpretation?

God wants us to love and serve him with all our heart, all our soul and all our mind. God wants us to use our minds when we interpret the Bible because we are dealing with communication that is written down and that cannot speak to us if it is not read, understood and applied. The function of the Holy Spirit is not to disregard our minds, but to renew them and to bring them under submission to God so that we will be able to understand the Bible even better.

The Holy Spirit was sent to glorify Jesus and we have already seen that Jesus is God's central message to us. It is therefore impossible that the Holy Spirit can be opposed to the message of the Bible! This point is clearly made by two passages that are not always used to state what they are actually saying:

The first one is 2 Cor 3:6. When Paul writes that 'the letter kills, but the Spirit gives life', he is certainly not contrasting the work of the Holy Spirit with the truth of the Bible. He is contrasting the New Covenant with the old one that some false teachers were holding to in spite of the fact that Jesus had come. The Holy Spirit does give life but it is as a result of what Jesus did for us on the cross whereby he introduced the New Covenant. The redemption that Jesus achieved and its implications are recorded in the Bible and indeed have to be read and understood with our minds.

The second passage is found in 1 Cor 2:6-16. When Paul writes that spiritual things must be discerned spiritually, he is not saying that the mind should not be used, nor is he suggesting that there are two classes of believers. He is telling us that only Christians, those who have the Holy Spirit, can 'understand what God has freely given us' (v12). This cannot be understood by everybody:

> None of the rulers of this age understood it, for if they had, they would not have crucified the Lord of glory. (v8)

and:

> The man without the Spirit does not accept the things that come from the Spirit of God, for they are foolishness to him, and he cannot understand them, because they are spiritually discerned. (v14).

The things that come from the Spirit are foolishness to those who have their own ideas about how to attain salvation:

> Jews demand miraculous signs and Greeks look for wisdom... (1 Cor 1:22).

God decided to act contrary to these expectations of either signs and wonders (false spirituality) or human ways of thinking (rationalism):

> ...but we preach Christ crucified: a stumbling block to Jews and foolishness to Gentiles, but to those whom God has called, both Jews and Greeks, Christ the power of God and the wisdom of God. (1 Cor 1:23-24).

It is the task of the Holy Spirit to glorify Christ who is the central message of the Bible, Christ 'who has become for us wisdom from God - that is, our righteousness, holiness and redemption.' (1 Cor 1:30).

From this it follows that it is impossible to isolate the working of the Holy Spirit from what Christ achieved for us on the cross through his death and resurrection. This is recorded in the Bible and the Holy Spirit wants to help us to understand that message with our minds.

3.3 The difference between God's Word and our guidance

Although we believe that the Holy Spirit is committed to communicate the contents of the gospel as recorded in the Bible, we are still left with questions as far as personal guidance is concerned. There are two questions that I would like to address in this regard.

The first question is, how does the Holy Spirit speak to me personally through the Bible?

The Holy Spirit wants to be actively involved in all Bible ministry, whether it is my personal quiet time or the public preaching of the Word. He can lead me to a specific passage of the Bible where the absolutes are specifically applicable to my circumstances. He wants to help me to interpret that passage and apply it to my circumstances.

An example of this is Rom 12:13 where Christians are instructed to offer hospitality. This is an absolute for all Christians of all times and is not only applicable when it is 'imparted' to me. However, at a specific time the Holy Spirit could lead me to that passage, convict me of my lack of hospitality and I could commit myself afresh to this general instruction from God. The commitment to this biblical absolute must influence my attitude and behaviour when a visitor arrives that afternoon for a cup of tea. I will then indeed be able to say that God spoke to me through his Word in this regard!

This application of the absolutes of the Bible to personal circumstances can take place in different ways and on various levels. For example the Word can speak to an individual during his personal quiet time, through public preaching or through personal instruction during counselling. Similarly the application could come to a whole group of people, like a church.

The more the biblical absolutes permeate our thinking and influence our behaviour, the more we will be able to make the right decisions when tempted and see with clarity what is right and what is wrong. This will keep a Christian from living in immorality and then appealing to God's guidance as a reason for seeking a divorce from his spouse. There are too many examples around of this type of 'guidance'!

The second question is perhaps a bit more difficult to answer: Can God also use a biblical passage to say something to me that the passage does not mean?

An example can illustrate this question. John Missionary has his personal quiet time. He is praying seriously about his need for financial provision and asking the Lord when he is going to answer his prayers. His Scripture reading takes him to Hag 2:19:

> Is there yet any seed left in the barn? Until now, the vine and the fig-tree, the pomegranate and the olive tree have not borne fruit." 'From this day on I will bless you.' "

John Missionary, being committed to interpret God's word responsibly, understands well that this passage is speaking about the blessings that God started to bestow on the returned exiles in Jerusalem for their obedience in rebuilding the temple. He realises that there is no absolute in the passage that indicates that God will provide in his needs on that day. However, he just senses that God is saying to him through that passage that he will experience provision for his needs that day.

I would dare to say that it is quite possible to hear God speaking in this way, for there are many testimonies of John Missionaries and Sarah Christians who have heard God correctly in this way. However, there are also many who have been wrong in thinking that they have heard God in this way with tragic consequences not only for themselves, but also for the faith of many others.

For this reason it is crucial to treat any impression that comes to one through a non-applicable biblical passage in exactly the same way as an impression that has come from a non-biblical source.

This distinction between personal guidance based on Bible passages that do not have applicable absolutes and those which do have applicable absolutes, should always be made. When we are dealing with an absolute, we should present it as such because God wants to speak with authority through his Word. If it is personal guidance, not based on an absolute, then it should be regarded as such and with humility because I could perhaps have misunderstood God's guidance! Not doing so could lead to the impression that the Bible is not trustworthy or that personal guidance is infallible.

3.4 Obedience as a requirement for biblical interpretation

There are two areas in which the Christian has to grow during his whole life: to understand the Bible better, and to obey its message more.

These two go hand in hand. They are like two lines that start off parallel and then need to move continually nearer to one another: the better I understand who God is and what he did for me through Jesus, the more I live in obedience and dependence on him. On the other hand, the more I love and serve him, the clearer the biblical message becomes as I draw from it daily. This process of growth in spiritual maturity could be illustrated as in figure 3.1.

FIGURE 3.1

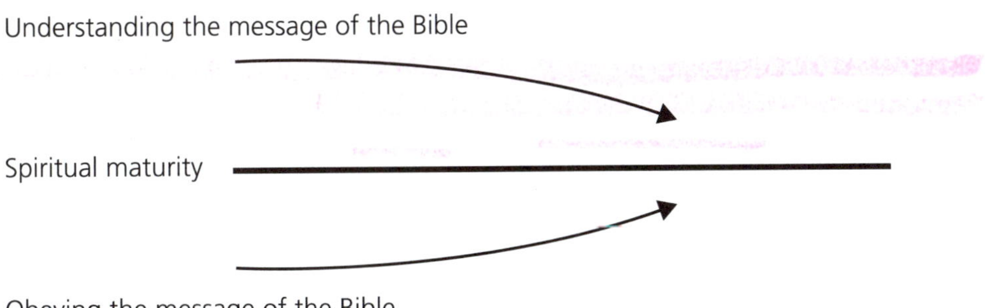

In this process of growth it is possible to become side-tracked by either concentrating on understanding at the expense of obedience, or to concentrate on obedience at the expense of understanding. The effect of either one should be obvious. If I want to understand the Bible well, but am not willing to obey it, then even that which I understand is worthless. For how long will the seminary professor in New Testament exegesis who lives in immorality (to use an extreme example!) be able to give a sound interpretation of the Bible? Similarly, for how long will the evangelist who bases his work on signs and miracles without himself understanding the gospel properly, be able to convert people without being deceived?

3.5 The dangers of liberalism and legalism

One can end up either with theological liberalism or legalism if wrong decisions are made during the process of hermeneutics. We will first cover the subject of hermeneutics again briefly and then from that background explain what is meant by liberalism and legalism.

When we first discussed hermeneutics (see 2.3), it was stated that it is the process by which the message to the original receivers is applied to the people of our time. In order to do so, it is necessary to go through the process of exegesis, through which the complete message to the original receiver is discovered. Then, through the process of hermeneutics (see figure 3.2), one must make a distinction between that part of the message which was only applicable to the original receiver (relatives) and that part which is applicable to all people of all times (absolutes). The absolutes are transferred to our time to become the message for everyone today. When those absolutes are applied to a specific target group, it becomes the message for that group.

FIGURE 3.2

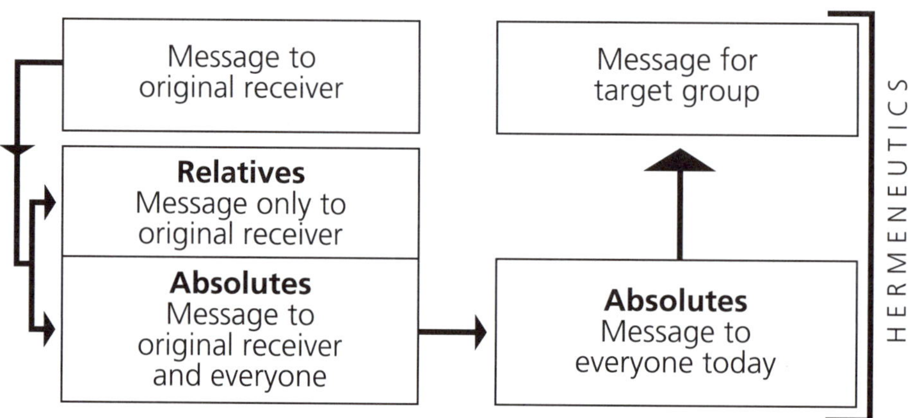

This process of hermeneutics is a very important one because of the decisions that have to be made about what is a relative and what is an absolute. A wrong decision can lead to what can be called theological liberalism or to legalism.

Theological liberalism is practised when those parts of the message that are absolutes, are perceived to be relatives, as shown as in figure 3.3.

FIGURE 3.3

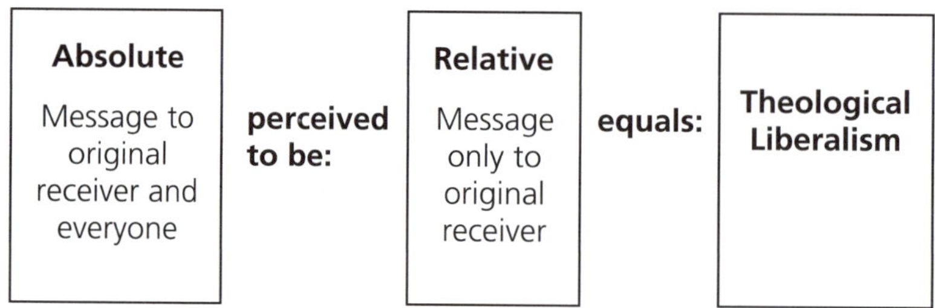

An example of theological liberalism is that of God's prohibition of homosexual practice as found in Rom 1:24-32. God prohibits it for all people of all time. When it is perceived to be only a command for the people of biblical times, we are certainly dealing with theological liberalism (illustrated in figure 3.4). Liberalism could even influence exegesis to such an extent that Rom 1:24-32 would not even be seen as applicable to the church in Rome, but only as Paul's own ideas!

FIGURE 3.4

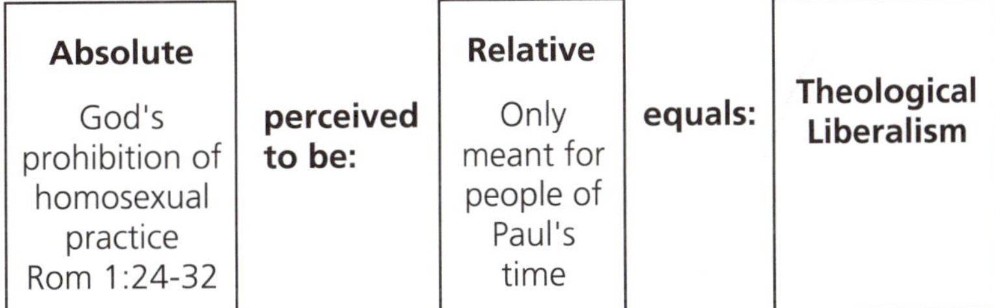

Theological liberalism is particularly active in the areas of morality and ethics, eg the sexual norms held in the church and the value of life before birth.

Legalism on the other hand will result when those parts of the message that are relatives, are perceived to be absolutes, as illustrated in figure 3.5.

FIGURE 3.5

Relative Message only to original receiver	**perceived to be:**	**Absolute** Message to original receiver and everyone	**equals:**	**Legalism**

An example of legalism is when the kiss with which Paul instructs the members of the church in Rome to greet one another (see 2.3), is perceived to be an absolute and as such, a form that all Christians of all cultures and times should adhere to (illustrated in figure 3.6). Just like theological liberalism, legalism could already start during the process of exegesis. This happens when the meaning behind a convention (form) in the Bible is incorrectly established or not even sought. An example is the wearing of head coverings that Paul requires in 1 Cor 11:5-6. If the meaning of that form of head covering is not correctly understood in its historical and cultural context, then only the form itself is seen as the message. And so there is a great risk of taking this as the absolute and all women in the church could end up wearing hats!

FIGURE 3.6

Relative Kiss as manner to greet	**perceived to be:**	**Absolute** Meant for Christians of all times	**equals:**	**Legalism**

Examples of legalism are found amongst others, in worship and in the practical outworking of growing in holiness:

In worship it happens when a distinction is not made between the form of worship and its meaning. The result is that one form with a specific meaning is exalted at the expense of another form with exactly the same meaning. For example,the rigid rule that no-one may lift their hands when worshipping, and the similarly rigid rule that everybody should lift up their hands in worship. In the end it does not matter whether hands are lifted up or not, but whether worship takes place with a commitment to God in Christ.

In the outworking of growing in holiness, legalism steps in when a form is kept without relating it to the meaning it originally had. An example is where a Christian is convicted to refrain from alcohol because it has started to control his life and has become an obstacle in his testimony to others. In this case the biblical absolutes underlying the form of abstention are that only Christ should control the Christian's life and that anything which hinders the Christian testimony should be stopped. If only the form of abstention is upheld without the underlying absolutes, it can soon become an illegitimate way to measure sanctification.

While the danger of liberalism or legalism can strike any Bible interpreter, those who are on either the tracks of rationalism or false spirituality (see 3.1), are even more susceptible because their framework of thinking gives them less of a safeguard against excesses.

3.6 Sound interpretation brings unity and purity

Sound biblical interpretation is largely the answer to the church's need for unity and also for purity. Biblical unity and purity are based on the centrality of Christ and on God's absolutes. We will first discuss the value of concentrating on the centrality of Christ and then that of concentrating on the absolutes.

The centrality of Christ will in time be challenged by both rationalism and false spirituality. In both cases a human faculty is placed above God's revelation of who Christ is as recorded in the Bible (see 3.1). Unfortunately people who agree in their approach to the gospel tend to gather together in groups that often reject those who are different from themselves. This can lead to division between real Christians.

On the rationalistic side, there is a real danger of false unity. This happens when fellowship with others is not based on the mutual confession of who Christ is, but on respect for one another's intellects and respectability. An ecumenism that incorporates even non-Christian religions could be, and sometimes is, the sad result!

Regarding false spirituality, there is a real danger of division between real Christians and a unity between those who share the same spiritual experiences. In its extreme form it is not a unity on the basis of the mutual confession of who Christ is, but on the basis of shared spiritual power and encounters. This could be extremely dangerous, especially in this time of New Age when supernatural phenomena are becoming more and more popular.

In contrast to rationalism and false spirituality, sound biblical interpretation challenges the true Christian to grow in his understanding of the centrality of Christ. Jesus is the content and source of his beliefs as well as his way of living. This leads to a basis of unity between Christians as they are prepared to have their pet presuppositions and doctrines continually challenged by the message of the Word.

A focus on the absolutes of the Bible underscores the centrality of Christ as the basis for unity and purity. In the practical life of the church such a focus can bring a unity between Christians on issues that should not bring divisions. Speaking in tongues can serve as an example. Christians can have unity if they are prepared to avoid theological liberalism as well as legalism. That is, if they could agree that it is a liberal view (or conservative, as preferred by some in this case) to state that speaking in tongues cannot take place today and that it is only meant for people of the time of the New Testament. On the other hand they will need to agree further that it is a legalistic view that every Spirit-filled Christian will speak, or should speak, in tongues.

On this same issue of speaking in tongues, a focus on the absolutes can lead to greater purity in the church. The speaking of tongues cannot be accepted as the proof of a Spirit-filled life, as is becoming clearer and clearer where there are so many who speak in tongues but do not portray the holiness brought about by the Holy Spirit. The biblical absolutes of holiness should certainly have priority over the relatives of any tradition when evaluating the spirituality of a person.

Another example of a practice in the church that causes a great deal of division, is that of christening. A focus on the absolutes can lead to unity between real Christians. The meaning of christening a child with believing parents may actually be exactly the same as the meaning of the dedication of a child of other believing parents. The meaning of the confirmation of a believer may be exactly the same as the meaning of the believer's baptism of another.

At the same time, in the case of christening, the focus on the absolutes can lead to challenging the non-commitment and superstition that so many times accompany the administering of christening. Many people want to have christening performed without adhering to the true meaning of it. An emphasis on the meaning of christening could lead to the purification of the church from superstition and non-committed people. In the process the conversion of many can take place.

Exercises

1. What are the similarities between the approaches of rationalism and false spirituality to Scripture?
2. How should personal guidance from the Bible be viewed, when it is out of context?
3. Explain graphically what the steps of hermeneutics are and show how unsound hermeneutics can lead either to liberalism or legalism. Give your own example of each.
4. What are the benefits of sound interpretation to the church?

part two

THE RELATIONSHIP BETWEEN FORM AND MEANING

CHAPTER FOUR

How to understand language

Objectives

1. To understand the process used when a passage is written and the process when it is interpreted
2. To grasp why it is necessary to analyse biblical passages
3. To comprehend the relationship between the form and the meaning elements of language
4. To understand the nature of the paragraph

Contents

STUDY TIP

This chapter gives the background for the steps of exegesis as explained in part three. Make sure you understand the concepts discussed in this chapter.

In part one of this book, we explained the processes of biblical interpretation. And in part three there will be a step by step explanation of the process of exegesis. When exegeting, it is necessary to keep in mind that the Bible is written in ordinary human language. Therefore, the principles that normally rule the understanding of language are also applicable as we aim to understand the text as the original receiver did.

The purpose of part two is to look at some of the principles that determine the relationship between the two main parts of language, namely form and meaning. This will serve as background for the proposed steps of exegesis in part three. It will also provide methods for discovering the meaning of words and phrases. A good understanding of these will be extremely valuable in exegesis and is presupposed in the explanation of the steps of exegesis.

4.1 The two elements of language

Language has both an element of form and of meaning:

The *form* element of language (also more technically called the surface structure of language) consists of two levels or hierarchies, namely the phonological level and the grammatical level.

The *meaning* element of language (also more technically called the semantic or deep structure of language) consists of the semantic level (see figure 4.1).

FIGURE 4.1

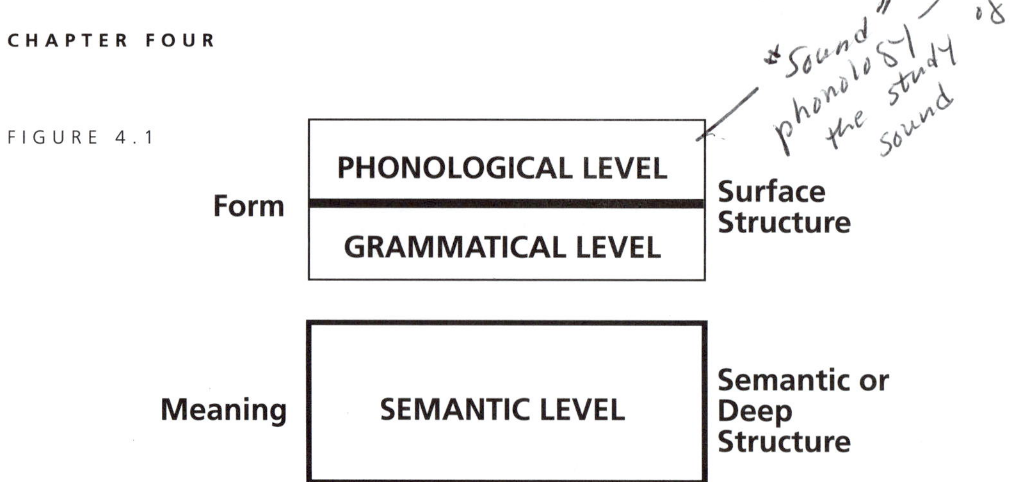

The phonological level is that part of language which encompasses the units of sound. Different sounds are brought together to form words that differ from one another. The study that is concerned with the analysis of these sound units is called phonology. Because we interpret the Bible as written communication, phonology is not used in the process of interpretation and for that reason will not be discussed in this book.

The grammatical level is that part of language which encompasses the structure of words, phrases, clauses and sentences. It also includes syntax, that is, the grammatical arrangement of words. The study that is concerned with analysis on the grammatical level is called grammar.

The semantic or meaning level of language is actually the most important one as it is served by the form level. Form is there to express meaning, it does not exist for its own sake. Semantics is the study that is concerned with meaning and the relationship between the form of a particular language and the meaning which that form represents.

4.2 Understanding language

When we interpret a passage we start with the words and sentences in front of us and end with understanding what it means. We actually move in the opposite direction from that which the author took when he wrote the passage. The writer started with what he wanted to communicate (meaning) and then put it into form, that is into words, sentences, paragraphs and combinations of paragraphs (see figure 4.2).

FIGURE 4.2

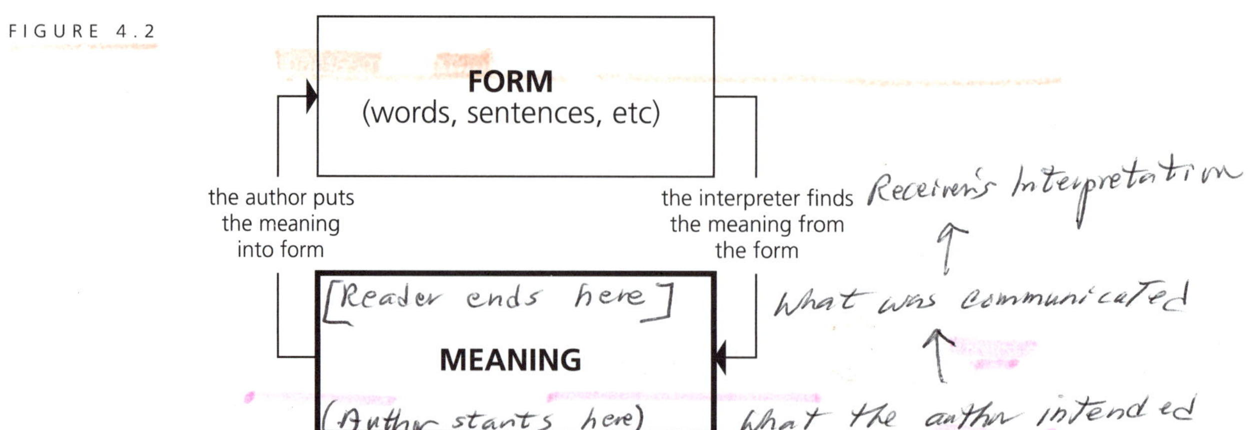

As the purpose of exegesis is to establish what the original receiver understood, how does his understanding differ from what the author intended to say? Right at the beginning of the process of communication there may be a loss of meaning between what the author intends to say and his actual communication of it. Perhaps we have all had the experience of writing something and then, when we look at it, wondering whether it really means what we wanted to communicate. There may be a further loss between the meaning of the communicated message and how it is interpreted by the receiver.

We do not have the human authors of the Bible available to explain what they actually meant with a specific passage. Neither do we have the original receivers available to explain what they actually understood from a specific passage. For this reason we are forced to accept the text in front of us as a true portrayal of what the author intended to say and also of what the original receiver would have understood.

4.3 Text analysis as the means of understanding

In order to understand a passage we have to establish its meaning from the form of the words and sentences in front of us. To do so we have to understand the relationships between the different linguistic components, like the words, phrases and sentences of the passage as they function together in a complex manner to present meaning. This always involves a process of analysis. When it is a very simple passage we would usually be able to see the relationships without much effort. So, the structure is clear and it is not necessary to go into a lengthy process of analysis. Actually we do analyse it, but do so mentally, like mental arithmetic.

Although we can take short cuts in our analysis when we see the relationships in a passage immediately, it is always dangerous to put too much trust in our immediate intuition or observations. A thorough linguistic analysis would safeguard against reading into the text what it does not say or against being deceived to read it as proof for our own preconceived views. 

A person who knows the style of a specific author or type of literature very well will obviously observe certain linguistic relationships more easily than a person who is not familiar with it. For this reason it can be very difficult for us to see the relationships in passages that would have been much easier for the original receivers to see because they were used to that specific style of writing. Although it may require effort to see the relationships in a specific Bible author's writings when analysing it for the first time, it will become easier with acquired experience.

We are going to follow, as part of our exegesis, a method of analysis called semantic discourse analysis (this analysis forms part of the steps of exegesis and will be described along with the other steps in part three).

4.4 The characteristics of semantic discourse analysis

In the relationship between the form and meaning structures of language, mismatching commonly occurs in all languages. Consider the following sentences:

a) The boy calls the dog.
b) The dog is called by the boy.

On the grammatical level the subject is different in each of these sentences:
In the first sentence the boy is the subject,
but in the second sentence the dog is the subject.

On the semantic level, however, the role of the boy is the same in both cases. He is the one who calls.

This is an example of the fact that the semantic role is independent of the grammatical function. Semantic roles are universal, that is, they can be applied in any language. Grammatical functions on the other hand are defined separately for each language according to the grammatical system of that specific language.

Not only are semantic roles universal, but meaning itself is universal. The same meaning could be expressed in all languages. Although meaning is universal, grammatical structure differs from language to language in the form (surface structure).

Semantic discourse analysis primarily aims to establish what the semantic relationships are between the units of language. This means that it aims to discern how linguistic units are arranged to express meaning. In more technical terms we can say that semantic discourse analysis aims to establish the underlying structure of a portion of language.

4.5 The paragraph as the basic unit for analysis

Traditional linguistics treats the word or sentence as the smallest unit for analysis. However, semantic discourse analysis follows more recent linguistic insights by treating the paragraph as the smallest unit of communication and thus the smallest unit for analysis. The analytical system that has paragraphs as a basis, is generally called discourse analysis. This approach can best be explained by first looking at what a paragraph consists of, and then how it is defined.

The paragraph consists of words and sentences. The word is the smallest independent linguistic unit able to indicate meaning. Letters in themselves, if not arranged to form a word, cannot indicate meaning and thus do not qualify as an independent unit.

Although the word is the smallest independent linguistic unit, it is never used on its own but with others to form sentences (except in one word sentences where it is completely dependent on the surrounding sentences to indicate its meaning). A word expresses only possibilities of meaning when used in isolation. For example the following words do not express meaning in themselves, but each one has only possibilities of meaning: 'bed', 'flowers', 'plants', 'woman'. When these words are placed in relationships, it could form the following sentence: 'The woman plants the bulbs in the flower bed.' With the additional information of the situation in which it is communicated and the context of the previous and following sentences, the meaning of this sentence should be as clear to the reader as the author intended it to be. We could thus say that the sentence forms the smallest unit for everyday usage.

Sentences combine together in specific relationships to form paragraphs. These relationships between sentences play an important role in the formation of the meaning of the whole paragraph. So that the meaning of the paragraph is more than just the sum total of the meaning of the individual sentences. Let us look for example at the following sentences:

The police broke the sad news.
The woman plants bulbs in a flower bed.
There was a terrible accident on the motorway.
Three people were slightly injured.
The wife did not suspect anything.
One man was instantly killed.

Each of the above sentences could be interpreted in isolation and each one expresses a specific meaning. Just to add the meanings together would not make much sense and could lead to quite a few different interpretations. However, when used together in a paragraph, the relationships between sentences are clearly expressed. The different sentences in our example could be put together in a paragraph (obviously with changes in form to express the different relationships):

> There was a terrible accident on the motorway. One man was instantly killed and three others slightly injured. When the police went to break the sad news to the unsuspecting wife, she was planting bulbs in a flower bed.

Thus we see that while words form sentences and sentences are in relationship with one another to form paragraphs, the paragraph in turn dictates the boundaries within which the sentences and words should be understood. This means that the meaning or semantic value of the smaller units are limited by the paragraph. In the isolated sentence 'the woman plants bulbs in the flower bed', any woman could be meant, doing it at any time. In the setting of our paragraph, it is not any woman, but the wife of a man who died instantly in an accident on the motorway. She was not planting at any time, but when the police came to break the sad news of her husband's death.

This relationship between smaller units and the paragraph could be compared to the relationship between an individual player in a game of football and all the other players on the field. Although what the individual player does is important, it only has meaning as far as it relates to the other players and the whole game. The player could for example give a long kick of the ball, but if it is in the wrong direction, it would not be considered a good kick at all!

Although the paragraph is the smallest unit of communication and therefore the smallest unit to analyse, it is too big a chunk to begin with in our analysis. Which is why we should start with smaller units and build up to the whole. Therefore, when we have analysed the smaller units of a paragraph, we need to find out how they link together to form the whole paragraph. From the perspective of the whole paragraph we in turn have to look at the roles of the smaller units.

In semantic discourse analysis we are actually involved in a process in which we constantly work from the smaller units to the whole and vice versa. Thinking of our illustration of the football match, analysis is like the live television coverage of such a match where the whole field is shown at times and then the camera zooms in again to show the movement of one specific player as he helps to shape the course of the match by what he does.

Exactly how semantic discourse analysis is done, will be explained and demonstrated in chapters 10 to 14.

Exercises

1. What is the difference between the process followed by an author and that followed by an interpreter?
2. Explain what is meant by the surface structure of language and what is meant by the deep structure.
3. A few descriptions follow. Select from the list of answers which part of language is referred to in each description:
   The smallest independent linguistic unit:
   The smallest unit for everyday usage:
   The smallest unit of communication:
   List of answers: sentence, word, paragraph

CHAPTER FIVE

How translations help us

Objectives

1. To understand that any translation has an underlying theory
2. To be able to name and explain the three main theories of translation
3. To understand which type of translation is the best for which purpose

Contents

STUDY TIP

If you understand the diagrams you understand the contents of the whole chapter. You may wish to draw the diagrams for yourself as they are explained.

We saw in chapter two that exegesis bridges the gap between the original receiver and ourselves so we can understand the message as he understood it. In that chapter the task was given to make a list of the types of differences between ourselves and a typical church member in Rome in the time of Paul. Possibly the biggest difference - as far as it influences communication - is the one of language.

In spite of what many people would like to believe, the Bible was not originally written in English! Most of the Old Testament was written in Hebrew, the language that was used by the Israelites in Canaan. Small parts of it (Dan 2:4-7:28, Ezra 4:8-6:18, 7:12-26 and two words in Gen 31:47) were written in Aramaic, a sister language of Hebrew. In the ninth and following centuries BC, Aramaic rapidly became the international medium for commerce and diplomacy. In Babylon at the time of Nebuchadnezzar, it was already in common use. And in the time of Jesus, Aramaic was spoken in Palestine and was the language in which he taught and communicated.

In the Near Eastern and Mediterranean lands in Roman times, the different peoples used Greek as a common language, similar to the way English is presently used worldwide as a means of international communication. Though often called Koine-Greek it was not a specific language in its own right, but rather a common label for the variants of Greek used in these lands. The whole New Testament was written in this type of Greek which explains the varieties of common Greek in the New Testament itself. It had been established over this wide territory by the conquests and cultural agenda of Alexander the Great and his successors. The official language of the Roman empire was Latin.

When Paul wrote his letter to the church in Colosse, a typical church member who knew Greek could probably understand quite well what he was talking about, (although Paul's use of Greek was rather sophisticated, especially when compared to that of Mark or John). Obviously it would be best for the purpose of exegesis if we could understand Greek just as well as the original receiver did - something that is not easily achieved!

Fortunately, nowadays, we have many excellent translations to help us bridge the language gap between us and the original writers of the New Testament. However, we cannot fully benefit from the use of translations unless we understand how they work. The fact that there are different translations available could be extremely confusing and lead to counter-productive discussions about which one is the best. In the end such discussions usually result in the profound decision that the translation that I use is the best!

What makes one translation good and another one bad? Let us look at three idioms (fixed expressions) from different languages, each one with the same meaning, that have been translated word for word into English:

He jumped into the flea case (Norwegian)
He went into the square field (Welsh)
He went into the trap (German)

Each one of these idioms means in its original language "to go to sleep".

In general it could be said that a translation that is likely to be misunderstood by the average reader is certainly not a good translation. Misunderstanding can be either the result of vagueness (as in the examples above) or the result of added comments and interpretations. A good translation is one that is likely to be understood by the average reader just as well as the original reader understood the original language.

In general there are according to the underlying theories, three main groups of translations, namely dynamic equivalent translations, literal translations and paraphrases.

5.1 Dynamic equivalent translation

With this kind of translation, success is measured according to the criterion of meaning. The reader of the translation should arrive as near as possible to the meaning received by the original reader. This does not mean that form is not important. Within each language it is the form that indicates the meaning. For this reason the translator has to study the form of the original text with the greatest attention to detail in order to arrive at the correct meaning. The translator then seeks accurately to express the meaning in the translation, using the appropriate forms of the language of the translation.

While the meaning of the translation will be very similar to the meaning of the original, the form of the translation will differ in many ways from that of the original text (see figure 5.1, where different shapes illustrate this). This is because, as we have seen in 4.4, languages differ in the way they express meaning. These differences may be in the length of sentences, in sentence construction, word order or grammar where for example nouns are translated into verbs.

FIGURE 5.1

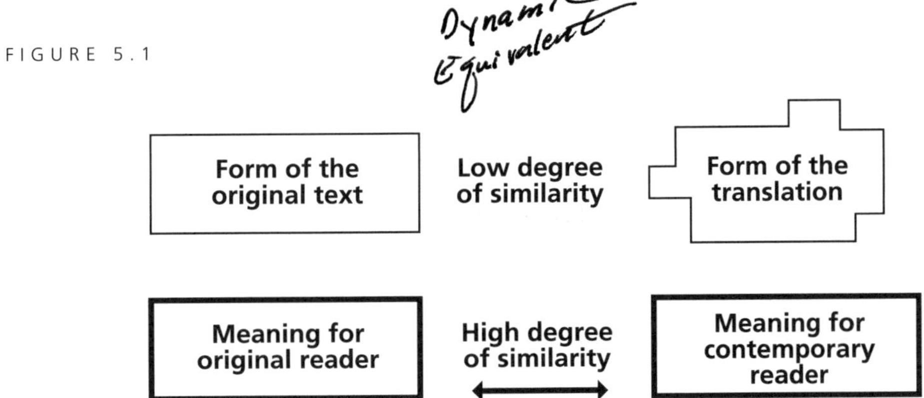

A dynamic equivalent translation of the three examples of idioms at the beginning of this chapter, could be 'he went to sleep', or if one wants to use an English idiom, the following are possibilities:

He turned in
He hit the hay
He hit the sack
He went into the arms of Morpheus

The dynamic-equivalent theory of translation is very effective in bridging some of the differences between the understanding of the original and the contemporary reader. But, and this is important to understand, it does not bridge all of them. These differences, as we have already seen at the beginning of chapter two, exist both in matters of language (words, grammar, and idioms) as well as in matters of culture, history, religious experience and understanding. In a dynamic-equivalent translation it is mainly matters on the linguistic level that are 'updated'. The distance in culture and history is kept and still has to be bridged by the process of exegesis.

5.2 Literal translation

With this kind of translation, great care is taken to be as faithful as possible to the original text (Greek or Hebrew) in preserving its form, yet trying to make sense. Thus if a particular word is used in the original language, it will almost every time be translated by the same word in the new language. If there is a long sentence in the Greek text, one will find a long sentence in the translation. Where nouns are used in the Greek, nouns are used in the translation, etc. It could be illustrated as in figure 5.2.

FIGURE 5.2

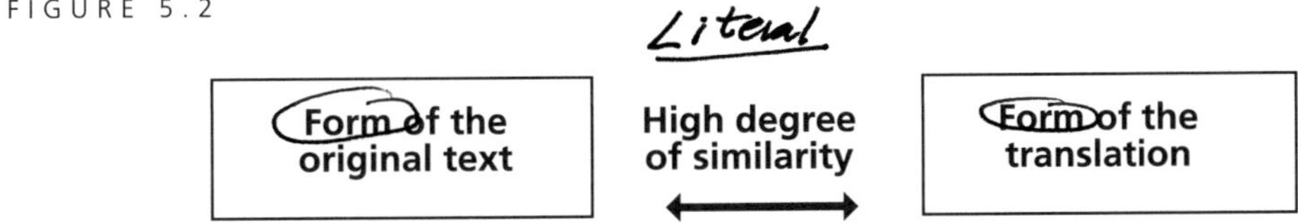

This kind of translation may appeal strongly to many. 'I want to stay as near as possible to the original' is the main argument used to defend the literal translation. It may be a valid argument, but only as long as there is not a loss of meaning in the translation due to the strong emphasis on preserving the form of the original in the translation. The reason being that God's intention with the Bible wasn't to give us a document of literary interest at the expense of the message that he wants to communicate through it. The message certainly has to be communicated by using language, but then again the language used is only the instrument and not an end in itself.

Unfortunately, when a passage is translated literally, there is often a loss of meaning, as illustrated in figure 5.3.

FIGURE 5.3

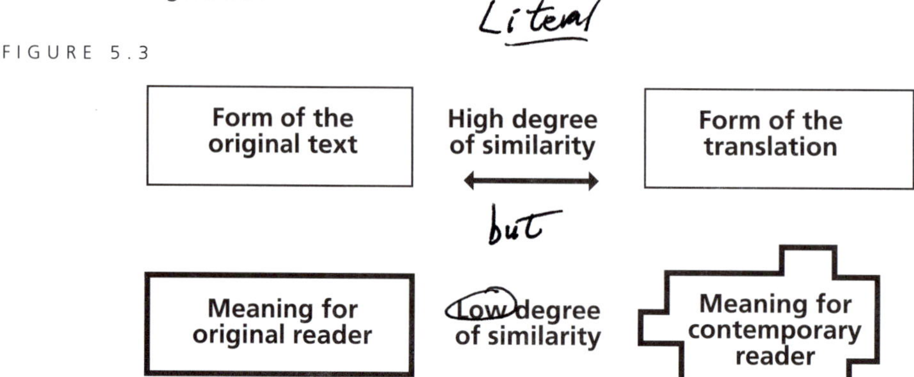

This loss of meaning is found for example when the New International Version (NIV) translates a Greek idiom in Rom 12:20 literally: '...you will heap burning coals on his head.' There is a high degree of similarity between the form of the translation and the form of the Greek. However, if one were to ask an average English speaker what it means, one can expect to find some interesting answers! The Good News Bible (GNB) translates it accurately as '...you will make him burn with shame.'

Another example is the literal translation in the NIV of Mt 20:22 where Jesus said to his disciples: 'Can you drink the cup I am going to drink?' The GNB translates it as: 'Can you drink the cup of suffering that I am about to drink?'

In each of these examples, many Christians might have been able to understand the literal translation, but then it is most probably because they have become used to 'biblical language'. Where it is also true that any new convert to Christianity will have to learn some new concepts that belong to his newly found faith, it would be unfortunate if in addition he has to cope with unnecessary archaic or alien words. There is also a real danger that the unnecessarily difficult language of some translations, overtly influences the language of the church. Sometimes, to such an extent that it loses the ability to explain the gospel message to outsiders in clear language.

5.3 Paraphrase

A paraphrase translates in a dynamic equivalent way but at times goes a bit further by also bridging some of the cultural and historical differences between ourselves and biblical times. An example is the Living Bible's translation of Rom 16:16: 'Shake hands warmly with each other'. A literal translation of the Greek is 'Greet one another with a holy kiss' (see chapter 2 where this verse is used as an example for a discussion of the relationship between exegesis, hermeneutics and homiletics).

When the historical and cultural distances are bridged, the reader receives to a certain extent a theological interpretation from the translator (and it should be treated as such). However, this certainly does not mean that a paraphrase should be viewed in exactly the same way as a commentary because good paraphrases do not always bridge the historical and cultural distances. In general they provide a good linguistic understanding of the text.

5.4 Evaluation

All translations could be placed more or less on a continuum, from literal translation, through dynamic equivalent, to paraphrases (see figure 5.4). This is done with the understanding that no translation could consistently follow its underlying theory.

FIGURE 5.4

literal				dynamic equivalent		paraphrase
KJV	RSV	NIV	JB	GNB	PHILLIPS	LB
NASB	NRSV	NAB				
		NEB				

(See a list of abbreviations of the translations at the beginning of the book.)

This brings us to the question of what kind of translation we should use for exegesis. In general, it could be said that you cannot really make do without a good dynamic equivalent translation, since its purpose is to bridge the linguistic differences between us and the original receivers. At the same time a more literal translation can be helpful in order to get an insight into what the form of the original text looks like. A paraphrase can shed more light on the meaning of the text and give insights into how to bridge the cultural and historical differences. The answer to our question therefore is that it is recommended that more than one translation should be used, each according to what it can contribute.

Fee and Stuart (1988:42) recommend the NIV, GNB and NAB as good translations:

> One would do well to have two or all three of these. The NIV is a committee translation by the best scholarship in the evangelical tradition; the NAB is a committee translation by the best scholarship in the American Catholic tradition. The GNB is an outstanding translation where the New Testament was done by a single scholar, Robert G. Bratcher, who regularly consulted with others and whose expertise in linguistics has brought the concept of dynamic equivalence to translation in a thorough way. The Old Testament was a committee translation.

In the method of exegesis that we recommend in this book, the NIV will be used as the basic translation from which we work. Because the NIV is fairly literal, it will help us to pick up some of the Greek forms that have been carried over into the English. This will make it possible for us to do some 'translating' ourselves - rewriting passages from the NIV into a more intelligible form. At the same time the NIV is not so literal that it becomes awkward to understand.

Exercises

1. Name the three main theories of translation and explain each one.
2. Read Phil 2:1-11 in a literal translation and in the GNB and make a list of the obvious types of differences that you find between the two.
3. Compare the following translation of 1 Pet 5:13 in the Living Bible (LB) with the NIV and make a list of the differences between the two:
   'The church here in Rome - she is your sister in the Lord - sends you her greetings; so does my son Mark.'

CHAPTER SIX

The relationship between words and meaning

Objectives

1. To grasp the nature of the relationships between words and meaning
2. To understand the implications of these relationships on practices traditionally followed in exegesis (eg word studies and historical meanings)
3. To know the correct approach to finding the meaning of a word

Contents

STUDY TIP

A good understanding of the issues discussed in this chapter will prove very helpful in all exegesis. Make certain that the logic is understood, especially if you only speak one language and are not used to translating - an activity through which one tends to become aware of the issues.

In chapter 4 you gained a general understanding of the relationship between form and meaning, and in chapter 5 we gave an explanation of the different types of Bible translations that are available. In this chapter we will look more in depth at the relationship between words and meaning and also show how and why the different kinds of translations differ in their translation of words. A good understanding of this relationship is essential before approaching exegesis.

6.1 One word with different meanings

Say your new neighbour who has little knowledge of English asks you the meaning of the word 'table'. You tell him that it is a piece of furniture that one sits around to have meals, and you even show him a table. The more you explain, the more perplexed he looks. He then reaches into his pocket and produces a letter from his child's new teacher:

> Dear Sir
>
> Could you please let me know which tables your child knows.
>
> Mrs Robinson

Suddenly, you realise that a different meaning is required. If the neighbour had shown the letter when asking his question, you would have been able to give him the right answer first time. If he asks you before leaving whether you could help him to carry a table upstairs, you would not even contemplate that he is referring to a mathematical table.

The Collins Cobuild Essential English Dictionary (1989) lists four possible meanings for the word 'table':

1. 'A table is a piece of furniture with a flat top that you put things on.'
2. 'A table is also a set of facts or figures arranged in columns or rows on a piece of paper.'
3. 'If you turn the tables on someone, you change the situation completely, so that they have the problems that they were trying to cause for you.'
4. 'If you table something such as a proposal, you say formally that you want it to be discussed at a meeting.'

The relationship between the word 'table' and these meanings, excluding the third one, is shown in figure 6.1.

FIGURE 6.1

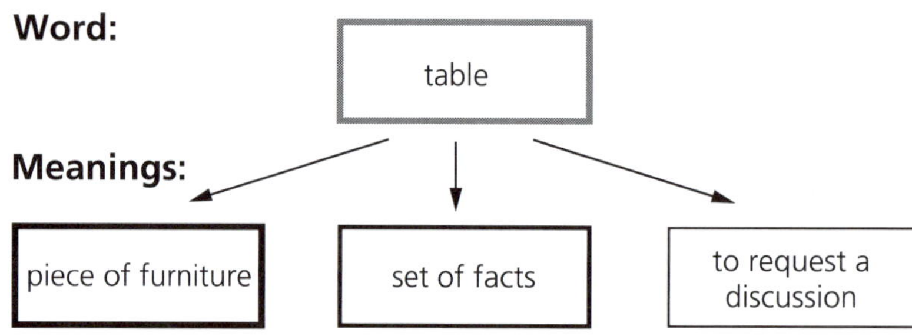

In the third meaning that was given by the dictionary, the word 'table' did not function on its own, but forms part of an idiom. For this reason we will not deal with it further.

The word 'table' can also have another meaning as it is used in the phrase 'the Lord's table', with the meaning "holy communion". Strictly speaking, we cannot say that "holy communion" is a normal or everyday meaning (called 'linguistic meaning') of 'table'. However, in this context it has indeed the meaning "holy communion", known as the 'contextual meaning'. The difference between these two types of meanings will be discussed more in depth in chapter 12.

The important facts that have arisen thus far from the discussion of the different meanings of 'table', are that;

a) one word can have more than one meaning, and
b) that these meanings are dependent on the context, whether it is the context in which it is communicated or the context of the other words with which it is used.

Looking at the different meanings of 'table' that we have discussed, it is clear that the meanings are not related to one another. In other words, they do not have anything in common as far as their meanings are concerned. However, there are cases where one word can have more than one meaning, of which some are related. The Greek word 'xulon' is a good example of a word with several possible meanings of which two groups could be made, each group consisting of related meanings.

In the NT the word 'xulon' is translated in the following passages with the following meanings:

Lk 23:31 :	tree	(NIV) - a large wooden plant
Rev 18:12 :	wood	(NIV) - a substance, part of a plant
Mark 14:43 :	club	(NIV) - a weapon used in fighting
Acts 16:24 :	stocks	(NIV) - an instrument to detain a person
Acts 5:30 :	cross	(GNB) - an instrument of execution

Although it may seem that there is a significant relationship between these five different meanings, for instance that they are all woody by nature, this is essentially of secondary importance. The first two meanings are related to one another as they describe things that belong to the meaning or semantic field of plants, while the last three belong to the semantic field of artifacts (see figure 6.2). Thus the first two meanings are related to one another and the last three meanings are related to one another, but the two groups of meaning are not related to one another - they belong to different fields of meaning.

FIGURE 6.2

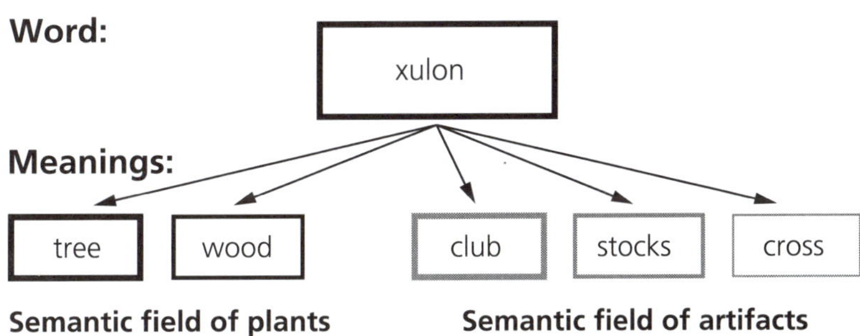

These examples of the meanings of 'table' and 'xulon' clearly illustrate the fact that a word may have more than one meaning - meanings that may be related or may not.

Usually dictionaries list possible meanings by means of single words. To apply such 'meanings' can be very misleading as it depends on the context in which the word is used. One should find out which one of the possible different meanings of a word is used in a particular context. How to use dictionaries and other linguistic helps to establish the meaning of words in the Bible will be discussed more in depth as one of the steps of exegesis in chapter 12.

In literal translations, the fact that one word can have different meanings, is not always taken into consideration. This is seen when one Greek word with different meanings in different contexts is translated by a single English word, even though the English word does not cover the same spectrum of meanings. The Greek word 'sarx', for example, is translated in various places in the KJV as the English word 'flesh'. However, in each case it has only one meaning and the reader has to establish what it is.

In a dynamic equivalent translation, words are translated according to their meaning in the specific context, and the reader can immediately see the meaning of a word or phrase. This difference between a literal and dynamic equivalent translation could be illustrated by looking at how 'sarx' is translated first by the KJV and then by a more dynamic equivalent translation:

Matt 24:22 : no **flesh** be saved
no-**one** would survive (NIV)

John 1:14 : the Word was made **flesh**
The Word became a **human being** (GNB)

Rom 9:8 : children of the **flesh**
natural children (NIV)

Heb 5:7 : in the days of his **flesh**
the days of Jesus' **life on earth** (NIV)

Rom 8:13 : live after the **flesh**
live according to the **sinful nature** (NIV)

Jude 7 : giving themselves over to fornication, and going after **strange flesh**
gave themselves up to sexual immorality and **perversion** (NIV)

Exercise

1. List five examples of a word that can signify more than one meaning, writing the word on one line and a few of the possible meanings below it (as is done in figure 6.1). (The meanings may or may not be related).

6.2 The same meaning expressed by different words

We have seen (6.1) that one word can have different meanings of which some may be related to one another and some not. Now we want to address the question whether different words can have the same meaning or meanings that are closely related.

Different words can express the same meaning, or fine nuances of the same meaning. The meaning of a "great number" for example can be expressed by the different words 'many', 'multitudinous' and 'numerous'. Thus we find that although they are three different words, the meaning expressed is very similar, as illustrated in figure 6.3. Numerous similar examples can be found.

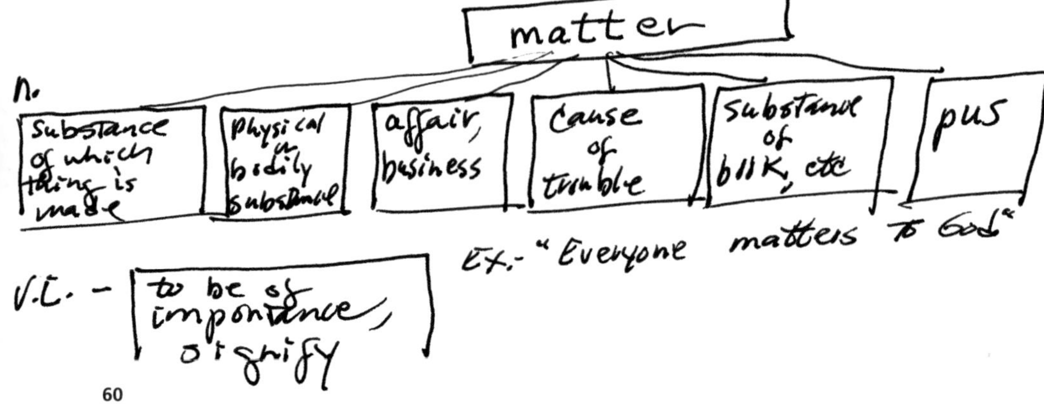

FIGURE 6.3

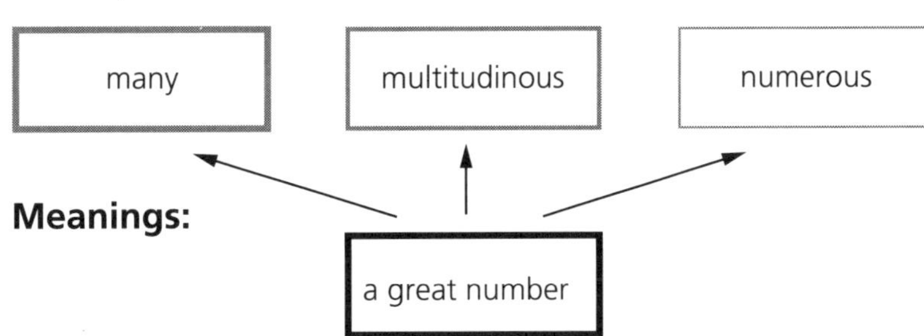

Exercise

2. Give five examples of a meaning that could be signified by more than one word, writing the different words above the meaning (as done in figure 6.3).

6.3 Think meaning

We have already seen that one word can have many different meanings. At the same time, one meaning can be expressed by different words. These facts lead to a complex network of relationships between different words and meanings in the same language. The examples of the words 'table', 'chair' and 'list' will be used to illustrate the point:

We saw in 6.1 that the word 'table' can have a number of possible meanings, of which three are:
1. "a flat piece of furniture",
2. "a set of facts" and
3. "to request a discussion".

These are three unrelated meanings.

The word 'chair' can have (among other things) the unrelated meanings of:
1. "a piece of furniture to sit on" and
2. "to lead a meeting".

The word 'list' can mean:
1. "a set of things written down" and
2. "a set of facts".

As illustrated in figure 6.4, the few listed meanings of these three words form a fairly complex network of relationships between the words and their meanings. The first meaning of 'table', "a flat piece of furniture" and the first one of 'chair', "a piece of furniture to sit on", are related, both belonging to what can be called the 'semantic field of furniture'.

The second meaning of 'table', "a set of facts", and that of 'list', "a set of things written down", are related, as they both belong to what can be called the 'semantic field of lists of facts'.

The last meaning of 'table', "to request a discussion", and the second meaning of 'chair', "to lead a meeting", are also related, belonging to what can be called the 'semantic field of meeting procedures'.

From this we see that the related meanings of different words are much nearer in meaning than the different unrelated meanings of the same word.

However, even those meanings that are related, do not have exactly the same meaning. For example, although 'table' (when meaning "set of facts") belongs to the same semantic field as 'list' (when it means "set of things written down"), each one has a distinct emphasis of its own.

FIGURE 6.4

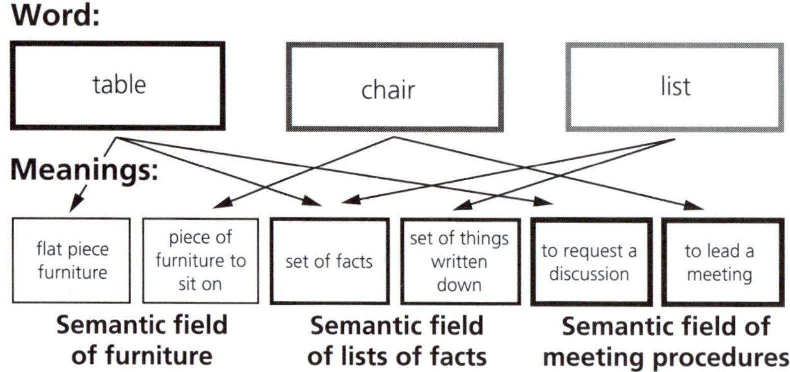

The fact that different words with the same or related meanings have more in common than the same word with different unrelated meanings, has important implications for the interpretation of the Bible. When studying a particular subject, we should seek its meaning and then trace the places where that meaning is found in the Bible. A specific meaning may very well be expressed by different words. If we do a strict 'word study' by indiscriminately following the same word through the Bible, we can very well end up grouping sheep and goats together as the same things! In addition, we are most likely going to miss quite a few passages where the same subject is treated, but with other words used.

One should always think of 'meaning studies'. When studying the concept of being born again, one would find that the words 'born again' are actually only used three times in the NIV, namely in Jn 3:3,7 and 1 Pet 1:23. Does that mean that these are the only places that the subject is mentioned in the Bible? The subject of the regeneration of the believer is indeed covered in many places in the Bible, but with various words that express the same concept. The believer is called a 'new creation' (2 Cor 5:17, Gal 6:15), is created in Christ Jesus (Eph 2:10), is born of God (1 Jn 2:29; 3:9; 4:7; 5:1), is united with Christ (Rom 6:1-14), etc.

6.4 Don't mix meanings

As one word can have different possible meanings, we have seen that the meaning in a particular sentence is dependent on the context. The question that we want to address here is whether a word used in context could refer to all or more than one of its possible meanings simultaneously. This question could be illustrated by referring again to our example of the word 'table'.

Let us say that we are analysing an English novel, and come to a place where the word table is used to refer to multiplication tables. Do we need to know that the 'table' can also refer to a piece of furniture, to understand what it means in this instance? By comparing these two meanings of 'table', we may conclude that both a multiplication table and a dining-room table are unchanging in their nature. They both share the property of staying the same, not changing. However, even though both 'tables' share this property, it is fairly obvious that multiplication tables and dining-room tables have absolutely nothing to do with each other.

Let us look at another English example, namely the word 'tear' in written form (not as it is pronounced). It could be used to refer to tears from crying or as a verb, for example to tear something up - two totally different meanings. It would not make any sense to say that the act of tearing has an element of grief, just because the same word could also be used for the tears you have when you cry!

We could mention many examples of mixing the different meanings in English, and its absurdity would be obvious to every one. When exactly the same thing is done in the interpretation of the Greek text of the New Testament, (although perhaps in a more subtle way than in our English examples!), it may be more difficult to spot that it is invalid and may even be seen to be scholarly. However, it is to be avoided! If we think back to our example of the Greek word sarx, we will remember that it has different meanings in six different places in the Bible (see 6.1). Just think of the interpretations one could arrive at by mixing some of those meanings and carrying them into a specific context.

As a rule, a word signifies one and only one meaning in the specific context that it is used. The exception is where a speaker purposely intends a play on meanings, eg in John's writings. But even then, if two meanings are purposely intended in a specific context, it only shows that the author wants his readers to acknowledge two readings of the particular sentence. Yet, in each reading the term will refer to only one meaning and not a 'mixture' of the two or more meanings.

Louw (1982:40-41) illustrates this point by referring to the opinions of different Bible translations and commentaries on the meaning of the Greek word 'katalambano' in Jn 1:5. Some choose the meaning "overwhelm" and others "understand". Both these meanings are possible and both fit the context. Because a play on words is characteristic of John's style, it is possible that the author intended both meanings. Even then meanings are not mixed, for if the context is understood in a specific way, the word signifies only one specific meaning. "Overwhelm" renders a feeling of joy - the darkness did not overwhelm the light; "understand" renders a sad tone - the darkness did not understand the light. In the context of Jn 1:5 the author sees the confrontation between light and darkness from two perspectives: triumph and melancholy. This does not mean that the meanings "overwhelm" and "understand" can be mixed to give an "overwhelming understanding"!

Even when the different meanings of a word are related, you should be careful not to carry all of them into a particular context. James Barr (1969:218) explains this by using the Greek word ekklesia (church) in the New Testament. If you were to ask what the New Testament teaches when using the term ekklesia, the answer may be given by adding up or compounding different statements about the ekklesia made in various passages. Thus we might say that 'the church is the body of Christ', 'the church is the first instalment of the Kingdom of God', 'the church is the Bride of Christ', and other such statements. The meaning of ekklesia in the NT could then be legitimately stated to be the totality of these meanings. However, when it is asked what the meaning of the word ekklesia is in a specific passage, the totality of these meanings may not be read into it (called 'illegitimate totality transfer'), but only the one applicable meaning according to that context.

You should learn to always ask the question: what does this word mean in this context?

Exercise

3. Complete the following golden rule for finding the meaning of a word:
One should learn to always ask the question: what does this word mean in this
Context ?

6.5 Meaning in the form of a word?

Since Socrates, it has been believed for many years that a word's meaning is closely related to its form. Thus if you want to arrive at the 'true meaning' of a word you should look for it in the form of the word. Fast movement or vehemence for example was believed to be expressed by the Greek letter 'rho' (r). Louw (1982:24) points out that the idea of fast movement or vehemence does not lie in the letter 'rho' but in the meaning of some words that happen to have the letter 'rho' in them. At the same time there are other words without a 'rho' in which the idea of fast movement or vehemence is expressed. There are also words with 'rho' in them that do not express fast movement or vehemence at all.

The ancient Greeks believed that if the form of a word does not readily offer the clues to the meaning of a word, then one should go back far enough into the word's history (called etymology) to find the 'real' or 'deeper' meaning.

An example of this quest for the 'real' meaning by going into the history of a word, is that of the Greek word for 'to sin', 'hamartano'. In the works of Homer, written more than eight centuries before the New Testament, 'hamartano' regularly occurs in situations referring to missing a target such as shooting an arrow at a target and missing it. The conclusion is then reached that to sin actually means to miss the target or purpose that God put us on earth for.

Three arguments could be brought against this method of interpretation:

1 The meaning of a word can change over a period of time. For example the word 'gay' was used some thirty years ago in everyday language as meaning lively and enjoyable. When saying that somebody is gay, you are actually expressing that he or she is lively and enjoyable to be with. The word 'gay' is not often used today with that meaning, but mostly with the meaning of homosexuality. If we make the mistake of trying to find the 'real meaning' of gay by going into the history of the word, we may very well arrive at the conclusion that homosexual people are actually lively and enjoyable people to be with because of their homosexuality. It is indeed not the previous meanings of a word that are relevant, but what it means at the time when it is used.

2 Even if you want to find a meaning in the history of a word, where will you stop in history - should you go back fifty, a hundred or three hundred years?

3 If you want to find a meaning in the history of a word, which one of the possible meanings at any given time in history should you choose?

It is clear from the above arguments that the use of the history of a word to establish its meaning can be very dangerous and indeed erroneous. A true life example is the story of a man who was in hospital, severely injured after an accident and wrestling with guilt about his sins. When a chaplain visited him and he expressed his need of forgiveness for his many sins, the chaplain told him not to be concerned about it because to sin 'actually means' only to "miss your target". And do not all of us miss our targets frequently?

Although it is obvious that a word at the time of its origin can be closely related to a specific occurrence or situation, it is in most cases impossible to track it down. Even if you are able to do so, it has generally been the case that as a word was rapidly established, its original meaning was lost. Louw (1982:25) illustrates this point by using an example Siertsema found in a study of the Yoruba of Nigeria. These people were inoculated for the first time in 1956, and they designated the process as 'ko nomba' because it appeared to them that a 'number was carved' on the people. At first the Yoruba connected this meaning with the process, but soon 'ko nomba' became the conventional term for inoculation. Later the Yoruba were amused to learn of the word's origin.

The principle that we should adhere to is that you should never use the form of a word to establish its meaning, as the relationship between form and meaning is arbitrary. This means that for example the word 'tape' could just as well have been 'teap'. It is only that the first form has been accepted by convention.

Even with compound words (made up of two separate words) you cannot assume that the total meanings of the different halves will give the meaning of the word. For some cases it may be true, but the meaning of the compound should first be established before you discover if this is the case. In English 'butterfly' cannot be associated with "butter" + "fly" or 'understand' with "under" + "stand".

The Greek word ekklesia (church) is sometimes explained as 'ek' + 'klesia'; "out" + "called". According to this explanation the church is the people called by God. This definition of ekklesia is not supported either by the meaning of the word in the New Testament, nor by its earlier usage and can more correctly be defined as "a congregation of Christians, implying interacting membership" (Louw & Nida 1988:126).

Exercise

4. Give three reasons why the meaning that a word had in history should not be used to establish its meaning today.

A. the meaning of a word can (& does) change over a period of time.

B. At which point ought one to stop to choose the "real" meaning? It's impossible to know

C. How many years back is the "correct" time?

Ex. 3 – Different words, similar meanings
Words

1) adult, complete, fit, full-grown, mellow, of age → **mature (adj.)**

2) captious, carping, censorious, fault-finding, finicky, niggling → **hypercritical**

3) agitation, delirium, frenzy, madness, panic, unreason → **hysteria**

4) attached, caring, devoted, doting, fond, warm-hearted, tender → **affectionate**

5) dead, empty, gathering dust, inactive, jobless, out of work, redundant, vacant → **idle** adj.

CHAPTER SEVEN

Explaining meaning in terms of semantic categories

Objectives

1. To know what is meant by semantic categories and to understand the value of looking at words from this perspective
2. To be able to name the four semantic categories and explain each one in your own words
3. To know the value of expressing (recasting) a word in a form according to its semantic category
4. To understand that a variety of relationships can be expressed by genitive constructions

Contents

STUDY TIP

Even if much of this is new to you, it should not be difficult to understand. Many examples are given and you should soon get the knack of it.

We have already seen how and why the different kinds of translations differ in their translation of words. We have also seen that a good understanding of the relationship between words and meaning is essential for exegesis. In this chapter we will continue with the same subject and explain how some translations differ from others, depending on whether words are translated according to semantic (meaning) categories or not.

The value of approaching the meaning of words according to their semantic categories is not only to understand better the differences between translations, but also to understand better the meaning of difficult words in the Bible.

7.1 Four semantic categories

As far as the grammar of language is concerned, we find different grammatical classes, eg nouns, verbs, pronouns, adjectives, etc. Various languages may have quite different sets of grammatical classes.

However, when we look at language from the level of meaning, or the semantic level, only four categories are found. These four categories cover all meanings in all languages and are thus universal. This means that all meaning can be divided into the categories of things, events (actions), attributes (descriptions) and relations, or combinations of any of these.

Things: This class refers to all things or objects, eg man, horse, kettle, etc. It also includes invisible objects, eg angel or spirit. It could also include things that exist only in the imaginations of people, eg dragon.

Events: This class covers all actions, processes and happening. This includes all movements whether voluntary or involuntary, and also mental processes, eg eat, run, drive, worship, think, fall, etc.

Attributes: This class includes words that give the qualities, quantities and degrees of things, events and other attributes, eg green, good, many, bad, lazy, (describing things); quickly, seldom, slowly, twice, often, (describing events); too, very, (describing other attributes).

Relations: This class contains the expression of the meaningful relationships between different kinds of terms. Relations may be expressed by words like a preposition or a conjunction: in, at, after. It may also be expressed by a morpheme like the English possessive suffix ('s): the boy's dog.

STUDY TIP

*The word TEAR may help you to remember the four categories, namely **Things**, **Events**, **Attributes** and **Relations**. If you know these four categories, it may save you a lot of tears during your exegesis!*

It is important to realise that the category in which a word falls, depends entirely upon each particular context. The same word may fall in different categories, depending on the context. Let us illustrate this by looking again at our example 'table'.

It could serve as an event:
He tabled a motion during the first ten minutes of the meeting.

It could serve as an attribute:
The top of the mountain is table flat.

It could serve as a thing:
The boy has to clear the table.

7.2 The relationship between semantic and grammatical categories

While keeping in mind that it could not be stated as an absolute rule, it could be said that the English language is easiest to understand when (illustrated in figure 7.1):
things are expressed by nouns,
events are expressed by verbs,
and attributes are expressed by adjectives and adverbs.

FIGURE 7.1

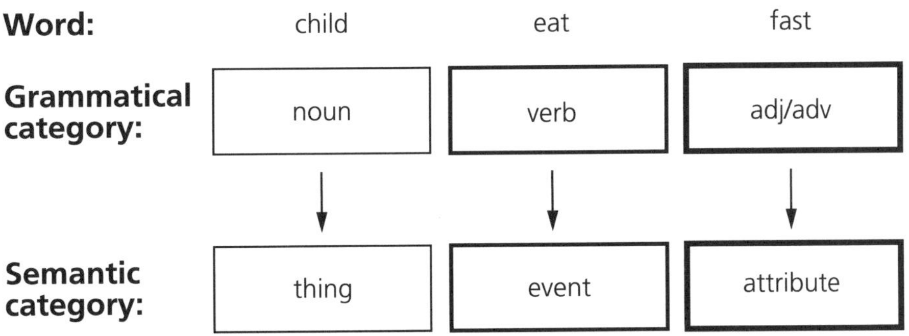

Unfortunately in practice there is not always a direct correlation between the different grammatical and semantic categories. Where events would normally be expressed by verbs, eg run, kick, bake, etc, we find that nouns can also express events. An example is the noun 'love', in the phrase 'God's love' in Rom 8:39 where it expresses an event, namely "God loves". We thus find a mismatching between the grammatical class of the word and the semantic category of its meaning, as shown in figure 7.2.

FIGURE 7.2

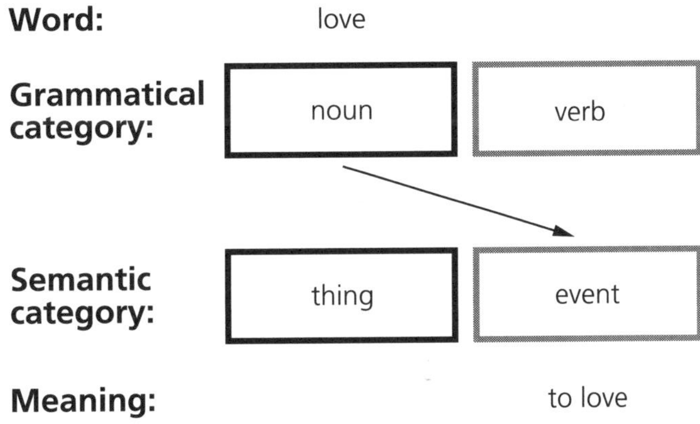

In cases of mismatching between grammatical classes and semantic categories, it helps to clarify the meaning of the word by changing the form of the word to match the semantic category to which its meaning belongs. In our example the noun 'love' will be changed or recast into a verb, namely 'loves', as illustrated in figure 7.3.

FIGURE 7.3

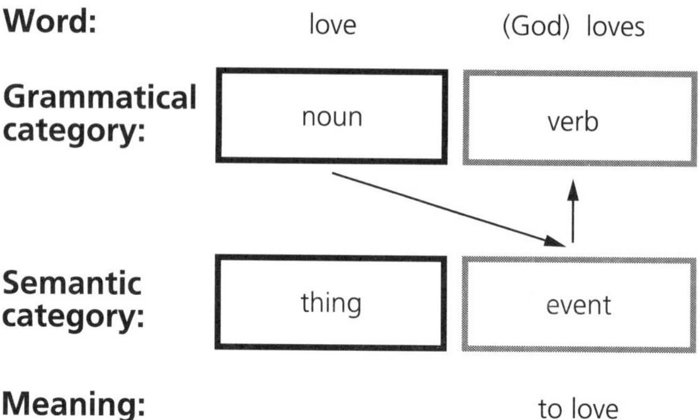

The following examples show how this process can make meaning much clearer.

Mark 1:4
NIV: And so John came...preaching a **baptism** of **repentance** for the **forgiveness** of sins.

GNB: So John appeared...preaching. "Turn away from your sins and be baptised," he told the people, "and God will forgive your sins."

NIV:	GNB:
baptism	be baptised
repentance	turn away from your sins
forgiveness (of sins)	God will forgive (your sins)

In this example three nouns that express events; 'baptism', 'repentance' and 'forgiveness', have been translated in the GNB using verbs. When an event is translated using a verb, the role of the different participants in the event can be seen more clearly. In the above example of 'forgiveness' we see that it is God who will forgive your sins.

Consider also the following examples where events are expressed using verbs (recast) in the second translation:

Heb 13:1
RSV: Let brotherly **love** continue
NIV: **Keep on loving** each other as brothers

Rom 1:16
RSV: For I am not ashamed of the gospel: it is the power of God for **salvation** to every one who has **faith...**
GNB: I have complete confidence in the gospel; it is God's power to **save** all who **believe...**

1 Tim 2:4
RSV: who desires all men to be saved and to come to the **knowledge** of the truth.
GNB: who wants everyone to be saved and to come to **know** the truth.

Mismatching may also occur where an attribute is expressed using a noun and not an adjective or adverb. An example will be given in 7.4.

7.3 Combinations of categories

There are cases when a word in its entirety can be classified into one semantic category but when it is broken up into its different components of meaning, falls into different categories. The word 'reconcile' is an example. As a whole it can be classified as an event. However, when it is broken down into its different components of meaning, it is an event as well as a relation: "to bring reconciliation between (persons)". Words that can be broken down into further components of meaning, should be recast into those components only if it helps you to understand their meanings more clearly.

Nida and Taber (1974:42-43) list the following types of combinations that occur frequently in English:

Thing-Event (T-E): The thing component performs the event, eg
disciple: one who learns
player: one who plays
heir: one who will inherit
sinner: one who sins

Event-Thing (E-T): The event happens to the thing component, eg
gift: that which is given
doctrine: that which is taught or believed

Event-Attribute (E-A): The event happens to someone or something which is implied. The attribute component qualifies what is happening (event) to the implied person, eg
sanctify: to make holy
justify: to declare innocent

Thing-Event-Attribute (T-E-A): The thing component performs the event that happens to someone (who is implied). The attribute component qualifies what is happening to the (implied) person, eg
sanctifier: person who makes holy
justifier: person who declares innocent

Event-Relation (E-R): The event component implies a relationship, eg
mediate: to act as an agent between others

It is also important to realise that event words can represent either simple events or complex ones. Nida and Taber (1974:43) use the example of the event words in the phrase: 'I am the resurrection and the life'. Both resurrection and life are events, but do not refer to the actions of rising and living, but to causative events, that is, to cause to rise and to cause to live. Thus this sentence actually means: "I am the one who causes people to rise from the dead and who causes people to live."

7.4 Genitive constructions

In English the genitive construction may have any of the following three forms:
the bag of the woman
the woman's bag
her bag

The genitive is frequently found in the Bible, especially in the epistles of Paul and can express different types of relationships between the parts of the construction. In many cases translations, especially literal ones, have not expressed these relationships in clear terms, but have carried the original Greek form over into the translation to make for a bit of 'biblical English'.

Genitive constructions are found with or without mismatching between the form of the words used and their respective semantic categories (see 7.2). When mismatching occurs, it is extremely helpful to recast the words according to their semantic categories. This will force you to clarify the underlying relationships, for example, who does what to whom.

It was mentioned at the end of 7.2 that mismatching can also occur when an attribute is expressed by a noun and not by an adjective or adverb. An example is 'the goodness of God'. This can be recast as 'God is good'. In this case the noun 'goodness' has been changed into an adjective 'good'.

We shall first look at relationships where genitive constructions don't need recasting, then where they do, because an attribute and/or an event is involved. In each case we will first list the genitive construction and its biblical reference, then express the relationship between the first part (A) and the second part (B) of the construction and then give its recast format. This is not an exhaustive list of the possible relationships that can be expressed by the genitive construction, but hopefully enough to be of help in analysing genitive constructions as they are found in the Bible. Beekman and Callow (1989: 249-266), from whom most of these examples are borrowed, is recommended for further examples.

Genitive constructions not needing recasting:
'the house of Philip' (Acts 21:8)
A is possessed by B - Philip's house

'the two wings of the eagle' (Rev 12:14)
A is part of B - the eagle's two wings

'brother of James' (Jude 1)
A is related to B by kinship - James' brother

'servant of the high priest' (Matt 26:51)
A is related to B by role - the high priest's servant

'Bethlehem of Judea' (Mt 2:1)
A is located in B - Bethlehem which is in Judea

'the city of Jerusalem' (Luke 24:49)
A is identified by B - the city which is called Jerusalem

'a cup of cold water' (Matt 10:42)
A contains B - a cup which contains cold water

'the mystery of Christ' (Col 4:3)
A is about B - the mystery which is about Christ

'a crown of twelve stars' (Rev 12:1)
A consists of B - a crown consisting of twelve stars

Genitive constructions needing recasting:
'the goodness of God' (Rom 2:4)
A describes B - God is good

'a crown of glory' (1 Pet 5:4)
B describes A - the crown is glorious

'the riches of the kindness' (Rom 2:4)
A indicates the degree of B - (he) is very kind

'the judgment of God' (Rom 2:3)
B does A - God will judge

'the love of the Father' (1 John 2:15)
A happens to B - (he) loves the Father

'the love of the truth' (2 Thes 2:10)
B describes the content of A - (they) love that which is true

'judgment of the great day' (Jude 6)
B indicates the time of A - (God) will judge (people) on that great day

'the day of the judgment' (1 John 4:17)
A indicates the time of B - when (God) will judge (men)

'the words of the grace' (Luke 4:22)
B describes how A is done - (he) spoke graciously

'a wisdom of word' (1 Cor 1:17)
A describes how B is done - (I) spoke wisely

'full of faith' (Acts 6:5)
A indicates the degree of B - (he) trusted in (Jesus) very much

'the law of Moses' (Acts 13:39)
B does the implicit event to A - the law which Moses wrote

'the God of peace' (Phil 4:9)
A causes the state of B - God who causes (you) to be peaceful

7.5 The value of recasting

When a word is recast it helps to clarify its meaning. Terms that Christians have become accustomed to and perhaps do not always understand the precise meaning of, take on new meaning. Compare the following readings:

Rom 1:17:
NIV: For in the gospel a **righteousness** from God is revealed...
GNB: For the gospel reveals how God **puts people right with himself**.

Rom 10:3:
NIV: Since they did not know the **righteousness** that comes from God...
GNB: They have not known the way in which God **puts people right with himself**

Not only does recasting help to clarify 'religious jargon' for the interpreter of the Bible, but it also makes it easier to communicate the gospel to the unsaved. Believers who listen to teaching and preaching will be helped by the recast form and become equipped to understand the Bible better when they use it themselves.

The four semantic categories are universal, and therefore are of great value in communicating the gospel cross-culturally. For example if a missionary knows that the term righteousness expresses semantically an event (put), thing (people), attribute (right) and relation (with), it will help him to communicate what 'the righteousness from God' means to any people group, whether the word 'righteousness' exists in their vocabulary or not.

It is important to remember that when recasting you are not adding anything, merely making explicit what is implicit in the word or combination of words.

7.6 The importance of the context in recasting

We have already seen (7.1) that the semantic category of a word depends on the context. The same word, eg 'table', can belong to three different categories, depending on the context in which it is used. For this reason it is extremely important to examine the context carefully when deciding on the semantic category and the relationship between the different elements involved. For instance, in Rom 8:39 and 1 John 5:3 we find the phrase 'love of God'. When we examine the context we find that in the first case it refers to God's love for us while in the second one it refers to our love for God.

Another example is the phrase 'worship of angels' in Col 2:18. Does it mean "the angels worship" or "to worship the angels"? Both views are held by commentators. It seems that the immediate context indicates that it is the latter meaning. This is also in line with the message of the whole of Colossians.

Exercises

1. List five examples in the GNB where the equivalent of a noun in the NIV is translated with a verb. Do it by first giving the Scripture reference, then writing down the text of both translations and underlining the noun in the NIV and the verb in the GNB.
2. List five places in the Bible where a genitive construction in the NIV is translated in the GNB without the genitive format. Do it by first giving the Scripture reference, then writing down the text of both translations and underlining the genitive construction in the NIV and the recast format in the GNB.
3. Look again at the possible combinations of categories that have been given under 7.3 and make certain that you understand why those words from the examples belong to those combinations of categories.

part three

THE STEPS OF EXEGESIS

CHAPTER EIGHT

Step 1: Research the communication situation

Objectives

1. To understand how the meaning of a passage is influenced by the communication situation
2. To know how to research the communication situation
3. To know how much time to allocate each step of exegesis

Contents

STUDY TIP
The emphasis of this chapter is to show the logical reason for this step.

We have already seen (2.2) that exegesis is the process by which we attempt to arrive at the message that the original receiver got from a passasge. To do so we get into our time machine called exegesis and put ourselves into the situation of the original receiver. In other words, we seek to bridge the differences between the original receiver and ourselves. This is best done by following specific steps towards that end.

8.1 Exegesis is done in steps

Although we can distinguish between different steps, all of them flow together to form one integrated process. It is almost like driving a car. You have to follow different steps, like pressing in the clutch, putting the gear in position, releasing the clutch and simultaneously putting pressure on the accelerator. The gentle flow of the one step into the other makes for a smooth drive or the lack of it!

The different steps of exegesis should not only add to one another, but also aim at the same end result, which will be a product of the integration of them all. It could be compared to baking a cake. Although different steps are used, they all combine to give an end product that is greater (more delicious!) than the different steps (ingredients).

There is a strong inter-relationship between the different steps of exegesis and sometimes it may be necessary to go back to a previous step. This may be either because a later step has influenced the findings of a previous one or because a later step requires some more information from a previous one.

It is important to budget one's time well when doing exegesis. It is always a temptation to be side-tracked into what is interesting but not important. The end goal of the process has to be kept in mind and accordingly time should be spent on each step of exegesis as it progresses towards that end goal.

The five main steps of exegesis are:

1. Research the communication situation
2. Establish the literary context
3. Analyse the passage (semantic discourse analysis)
4. Relate the message to the broader biblical and theological framework
5. Read the interpretations of others (eg commentaries)

These five steps are the same for all the different types of literature in the Bible. However, there will be some adaptations required to step three, 'analyse the passage', according to the type of literature (the different types of literature will be discussed in some detail in the next chapter). In this part of the book (part three) exegesis will be discussed for exposition/exhortation, the literature type predominantly used in the New Testament epistles. In part four we will show how the steps are to be adapted for poetry and in part five for narrative.

Figure 8.1 shows the steps of exegesis for exposition/exhortation. Just as in figure 2.3, the process of exegesis is illustrated here starting from the top with the text of the Bible itself and moving towards the deeper level of meaning by bridging all the differences of language, culture and history that exist between us and the original receivers.

The different steps of exegesis are indicated by boxes that differ in length, according to the proportion of time that should be spent on each. According to this, most of the time should be spent on the analysis of the text. Obviously these should not be seen as absolutes, but only as guidelines. The proportion of time spent on each step may also differ according to the passage you are working on.

In this, and the next eight chapters (chapter 8-16), all the steps of exegesis will be discussed, explained and illustrated. For illustrative purposes, the exegesis will be on a paragraph from Colossians (1:21-23). In this chapter we will discuss the first step of exegesis, namely researching the situation in which the communication took place, called the communication situation, or context of communication.

FIGURE 8.1
The steps of exegesis

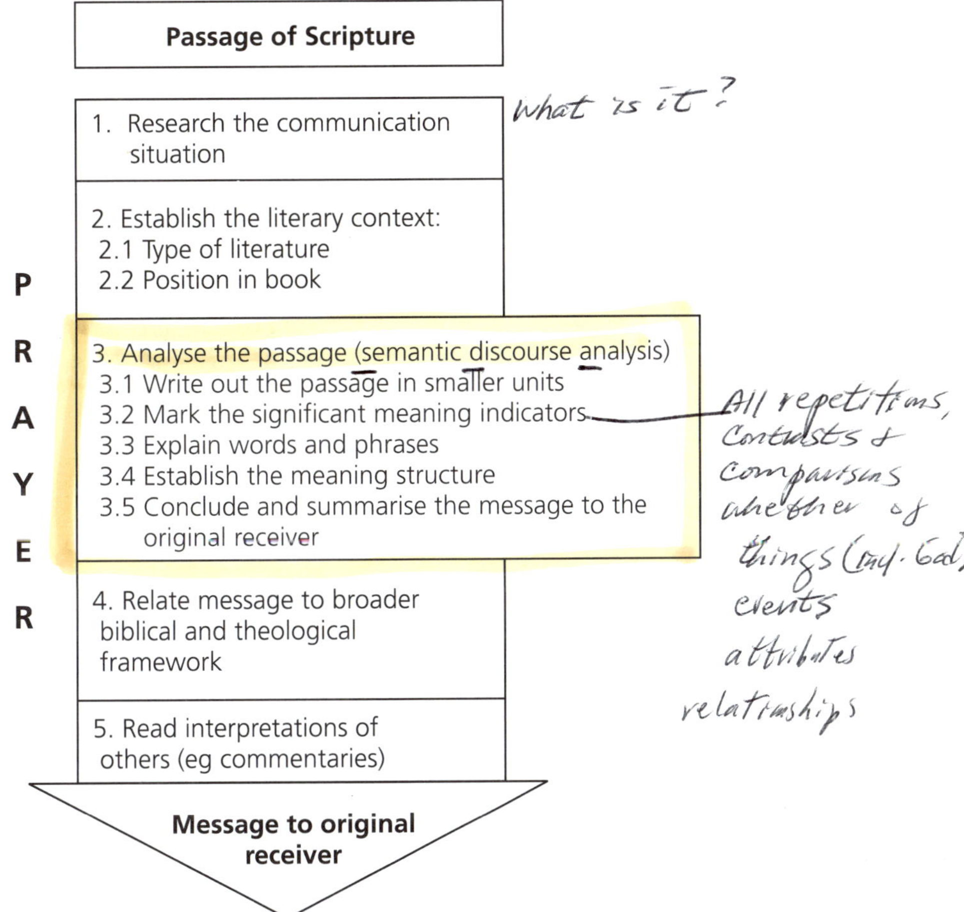

8.2 How the communication situation influences meaning

The same combination of words can have different meanings according to the situation (context) in which they are used. The meaning of sentences may depend on the people who use them and on the relationships between the participants in the process of communication, eg the sentence 'I love you' can have different meanings when used by the following people:

A boy saying it to his mother
A teenage boy saying it to a teenage girl
A husband saying it to his wife
A minister/pastor saying it to his congregation

STUDY TIP
It may help to use a bit of imagination to put yourself in each situation when these different examples are used.

The meaning does not only depend on the persons who are communicating, but also on the specific circumstances in which it takes place. If we take the first example of the boy telling his mum that he loves her, it will have a different meaning when it is said in the following circumstances:

> The mother has just prepared a nice meal.
> The mother has just told her son off.

In the first case the boy expresses his appreciation to his mother for what she does for him. In the second case he attempts to make up for his wrong behaviour and to be reconciled to her.

In the example of the teenage boy saying to the teenage girl that he loves her, consider the differences of meaning if said against the following different backgrounds:

> They are out on a date and it is a beautiful moonlit evening as they walk through a park.
> They are in a church youth meeting and the leader has just encouraged everybody to express their Christian love to one another.

Strongly linked with the circumstances is the purpose of the communication. This may not always be that easy to establish in every day life, but it can make a radical difference to the meaning. In the above example of the boy saying to a girl in the park that he loves her, the meaning of the utterance will depend largely on his motives. One possibility is that he says it to gain her favour in order to take advantage of her physically. In this case the sentence 'I love you' actually expresses "I feel physically attracted to you and would like to have a physical relationship with you".

The cultural distinctions against which the communication takes place also need to be considered as part of the communication situation. When thinking about the example where teenagers are encouraged to show their Christian love for one another, we can only think of the different ways in which it could be done by Christians from different cultures and how that could lead to misunderstanding. A real life example of this is where teenagers from different cultures were together in a Christian discipleship course. The leader encouraged them to express their Christian love to one another. The outcome was that the father of a young man from a non-Western background who was in the group, contacted the father of a Western fellow student the next week, proposing that they arrange a marriage between their children. What the girl wanted to communicate was "I love you as a Christian brother". The young man understood: "This girl loves me so much that we can get married."

From the above examples of everyday life we have seen how drastically the elements that form the communication context (situation) could influence the meaning. For this reason, in exegesis, we have to discover all the necessary information about the communication situation that may influence the meaning of the text.

In researching the communication context of a Bible book, it is important not only to answer questions about people, circumstances and cultural distinctions, but also about the theological understanding of the people involved. The main categories that we find here are those of Old Testament times and those of the New Testament. In the Old Testament times the Lord required from his people to live with an expectation of the coming of the Messiah. In New Testament times people live in response to the fact that he has come.

In enquiring what a passage of Scripture said to the original receivers, we cannot assume that they understood what we understand today. Although the prophets from Old Testament times, for example, expected the coming of the Messiah and prophesied about it through the working of the Holy Spirit, they could not have known as much about Him as we do, because we have the privilege of looking back on his advent. For this reason, in our exegesis, we need to limit our findings to what the original receivers must have understood.

While we limit ourselves at this stage to the theological understanding of the original receivers of the passage, our end findings should obviously fit into the broader framework of the consistent message of the Bible. We will actually test our end findings by comparing how they fit into the broader framework of the whole message during step four of exegesis.

The better you understand God's growing revelation of himself and his purposes in the unfolding of history, the easier you will find it to limit yourself to the understanding of the specific original receivers. At the same time, it will also be easier for exegesis to be done in such a way that the message will indeed fit into the broader framework of God's revelation throughout history.

8.3 How to research the communication situation

Our first source of information for the context of communication is the explicit information that the particular Bible book itself contains. If we take the letter of Paul to the Colossians as an example, we will find that it provides us with answers to the questions of

- who wrote it
- to whom
- under which circumstances
- for what purpose.

In addition to this we could find some other explicit information about people, places, movements of people, etc in the book itself.

More details about people and places can often be obtained from other Bible books, for example where a person is mentioned in more than one book. The name of Timothy can be found in 10 different books. This list of references can be obtained from a study Bible or a concordance. If we want to know more about Timothy we can read all these references.

Sometimes it is difficult to find explicit information about the author's purpose and the problems that he addressed, but we can get a good indication of it by researching carefully the content of the book itself. For example, we possess very little information about the heresy in Colosse that Paul is writing against because the nature of it is not explicitly described. However, we get some indication of what it might have been by considering what Paul says to correct it.

In addition to the Bible we sometimes find information about the communication context from outside sources, like the writings of the early church fathers, secular historians, writers and everyday literature of that time, as well as reports about archaeological findings. In most cases study Bibles, Bible dictionaries and encyclopaedias will provide an adequate selection of this outside or extra-biblical information.

8.4 How far to go in my research

When researching the communication situation of a specific passage, it is important to know how far to go in one's research. Theoretically it could become a never-ending exercise and much valuable time could be spent on this. The principle is to obtain information that could influence the interpretation of the specific passage.

Most of the time, when you start with exegesis, it is impossible to know how much information you will need as it will differ from passage to passage. As a guideline, you don't want to spend too much of the available time on research at the beginning of the exegesis. Be prepared to return to this step later on if it becomes clear that more information is needed.

It is best if you can research the communication situation from the Bible itself, but it is not always practical time-wise to do so. Again, reference works like Bible dictionaries and encyclopaedias can be very helpful in giving a summary of the biblical and extra-biblical information. You must find out whether the reference works treat the information that is found in the Bible as reliable or not, so that you can decide what to accept and what to reject.

Sometimes it is impossible to find the necessary information about a specific communication context in the Bible. In cases like this you should be careful not to base your interpretation on mere speculation about the communication situation, but take care to interpret the particular subject in the light of other Scripture passages that deal with it.

Be encouraged to know that as you continue to interpret the Bible over a period of time, you build up a valuable framework of knowledge of the communication context and become more sensitive to it.

8.5 The communication situation of Colossians

From Colossians itself we find the following information about the context of communication:

- Paul wrote it (1:1).
- Timothy was with Paul when he wrote it (1:1). Although it could appear from this verse that Paul and Timothy were co-authors, it is unlikely, as Paul uses the first person singular (I) later in the letter.
- It was written to the Christians in Colosse (1:2).
- The church in Colosse was most probably planted by Epaphras (1:7-8). Epaphras was with Paul when he wrote the letter (4:12) and also took some kind of responsibility for the churches in Laodicea and Hierapolis (4:13). It seems that Epaphras brought Paul up to date with the situation in Colosse (1:8 and 4:12).
- Paul was in prison when he wrote this letter as he refers to a 'fellow-prisoner' (4:10) and asks them to 'remember his chains' (4:18).
- As far as the purpose of the book is concerned, it is clear that Paul addresses some heresies that were a threat to the church (2:8). Their teachings are not stated explicitly.
- Tychicus most probably took the letter to the Colossians, accompanied by Onesimus (4:7-9).

In some of the other books of the Bible we can find more information that adds to the picture of the communication situation:

- In Acts, as well as in Paul's other letters, we can come to know him and his colleagues better.
- In Acts 19:9-10 it is mentioned that Paul had discussions daily with the disciples and that it 'went on for two years, so that all the Jews and Greeks who lived in the province of Asia heard the word of the Lord.' Was this perhaps the time that the church in Colosse was planted?
- In Philemon 23 there is a reference to Epaphras as Paul's 'fellow-prisoner in Christ Jesus'.

Paul does not tell us what the heresy addressed was, but we can infer from the content of Colossians that:

- It required circumcision (2:11).
- It required strict adherence to rules about the use of food and the keeping of religious festivals of a Judaistic nature (2:16).
- It involved the worship of angels and most probably the seeing of visions (2:18).
- Harsh treatment of the body, perhaps in the form of asceticism, was required (2:23).
- According to these characteristics it certainly did not adhere to the centrality of Christ. This can also be derived from the fact that Paul found it necessary to emphasise the supremacy of Christ (1:15-20).

Finally we can turn to outside sources for some more information on the context of communication. The NIV Study Bible (1987:1776) for example, has the view that the heresy in the Colossian church might have been a mixture of an extreme form of Judaism and an early stage of Gnosticism. The NIV Study Bible (1987:1866) gives as introduction to 1 John the following helpful description of Gnosticism:

> One of the most dangerous heresies of the first two centuries of the church was Gnosticism. Its central teaching was that spirit is entirely good and matter is entirely evil. From this unbiblical dualism flowed five important errors:
>
> 1. Man's body, which is matter, is therefore evil. It is to be contrasted with God, who is wholly spirit and therefore good.
> 2. Salvation is the escape from the body, achieved not by faith in Christ but by special knowledge (the Greek word for "knowledge" is gnosis, hence Gnosticism).
> 3. Christ's true humanity was denied in two ways: (1) Some said that Christ only seemed to have a body, a view called Docetism, from Greek dokeo ("to seem"), and (2) others said that the divine Christ joined the man Jesus at baptism and left him before he died, a view called Cerinthianism, after its most prominent spokesman, Cerinthus. This view is the background of much of 1 John (see 1:1; 2:22; 4:2-3).
> 4. Since the body was considered evil, it was to be treated harshly. This ascetic form of Gnosticism is the background to part of the letter to the Colossians (2:21-23).
> 5. Paradoxically, this dualism also led to licentiousness. The reasoning was that, since matter - and not the breaking of God's law (1 Jn 3:4) - was considered evil, breaking his law was of no moral consequence.

The Gnosticism addressed in the NT was an early form of the heresy, not the intricately developed system of the second and third centuries. In addition to that seen in Colossians and in John's letters, acquaintance with early Gnosticism is reflected in 1, 2 Timothy, Titus, and 2 Peter and perhaps 1 Corinthians.

Exercises

Research the communication situation of Paul's letter to Philemon in the following way:

1. Read only the text of Philemon and list the explicit information on the communication context that you were able to find.
2. Use the rest of the Bible to see whether you can find more information about the people and places mentioned in Philemon (it is not necessary to do that for Paul!).
3. Study the text of Philemon carefully in order to find out what the purpose of the letter was and which problems are addressed in it.
4. Use helps like Bible dictionaries and encyclopaedias to research the communication situation and compare your findings with theirs.

CHAPTER NINE

Step 2: Establish the literary context

Objectives

1. To understand that the kind of literature that a passage is written in, influences its meaning
2. To identify the major forms of discourse
3. To identify the major discourse types and their characteristics
4. To recognize the importance of exegeting a passage in the context of its position in the whole Bible book

Contents

STUDY TIP

The content of this chapter is explained using examples. Make certain that as the different terms are introduced, you understand how one differs from the other, eg major forms of discourse, major discourse types and different genres.

By researching the communication situation, we put ourselves in the situation of the original receiver and are now able to see the Bible passage that we are exegeting in its communication or historical context.

With the second step of exegesis, establishing the literary context, we turn to the text itself. Firstly, we need to find out what kind of literature we are dealing with (step 2.1). Then we need to discover how the particular paragraph which we are dealing with relates to the whole Bible book (step 2.2).

We will firstly deal with step 2.1, the significance of the kind of literature used (9.1 to 9.6) and then with step 2.2, the position of the passage in the rest of the Bible book (9.7 & 9.8).

STUDY TIP

Be careful not to confuse references to steps of exegesis, eg step2.1, with references to the subheadings of chapters, eg 2.1 (The three processes of interpretation).

9.1 The kind of literature influences the meaning

If we compare the texts of Judges, the Psalms and of one of Paul's epistles, it would not require much analysis to see that they are not the same. The style of Judges is very similar to that of a story, the style of Psalms is very similar to that of poetry and Paul's epistles look similar to the style of an essay. These differences in style (or kind) of literature in which a biblical passage is written, have to be taken into account when exegeting.

From our daily experience of reading the newspaper, we know how to differentiate in our interpretation between a news report, an editorial and a comic strip. We do not give the same value to what is written in a comic strip as we do to the main report on the front page. The comic strip is evaluated according to its entertainment value and the main report according to its portrayal of the truth.

The fact that the kind of literature contributes significantly to the meaning of the passage, is clearly illustrated in the following example used by Nida et al (1983:56-57):

Format A:

After years of stock car racing, running rifles to Cuba, money from Rio, high diving from helicopters into the Gulf; after life at gunpoint, on the dare, my father can't make the trip out of Miami.

Format B:

After years of stock car racing, running
rifles to Cuba, money from Rio, high
diving from helicopters into the Gulf;
after life at gunpoint, on the dare,
my father can't make the trip out of Miami.

In format A one immediately assumes that this is a factual description about somebody's father who has difficulties in overcoming fear at an advanced age despite his earlier dare-devil existence.

When looking at format B, the meaning changes considerably. Although the content is the same, the poetic format suggests that there is more involved than meets the eye. An emotive and an evaluative element is brought into the interpretation.

Nida et al (1983:56-57) reveal that format B is actually the correct reproduction of the first paragraph of a poem by Daniel Mark Epstein entitled 'Miami' (printed on page 202 of The American Scholar for the Spring, 1982).

9.2 The major forms of discourse

When we look at the different kinds of literature in the Bible, we will see that the two main forms are poetry and prose. Either form could be used for the same purpose, for example to explain, to exhort, or to tell a story. The decision whether to use poetry or prose is usually culturally determined.

In Hebrew literature, poetry was used very effectively for songs and hymns, curses and blessings, judgments of God and announcements that punishment was coming. Not every language uses poetry in all these ways and for that reason there is a strong argument not always to translate poetic parts of the Bible into poetry in other languages, but in the form that will best suit the language into which it is translated (De Waard & Smalley 1979:15-16).

For example, that is the reason why the GNB translates most of the book of Amos into prose and not into poetry, in which the Hebrew text was written. The translators believed that the message of Amos would actually be better communicated to readers of modern day English if translated into prose and not poetry.

9.3 The major discourse types

Once an author has decided whether he wants to use poetry or prose, he starts to organise his writing according to the purpose that he has in mind. This will lead to the selection from the four major discourse types: exposition, exhortation, procedure and narrative.

The combination of two characteristics determines which one of the four major discourse types we are dealing with. These characteristics are chronology and prescription (Beekman et al 1981:35-40). When chronology is present, events are mentioned in sequence. When prescription is present, it expresses explicitly in the discourse type what should be done. All four discourse types have logical relations, but two of them have their logical relations within a chronological framework and two do not (see figure 9.1).

FIGURE 9.1
The main characteristics of the discourse types

	Nonprescriptive	**Prescriptive**
Chronological framework	Narrative	Procedure
Non-chronological framework	Exposition	Exhortation

It should be mentioned right from the beginning that these discourse types should not be seen as pure forms. This is because there is a tendency for overlapping and mixing of discourse types. Certain texts may reflect primarily one specific discourse type, but most discourses are a mixture or blend of these four major types. For example, exposition may contain some narrative while exhortation may contain procedure as well as exposition.

STUDY TIP
How do you tell which discourse type you are dealing with? The presence or absence of chronology and prescription provides the answer. Keep an eye out for this in the following examples.

An example of narrative in the Bible is the book of Ruth. It has a chronological framework - it records one event after another in the life of Naomi and her daughter-in-law, Ruth. It is nonprescriptive as it does not explicitly give instructions to the reader. In spite of this fact it has a specific message from God to the original receivers of the book as well as to Christians of all times. This message is not always easy to find in narrative and requires precise exegesis.

An example of procedure in the Bible is Num 8:5-14 where God gave Moses instructions on how to set apart the Levites. It is prescriptive and simultaneously chronological because one step has to be done after another.

An example of exposition is the first part of Col up to 2:5. Paul gives no explicit instructions and thus writes nonprescriptively. He does not put his statements in chronological order, but builds one doctrine upon another as he continues to bring his message.

An example of exhortation is the last part of Col, from 2:6. Paul writes in directly prescriptive terms, telling the Colossian Christians how they should behave. It is not in a chronological framework because he does not give them instructions to be followed in a specific order.

The discourse type of a particular Bible book can be classified according to the type that provides the framework of the book. That does not mean that the specific discourse type is necessarily found more often, but that the overall structure of the book is provided by the characteristics of a particular discourse type.

9.4 The different genres in the Bible

The different discourse types can be used in specific genres. For example Paul uses mainly exposition and exhortation, but he writes in the format or genre of a letter. He could just as well have written an essay, but obviously felt that letters would suit his purposes better, in communicating his message in a more personal form.

The principal genres of the New Testament are dramatic history, letters and the apocalyptic.

Dramatic history is a genre of the narrative discourse type. It may either focus upon an individual, as in the gospels, or on the activities of a group of people, like the Acts of the Apostles. Its characteristics will be discussed in more detail in Chapter 19.

Letters are either personal and addressed to a specific group of people, or written to a wider group of Christians and therefore more general. This will be discussed in more detail in chapter 29.

Apocalyptic text is a genre of the narrative discourse type. It is distinct in its heavy symbolism, veiled allusions, and its involved series of sequences that reflect relationships in time and space. It will be discussed in more detail in chapter 30.

A specific genre usually characterises a Bible book, although other kinds of literature might be found within (embedded in) it, eg Paul's letter to the Colossians also contains an early Christian hymn (1:15-20), that should be treated as such when analysed.

The primary embedded genres of the New Testament are miracle stories, parables, allegories, conversations, speeches (teaching, sermons, legal pleas), liturgical fragments and quotations.

9.5 The value of different kinds of literature

Different literature forms, discourse types and genres exist in all literate cultures and one might very well wonder what their real value is. Why is everything not written in poetry? The reason is that it gives writers the opportunity to use the type of text that will best suit their specific purpose and material according to the circumstances and culture in which they communicate. If a writer today wants to communicate news to a nation, he would not use poetry but a news report as it best serves his purpose and circumstances.

The receivers know the use and function of the different types of text and read them accordingly. When you want to know how to prepare a certain dish you turn to a recipe. From a recipe you expect certain elements, eg a list of the ingredients needed to prepare the dish and instructions of how to do so. To have a text type like a recipe thus serves not only the writer, but also the reader in his interpretation.

Although it is true that particular kinds of material can more readily be expressed in specific kinds of literature, it should never be thought that a specific idea can only be expressed by one kind of literature. For example to deal with the subject of romantic love, one can employ a poem, a story, a proverb or a parable. Although these different kinds of literature could be used to express the same idea, each one would add its own significant dimension to the theme.

The exact significance of each kind of literature is not always easy to define, although readers would readily be aware of the contrasts and similarities between different ones.

One kind of literature can serve different functions. For example a letter could be used to tell a story, describe something, or defend a view by means of argument. Similarly a poem could be used for exactly the same functions, and accordingly we find different kinds of poetry.

9.6 Read the Bible according to the kind of literature used

Just as we daily read texts, (such as the newspaper), according to the kind of literature in which it is written, we should also interpret passages of the Bible according to their literary style.

To find out what kind of literature a passage is written in, we need to ask ourselves a series of questions. Here, we will look specifically at Col 1:21-23:

Q1: In which form of discourse is the passage written?
Answer: It can be either prose or poetry. In our example it is written in prose.

Q2: In which major discourse type is the passage written?
Answer: It can be narrative, procedure, exposition or exhortation. In this case it is exposition.

Q3: In which genre is the book written?
Answer: There are a number of possibilities, like a parable, miracle story or letter. Colossians is a letter that is addressed to a church (not an idividual).

Q4: Is the specific paragraph written in an embedded genre?
Answer: Col 1:21-23 is not, but there are strong indications that the previous paragraph, Col 1:15-20, is an early Christian hymn.

Because the form of discourse and the discourse type influence how we read a particular passage in the Bible, it will also influence how we analyse a passage (step three of exegesis). Although the steps of analysis are principally the same, they are adapted for three main types of analysis; poetic, expositional and narrative analysis.

Poetic analysis will be used where the form of the text is explicitly poetic (with the text printed in poetic lines) in the Bible.

If the text does not require poetic analysis, then either expositional or narrative analysis will be used.

Expositional analysis is used when the the work is not set in a chronological framework and will be applied to the major discourse types of exposition and exhortation.

Narrative analysis is used when the events are set in a chronological framework and so will be applied to the major discourse types of narrative and procedure.

Each of these methods of analysis will in turn need 'fine tuning' and adaptating according to the specific genre. At certain times it may even be necessary to use a combination of methods. For example, with the interpretation of some of the prophets, where the form is poetic and the discourse type partly narrative and partly exposition.

In this section of the book (part three, chapters 8-16) we are dealing with expositional analysis that is especially applicable to exposition and exhortation. In part four (chapters 17-18) we deal with exegesis of poetry and in part five (chapters 19-20), narrative exegesis.

Exercise

1. Find a chapter in the Bible where each one of the major discourse types features predominantly, eg one chapter where narrative is used predominantly, etc.

9.7 Read in the context of the whole

We are all aware of the danger of misusing the words of someone, by quoting something in the absence of what has come before or after - out of the context of the whole. This practice can lead to much damage and we would all agree that it is to be condemned, especially when it is done with something that we have said!

When interpreting the Bible, we need to make sure that we don't do exactly the same. Because the author communicated his message as a whole in one book, our exegesis of a particular passage must be in the context of the book from which it comes. For instance, when we read Paul's letters, we will find that every one of them forms a wonderful unity in its composition. Passages are usually built on what has come before and also form the basis for what comes later.

There is a temptation to do with Bible books what we would never do with other literary works, eg those of Shakespeare, namely to take small parts of it and interpret it out of context. One of the reasons for this may be that the different 'chapters' and 'verses' of the Bible may encourage us to view them as separate and independent units. It should be remembered that the chapter and verse divisions as we know them today are not original. For example the New Testament books were only divided into our numbered verses in 1551. This was done by the Swiss printer and publisher Stephanus. According to legend some parts of the work were done on horse-back - a legend that probably wanted to say that he did it haphazardly as if on horse-back.

It may take some reorientation for many Christians to realise that the best way of reading the Bible is actually doing it book by book. Each book forms a wonderful unity in its content and the structure in which it is written.

9.8 How to discover the structure of a Bible book

You can get an idea of the structure of a book by reading through it in one sitting, ignoring the chapter and verse divisions, and following the flow of thought as it develops from the beginning to the end of the book. As the paragraph is the smallest unit of communication and the basic unit for analysis (see 4.5), we need to see the flow of thought of the whole book, as it develops from one paragraph to the next. This implies that you need to have a good understanding of the central meaning of each paragraph.

Although it is possible to get an idea of the structure of a Bible book written in exposition/exhortation by reading through it, you will be limited in understanding it well because of the need to have a good understanding of the central meaning of each paragraph - something that is usually only obtained by a thorough analysis of it.

As the message of each paragraph of a book is analysed, it is necessary to see what its boundaries are, in other words where it starts and where it ends. This is done by looking at the content of the individual paragraph, making certain that every part of it belongs together to contribute to its central message. At the same time, one has to look at the content of the neighbouring paragraphs to make certain that sentences at the end of the previous paragraph and at the beginning of the next one do indeed belong to those paragraphs. This is done by looking at how the neighbouring paragraphs differ from the paragraph that is being interpreted.

As the line of thought of a book develops from one paragraph to the next, some paragraphs will be more related to one another than to others. When neighbouring paragraphs are very closely related, they can form a 'block' of thought (we can call this a 'block of paragraphs'). In the proposed structure of Colossians (see figure 9.2), 1:3 to 2:5 form such a block of paragraphs, with the central meaning that the beliefs and life of the Colossians and Christians are based on Christ.

Similarly 2:8-2:23 link together as exhortation not to follow false teaching, and 3:1-4:6 as exhortation to live a holy life. The paragraph 2:6-7 forms the introduction to these two blocks.

The opening greeting of the letter is 1:1-2, while 4:7-18 serve as the final greeting with news and commendations.

The paragraph divisions of the NIV have been followed except in three cases (1:9-14, 2:1-5, 4:2-6) where each paragraph has been split into two separate paragraphs - as indicated in figure 9.2. All the paragraphs in 3:18-4:1 have been summarised together because of the strong links between them and because some of them are one line paragraphs. The same has been done with 4:10-18.

In the overall structure of a book, blocks of paragraphs can function on different levels. Theoretically, blocks can group together in an unlimited number of levels. The structure of Colossians that I propose (figure 9.2) functions on four levels. For example, the block of paragraphs formed by 3:12-4:6 functions on the fourth level. On the third level this block forms part of the block of paragraphs 3:1-4:6. On the second level it forms part of the block of paragraphs 2:6-4:6. On the first and final level it forms part of the whole book.

It is possible for a particular paragraph not to form part of any block of paragraphs, but to relate directly to the overall structure of the book. An example of this is Col 1:1-2 that does not relate directly to neighbouring paragraphs but to the overall structure of Colossians.

Although neighbouring paragraphs can be related to form blocks of paragraphs, it is also possible for paragraphs that are removed from one another to be related. An example is found in the structure of the paragraphs that make up the block 1:3-2:5. The three paragraphs from 1:24 to 2:3 belong together to form a paragraph block (level 3). Looking at the relationships between the paragraphs of the whole block, it seems that they are related

FIGURE 9.2
The structure of Colossians

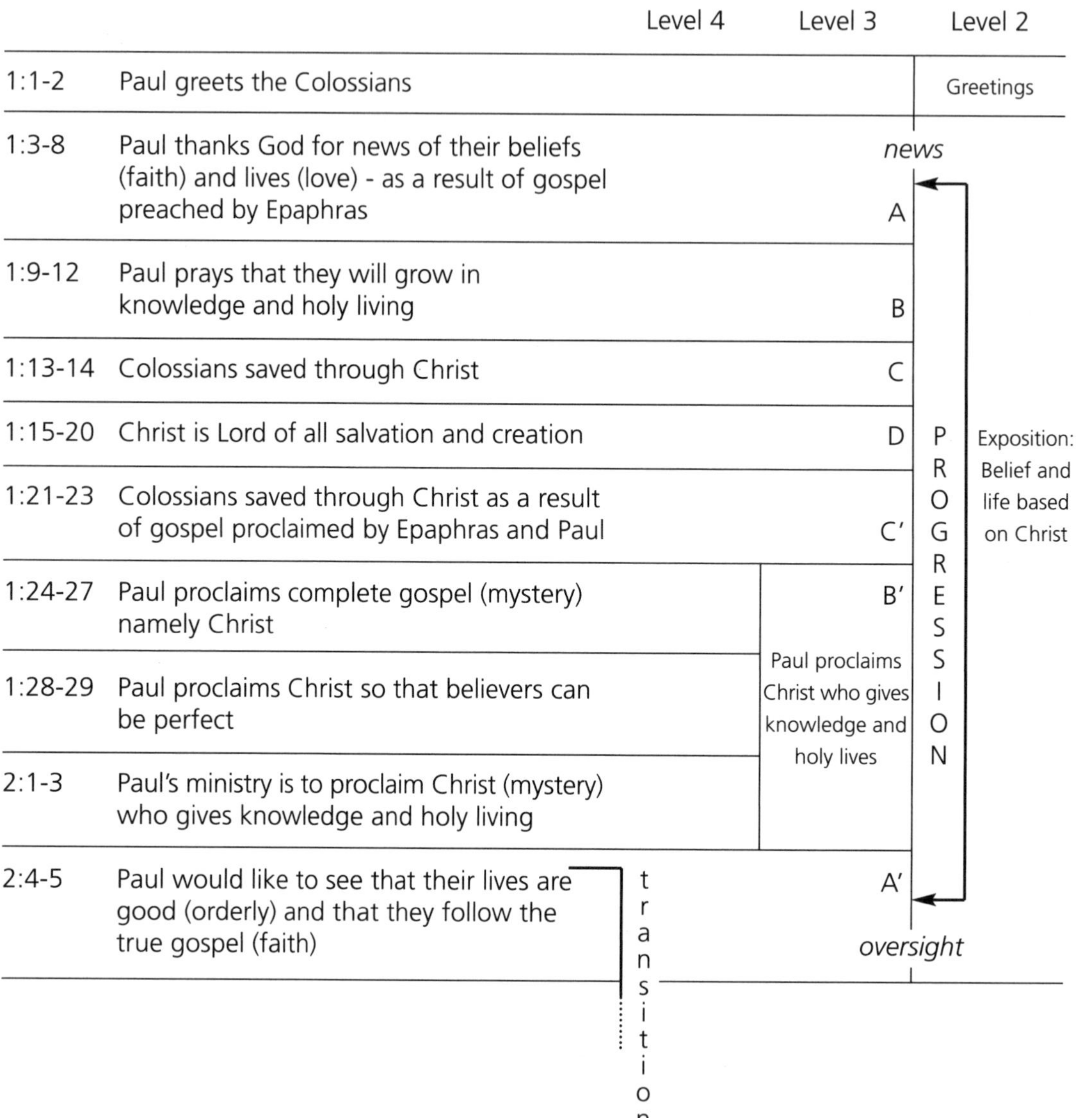

FIGURE 9.2
The structure of Colossians

Passage	Content	Level 4	Level 3	Level 2
2:6-7	They must live (X) in union with Christ and follow the true gospel (Y) (faith)		Introduction	Exhortation: Base belief and life on Christ
2:8	They must not follow false teaching (based on human tradition and 'basic principles')		Y Do not follow false teaching – you have victory in Christ	
2:9-12	They have all blessings in Christ - victory over sinful nature			
2:13-15	They are saved and forgiven - Christ conquered the legalistic system and demonic forces			
2:16-19	They must not be judged by the legalistic system or enticed by beliefs in angel worship			
2:20-23	They have victory with Christ over 'basic principles' and must not follow the human legalistic system that lacks holiness	transition		
3:1-4	Identified with Christ - aim at his standard of holiness		X Live a holy life	
3:5-11	Make an end to sin because you have a new life			
3:12-14	Love one another	Live in good relationships		
3:15-17	Live peacefully, be caring and thankful			
3:18-4:1	Relationships in family should be pleasing to God			
4:2-4	Personal request for prayer			
4:5-6	Witness to non-Christians with deeds and words			
4:7-9	Paul sending Tychicus and Onesimus with news			Greetings, news and commendations
4:10-18	Personal news and greetings			

to one another in reverse order (chiastic parallelism): 1:3-8 (A) to 2:4-5 (A*); 1:9-12 (B) to 1:24-2:3 (B*); 1:13-14 (C) to 1:21-23 (C*); with 1:15-20 (D) standing on its own.

According to the above structure in this block of paragraphs, the emphasis on the supremacy of Christ is made not only by the content of paragraph D, but also by its central position in the structure of the block of paragraphs. This leads us to the important point that meaning is not only communicated by the content of the paragraphs, but also by the way in which they are arranged.

The implication of this structure of related paragraphs that are removed from one another, is that each paragraph should actually be read together with its corresponding one, without losing the flow of thought of the normal sequence of the book. The corresponding paragraph may give valuable information on the related theme. At the same time there may be another underlying theme that is developed. In Col 1:3-2:5, the last example that we looked at, the theme of the relationship of Paul to the Colossians is developed. He starts off by thanking God for the news of their belief and holy lives (A) and then prays that they will grow in both (B). In C he states the fact of their salvation. After the paragraph on the supremacy of Christ (D) Paul mentions again the salvation of the Colossians (C*), but this time he states that they are saved by the same gospel that he proclaims. In B* he states that he also has a responsibility for the well-being of the Colossians as far as their beliefs and lives are concerned. This responsibility develops into A* where the Colossians are actually held accountable by him for their beliefs and lives. Thus we can see a progression from A to A*.

Just as paragraphs that are not adjacent to one another can be related in meaning, it is also possible for combinations of paragraphs to be similarly related. For example De Waard and Smalley (1979) propose such a relationship for the structure of the whole of Amos where it starts with A and develops to the central message of J to work in reverse order back to A*.

If I want to exegete only a few paragraphs and am not able to do a detailed analysis of the whole book myself, I may borrow from the work of others who have done so. Even then I should read at least once through the whole book in one sitting, in order to see the portion of Scripture that I am working on, in the context of the whole.

The problem with borrowing from the structures of others is that it can be hard to assess whether a particular structure is good. This is especially true in the light of a statement by Cotterell and Turner (1989:36) that they are aware of only two commentaries that, at that time, 'constantly appeal to approaches informed by linguistics', namely one by W. Schenk on Philippians and one by J.P. Louw on Romans. Until we have structures available that are based on detailed linguistic analysis of the original text, we will need to be careful in selecting the most feasible one.

Exercises

2. Read once through the whole of Colossians in one sitting, ignoring all the chapter and verse separations in order to follow the general flow of thought.
3. Read through Colossians a second time while following the structure in fig 9.2, making sure that you understand the structure of the book.

CHAPTER TEN

Step 3.1: Write out the passage in smaller units

Objectives

1. To understand that we start our analysis with the form of the text and then progressively work through steps in order to establish the meaning of the paragraph
2. To understand the need to divide paragraphs into smaller units
3. To be able to write out a paragraph in smaller units

Contents

STUDY TIP
This step is not difficult if you follow the way recommended in 10.3.

With this step, step 3.1, we begin the process of text analysis, using the approach of semantic discourse analysis as discussed in chapter four. Five different chronological steps for text analysis are presented in this and the following chapters:

3.1. Write out the passage in smaller units (Chapter 10)
3.2. Mark the significant meaning indicators (Chapter 11)
3.3. Explain words and phrases (Chapter 12)
3.4. Establish the meaning structure (Chapter 13)
3.5. Conclude and summarise the message (Chapter 14)

Although we can make a distinction between these different steps of text analysis, we cannot separate them. One step flows into the other and each one is dependent on the other. This means that a later step may influence and even change the findings of a previous step. For example, we may decide under step 3.2 that certain words express related meanings, but later, as a result of the findings of step 3.3, realise that the meanings are not related. However, this should not keep us from starting at a certain point in our analysis and proceeding towards a conclusion.

Semantic discourse analysis can be done by following different methods. The steps of text analysis that are proposed here are simplified in such a way that they can be picked up quickly. However, they are certainly detailed enough to provide results that will be adequate for sermon and Bible study preparation. It is recognized that the method of semantic discourse analysis proposed in this work, just like any other method, has its own strengths and weaknesses as it is virtually impossible 'to find a single straightforward and uniform method of analysis which can be easily employed to account for all the subtleties of language' (Louw 1987:3).

10.1 Starting on the syntactic level

Text analysis involves establishing relationships within and between the different units of language. As the type of discourse analysis used here is primarily semantic, we are interested in finding what the meaning relationships are. These meaning or semantic relationships are based on the surface structure or form of the text, since the author put the meaning he wanted to communicate in written form.

We begin our analysis with the surface structure, analysing the form of the text carefully as we move ahead to establish the semantic content or meaning. This type of analysis, with its emphasis on starting at the syntactic level, can be called 'progressive' semantic discourse analysis. We move, with each step of analysis, further towards establishing the semantic relationships.

10.2 The need to work with smaller units

In chapter four (4.4) we saw that while the smallest unit for everyday usage is the sentence, the smallest unit for analysis is the paragraph. This means that we need to analyse a paragraph at a time. However, when we look at how loaded a paragraph can be, we can see that the paragraph is too big a chunk with which to start our analysis. Even single sentences in fairly literal translations can be too loaded to start with. For example, when reading the first paragraph/sentence of Titus in the NIV, we will find it difficult to see at once how its different parts relate to one another:

> Paul, a servant of God and an apostle of Jesus Christ of the faith of God's elect and the knowledge of the truth that leads to godliness - a faith and knowledge resting on the hope of eternal life, which God, who does not lie, promised before the beginning of time, and at his appointed season he brought his word to light through the preaching entrusted to me by the command of God our Saviour,
>
> To Titus, my true son in our common faith:
>
> Grace and peace from God the Father and Christ Jesus our Saviour.

In order to see the relationships within the paragraph more clearly, it is helpful as a first step to break it up into smaller units. We can then focus on the relationships within each unit as well as on the relationships between the different units. If we think of the illustration of the paragraph as a football match (see 4.5), it will be like looking at the whole game at a specific moment from the perspective of the relationships within smaller groups of players, some busy to attack, others to defend, and others ready to back up. At the same time, the relationships between these different groups as they are interacting have to be observed, in order to get a picture of the whole game.

There are different ways in which the text can be written out. It can be done either on the form level or on the semantic level. For example on the semantic level it could be done by first recasting all event words into verbs and then to break the text into units around these and the other verbs. The disadvantage of this method is that one works with the recast forms and not with the original form or surface structure of the passage.

In our approach, we will break up the surface structure of the text according to syntax, that is, the grammatical arrangement of the different parts of a sentence.

The 'breaking up' of the text into the smaller syntactic units is nothing more than mapping it in such a way that the syntactic relationships of the different units can be seen clearly. These syntactic relationships point to the semantic content.

Writing out the text into smaller syntactic units can be done in various ways, two of which are:

- Take a sentence at a time, and write it out into smaller and more manageable parts;
- Make a diagram of the paragraph, separating it into smaller units according to set rules and definitions.

In this chapter we are going to present the first way of writing out the paragraph. To write out the passage is easy to do and does not require much instruction. Yet it is adequate for analysis of a high standard.

The second way, 'diagramming', has the advantage of showing more clearly the relationships within a sentence than is the case with writing it out. However, it is complex to learn. We as authors have spent a lot of time in the past teaching students how to do it. Taking everything into consideration, we have come to the conclusion that it is not worth the extreme effort to learn diagramming. Therefore it will not be introduced in this book.

10.3 How to write out the passage in smaller units

There are no fixed and firm rules for writing out a paragraph. The main idea is that each sentence should be broken up into its natural smaller parts, that is, groups of words that belong together. These smaller units, each one written on a line, should not be too long. At the same time, words that are closely related, should, as far as possible, not be separated.

In practice, it means that every new sentence will start on a new line. If a sentence consists of more than one clause and/or phrase, each of these will usually be written on a separate line. A clause is a group of words containing a verb, eg L1 and L2 in figure 10.1. contain one clause each. A phrase is a small group of words which form a unit within a sentence, but does not contain a verb, eg L3.

The best way to describe how to break up a passage like Col 1:21-23 into smaller units, is by illustrating it as in fig 10.1.

FIGURE 10.1
Col 1:21-23 written out in smaller units

1 21] Once you were alienated from God

2 and were enemies in your minds

3 because of your evil behaviour.

4 22] But now he has reconciled you

5 by Christ's physical body

6 through death

7 to present you

8 holy in his sight,

9 without blemish

10 and free from accusation

11 23] - if you continue in your faith,

12 established and firm,

13 not moved from the hope

14 held out in the gospel.

15 This is the gospel that you heard

16 and that has been proclaimed to every creature under heaven,

17 and of which I, Paul, have become a servant.

Exercises

1. Look carefully at how Col 1:21-23 is written out in smaller units (in figure 10.1) and make certain that you understand why it is done in this way.
2. Write out Col 3:5-11 in smaller units.

CHAPTER ELEVEN

Step 3.2: Mark the significant meaning indicators

Objectives

1. To understand the purpose of marking the significant meaning indicators
2. To know how to mark the meaning indicators

Contents

STUDY TIP
It is recommended that you use felt tips or coloured pencils to mark the significant meaning indicators. Using different colours will make it easier to see the patterns that need to be observed during this step.

Because the paragraph is the basic unit for analysis, we turn to it as a whole when we mark the significant meaning indicators. We thus mark them in the light of their relationship to one another within the boundaries of the paragraph.

11.1 The purpose of marking the meaning indicators

There are basically three types of significant meaning indicators that need to be marked:

- Those that indicate things (including people), events and attributes involved in the paragraph, in order to see how they interact
- Those that indicate stylistic features
- Those that indicate relationships between the different syntactic parts

The first type of significant meaning indicators helps us to identify the different participants in the paragraph and the scope of the events and things. This should be done because the paragraph is based around a specific theme. Although this theme can be made up of different elements, these will nevertheless link together to deal with the theme. The types of related meanings, as well as the practical ways of marking them, will be discussed in sections 11.2 to 11.5.

The second type of significant meaning indicators serves to identify the stylistic features of the paragraph, in particular concerning repetition in form or meaning. This will be discussed in 11.6.

The third type of significant meaning indicators points to the relationship between the various syntactic units of the paragraph. This will be discussed in 11.7.

11.2 Meanings group together in fields

The meanings of words in a paragraph can be grouped together according to their similarities or differences. It is a characteristic of any language that meanings can be grouped together in categories.

All meanings can be grouped together into the four semantic categories of things, events, attributes and relations. In each of these categories the meanings can in turn be grouped into sub-categories, or 'semantic fields'. We will now examine how, and according to which principles, the meanings are grouped together. This should make it easier to see which words can be marked as belonging together in a particular paragraph.

A word has in each of its possible meanings, different elements or components of meanings. When a number of words have shared elements of meaning with one another, they belong to the same semantic field. For the group 'cow', 'dog', 'cat' and 'elephant' the shared element of meaning is "animal".

The meaning of a word is not only determined by the elements of meaning it shares with other words within the same general area of meaning, but also by the contrasting elements of meaning between them. Although 'cow', 'dog', 'cat' and 'elephant' share an element of meaning, they also have contrasting elements of meaning by which each one's meaning is distinguished from the others in the same field. The meaning of 'elephant' contrasts with the other members of the set, in the sense that it is a large and wild animal. 'Cow' has the contrasting element that it produces products that can be sold. Similarly 'cat' and 'dog' each have further contrasting elements of meaning.

The shared and contrasting elements of words can be defined according to the meaning of the words in the context of a specific paragraph. For example, in a certain paragraph the words 'brother' and 'father' could be grouped together for their shared element of meaning as family members. Their distinguished meanings can be based on the contrasting element that 'father' is a generation above 'brother'. However, when we look at these same words in another paragraph like in Col 1:1-2, they do not refer to family membership. Here we need to use authority and intimate relationship as the meaning elements of 'Father'. For 'brother' we need to use the meaning elements of equality and intimate relationship.

When a different set of meaning elements is applied to a word, like in the case of 'Father', we actually deal with a different meaning of the word. There are even further sets of meaning elements for 'father' that could be used, for example with the focus upon status, like in Mt 23:9: 'And do not call anyone on earth 'father'...'

11.3 Some words are more general than others

Within any semantic field or sub-field, meanings can be found that are more general or generic than others. For example 'furniture' is generic whereas 'table' is specific. The two have some shared elements of meaning and all the meaning elements of 'furniture' can be found in 'table'. 'Table' is in turn more generic than 'dining room table' as all the meaning elements of 'table' can be found in 'dining room table':

generic		**specific**
furniture	⟶	table
table	⟶	dining room table

In our example of 'furniture' and 'table' there are no contrasting meaning elements between the two. However, 'table' has some shared and contrasting meaning elements with other words on the same level, for example 'chair', 'wardrobe' and 'bed'. They all share the fact that they belong to the field of furniture, but have the contrasting meaning element of function and design as they differ in their specific function and design:

generic		**specific**
furniture	⟶	table, chair, wardrobe, bed

11.4 How to mark the significant meaning indicators

When we mark the significant meaning indicators, we look for words that are related through their shared or contrasting elements of meaning in the paragraph (11.2), or because they have a generic-specific relationship (11.3). Words with related meanings are marked in such a way that it can easily be seen that they are related. We start with any grouping of meanings and move on to another one when all the words within that grouping have been marked. It will be illustrated in this point and the next with our example of Col 1:21-23.

In Col 1:21-23 (figure 11.1) we see that God and certain people are explicitly referred to in the paragraph: God the Father (lines (L) 1,4,8), Christ (L5), the Colossians (L1,2,3,4,7,11,15), Paul (L17) and 'every creature under heaven' (L16).

We mark all the words that refer to these participants in the same way. It is important to note that not all the words we mark as having related meanings 'mean' the same thing. For example, we cannot say the meaning of 'he' is "God". However, 'he' in L4 does refer to God in the context of this paragraph. For that reason we will mark 'he' in L4 in the same way as 'God' in L1.

Once we have done so, it is easy to observe that the Colossians are mentioned throughout the paragraph, God predominantly at the beginning, and Paul and 'every creature under heaven' only once each at the end of the paragraph.

When we turn to the things, events, attributes and relations in the paragraph, we mark those that are related in meaning. They can be related because of a similarity in their meaning - eg 'alienated' and 'enemies' (L1,2). They can also be related because of a contrasting element - 'alienated' and 'enemies' together are related to 'reconciled' (L4) because 'reconcile' means "to re-establish friendly interpersonal relations", that is to cancel out the "alienation" and "hostility". When marking 'alienated', 'enemies' and 'reconciled', the first two will be marked in the same manner (with white diamonds in figure 11.1) and then with 'reconciled' all three will be marked in the same way (with black diamonds) to show that they are related.

Another group of related meanings to be marked in Col 1:21-23 is 'holy', 'without blemish' and 'free from accusation' (L8-10). They are related because they express the similar meaning of "a status of being morally irreproachable". Although they have similar meanings, they are not exactly the same, as each one has its own specific nuance of meaning (which will be explained in step 3.3).

Another group of words in our example with similar meanings is 'continue', 'established', 'firm' and 'not moved' (L11-13). Each one of these words expresses the idea of challenging the Colossians to continue in their faith.

The 'gospel' and all the words that refer to it should also be marked: 'gospel' (L14), 'this', 'gospel', 'that' (L15), 'that' (L16) 'which' (L17).

The meanings of 'heard' and 'proclaimed' (L15-16) are related as they both refer to the communication of the gospel - receiving and communicating it.

'Once' (L1) and 'now' (L4) are related as they serve to bring out the contrast of time and events.

The words 'faith' and 'hope' (L11,13) are related. They both express placing trust in God; 'hope' with the element of looking to the future.

FIGURE 11.1
Meaning indicators of Col 1:21-23 marked

1 21] Once you were alienated from God
— • ♦◊♦◊ *

2 and were enemies in your minds
— ♦◊♦◊ • ∞∞∞

3 because of your evil behaviour.
— ∞∞∞∞∞∞∞∞∞∞∞∞

4 22] But now he has reconciled you
— * ♦♦♦ •

5 by Christ's physical body
× ∩∩∩∩∩

6 through death
∩∩∩

7 to present you
•

8 holy in his sight,
⊂⊂ *

9 without blemish
⊂⊂⊂⊂⊂⊂⊂⊂⊂⊂

10 and free from accusation
— ⊂⊂⊂⊂⊂⊂⊂⊂⊂⊂⊂

11 23] – if you continue in your faith,
— • ≡≡≡ •

12 established and firm,
≡≡≡≡≡ ≡≡

13 not moved from the hope
≡≡≡≡≡≡

14 held out in the gospel. –
▽▽

15 – This is the gospel that you heard
▽▽ ▽▽ ▽▽ • ≤

16 and that has been proclaimed to every creature under heaven,
— ▽▽ ≥≥≥≥≥≥ ⊕⊕⊕⊕⊕⊕⊕⊕⊕⊕⊕⊕⊕⊕⊕

17 and of which I, Paul, have become a servant.
— ▽▽ ↑ ↑↑↑

11.5 Communication situation influences significance

When we mark the significant meaning indicators in a paragraph, it should be done according to what was significant for the original receiver. In other words, the communication context has to be taken into consideration.

In our example of Col 1:21-23 we should look at the meaning indicators from the perspective that the Colossian church was under heretical attack when Paul wrote the letter to them. As we saw in 8.5 the heresy was most probably Gnostic in nature and denied the fact that Christ died as a physical human being. Two possibilities for the nature of his death were offered by the heretics: Jesus did not have a real body, but something like a 'spiritual body'. The other possibility was that he entered a physical body only with his baptism and left it again before his crucifixion.

With this background information in mind, we can see the significance of the words used in L5 and L6, 'by Christ's physical body through death'. By qualifying the death as physical, Paul wants to make sure that his readers know that their salvation is as a result of the fact that Christ died a physical death.

The heretics of Colosse also held to the belief that one gains salvation through 'secret knowledge'. For them, the body in itself was evil, and the 'spirit', including the secret knowledge that they kept in their minds, was good. It was important to escape from the body by treating it harshly. However, at the same time, it did not matter that one indulged in immorality because the body was seen as evil.

In the light of this dualistic view of man, it is significant to observe that Paul makes a connection between their 'minds' (L2) and their 'evil behaviour' (L3). From the Christian perspective these two cannot be seen in isolation, in the sense that a person cannot be pure in mind and at the same time live a sinful life.

11.6 Indicators of stylistic features

Once we have marked the related meanings, it is necessary to see whether they appear in a particular order or sequence. The two most regularly found patterns in the New Testament are parallelism and chiasm.

Parallelism is when at least two different meaning indicators are repeated at least twice in the same sequence, leading to the following pattern: a b a b. When there are three different meanings, the pattern will be: a b c a b c. An example of parallelism is found in 1 Cor 1:22-23, with the repetition of 'Jews' and 'gentiles':

Jews demand miraculous signs	a
and Greeks look for wisdom,	b
but we preach Christ crucified:	
a stumbling-block to Jews	a
and foolishness to Gentiles,	b

Chiasm is when at least two different meaning indicators are repeated in an inverted sequence, leading to the following pattern: a b b a. An example is the first four groups of people mentioned by Paul in Col 3:11:

Here there is no	- Greek	a
	- or Jew,	b
	- circumcised	b
	- or uncircumcised	a

In the first example we have seen the repetition of the same word, 'Jew' and the repetition of the related meanings, 'Greek' and 'Gentiles'. In the second example we do not find the repetition of the same word, but the repetition of the same concepts, "Jews" and "Gentiles". It is also possible to find repetition of the same form, for example a few verbs that are all participles.

Because we are working with a translation, at times it may be impossible to see the repetition of form that the author of the Greek text used. We should also be cautious not to attach too much value to the type of repetition, namely whether it is parallel or chiastic. This is because the sequence may have changed in some translations, with the result that the repetition is chiastic in the English translation while it is parallel in the Greek. However, what matters is that we realise that we are dealing with repetition and can discern which elements are repeated. These point towards the meaning structure of the paragraph, as will become clearer in step 3.4.

In Col 1:21-23 we do not find any significant chiasms or parallelisms.

11.7 Indicators of relationships between syntactic units

The syntactic units of the paragraph are those words that belong grammatically together. They could be either sentences, clauses or phrases. These are grammatical in nature, and at this stage the main purpose is to discover the obvious relationships between the syntactic units of the paragraph. It is true that there can also be a number of relationships within a clause or phrase, especially when event words are present, but those relationships will be dealt with in step 3.3. In step 3.4 all the relationships in the paragraph will be taken into consideration.

In order to discover the relationships between the different syntactic units, we have to look out for conjunctions like 'and', 'but', 'although', 'if', 'when', 'because', etc. These will indicate the nature of the relationship.

The relationships can be divided broadly into three main categories:

- those with a focus on time
- those with causality as the basis
- those that are descriptive

The first two categories of relationships, time and causality, carry the message forward. The descriptive category dwells for a moment on a thought and expands or emphasises it (Callow 1989:136, 149). The first two could be compared to a road on which you drive from one place to another, along the line of either time or causality. The descriptive relations then, are like the filling stations, restaurants and picnic areas along the road. These three categories will be described only briefly now. A more detailed and complete description of the different types within these categories can be found in appendix A.

With time relationships, elements are related to one another within the framework of time. It is not that the time of a specific event is given, (that will fall into the category of description), but that the elements are co-ordinately related to one another in the framework of time. The events can either take place simultaneously or one after the other, eg

> While John kicked the ball, his sister baked a cake.
> John kicked the ball after he had done his homework.

In relationships with causality as the basis, two or more elements are related as cause and effect of one another. Several different types of this kind can be found, eg

> It rained, **therefore** John could not play football.
> **Because** his father encouraged him, John played football.
> **If** John gets his boots in time, he will play football.

With these two main groupings of relations, we find that the message is carried forward, either with the focus on time or on causality. Descriptive relationships are quite different. Their purpose is not to carry the message forward, but to expand on it, or in some other way make sure that the communication is understood clearly, eg

John will play **in London**.
John played **well**.
John played **while it was raining**.

Let us return to Col 1:21-23 by marking those significant meaning indicators (figure 11.1) that give an indication of the relationship between the syntactic units. We look in particular for conjunctions:

'and' in L2: It links L1 and L2 in a co-ordinate way, that is on an equal level. Both these lines describe what the Colossians were like before their conversion.

'because' in L3: It links L3 to the previous two lines and gives the reason for the relationship of enmity and hostility between the Colossians and God.

'but' in L4 links the first two sentences of the paragraph together in a relationship of contrast. Although there is a time sequence involved, especially expressed by the 'once' of L1 and the 'now' of L4, the focus is on the contrast between how the Colossians were and how they are now. The relationship is therefore descriptive.

'and' in L10: It links L10 with L9 and L8 in a co-ordinate way. All three of these lines describe the condition of the Colossians, as a result of their salvation.

'if' in L11: The rest of the sentence that follows gives the conditions for the status that the Colossians enjoy and is causative.

'and' in L16 and L17: It links L15, L16 and L17 in a co-ordinate way. All three of these lines describe the gospel through which the Colossians have received their salvation.

Exercise

1. In the exercises at the end of the previous chapter you were asked to write out Col 3:5-11 in smaller units. Use this to mark the significant meaning indicators and look for patterns of repetition. Mark the patterns, using letters of the alphabet (see 11.6 as an example).

STUDY TIP

Because marking the significant meaning indicators has to be done in the context of steps one and two of exegesis, it is recommended that you first review the communication situation of Colossians and study the position of Col 3:5-11 in relation to the structure of the whole book (see figure 9.2).

CHAPTER TWELVE

Step 3.3: Explain words and phrases

Objectives

1. To know how to find the meaning of words and phrases
2. To understand which type of lexical reference works should be avoided
3. To understand which type of reference book could be useful

Contents

STUDY TIP

You may find it helpful and even necessary to do revision of chapter six (the relationship between words and meaning) and chapter seven (semantic categories) before or as you continue with this chapter

With step 3.2, mark the significant meaning indicators, we focused on the words of the paragraph by marking those that express related meanings. In this step we will concentrate again on the words by establishing the meaning of the words and phrases of the paragraph.

12.1 What the original receiver undestood

The main task here is to find out how the original receiver understood the words and phrases of the paragraph. This implies two things. Firstly, that we should establish the meaning for the specific time and circumstances that the words were used (communication situation). Secondly, it means that we need to establish meaning in the context of the paragraph and the whole book (literary context).

This meaning is called the 'contextual' meaning because the context of the whole book and paragraph, as well as the communication context, determine the actual meaning. If we hold to this definition of the meaning of words, it will protect us from the danger of isolating words and finding their meanings in the form or history of the words themselves (6.5), from mixing different meanings and carrying them into the passage (6.4) or from carrying too much meaning into a passage (illegitimate totality transfer) (6.4).

Cotterell and Turner (1989:165) illustrate this emphasis by using the example of 'baptism' in Col 2:12. They caution against using the generally accepted meaning of "Christian initiatory water-rite" because this is too narrow to express the emphasis of meaning in this context. On the other hand, they warn against reading into this occurrence of the word 'baptism'

Paul's whole theological concept of it. In this passage baptism is, for Paul, an expression of the uniting of the believer with the crucified and risen Lord.

In establishing the contextual meaning, we will need to be aware of how the meaning of specific terms were influenced by the communication situation. When Paul wrote to the Colossians, it was in the context of the false Gnostic teaching that he sought to correct. For this reason he uses terms that were part of the Gnostic vocabulary, but he filled them with new meaning. An example of this is Paul's use of the word 'mystery' in Col 1:26. This was a term that was used by the Gnostic thinkers to refer to the secret knowledge which was known only to a few. When Paul uses it here he does so together with the word 'disclosed', and fills it with the meaning of God's plan of salvation that was not known before, but is revealed now through what Jesus did.

Sometimes a biblical author uses a particular term in a book and then specifies the meaning of that term in another place in the same book. An example is the use of the word 'wisdom' in James 1:5. The same word is also used in the form of a noun or an adjective in James 3:13, 15 and 17. In these instances the meaning is made more explicit and 'wisdom' could accordingly be defined as "the capacity to understand and, as a result, to act wisely" (Louw & Nida, 1988:384). So it is helpful to find out how a term is used by an author in the book in which it is found, and even in other books by the same author. However, you should make certain that you work with the same meaning of that word because an author may use the same word, even in the same book, with different meanings.

In addition to the fact that a particular author could have used a specific term in such a way that it acquires a meaning specific to his usage, it is also possible that a term could have acquired a 'specialised' meaning over a period of time. Cotterell and Turner (1989:166) state that Paul's teaching on issues like baptism, righteousness, charismata, etc, gradually built up meanings that were common to the churches influenced by him. The result is that such specialised meanings are not purely Paul's personal usages nor the generally established meaning of the words, but the meaning commonly understood by a specific church or group of churches.

12.2 Recast according to semantic categories

In chapter seven we showed that all meaning can be divided into the four categories of things, events, attributes and relations. This knowledge is invaluable in establishing the meaning of difficult words, while the method of recasting (7.2) is invaluable for explaining the meaning of difficult words and phrases.

We can illustrate this using the word 'forgiveness' in Col 1:14. In grammatical form it is a noun. Semantically it is an event as the action of forgiving is expressed by it. Once we have established this, the meaning can be made more explicit by recasting the event into a verb form: 'to forgive'.

'Forgiveness' does not stand on its own in the sentence but is part of a genitive, 'the forgiveness of sins'. In explaining the meaning of this phrase, it is necessary to find out what the relationship is between 'sin' and 'forgiveness'. In this context it means that "sins are forgiven".

The word 'sin' can in this context be explained as "the moral consequence of having sinned" or as "guilt" (Louw & Nida 1988:776). The meaning of the whole phrase can thus be stated as "the guilt resulting from your sin has been cancelled".

12.3 Evaluation of lexical reference works

There is a great variety of lexical works available which present themselves as books that can provide us with the meanings of words in the Bible. We will discuss the value of these reference works by first defining what type of book we need in order to establish the meaning of words and phrases and then compare it to what dictionaries, word studies and encyclopaedias provide. As we discuss these types of reference works, it will become clear that it is not only a matter of what to use, but also what to avoid!

We want to establish the contextual meaning of a word (12.1). Outside sources can show us what the words - in and of themselves - contribute linguistically to the content of the passage (the lexical meaning). From this information we ourselves can establish what the contextual meaning is by taking the communication context, the structure of the whole Bible book, and the structure of the specific paragraph into consideration.

We would usually expect dictionaries to provide this information. Unfortunately, such helps are not as useful as one might expect. Louw (1985:80) summarises this in his article 'What dictionaries are like':

> What is perhaps most remarkable is that though all dictionaries are regarded as books on the meanings of words, meanings in the strict linguistic sense seldom enjoy proper treatment. This is mainly due to the fact that semantics as a linguistic discipline is, in a sense, still a fairly new science.

If this is true of dictionaries in general, then it is even more true of Hebrew and Greek dictionaries dealing with the Old or the New Testament. These have traditionally been written by theologians whose theological interests have influenced the treatment of the Hebrew and Greek words. The result is confusion between the linguistic meaning of the words and the theological concepts to which they refer. This makes such dictionaries very unreliable to use as helps in exegesis since it takes a trained linguist to distinguish the lexical meanings. It can be very misleading if you believe that you are dealing with the 'meaning' of a specific Greek word, while in reality it is someone's theological interpretation of it.

If this is the state of dictionaries, then what about word studies? In a well researched chapter with the title 'The use and abuse of word studies in theology', Cotterell and Turner (1989:106) state that future generations may very well call the last hundred years or so the 'Era of Theological Word Studies'. It most probably started with the publication of Cremer's 'Biblico-Theological Lexicon of New Testament Greek' in 1867. As far as the termination of the era of word studies is concerned, Cotterell and Turner (1989:106) remark:

> The precise date of its decease would be uncertain; perhaps all that could usefully be said of it is that in 1961 Dr. James Barr pronounced the patient severely ill, and gave it but a short time to live.

These word studies were produced in 'scholarly' formats like Kittel's 'Theological Dictionary' and also in more popular ones like Vine's 'Expository Dictionary of Bible Words'. Unfortunately, a variety of wrong linguistic theories were employed to a greater or lesser degree, with the result that one would do well to avoid word studies in general. These wrong linguistic theories include the use of etymology and the word form to establish meanings (6.5), the mixing of meanings (6.4) and illegitimate totality transfer (6.4).

Biblical encyclopaedias go further in their purpose than the lexical meaning and discuss the concept to which a word may refer. They give the type of information that one gains through exegesis of a concept found in different places in the Bible and placing it in a broader biblical and theological framework. Some may even go further by additionally discussing how a concept, such as baptism, has featured in the church, past and present. The result is that encyclopaedias should be viewed, in most cases, as similar to commentaries and used accordingly.

12.4 Recommended helps to establish the meaning

One of the greatest breakthroughs in helps for finding the meaning of words in the New Testament, was the publication of the Greek-English Lexicon of the New Testament by the United Bible Societies in 1988. It is also available for computers. The editors, Louw and Nida, classified all the meanings of the New Testament vocabulary into 93 domains or fields of meaning, each with sub domains.

The Greek-English Lexicon comes in two volumes and is used by looking up the specific Greek word in question. The lexicon lists the possible meanings of each word with a number behind each meaning. (It also contains an English list of words that makes the dictionary a useful help for those who do not understand Greek.) For example for the Greek adjective 'sofos' the following are listed:

a	skilful	28.9
b	wise	32.33

The letters 'a' and 'b' refer to two meanings often translated as 'skilful' and 'wise'. The numbered references '28.9' and '32.33' refer to the domains 28 and 32, and the subdomains 9 and 33 wherein meanings are discussed. When 'sofos' has the translation equivalent of 'wise', it belongs to the domain 'understand' and the subdomain 'capacity for understanding'. It shares that domain with a number of other words and has its meaning clearly defined and distinguished from that of the other members of that subdomain as "pertaining to understanding resulting in wisdom". It also lists 'prudent, wise, understanding' as translation equivalents. Its more precise meaning can be established by comparing its meaning with the meanings preceding and following it.

The United Bible Societies have published Translator's Handbooks on a number of Bible books and these are extremely helpful in establishing the meaning of words and phrases as they are treated in the context of the paragraph and the Bible book.

The use of different translations to establish meaning should not be underestimated. Especially in dynamic equivalent and free translations, the word choices of the translators may give an indication of the possible meaning for that context. The New Testament in the Good News Bible is to be highly recommended as it translates many Greek words in their recast format and difficult terms with their contextual meaning.

Cotterell and Turner (1989) and others have pointed out the need for sound linguistic insights on biblical interpretation. We can only trust that the influence of these insights will grow and lead to the publication of more lexical helps on the academic and popular level.

12.5 Explanation of words and phrases in Col 1:21-23

In explaining the meaning of words and phrases in this paragraph, we must turn back to figure 11.1 where the outcome of all the previous steps of text analysis is shown. Why? Because this step must be done in the light of the findings of previous steps. Here, the word or combination of words will be listed in each case, followed by alternative words which express the meaning more clearly. Also mentioned is the semantic category or combination of categories that the meaning of a term belongs to, thing (T); event (E), attribute (A) or relation (R).

alienated: being in a wrong (A) relationship (R) (with God)

enemies: being in a hostile (A) relationship (R) (with God)

in your minds: in the manner that you were thinking (E)

your evil behaviour: you did evil (A) deeds (E)

reconciled: put (E) in a right (A) relationship (R)

by Christ's physical body through death: by the fact that Christ died (E) physically

to present you: to make you to be (E)

holy in his sight: morally pure (A) in how God views (E) them

without blemish: without moral defect or fault (A)

free from accusation: cannot be accused (E) of anything wrong (A)

continue in your faith: continue to believe (E) the right (A) message (T) which Christians (T) believe (E)

established: well (A) founded (E)

firm: standing (E) strongly (A)

not moved from the hope: continue confidently (A) to expect (E)

held out in the gospel: that which the gospel teaches (E)

proclaimed: preached (E)

every creature under heaven: everywhere (hyperbole to express the fact that the gospel they heard is the same one that is preached everywhere)

servant (of the gospel): person (T) who works (E) to spread (E) (the gospel)

Exercise

1. Explain the meanings of the words and phrases of Col 3:5-11.

CHAPTER THIRTEEN

Step 3.4: Establish the meaning structure

Objectives

1. To understand what is meant by the meaning structure
2. To know how to identify the meaning blocks

Contents

STUDY TIP
As with the other steps of exegesis, the more practice you have, the easier it will become to establish the meaning structure. This step may require spending a good deal of time, as the findings of all the previous steps have to be carefully taken into consideration when proceeding with this one.

A paragraph does not consist of an unlimited number of concepts, but is limited in the scope of meaning it expresses. The concepts found in a paragraph are closely related and build up towards a central integrated meaning structure.

13.1 Identify the main meaning blocks

During this step of text analysis, we want to identify the main elements that function together to give the meaning of a paragraph. These main elements can also be called 'meaning blocks'. These blocks form a network of relationships with each other. So, the meaning of a paragraph is more than just the sum total of the individual blocks of meaning.

In identifying the main meaning blocks, it is necessary for the findings of all the previous steps to be considered. This is because the meaning that the author wants to express is not transparent, as in mathematical statements, but encoded into a surface structure or form of his own choice. All the details of this surface structure have to be taken into consideration to draw final conclusions as to the meaning of the paragraph. The function of the previous steps of text analysis was to lead us from the surface structure to the meaning structure.

In step 3.1 (chapter 10) the passage is written out in smaller units to make it easier to work on.

In step 3.2 (chapter 11) the significant meaning indicators are marked in order to achieve three purposes: to identify the related meanings, to discover the stylistic features, and to establish the main syntactic relationships. In particular, the repetition of both the meaning and the stylistic features of the paragraph point to the blocks of meaning to be identified in step 3.4. However, these indicators have to be taken into consideration together with the information provided by all of the other steps.

During step 3.3 (chapter 12) the meaning of the words and phrases is established. This is done in the light of the findings of the previous step as it gives indications of the meaning and actually helps you to find the meaning of specific words in the context of the paragraph. In turn, during step 3.3 you can check whether the preliminary findings of step 3.2, that certain words are related, are correct.

With the completion of all these steps the necessary information has been gathered to move to step 3.4 (chapter 13), identifying the meaning blocks.

13.2 How to identify the meaning blocks

In identifying the blocks of meaning, we will return to our example of Col 1:21-23 (see figure 13.4).

The first meaning block is formed by L1-3. They group together to show that the Colossians were once lost as a result of their sinfulness in their thoughts and deeds. It can be summarised briefly as 'Colossians lost because of their sin'.

The second meaning block is formed by L4-6 and states that there is reconciliation between the Colossians and God as a result of the death of Christ. It can be summarised as 'saved because of Christ's death'.

The third meaning block is formed by L7-10 and refers to the status that the Colossians have (and will have) before God as a result of their reconciliation with him. It can be summarised as 'morally pure in how God views them'.

The fourth meaning block consists of the rest of the paragraph. It exhorts the Colossians to continue following correct beliefs (L11-13). These beliefs are based on the gospel (L14) that they heard (L15), that is universally preached (L16) and is also preached by Paul (L17). This block could be summarised as 'they should continue with the correct gospel'.

These meaning blocks are not difficult to identify because of the strong grouping of related meanings within each block as observed during step 3.2. The observation that the last meaning block (L11-17) starts with the last part of the second sentence and includes the third sentence, is validated by step 3.2 which showed that the third sentence elaborates on 'gospel' which is already introduced at the end of the second sentence.

13.3 Stylistic features point to meaning blocks

The stylistic features of parallelism and chiasm can point to the meaning structure. This was covered in 11.6 where we discussed the parallelism found in 1 Cor 1:22-23, with the repetition of 'Jews' and 'gentiles'.

The repetition of these two concepts is also found in the two verses that follow, as shown in figure 13.1.

FIGURE 13.1

22)	Jews demand miraculous signs	a
	and Greeks look for wisdom,	b
23)	but we preach Christ crucified:	
	a stumbling-block to Jews	a
	and foolishness to Gentiles,	b
24)	but to those whom God has called,	
	both Jews	a
	and Greeks,	b
	Christ the power of God	a
	and the wisdom of God.	b
25)	For the foolishness of God is wiser than man's wisdom,	b
	and the weakness of God is stronger than man's strength.	a

The clear repetitive pattern of 'Jews' and 'gentiles' in verses 22, 23 and the beginning of 24 helps us to see that this pattern is actually taken through to the end of verse 24: 'Christ the power of God' is the answer for the Jews who wanted to see the power of God through miracles. Similarly 'Christ...the wisdom of God' is the answer for the Greeks who wanted to see God revealing himself to them through what they perceive to be wisdom.

In verse 25 we find the repetition in reverse order (chiastic). The power of God is revealed through the apparent weakness of the crucifixion of Christ (verse 23). Similarly, the wisdom of God is revealed through the apparent foolishness of the crucifixion of Christ.

Once we have spotted these patterns of repetition it is easier to see the blocks of meaning as indicated in figure 13.2.

FIGURE 13.2

22)	Jews demand miraculous signs	a
	and Greeks look for wisdom,	b
23)	but we preach Christ crucified:	
	a stumbling-block to Jews	a
	and foolishness to Gentiles,	b
24)	but to those whom God has called,	
	both Jews	a
	and Greeks,	b
	Christ the power of God	a
	and the wisdom of God.	b
25)	For the foolishness of God is wiser than man's wisdom,	b
	and the weakness of God is stronger than man's strength.	a

Verses 22 and 23 form the first meaning block with Christ emphasised as the answer that the Jews and the gentiles are not looking for, because of their quest for power and wisdom.

Verses 24 and 25 form the second meaning block with Christ again emphasised as God's answer for those Jews and Greeks who are willing to accept him as such. Christ is this answer because God's provision which appears to be weak and foolish, is actually powerful and wise.

13.4 Look for repetition of meaning blocks

In the example of Col 1:21-23, the four meaning blocks follow one another without a repetition of any one block within the paragraph. Sometimes there can be a repetition of meaning blocks in a paragraph. This repetition can take different patterns, such as forming a chiastic or parallel structure. The author decided to organise the meaning blocks in such a pattern for reasons such as emphasis or clarity (more about the significance of meaning block repetition is to be found in the next chapter).

An example of the repetition of meaning blocks is found in Col 1:3-8. The pattern of repetition is chiastic.

FIGURE 13.3

We always thank God, the Father of our Lord Jesus Christ, when we pray for you, because we have heard of your faith in Christ Jesus and of the love you have for all the saints	A
- the faith and love that spring from the hope that is stored up for you in heaven and that you have already heard about in the word of truth, the gospel that has come to you.	B
All over the world this gospel is bearing fruit and growing	C
just as it has been doing among you since the day you heard it and understood God's grace in all its truth. You learned it from Epaphras, our dear fellow-servant, who is a faithful minister of Christ on our behalf,	B*
and who also told us of your love in the Spirit.	A*

The meaning blocks of this passage can be summarised as follows. After a short introduction by Paul, stating that he always thanks God when he prays for the Colossians, the following blocks of meaning occur:

A Heard of confidence (faith) in Jesus and love for other believers that the Colossians have
B Confidence and love are because of the gospel that has come to them
C The gospel is producing positive results everywhere
B* Positive results in Colossians' lives are because of the gospel that has come to them - gospel came through Epaphras
A* Heard of the love that the Colossians have - heard from Epaphras

The significance of this arrangement of meaning blocks in this paragraph will be discussed in 14.2.

13.5 Structure shows paragraph boundaries

The cohesion of a group of meaning blocks will determine whether they belong together in a single paragraph or not. The cohesion is strongly influenced by the pattern of arrangement within and between the meaning blocks in question. For example, if the meaning blocks being analysed form part of a chiastic or parallel arrangement, as in our example of Col 1:3-8 in 13.4, then it is most likely that they belong together to form one paragraph.

FIGURE 13.4
The meaning structure of Col 1:21-23

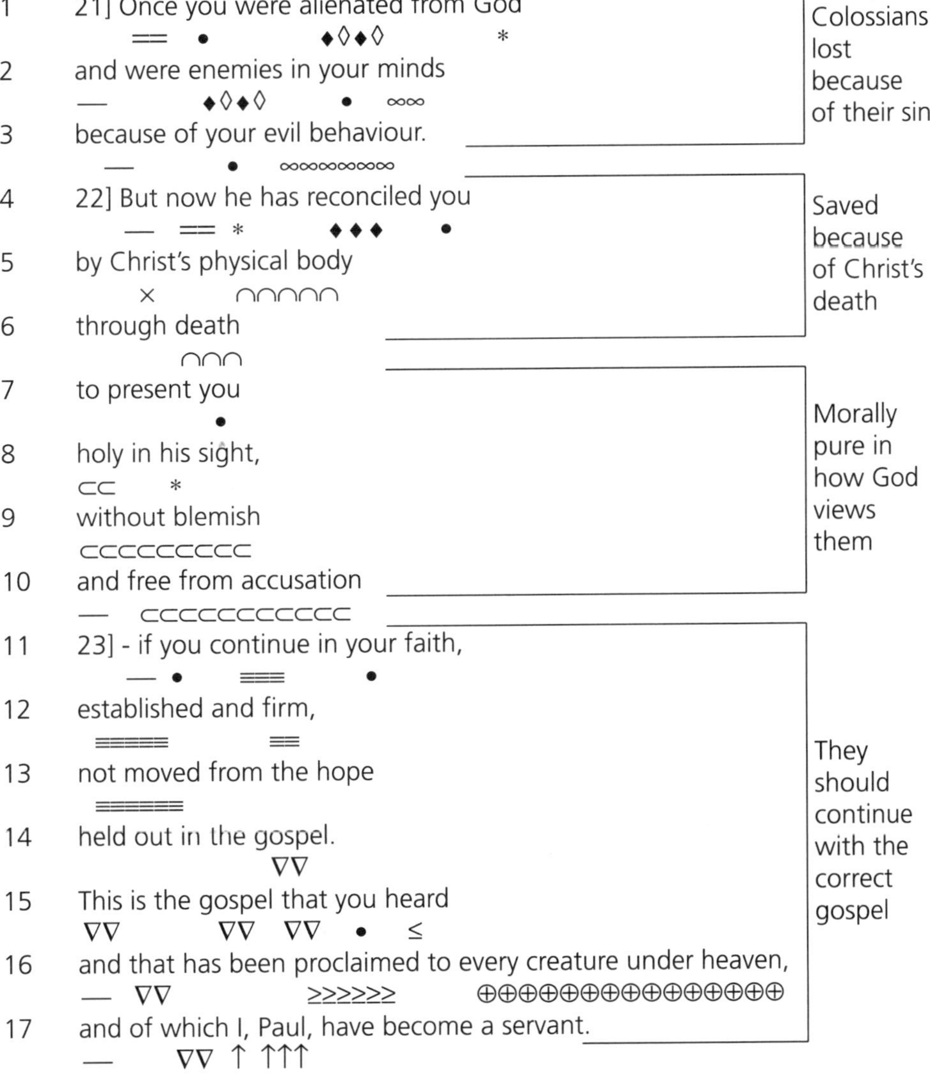

Exercise

1. Establish the meaning structure of Col 3:5-11.

CHAPTER FOURTEEN

Step 3.5: Conclude and summarise the message

Objectives

1. To know how to conclude and summarise the message
2. To be able to take the significance of the arrangement of meaning blocks into consideration when concluding and summarising the message

Contents

STUDY TIP

The content of this chapter is very much taught by way of example. Make certain that you understand what is done and be patient in developing the skills.

During step 3.4 the meaning blocks of the paragraph were identified, summarised, and their arrangement in the paragraph determined. In this final step of text analysis the message of the whole paragraph will be concluded and summarised.

14.1 All the findings integrated

The different steps of text analysis follow one another, with each step building upon the findings of the previous one until the message of the paragraph is finally established in this step. The steps are progressive in the sense that each one in turn leads you nearer to establishing the meaning of the paragraph.

The meaning blocks have already been identified in the previous step. In this one we have to determine how they function together in a paragraph to give it its meaning. This will be done in our example of Col 1:21-23 (please refer back to figure 13.4) for which the meaning blocks have been identified as follows:

Colossians lost because of their sin
Saved because of Christ's death
Morally pure in how God views them
They should continue with the correct gospel

In this paragraph Paul contrasts the state of the Colossians when they were lost, to their state after being saved by Christ. This salvation gives them the blessing of being morally pure before Christ. All of this is actually the message of the gospel with which they must continue. The condition for receiving these blessings is that they should continue to believe the gospel. If they do not, but adhere to a false one, then they obviously miss its blessings.

Just as in the previous steps of text analysis, this step must also take into consideration the communication context (step one of exegesis) and the literary context (step two). This is because the purpose of exegesis is to discover what the meaning of the passage was for the original receiver in the context of the whole book.

Once the message to the original receiver is established, the findings can be presented in a summary. Such a summary should show the content of each meaning block as well as the relationships between them. This summary is used when the message is applied to our time, through the process of hermeneutics.

The message of Col 1:21-23 could be summarised as follows:

> The Colossians were lost because of their sinful deeds and thoughts, but are saved by Christ, with the result that they are morally pure in God's view. This salvation and purity depend on the gospel concerning Christ with which they should continue faithfully.

When summarising the message, there is always the temptation to not integrate the findings of step 3.3 ('explain words and phrases'). The importance of stating the message in clear language cannot be over emphasised. If it is not done, the message can so easily be obscured by church jargon. For this reason, in the above summary of the message of Col 1:21-23, the word 'holiness' was avoided and 'morally pure' was preferred.

This step of text analysis takes us to the end of the process of exegesis, except for steps four and five, namely to put the findings in the broader biblical and theological framework and to read the interpretations of others. These two last mentioned steps actually serve as an opportunity to test the results of our exegesis.

14.2 The significance of the structure of the paragraph

With step 3.4, the task is to identify the meaning blocks and to see whether there is a specific pattern of arrangement within the paragraph. The task in step 3.5 is to find out what the influence of the arrangement of meaning blocks is on the meaning of the paragraph. This influence then has to be taken into account when summarising the meaning of the paragraph.

In seeing how this is done, we will again refer to Col 1:3-8, where we identified the following meaning blocks:

A Heard of confidence in Jesus and love for other believers that the Colossians have
B Confidence and love are because of the gospel that has come to them
C The gospel is producing positive results everywhere
B* Positive results in Colossians' lives are because of the gospel that has come to them - gospel came through Epaphras
A* Heard of the love that the Colossians have - heard from Epaphras

This chiastic arrangement of the meaning blocks serves to clarify those parts of the paragraph that may at first glance seem unclear. For example in block C it is stated that the gospel is producing positive results ('bearing fruit') everywhere ('all over the world'). What does that mean? In what way is the gospel producing positive results? In block B* it says it is doing so in the same way as it has been doing among the Colossians. Block B tells us how this has happened in the lives of the Colossians - through love and confidence. According to block A it is love for the other believers and confidence in Jesus that the Colossians have.

From the way in which the content of the paragraph is arranged, we can therefore see that the acceptance of the gospel is leading (everywhere) to confidence in Jesus and love for other believers.

The chiastic arrangement in this paragraph also serves to emphasise the fact that the same gospel that was preached to the Colossians, is also preached everywhere, and is producing the same results. This fact is important in the light of the communication situation of a heretical attack on the gospel originally preached to the Colossians by Epaphras. Paul wants to stress that this original gospel is the same one that is preached everywhere. He does this by referring to their good lives at the beginning and the end of the paragraph (blocks A). Directly next to these blocks, he states that their lives are like this because of the outworking of the gospel (blocks B) and in the centre he says that this same gospel has the same effects everywhere (block C) - placing the gospel that was preached to them on the same level as the one preached everywhere.

This brings us to the third point to be observed about the chiastic arrangement of this paragraph. Although there is repetition in reverse order, there is also development of the theme. Paul starts in a way that must have pleased the Colossians by referring to their good lives (block A). He then moves on in block B to state that this is as a result of the gospel that came to them. He emphasises that it is the same gospel that is preached everywhere (block C) and then returns in block B* to the fact that it is the gospel that has produced the positive elements in their lives. However, this is not merely repetition, because he adds that this gospel was communicated to them by Epaphras, the leader of their church. He then returns to the theme of block A and the fact that he knows about their good lives. But in block A* again brings Epaphras into the picture by stating that he heard the news about them from him (A*). Through this chiastic arrangement and the additions in blocks B* and A*, Paul clearly makes the point that Epaphras is the proclaimer of the correct gospel and also the bearer of the good news about the Colossians. As the false prophets were obviously trying to discredit Epaphras and his message in the Colossian church, Paul not only affirms Epaphras' message but also his position.

We need to keep in consideration the structure or arrangement of the meaning blocks of a paragraph and incorporate it into the summary:

> Paul thanks God for the confidence in Jesus and the love for other believers that the Colossians have. Epaphras told him about this. They have this in their lives because of the correct gospel that has come to them through the ministry of Epaphras. It is this same gospel that produces the same results everywhere in increasing measure.

Exercise

1. Conclude and summarise the message of Col 3:5-11.

CHAPTER FIFTEEN

Step 4: Relate message to broader biblical and theological framework

Objectives

1. To understand the value of relating our findings to the broader biblical and theological framework of the Bible and to know how to do it

Contents

STUDY TIP
This chapter and the next bring us to the last two steps of exegesis. Make certain that you've memorised all the steps when you come to the end of these chapters.

At the end of step three we completed our exegesis by establishing what the original reader understood from the text. Steps four and five give the opportunity to test or evaluate this interpretation. The outcome of this could mean that we may have to return to the first three steps of exegesis.

15.1 Why and how to relate your findings

By posing the question of what the passage meant to the original receivers, we have limited ourselves up to now, to a specific 'cut' in God's ongoing revelation of himself and his purposes. Although we have limited ourselves, our exegesis throughout has been within a wider context. It has been:

- in the context of the communication situation (step 1)
- in the context of the whole book (step 2)
- in the context of one paragraph at a time (step 3)

The findings from these three steps still have to be put through step 4 in order to place them in the context of the overall message of the Bible.

This step serves two main purposes. The first is to test our exegesis. If our findings are consistent with what the Bible teaches in other places, it serves as confirmation of them. If they are not consistent, we need to find out why, and re-evaluate our exegesis. The answer could be that there is only an apparent inconsistency or that our exegesis of the passage is incorrect. The Bible itself is consistent!

The second purpose is to consider the significance of the message in the passage. How does the message of this passage influence the meaning of other passages? How does this passage fit into the broader message of the Bible? What specific contribution does this passage make to the broader understanding of the Christian faith?

As an example of the practical application of step 4 of exegesis, we shall look at James 2:14-26.

Firstly, we can compare our findings with other passages that deal with the same subject to see whether the findings are consistent. Let's say we have arrived at the conclusion that salvation is the result of one's good works. We would now compare these findings with other passages that deal with the same subject, like Eph 2:1-10. We can also compare it with the general 'line' of teaching on this subject in the whole Bible. This will lead to the understanding that something is wrong with our exegesis of the passage and send us back to the earlier steps of exegesis.

Once we are satisfied that our interpretation is now in line with the message of the rest of the Bible, we can establish the significance of the message of the passage. In the case of Jas 2:14-26 the correct interpretation, that one is saved by faith, and that saving faith will necessarily lead to good deeds, will have important implications for the interpretation of other Scripture passages. For instance, it could safeguard us from wrongly interpreting Jn 3:16-21 as God requiring only the intellectual acceptance that Christ died for the salvation of mankind.

The message of Col 1:21-23 as summarised under step 3.5 is consistent with the overall message of the Bible of salvation in Christ. The requirement of perseverance according to verse 23 is in line with the message of the gospel: Rom 11:22; 1 Cor 15:20; Heb 3:6; etc.

As Col 1:21-23 presents in a single passage a summary of the message of salvation, it can serve as a framework to refer back to when other passages about salvation are interpreted.

The more exegesis we do, the better we will understand the overall message of the Bible. This in turn will help with our exegesis. Also, the more we work on Paul's writings, the better we will understand the message that he communicates and thus be able to exegete his writings better. For example, Paul relates our complete salvation to the redemptive deeds of Christ, as the believer is identified with Christ in his death and resurrection. If we understand how Paul applies this to the life of the believer, then we will find similar passages easier to interpret.

Exercises

1. Relate the message of Col 3:5-11 to the broader biblical and theological framework.

CHAPTER SIXTEEN

Step 5: Read interpretations of others

Objectives

1. To understand the value, and also the limitations of reading others' interpretations

Contents

STUDY TIP
This chapter brings us to the last step of exegesis. Make certain that you have memorised all the steps when you come to the end of the chapter.

16.1 The value of reading commentaries

During the previous steps of exegesis we could have used various different sources such as dictionaries, Bible dictionaries and encyclopaedias. These sources provide us with specific information as we need it during the different steps of exegesis. The exegesis itself, however, was our own work. With this last step of exegesis, we compare our end product with the end product of others. Where does it agree and where does it disagree?

If our own findings differ from those of others it is not necessarily ours that are wrong! As a first step we should try to establish how and why the other person has arrived at his conclusion. We should also make sure that we know how and why we have arrived at ours. Then we can make a considered decision on which interpretation we prefer and why. This not only gives us the opportunity to evaluate and reconsider our own findings, but also to learn from others in their methodology as well as from their findings.

Exercises

1. Read the interpretations of a number of commentaries on Col 1:21-23 and compare them with the findings we arrived at in step 3.5.
2. Read the interpretations of a number of commentaries on Col 3:5-11 and compare them with your own findings.

part four

THE EXEGESIS OF POETRY

CHAPTER SEVENTEEN

The characteristics of poetry

Objectives

1. To understand the characteristics of biblical poetry
2. To know how to identify and analyse stylistic features in biblical poetry

Contents

STUDY TIP
This chapter builds on what has come before. Therefore, you need a clear understanding of the first three parts of the book in order to get the most from this chapter and part four.

> Poetry is the art which uses words
> as both speech and song to reveal the realities
> that the senses record,
> the feelings salute,
> the mind perceives,
> and the shaping imagination orders.
>
> *Babette Deutsch*

We saw in chapter 9 (9.2) that there are two major forms of discourse, poetry and prose. In the example used in 9.1 it was shown how the same sentence, when changed from prose to poetic form, has a changed meaning. This alerts us to the fact that the poetic form itself can make a significant contribution to the meaning. The way in which it does so needs to be established in each particular passage that is analysed. We also saw (9.2) that the function of poetry in a particular culture at a particular time, has to be taken into consideration.

Just as the form of language used points to the meaning it expresses, we need to understand the characteristics of the forms that poetry employs. Once we understand what the forms are, and we are able to identify them, we need to be able to identify how they influence the meaning.

The purpose of this chapter is to orientate the reader with the characteristics of biblical poetry. Examples will be used to illustrate how the stylistic features of biblical poetry contribute to its understanding.

The steps for exegeting poetry are the same as those explained and applied to exposition and exhortation in Part Three. As mentioned, poetry has some distinctive stylistic characteristics which should be taken into account in your analysis. This will be examined carefully in this chapter.

17.1 The stylistic features of poetry

The writer creates his poem by, among other things, his choice and arrangement of stylistic or distinctive features from those available in his language and his poetic conventions. The stylistic features of biblical poetry can be grouped under the three headings of **syntactic elements, figurative expressions** and **rhythm.** This can be shown schematically as follows:

FIGURE 17.1
Stylistic features

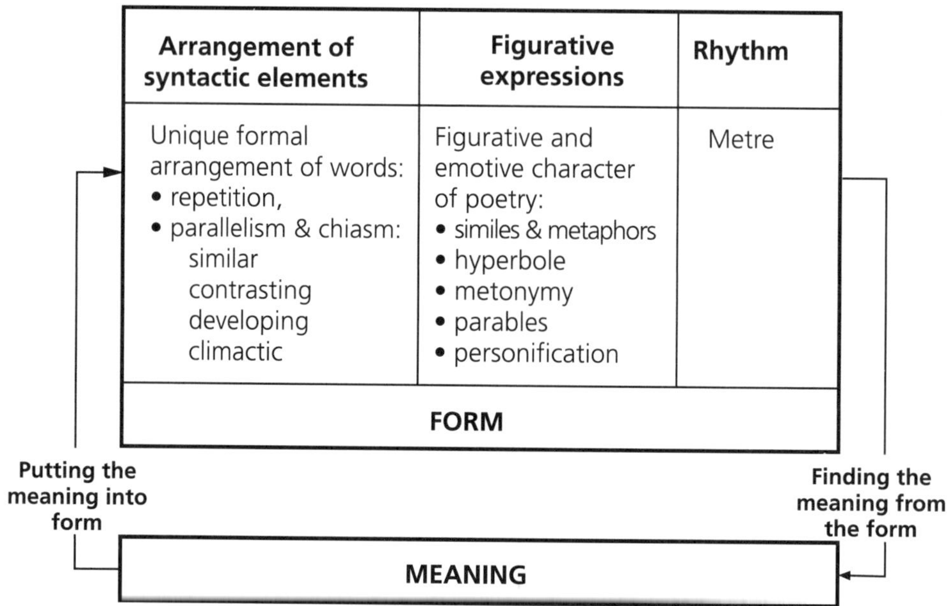

We see clearly from figure 17.1 that in exegesis attention should be given to figurative expressions with their emotive character, as well as to the formal syntactic arrangements of biblical poetry.

We will now take a closer look at each of the three groups of stylistic features, namely the arrangement of syntactic elements (17.2), figurative expressions (17.3) and rhythm (17.4).

17.2 Arrangement of syntactic elements

17.2.1 Repetition

Repetition plays a major part in Hebrew poetry and in other kinds of literature in the Bible (see 11.6). The following two verses in Ps 93 clearly highlight this aspect.

Ps 93:3,4
The seas have lifted up, O LORD
The seas have lifted up their voice;
The seas have lifted up their pounding waves.
Mightier than the thunder of the great waters,
mightier than the breakers of the sea -
the LORD on high is **mighty**.

Observe the effect of repetition in the next psalm:

Psalm 13
How long, O LORD? Will you forget me forever?
How long will you hide your face from me?
How long must I wrestle with my thoughts
and every day have sorrow in my heart?
How long will my **enemy triumph** over me?

Look on me and answer, O LORD my God.
Give light to my eyes, or I will sleep in death;
my **enemy** will say, "I have **overcome** him,"
and my **foes** will rejoice when I fall.

But I trust in your unfailing love;
my heart rejoices in your salvation.
I will sing to the LORD,
for he has been good to me.

17.2.2 Parallelism

One of the primary characteristics of biblical poetry, as indeed of poetry generally, is the sense of balance. One element, in various ways, matches or balances another element 'like a piece of music in which the same theme is repeated over and over again, each time with slight variations of mood' (Drijvers 1964: chapter 1).

When this repetition is found in a sequence, we are dealing with parallelism (see 11.6) which is a common feature in Hebrew poetry.

Parallelism can be found where a number of elements of one line closely resemble those of another line in both content and form. This repetition within the lines then holds the two lines in balance, rather like the two arms of a pair of scales - they are both needed for the full expression of the idea. Consider how the 'arm' of one line is 'balanced' by another line in the following examples:

Ps 15:1
a b c
[LORD], [who] [may dwell] [in your sanctuary]?
a b c
[Who] [may live] [on your holy hill]?

Ps 15:2

a b c
[He whose] [walk] [is blameless]
a b c
[and who] [does] [what is righteous],

Gen 4:23,24

Lamech said to his wives,

a b
"[Adah and Zillah], [listen to me];
a b
[wives of Lamech], [hear my words].
c d
[I have killed a man] [for wounding me],
c d
[a young man] [for injuring me].
e f
[If Cain is avenged] [seven times],
e f
[then Lamech] [seventy-seven times]."

Parallelism is not only found when elements of one line correspond closely with those of another. Lines themselves can also be repeated in a pattern of parallelism, as seen in **Amos 5:3**:

The city that marches out a thousand strong for Israel]A

will have only a hundred left;]B

the town that marches out a hundred strong]A

will have only ten left.]D

When the repetition unfolds cyclically, ending at the point where it began, it is called chiasm. **Ps 134:1-2** is a fine example of this kind of concentric movement:

Praise the LORD, all you servants of the LORD]A
who minister by night in the (house of the LORD)]B
Lift up your hands in the (sanctuary)]B
and **praise the LORD**]A

Chiasm is the same as parallelism, except that it is repetition in reverse order. Therefore, as one finds different types of parallelism (eg contrasting parallelism), one also finds similar types of chiasm (eg contrasting chiasm). For that reason only the different kinds of parallelism will be listed and explained below, with the understanding that the same patterns could be found in a chiastic arrangement.

17.2.2.1 Similar (Synonymous) Parallelism

The first type of parallelism we will look at is similar parallelism. The thought or expression of the first line is repeated by the second line in different words.

Ps 6:1

a b c
[O Lord], [do not rebuke me] [in your anger]
b c
[or discipline me] [in your wrath].

Ps 6:2

a b
[Be merciful to me, Lord], [for I am faint];
a b
[O LORD, heal me], [for my bones are in agony].

Ps 6:5

a b c
[No-one remembers] [you] [when he is dead]
a b c
[Who praises] [you] [from his grave]?

Ps 6:6

I am worn out from groaning;
a b c
[all night long] [I flood my bed] [with weeping]
b c
[and drench my couch] [with tears].

Exercise

1. Read Ps 147 and indicate the similar parallelism.

17.2.2.2 Contrasting (Antithetic) Parallelism

In similar parallelism we had the same thought or idea in both lines. In contrasting parallelism we have the opposite thought or meaning in line two. Therefore line one **contrasts** with line two. The word 'but' is usually found at the beginning of line two, to indicate the contrasting thought.

Ps 18:26

a b c
[to the pure] [you show yourself] [pure],
a b c
[**but** to the crooked] [you show yourself] [shrewd].

Ps 18:27

a b
[You save] [the humble]
a b
[**but** bring low] [those whose eyes are haughty].

Exercise

2. Read Proverbs chapters 14-15 and note down a few examples of contrasting parallelism.

17.2.2.3 Developing (Synthetic) Parallelism

In developing parallelism, the second line develops and completes the thought of the first line. There is therefore an extended or expounded thought in the second line of the parallelism.

Ps 142:1

a b
[I cry aloud] [to the LORD;]
a b c
[I lift up my voice] [to the LORD] [**for mercy**].

Ps 1:2

a b
[But his delight] [is in the law of the LORD,]
b c
[and on his law] [**he meditates day and night**].

17.2.2.4 Climactic Parallelism

Climactic parallelism is also known as repetitive or staircase parallelism. One or more elements from the first line are repeated in the second (or third) line and the **main emphasis** or 'climax' comes at the **end** of the second line. We find an example in the last line of the following passages:

Judges 5:24-27

Most blessed of women be Jael,
the wife of Heber the Kenite,
most blessed of tent-dwelling women.
He asked for water, and she gave him milk;
in a bowl fit for nobles she brought him curdled milk.
Her hand reached for the tent peg,
her right hand for the workman's hammer.
She struck Sisera, she crushed his head,
she shattered and pierced his temple.
At her feet he sank,
he fell; there he lay.
At her feet he sank, he fell;
where he sank, there he fell - **dead**.

Ps 93:3,4

The seas have lifted up, O LORD,
the seas have lifted up their voice;
the seas have lifted up their pounding waves.
Mightier than the thunder of the great waters,
mightier than the breakers of the sea -
the LORD on high is mighty.

Note: Climactic parallelism will most often be at the end of a strophe (a strophe is a grouping of lines that form a unit within a poem, and can also be called a verse).

17.2.3 The purpose of parallelism and chiasm

The different types of parallelism are there for specific purposes, some of which may be combined in a particular context. Some possibilities are (what applies for parallelism also applies for chiasm):

Creates balance and beauty: It creates a balance between the two (or more) lines that make a similar statement eg Gen 4:23,24.

Helps us to focus on the topic: The repetition of parallelism helps one to focus on the topic, eg the three lines in Ps 1:1 focus attention not on three individual characteristics, but rather on the entire lifestyle and conduct of the ungodly man.

Helps clarify the meaning: A complex meaning can be expressed concisely by two or more parallel lines, and therefore helps to give a better understanding of that meaning.

Emphasis: By means of repetition, which is the essence of parallelism, emphasis is provided and helps one to remember content. This was especially true for the original Hebrew readers who had a strong oral tradition.

Involves emotions: By setting things in contrast, tension is created. Sometimes even doubt, or imagination is stimulated.

Highlights the theme: Parallelism assists the exegesis of texts. It helps the reader, through the association of words, to see new connections and to follow the unfolding theme with greater ease.

One main difficulty that we have when discussing and analysing poetry is the fact that we analyse a text which is a **translation**. Nevertheless, the most dominant stylistic features of Biblical poetry namely parallelism, chiasm, similes, metaphors and rhetorical questions have been preserved as faithfully as possible by the translators of the NIV. Bliese notes (1990:319): 'For Bible translators the main point to keep in mind is that biblical poetry is not just a random series of lines, but that it has a beautiful symmetry. The need, then, is to look for a comparable form to convey a poetic standard in the translation as well'. He claims that most of these poetic features mentioned will transfer normally in the receptor language (translation). This is certainly the case with the NIV translation, as the poetic features can easily be observed. Translators also agree that printing variations can also be used to mark important and different lines. In the case of the NIV the second and third lines in parallelism are slightly indented compared to the first, as a rough distinction that will assist the reader.

To summarise, we can say that arrangements of words were an aid to convey the full meaning, aesthetic beauty and emphasis in the original text. Present day translators are well aware that they should work at making beauty and content clear to their readers. With this understanding, translations can be used in the marking and analysis of content and stylistic features in order to derive the meaning of a biblical poem or psalm.

17.3 Use of figurative expressions

Our second type of stylistic feature found in poetry is that of figurative expressions (figure 17.1). Figurative expressions are based on associated ideas. A word is used that has a particular meaning, but in the specific context a less frequently used meaning is intended. For example, to refer to a person as a fox. The meaning of 'fox' in this context is "slyness". Figurative expressions are used for various purposes which will be discussed below.

17.3.1 Similes and metaphors

A simile is a figure of speech which involves a comparison.

eg The baby's skin is **as smooth as silk**.
He ran **like the wind**.
I'm **as hungry as a hunter**.

Ps 37:1

Do not fret because of evil men
or be envious of those who do wrong;
for **like the grass** they will soon wither,
like green plants they will soon die away.

A metaphor is also a comparison. The only difference between a simile and metaphor is that in a simile the comparison is explicitly stated, usually by a word such as 'like' or 'as' while in a metaphor the comparison is just implied, eg:

Metaphor: Benjamin is **a ravenous wolf** (Gen 49:27)
Simile: Benjamin is **like a ravenous wolf**.

Metaphors: John is **a tower of strength** to me.
That child really is **a greedy little pig**!

Ps 23:1

The LORD is my **shepherd**, I shall not be in want.

Ps 3:3

But you are a **shield** around me, O LORD;
you bestow glory on me and lift my head.

Similes and metaphors are used for various reasons. They could be used to clarify and illustrate a teaching point. This can clearly be seen in the teaching of Jesus when he illustrates the concept of the kingdom of heaven as a treasure hidden in a field (Mt 13:44-45).

Secondly, they are used to catch and hold the attention of the hearer, like when Job has to brace himself 'like a man' (Job 38:3). This simile is again repeated in ch 40:7.

Thirdly, similes and metaphors can be used to arouse a certain emotional response in the hearer. The highly exaggerated poetic imagery in Job 41:12-34 highlights the fierceness of the leviathan.

When analysing metaphors and similes it is helpful to know that each one has three elements:

- the topic - the actual thing which is being talked about;
- the illustration - the thing to which the topic is compared;
- the point(s) of similarity - the components of meaning which the topic and the illustration have in common.

After you have analysed the metaphor, it is helpful to rewrite it in non-figurative language in order to clarify the meaning for yourself.

Examples:

a) For the simile, 'I feel like a wet rag'

• the topic is	a person (I)
• the illustration is	a wet rag
• the point of similarity is	limpness
Non-figurative equivalent:	I feel very tired

b) For the metaphor, 'Benjamin is a ravenous wolf'

• the topic is	Benjamin
• the illustration is	a hungry wolf
• the point of similarity is	fierce and destructive (the meaning that the topic and the illustration have in common in the particular context)
Non-figurative equivalent:	Benjamin is fierce and destructive

Another example is Gal 5:15, 'If you keep on **biting and devouring** each other, watch out or you will be destroyed by one another'.

• the topic is	behaviour of members of the church in Galatia
• the illustration is	behaviour of wild animals
• the point of similarity is	bitter conflict (just as wild animals in conflict bite and devour one another, the church members in Galatia are destructively criticising and slandering one another)
Non-figurative equivalent:	destructively criticising and slandering one another

Notice that while sometimes all three parts of the simile or metaphor are explicitly stated in the text, sometimes one (or even two) of the parts is left implicit. Quite often it is the **point of similarity** which is left implicit, but is understood because of the surrounding context.

The topic may either be a thing (including persons or objects) or an event (an action, happening or movement) (see ch 7). If the topic is a thing, then the illustration will also be a thing. Similarly, if the topic is an event, then the illustration will also be an event, together with the appropriate participants.

The correct understanding of any simile or metaphor depends on correctly identifying the point of similarity between the topic and the illustration. The topic and the illustration are not similar in all aspects of their meaning, but only in **one particular component** of their meaning.

In different contexts, different components of meaning may be in focus. The illustration of **sheep** can be used, where the point of similarity with the topic is different in each passage:

Is 53:6:	"We all, like sheep, have **gone astray**."
Is 53:7:	"he was led like a lamb to the slaughter, and as a sheep before her shearers **is silent**..."
Mic 2:12:	"I will bring them together like sheep in a pen, like a flock in its pasture."

Therefore, careful attention should be given to analysing not only words and phrases, but figures of speech too.

Rev 3:3: "I will come like a thief"

the topic is	the coming of Jesus
the illustration is	will be like that of a thief
the point of similarity is	unexpected (not in respect to other components of the meaning of 'thief')
Non-figurative equivalent:	I will come at a time when you do not expect it at all.

Exercises

3. Look at the following lines and see if you can identify the implied metaphor:

Ps 3:3:	But you are a shield around me, O LORD.
Jas 3:6:	The tongue is a fire.
Jn 10:9:	"I am the gate".

4. Analyse the following three expressions according to the topic, illustration and point of similarity:

Is 53:6:	We all, like sheep, have **gone astray**.
Is 53:7:	he was led like a lamb to the slaughter, and as a sheep before her shearers **is silent**...
Mic 2:12:	I will bring **them together** like sheep in a pen, like a flock in its pasture.

17.3.2 Hyperbole

Hyperbole is a deliberate exaggeration in order to create a dramatic effect, eg, 'I'm starving' often means "I'm very, very hungry".

Mt 11:18: 'For John came neither eating nor drinking ...' Obviously, John did eat and drink, as is evident in Mk 1:6 where it is mentioned that he ate locusts and wild honey. The point is that John ate very simply, often fasted and drank no wine.

Jn 12:19: So the Pharisees said to one another, 'See, this is getting us nowhere. Look, the **whole world has gone** after him'. This hyperbole states the fact that many people in the area of Jerusalem believed and followed Jesus.

Exercise

5. Identify the hyperbole in the following clauses. Try to re-express each one avoiding the use of the hyperbole, but retaining the emphasis of the hyperbole. It is important to look at the broader context in which each one of these clauses occurs.

- Acts 19:27: Artemis...who is worshipped throughout the province of Asia and the world
- Num 13:27: it (the land) does flow with milk and honey

17.3.3 Rhetorical questions

There are about 1000 utterances in the form of a question in the original text of the NT. It is estimated that about 300 of these are 'real' questions which therefore ask for information and require a specific answer. The remaining 700 'questions' do not ask for information and in most cases, do not require an answer. Their function is rather to give information, including information about the speaker's attitude and opinions. Sometimes they aim to stimulate a particular response in the hearer. They also highlight and introduce a new subject or a new aspect of the same subject (Beekman & Callow 1989:238). These are called rhetorical questions.

The biblical psalmists, authors and prophets made ample use of this figure of speech. It is nowhere more beautifully highlighted than in Job 38-41, in which God's response to Job is almost entirely in the format of rhetorical questions. The purpose of these questions is also evident, as we see that they not only give information about God, but evoke a certain response and attitude in Job towards God.

Ps 94:20

Can a corrupt throne be allied with you -
one that brings on misery by its decrees?

The purpose of this rhetorical question is to express certainty - the writer is certain of the fact that God will have nothing to do with people in authority who are corrupt. He wants to emphasise this by employing a rhetorical question. We could restate this rhetorical question with a statement of certainty:

Surely, a corrupt throne will never be allied with you -
one that brings on misery by its decrees.

17.3.4 Metonymy

Metonymy is the substitution of a word to stand in place of another, closely related idea eg The **kettle** is boiling.
'Kettle' stands in the place of water.

Ps 132:17: 'Here I will make a **horn** grow for David'.
'Horn' stands in the place of power.

Ps 78:67: 'Then he rejected the **tents of Joseph**'.
'Tents of Joseph' stands for descendants or family of Joseph.

17.3.5 Parable

A parable is an extended comparison in which the story is realistic, even if it is fictional.

Is 28:23-29 is a wisdom poem written as a poetic parable. Isaiah emphasises his arguments and predictions concerning the judgment of Israel.

the topic is	God's judgment of Israel
the illustration is	farming
the point of similarity is	God who teaches the farmer is not less wise and skilful in the way he maintains Israel
Non-figurative equivalent:	God knows how to deal with Israel

Emphasis is laid upon the fact that farmers, to get the best results, must apply a variety of different procedures. In particular, farmers have to apply a measure of violent activity to achieve results (v27), but they dare not use too much force or everything would be lost (v28). The point the parable stresses is that God must punish Israel, and his actions will be as measured and as well-timed as a farmer's. There is, therefore, a purpose in the actions he is about to take.

17.3.6 Personification

This is where an abstract idea, or something which is not alive, is referred to as if it were a person. The purpose of personification is to bring stylistic variation or to make a condensed, attention-grabbing statement. In Prov 8, wisdom is not only personified, but represented as a woman.

In Ps 23:6 the psalmist declares 'Surely goodness and mercy shall follow me' in which mercy is personified to follow or pursue him. He expresses thereby that God will continually be good and merciful to him.

In Rev 16:20 it is said that 'Every island fled away and the mountains could not be found'. In this verse the islands are personified as fleeing, and the mountains as hiding, thus meaning that all the islands and mountains disappeared.

Exercise

6. Look at Prov 7-8 and identify the way wisdom is personified.

17.3.7 The purpose of figurative expressions

Figurative expressions can be used for different purposes. Sometimes they appeal to our senses and imagination, and thus establish connections between phenomena around us that were previously hidden. This enables us to look upon the world with new eyes.

Secondly, they can appeal to our emotions, and so instil certain attitudes towards the subject addressed.

Finally, figurative expressions can express ordinary and commonplace phenomena, things and events in a striking and unusual way, which forces the reader to contemplate their truth and application.

Exercise

7. Study Ps 103:15-16 and list the purpose of the figurative expression.

Ps 103:15-16
As for man, his days are like grass,
  he flourishes like a flower of the field;
the wind blows over it and it is gone,
  and its place remembers it no more.

17.4 Use of poetic rhythm

A third type of stylistic feature (see figure 17.1) has to do with rhythm and 'verbal music'. A large portion of OT poetry consists of lyrical poems and religious songs that were meant to be sung with accompaniment, as is evident from the Hebrew titles and superscriptions of the Psalms. Thus musicality and rhythm are commonplace to all Old Testament poetry.

However, the question of whether classical Hebrew poetry had metre, in the sense of repeated patterns related to time intervals, is a matter of dispute among many scholars today.

Due to the fact that we are not working with the Hebrew text itself, I refrain from any more discussion on this matter.

CHAPTER EIGHTEEN

The steps of exegesis applied to poetry

Objectives

1. To understand how the steps of exegesis should be applied to poetry in the light of its distinctive stylistic characteristics
2. To know how to do exegesis of poetry

Contents

STUDY TIP

This chapter follows on from the previous chapter which described the characteristics of poetry and therefore should be read together with it. As this chapter teaches the practical steps of the exegesis of poetry, it builds on the first three parts of the book. It will be assumed that the skills and knowledge in the first three parts of the book have been mastered already.

The aim of this chapter is to show how to exegete biblical poetry. The steps of exegesis for poetry are the same as the steps for exposition/exhortation that have been explained and applied in Part Three of this book. In chapter 17 we have seen that poetry has some distinctive stylistic characteristics which should be taken in account in your analysis. Therefore the steps of exegesis (see figure 8.1) will be adjusted for poetry. Ps 1 is used to explain and apply the steps of exegesis of biblical poetry. In chapter 23, Ps 100 will be used as another example of the exegesis of poetry.

18.1 Step 1: Research the communication situation

STUDY TIP
It would be good for you to quickly glance through the notes in 8.3 again. We need to find answers to the questions of ***who*** *wrote to* ***whom****, under* **which circumstances***, for* ***what purposes****.*

18.1.1 The Bible as a source

Our best source for researching the communication situation of a specific psalm or poetic passage of Scripture is the Bible itself (see 8.3). Let us consider three examples where the Bible itself gives understanding concerning the communication context in biblical poetry.

Ex 14 is a narrative account describing the destruction of the Egyptian army in the sea while they were pursuing the Israelites. These same events are expressed in poetical form in Ex 15, entitled the 'The Song of Moses and Miriam'. It is the worthy expression of a nation's joy at being delivered when 'your right hand, O LORD, shattered the enemy' (Ex 15:6). This lyrical poem possesses in form, content and spirit, the characteristics of Hebrew poetry. It was sung and danced to the music of the maidens playing upon the tambourines and timbrels (v20), and was sung in antiphonal measures, that is, one chorus answering the other (v21). Thus we discover the historical context from the poetic part itself, as well as from the narrative that comes before it.

The second example is one of the greatest poems that survived Israel's time in the wilderness; Ps 90, 'A prayer of Moses the man of God'. The narrative accounts of Moses' life from Exodus to Deuteronomy shed much light on Ps 90, as they reveal to us the background against which it was written. It is touched with the profound melancholy of one who endured difficult trials; who buried his relatives in the desert; who had led the people out of Egypt and knew the anger of God; who came to the borders of the Promised Land; looked upon it but was not allowed to enter it. Psalm 90 is an expression of a faith purified by adversity. A faith which, having seen every human hope destroyed, clings with a firmer grasp to Him of whom it can be said 'From everlasting to everlasting you are God' (v2).

The third example comes from the great era of lyrical poetry which began with David. The poems of David throw comparatively little light on the external circumstances under which they were written, but throw much light on his inner life. In the psalms we see David as we see few men, his heart laid open in communion with God. For example in Ps 51 we find David opening his heart to God as he confesses his sin and sinfulness. The historical background of this confession, namely his double crime of adultery and murder is narrated in 2 Sam 11:1-12:25. It is when we read these verses, that we understand better what David must have felt when he wrote Ps 51.

In the above three examples, we see that historical narrative in the OT enhances our understanding of some of the poetic parts of Scripture. Where poetry is embedded in prose sections, it is usually after a description of God's salvation, eg Ex 15, Judg 5 and 1 Sam 2.

18.1.2 Function of biblical poetry in Israel

Poetry, especially in the form of songs or hymns, occupies an important place in Hebrew literature. The Israelites were evidently a music-loving people and famous for their songs (Psalm 137).

Little of their secular poetry has remained, but references in the OT seem to indicate that it was of considerable volume. The 'Song of the Well' (Num 21:17-18) was probably a work-song used at the well or by well-diggers. Other occupations probably had special songs, like reaping (Is 9:3) or wine-treading (Is 16:10). Songs were also used for special occasions, eg Laban would have made use of songs at a farewell for Jacob (Gen 31:27). No marriage feast would be complete without them (Jer 7:34). Laments for the dead were often in poetic form (2 Sam 1:19-27; 2 Sam 3:33-34). The short lament over Absalom has been called a 'masterpiece of rhythm' (2 Sam 18:33).

Songs were nearly always accompanied by instrumental music (Ex 15:20; 1 Chr 25:6).

18.1.3 The communication situation of Psalm 1

STUDY TIP
The communication context of the psalms can be problematic at times, in that very little background information may be available. If this is the case, don't be put off by this, but carry on with the further steps of exegesis.

- The author and date are unknown.
- Wisdom psalm - not worship but didactic - meant to instruct and teach. Ps 1 is therefore a didactic poem. The setting is not religious or social, but its primary setting is literary, because it forms an introduction to the Psalter as a whole.
- This is a practical prologue to the rest of the Psalter, because it clearly gives, by way of instruction, the two destinies of man.

18.2 Step 2: Establish the literary context

18.2.1 Poetic genres and their structures

In chapter 9 (see 9.4 & 9.5) we have seen that the writer uses a particular genre that will best suit his specific purpose and material. In Old Testament poetry, the poet's situation determines his mood and influences his choice of a particular poetic genre. For instance, David wrote a song of lament (2 Sam 1:19-27) when he heard of Saul's and Jonathan's tragic deaths. At an occasion of great military and political success he wrote songs of victory (I Sam 18:7, 21:11, 29:5) which were sung right at the place where the salvation had been experienced. During the Passover, the 'Hallel' (Ps 113-118), a song of praise, was sung in the family context. In Luke's Gospel the songs of praise by Mary (1:46-55) and Zechariah (1:68-79) were recorded for us in memory of Jesus' birth. The author of Song of Songs wrote love songs for the wedding of a young couple. In Lamentations, sorrow at the fall of Jerusalem and the loss of freedom and of the land is expressed.

Although all the poems use the principle elements of the genres to which they belong (eg song of praise or lament), each poem has an identity of its own. We will now look at the basic structures of religious songs, songs of lament and songs of praise.

Most of the Psalms were **religious songs** (see figure 18.1), and many have a common basic structure. This common structure may be schematically represented in the form of a diamond (Burden 1986:55-56):

FIGURE 18.1
Form of a religious song

Introduction
Body
Conclusion

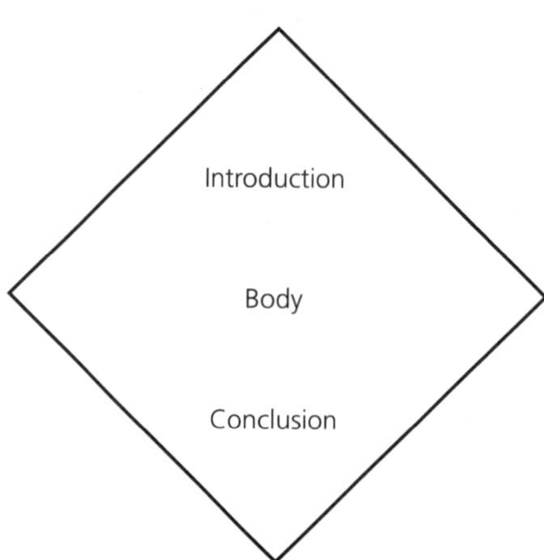

A **lament** always more or less follows a standard pattern, whatever the particular reason for it. This form may be briefly set out as seen in figure 18.2.

FIGURE 18.2
Form of a lament

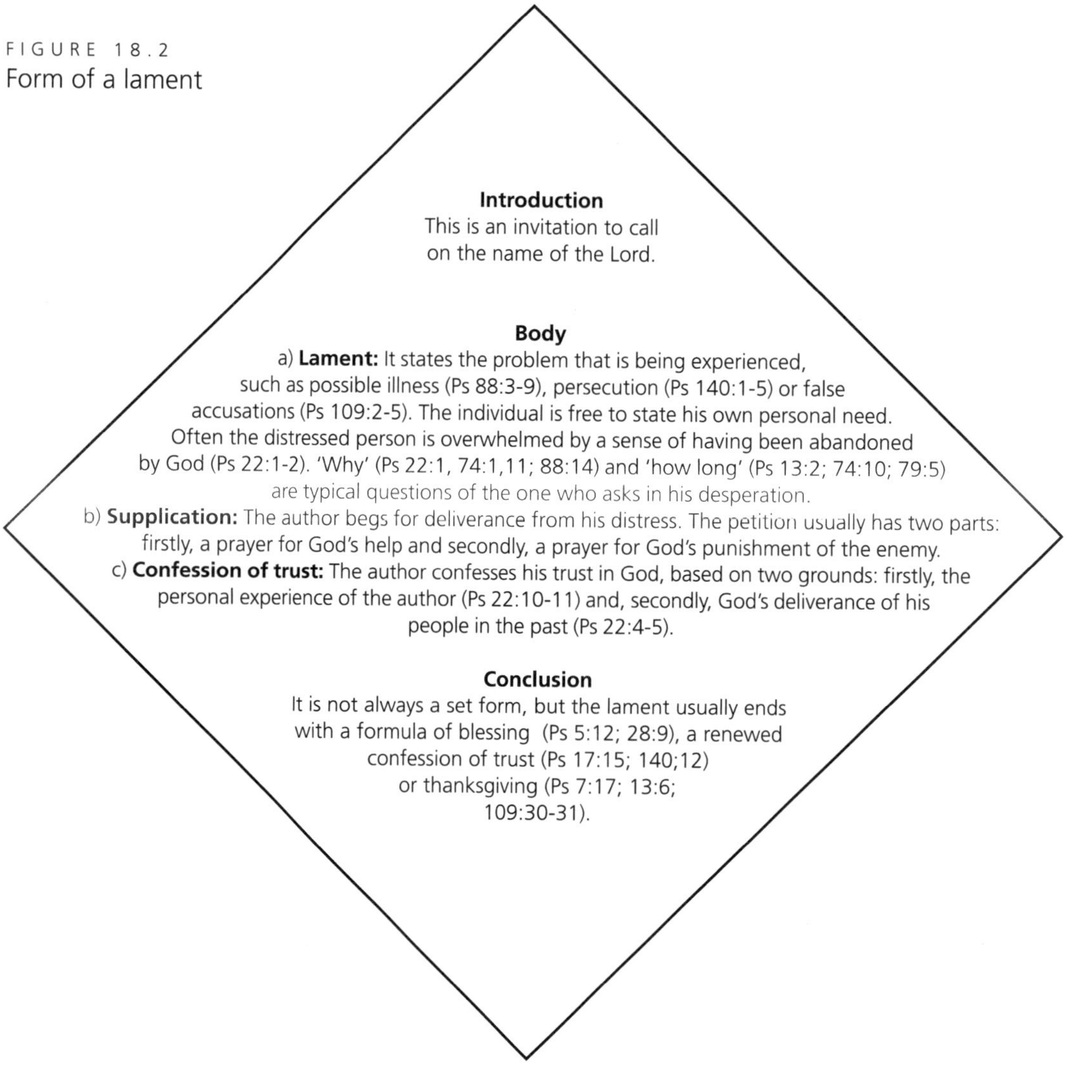

Introduction
This is an invitation to call on the name of the Lord.
Body
a) **Lament:** It states the problem that is being experienced, such as possible illness (Ps 88:3-9), persecution (Ps 140:1-5) or false accusations (Ps 109:2-5). The individual is free to state his own personal need. Often the distressed person is overwhelmed by a sense of having been abandoned by God (Ps 22:1-2). 'Why' (Ps 22:1, 74:1,11; 88:14) and 'how long' (Ps 13:2; 74:10; 79:5) are typical questions of the one who asks in his desperation.
b) **Supplication:** The author begs for deliverance from his distress. The petition usually has two parts: firstly, a prayer for God's help and secondly, a prayer for God's punishment of the enemy.
c) **Confession of trust:** The author confesses his trust in God, based on two grounds: firstly, the personal experience of the author (Ps 22:10-11) and, secondly, God's deliverance of his people in the past (Ps 22:4-5).
Conclusion
It is not always a set form, but the lament usually ends with a formula of blessing (Ps 5:12; 28:9), a renewed confession of trust (Ps 17:15; 140;12) or thanksgiving (Ps 7:17; 13:6; 109:30-31).

FIGURE 18.3
Form of a song of praise

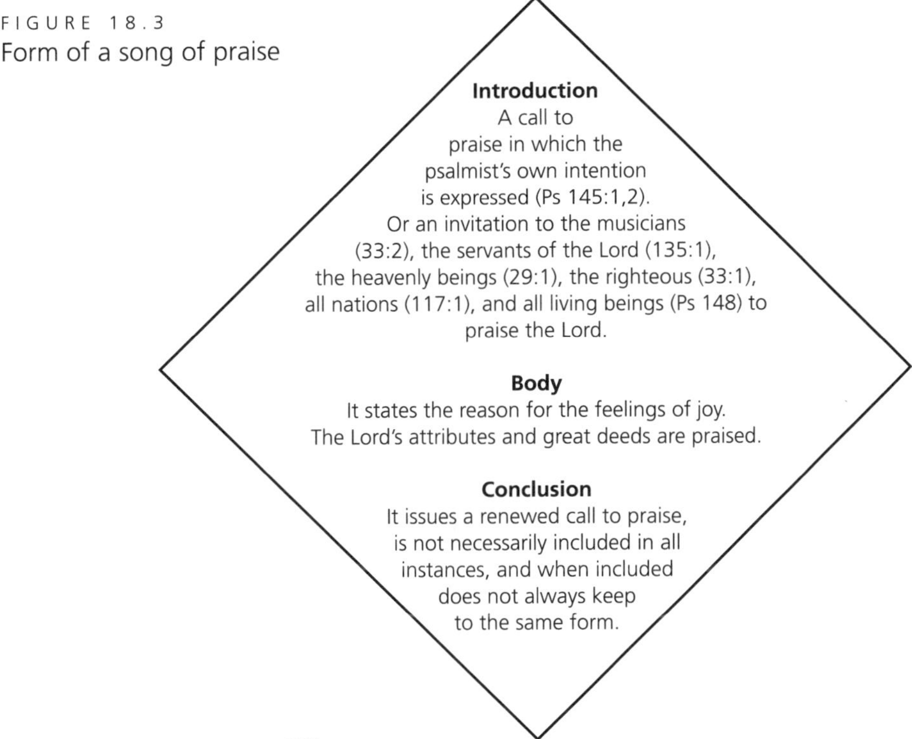

18.2.2 Step 2.1: Type of literature

The genre of Ps 1 is a wisdom psalm.

Common features of wisdom psalms:

- they set a high standard for the way in which one conducts one's life
- the ideas are arranged in a characteristically compact way
- they are didactic as their aim is to teach
- they refer to and glorify the law in its broadest sense
- they are warm in their praise of the man who walks Yahweh's way and unsparing in their condemnation of him who departs from it.

Other wisdom psalms are Ps 37, 49, 73, 112, 119, 128, 127, 133.

The specific features of Ps 1 are:

- It deals with principles which are fundamental and general in application.
- Five very important theological terms are found in this psalm which are also a feature of wisdom poetry, namely 'wicked ones', 'sinners', 'law', 'judgment', 'righteous'.
- It forms part of the 'torah-psalms' (Ps 1, 19, 8-15, 119) which means that these psalms show a clear reference to the Law of Moses. In line 5 we see the reference to the **law** (torah). It is very important to notice that the word **law** implies much more than just the Ten Commandments (Ex 20). It implies divine and godly instruction, and guidance in the righteous way (Ps 119:105). This law encompasses a covenant relationship with God (see 18.6: Line 1-4).

18.2.3 Step 2.2: Position in the book

When we look at the position of Ps 1 in the whole of the Psalter (book of Psalms), we see that it has been placed right at the beginning, serving as an introduction to the whole book. It demonstrates that the whole collection of psalms is a book of instruction for true spirituality and ethics, and not just a book of liturgy for worship. The significance of the grouping of psalms will be discussed in chapter 23.

18.3 Step 3: Analyse the passage

In exposition, the paragraph is treated as the smallest unit of communication and therefore the smallest unit for analysis (see 4.5). What the paragraph is in exposition, the strophe is in poetry. A strophe is a grouping of lines that form a unit within the poem. In Ps 1 (see 18.4), L1-10 form one strophe, L11-15 another and L16-17 a final one. As the paragraph is marked by indentation in prose, so the strophe is indicated with spaces in the NIV.

18.4 Step 3.1: Write out the passage in smaller units

Some modern translations, such as the NIV and Good News Bible, have preserved the poetic form of Hebrew poetry in the Psalms. The psalms are therefore written in lines in the Bible, and we don't have to write them out in smaller units. In this step we only have to number the lines to help us to refer to features, words or phrases in a particular place.

1 Blessed is the man
2   who does not walk in the counsel of the wicked
3 or stand in the way of sinners
4   or sit in the seat of mockers.
5 But his delight is in the law of the Lord,
6   and on his law he meditates day and night.
7 He is like a tree planted by streams of water,
8   which yields its fruit in season
9 and whose leaf does not wither.
10   Whatever he does prospers.
11 Not so the wicked!
12   They are like chaff
13   that the wind blows away.
14 Therefore the wicked will not stand in the judgment,
15   nor sinners in the assembly of the righteous.
16 For the Lord watches over the way of the righteous,
17   but the way of the wicked will perish.

18.5 Step 3.2: Mark the significant meaning indicators

This step is explained in chapter 11. In 11.1 the three basic types of meaning indicators are discussed;

- Those that indicate the events, people, things and attributes involved in the poem in order to see how they interact
- Those that indicate the relationships between the different syntactic parts
- Those that indicate stylistic features

Due to the aesthetic nature of biblical poetry, we need to analyse carefully and note the **stylistic features** (chapter 17) involved. Repetition, parallelism and chiastic sequences, metaphors, rhetorical questions and other stylistic features need to be marked in order to see how they assist in conveying meaning (ch 17).

We will now identify the arrangement of the syntactic elements of Ps 1 and combine the lines according to these arrangements and the meaning of the lines.

1 Blessed is [the man]

similar parallelism/triple parallelism:

a b c
2 [who] [does not walk] [in the counsel] [of the wicked]
a b c
3 [or stand] [in the way] [of sinners]
a b c
4 [or sit] [in the seat] [of mockers].

developing parallelism:

a b c
5 [**But** his delight] [is in the law] [of the Lord],
c b d **hyperbole**
6 [and on his] [law] [he meditates day and night].

developing/climactic parallelism:

a b c
7 [He is like a tree] [planted][by streams of water], - **simile**
a d
8 [which] [yields its fruit in season]
a d
9 [and whose] [leaf does not wither].
a e
10 [Whatever he does] [prospers].

developing parallelism:

a
11 Not so [the wicked]!
a
12 [They are like chaff] - **simile**
a b
13 [that] [the wind blows away].

similar parallelism:

a b c
14 [Therefore the wicked] [will not stand] [in the judgment],
a
15 [nor sinners] [in the assembly of the righteous].

contrasting parallelism/chiasm:

a b
16 [For the Lord watches over] [the way of the righteous],
b a
17 [but the way of the wicked] [will perish].

We see that different kinds of parallelism are employed. By taking them and the content into consideration, the following groupings can be identified:

L1-4, L5-6, L7-10, L11-13, L14-15, L16-17.

We now mark those words that have related meanings because of their shared or contrasting elements of meaning in the poem (see 11.4). Please mark these elements yourself in the psalm on the previous page.

In Ps 1 there are two main contrasting groups of people:

'Righteous man' (L1,16), 'who' (L2), 'his' and 'he' (L5,6,10).

'Wicked man' (L11,14,17) and 'they' (L12) could strongly be linked with 'wicked' (L2), 'sinners' (L3,15) and 'mockers' (L4).

Another group of words refer to an assembly of people namely 'in the judgment'(L14) and 'assembly' (L15).

'Law' (L5,6) is also a vital meaning indicator in this wisdom psalm.

The event words 'walk' (L2), 'stand' (L3) and 'sit' (L4) show the way of conducting one's lifestyle.

The event word 'watches' (L16) stands in contrast to 'perish' (L17). It can also be linked in some way to 'will not stand' (L14), indicating an outcome of certain lifestyles.

We will now mark those meaning indicators that show relationships between the different syntactic parts:

'or' (L3,4) links lines 1-4. Lines 2-4 describe the man who is blessed (L1).
'but' (L5) indicates a contrast between what the blessed man does not do (L2-4) and what he does (L5-6).
'not so' (L11) indicates contrast to the previous strophe.
'therefore' (L14) gives a result (cause and effect).
'for' (L16) gives a result and conclusion.
'but' (L17) contrasts the outcomes and destinies of the righteous and the wicked.

18.6 Step 3.3: Explain words and phrases

STUDY TIP
It is important that not only the words, but metaphorical words and literary images are recast properly in order to understand the psalm or poem.

LINES 1-4
Blessed: meaning "happy" or "fortunate"

is the man: "any person who" or "the people who"
The formula 'blessed is the man' is a typical expression of wisdom literature. This wisdom formula occurs in Job 5:17, Prov 8:32.

Lines 2 - 4: Three parallel lines are poetically similar and all describe, in slightly different ways, the evil company which should be avoided by the righteous man. The function of these three lines is to emphasize the full picture of what should be avoided. It stresses a teaching point.

who does not walk in the counsel of the wicked: 'walk' means "live according to" and the whole phrase could be restated as: "they refuse to listen to what evil men tell them to do".

or stand in the way of sinners: 'the way of sinners' means "the way in which sinners live" and 'stand' has the sense of "participate in". The meaning of the whole phrase is: "they don't do what sinners do".

or sit in the seat of mockers: 'sit in the seat' means "participate in the deliberations of", or "join in the discussions of". The meaning of the whole phrase is: "they do not spend their time with those who reject God".

Sinners, mockers and the wicked, refer to the same group of people. It is used in a restricted sense for those who are opposed to God and righteous people. In Old Testament terms the word 'wicked' usually refers to unreliable, arrogant and often influential people (Ps 73). The word 'sinners' does not refer to people committing a particular sin, but more to people who are disqualified from, or ineffective to function in a specific relationship - the relationship of the covenant commitment, fellowship and intimacy with God which is expressed through the covenant law.

LINES 5-6

but: this word is drawing a sharp contrast between that which the blessed man avoids in L2-4 and how he lives in L5-6.

his delight is in the law of the Lord: 'his delight' means "he finds his joy in". To find joy in the law means essentially that it is a joy to obey it. The law means "instruction" and particularly "the instruction that God gives to mankind as a guide for life".

This psalm is written in the context of the covenant, a living relationship between God and man, which finds expression in daily obedience and victorious living, because the covenant asked complete commitment and loyalty. An understanding of the law contributed to long life, peace and prosperity (Prov 3:1-2).

and on his law he meditates day and night: means "actively and thoughtfully study and read".

day and night: means "habitually". He uses a hyperbole (exaggeration) to emphasize this regular or habitual action.

LINES 7-10 (a simile)

he is like a tree planted by streams of water: Palestine had deserts with oases and therefore this is a particularly vivid picture for the Israelites.

which yields its fruit in season: means "that it bears fruit when the time for fruitbearing comes".

and whose leaf does not wither: that is, "they never suffer in drought".

whatever he does prospers: 'Prospers' has a general sense of "turn out well", so it is more than just material terms. 'He' refers to the righteous man.

The topic is	the righteous man
The illustration is	tree planted by water
Point of similarity is	fruitful and reliable
Non-figurative language:	a righteous person consistently lives a good life.

Line 10 summarises and explains this comparison in a non-figurative way.

The state of blessedness or happiness is not a reward - rather it is the **result** of a particular type of life.

LINES 11-13

not so the wicked: those who are opposed to God and righteous people.

they are like chaff: another simile, but shorter than the previous one describing the conduct of the righteous man. It is most significant when we look at the comparison itself.

The topic is	the wicked man
The illustration is	Chaff (the straw and husks of grain left after the seed has been removed. The grain would be tossed into the air with a pitchfork at the village threshing floor; the wind would separate the light chaff and husks and blow them away, while more substantial grain fell back to the floor. Chaff is useless and light (a part of the crop, but a part to be disposed of by the farmer (Lk 17:3)).
Point of similarity is	worthless and to be removed
Non-figurative language:	condemned and to be destroyed

Lines 14 and 15 help us to identify the point of similarity.

LINES 14-15

Lines 14-15 reflect essentially the same thought as L11-13, using similar parallelism.

Therefore the wicked will not stand in the judgment: 'in the judgment' implies the place of judgment (Deut 25:1) ie "the wicked will have no respect in the courts of law, where justice and righteousness are applied". 'Will not stand' means "they will not be declared innocent but will be condemned". Such a meaning is strongly implied by the second line of the similar parallelism in L 15. However, some commentaries do interpret 'judgment' as "God's action condemning sinners and those living unrighteously".

or sinners in the assembly of the righteous: 'righteous' refers to the idea that "they are people who belong to God". Those who are not able to stand in the congregation of the righteous are, then, those who are not allowed to participate with God's chosen people (Deut 25:7; Prov 31:23; Amos 5:12). Every Israelite had to participate in the assembly of the righteous, and if you were excommunicated, it foreshadowed the final judgment.

LINES 16-17

For the Lord watches over the way of the righteous: means that "God will protect/preserve the righteous person's life".

but the way of the wicked will perish: stands in contrast to the previous line. Whereas the Lord will protect and prosper what the righteous do, the wicked will be destroyed.

Each 'way' is presented as the natural outcome of a way of life which has been chosen. The lifestyle of the righteous is a response and answer to the covenant. Life outside the covenant meant death, physically and spiritually.

18.7 Step 3.4: Establish the meaning structure

A poem, like a paragraph, does not consist of an unlimited number of concepts, but is limited in its scope of meaning. The concepts found in the poem or psalm are closely related, and build up towards a central integrated meaning structure (see chapter 13 and 17.2.3). In articles on the structural meaning of the psalms, Bliese (1990:265-322) and Graber (1990:322-353) show clearly that biblical poetry is not just a random series of lines, but it has a beautiful, complete meaning structure.

In this step, we look for main elements (or meaning blocks) in the lines.

STUDY TIP

If needed, read through the notes in chapter 13 to refresh your memory on the concept of 'meaning structure'.

Psalm 1

1	Blessed is the man	A
2	who does not walk in the counsel of the wicked	
3	or stand in the way of sinners	
4	or sit in the seat of mockers.	B
5	But his delight is in the law of the Lord,	
6	and on his law he meditates day and night.	
7	He is like a tree planted by streams of water,	
8	which yields its fruit in season	C
9	and whose leaf does not wither.	
10	Whatever he does prospers.	
11	Not so the wicked!	A*
12	They are like chaff	
13	that the wind blows away .	C*
14	Therefore the wicked will not stand in the judgment,	
15	nor sinners in the assembly of the righteous.	
16	For the Lord watches over the way of the righteous ,	D
17	but the way of the wicked will perish.	D*

Meaning blocks in Psalm 1:

The first meaning block is L1 (called A) and L11 (called A*). There are two main groups of people that are discussed; the righteous (L1) and the wicked (L11). L1 has therefore been marked with an A, and L11 with A* as contrast to the righteous man in L1, indicating the psalm's introductory statement concerning the righteous man and the wicked man.

The second block is L2-6 (B) which states the conduct and lifestyle of the righteous man, which is rooted and fulfilled in God's law and his revealed will. It is important to note that there is no contrasting B*, because the lifestyle and conduct of the sinner and the wicked are not described. The omission of B* in the structure of this psalm, underlines the fact that it is worthless talking about the conduct and lifestyle of the wicked man.

The third block is L7-10 (C) and L12-15 (C*). The result and fruit of a godly lifestyle is contrasted by the fruit of the sinner without God. It is significant to notice that both C and C' are introduced with a metaphor. The form here again contributes to the meaning and message of the psalm.

The fourth block is L16-17 (D and D*) in which the destinies of the righteous man and the wicked man are contrasted. L16 and 17 is a final peak marked by chiasm to underline the contrast in outcome (see 18.6: Line 16 and 17). This block summarises the message of A to C and A* to C*.

18.8 Step 3.5: Conclude and summarise the message

The meaning blocks have been identified, summarised and their arrangement in the paragraph determined. In this final step of text analysis the message of the whole psalm will be concluded and summarised.

AA*+B: The person who belongs to God should not adopt the lifestyle and attitude of the wicked (sinner), but should find his fulfilment in knowing and being totally committed to God's revealed will and instructions for living.

CC*+DD*: The result, and therefore outcome of a godly lifestyle governed by God, is well-being and protection from God. In contrast, the man's life without God is totally meaningless and leads to destruction.

18.9 Step 4: Relate message to broader biblical and theological framework

This step is necessary in order to test or evaluate your interpretation (see chapter 15). The findings need to be put in the context of the overall message of the Bible.

In the summary of CC*+DD* we see that God takes notice of, and has regard for, the godly way in which those who belong to him conduct their lives. There may not necessarily be a material and physical advantage to a life marked by right conduct and attention to God's instruction. However, such a life is noticed by God and he cares for people living in a right relationship with him. The absolute principle of this psalm is that the life of the righteous is sustained by the Lord. This is in line with the message of the rest of Scripture. In the 'beatitudes' (Mt 5-7), Jesus also linked blessing to following God's instructions and law. Jesus speaks of two gates. A broad gate that leads to destruction and a narrow gate that is 'the way that leads to life' (Mt 7:13-14). The principles of Jesus' teaching are essentially those of Ps 1. Joy and reward are also found (Mt 5:5-9), but not necessarily separate from persecution and suffering (Mt 5:10-12).

It is interesting that this psalm does not state explicitly what God does concerning the wicked man. There is no word of divine action, simply the statement that immoral conduct and the disdain for God's instruction cannot be ultimately sustained, and finally comes to an end. While there are many biblical passages concerning God's judgment upon the wicked and unbelievers, we sense in this psalm that the natural outcome for the wicked is failure and destruction. We can see many examples of this in the Old and New Testament because the world is shaped and governed by God's moral order (Rom 1:18-32).

18.10 Step 5: Read interpretations of others

In this last step of exegesis we compare our end product of exegesis with the end product of others (chapter 16). This gives us an opportunity to evaluate and reconsider our own findings.

18.11 Hermeneutics

The hermeneutics of the Psalms does not fall within the scope of this chapter and will be discussed in more depth in chapter 24.

part five

THE EXEGESIS OF NARRATIVE

CHAPTER NINETEEN

The characteristics of narrative

Objectives

1. To be able to identify narrative
2. To be able to identify the different genres of narrative
3. To understand that the different genres of narrative determine our approach to exegesis
4. To be able to discover the author's message to the original receiver in dramatic history
5. To recognise episodes
6. To grasp the importance of exegeting the whole story in order to understand its message

Contents

Part five, beginning with this chapter, will teach how to interpret narrative. We learned in chapter nine that the type of literature and, in particular, the discourse type (ie exposition, exhortation, narrative and procedure) influences our approach to exegesis. Although the steps of exegesis will be the same as explained in part three (exegesis of exposition/exhortation), this and the next chapter's overall purpose is to help you fine-tune the steps for narrative.

STUDY TIP
To help you understand section 19.1, review figure 9.1, making sure you understand the distinctive characteristics of the major discourse types.

19.1 The main characteristics of narrative

Large parts of the Bible are written in the narrative discourse type. We explained in chapter nine the two characteristics which determine the narrative discourse type: firstly, its events are described in sequence (the chronological framework), and secondly, it is non-prescriptive, that is, no explicit instructions are given to the reader. Finding these two characteristics in any text will help us in determining what kind of literature we are dealing with. We will now explain the chronological framework of the narrative discourse type. Later on in this chapter more will be said about how the 'non-prescriptive' characteristic influences our interpretation of narrative.

Figure 19.1 illustrates what is meant by the chronological framework of the narrative discourse type. It is simply a series of events taking place in chronological order. For instance, John got up and washed himself, and after he ate breakfast he put on his tie. This series of events is graphically illustrated along a time line in figure 19.1.

FIGURE 19.1

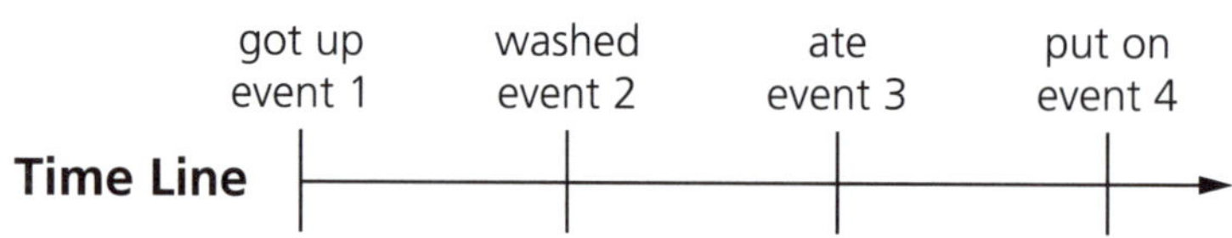

The time line is the back bone of narrative. The chronological order is usually indicated by conjunctions and prepositional phrases linking the events. It could also be indicated without such words, in which case the context indicates the relationships.

As in the following examples, events taking place in sequence are indicated with such words as then, and, after, afterwards, etc. There is no time overlap between such events.

Examples:

'So she went out **and** (means "and then") began to glean in the fields...' (Ruth 2:3).
'**When** she sat down with the harvesters, he offered her some roasted grain' (Ruth 2:14)
'So Ruth gleaned in the field.... **Then** she threshed the barley...' (Ruth 2:17).
Bill always does his chores **before** he goes to school.
The team's victory **was followed by** great celebrations.

Events that take place simultaneously are indicated with words and phrases like while, meanwhile, at the same time, etc. These events either take place at the same time or overlap partially.

Examples:

'**As** she got up to glean, Boaz gave orders to his men...' (Ruth 2:15)
While Bill was doing his chores, Mary was reading a book.
Mum was cooking dinner **and** Dad was working in the garden.

At a certain stage in the narrative we may of course find events recounted that took place earlier than the events around them. This is a 'flash-back' and will also be indicated in some way. An example of this is found in Acts 11:19: 'Now those who **had been scattered**...' (past perfect tense).

Deviation from the time line by means of a flash-back or elaborating and describing an event in detail, should be noted carefully. This may be significant and should be evaluated carefully. It may help us to better understand the structure and/or message of the narrative. The example of Acts 11:19 is relevant here. It hints that a new block of thought begins at this stage of the narrative.

Exercises

1. What main characteristics distinguish narrative from the other main discourse types?
2. What are the discourse types of the following passages? Ex 2:1-10; 1 Sam 13:23-14:14; Jer 36.

19.2 The different genres of narrative

STUDY TIP

Reviewing chapter 9.4 may help you understand this section more easily.

In figure 19.2 there is a list of narrative genres found in the Bible, each one with its own distinctive feature. We will now discuss the various genres, including the special case of conversational genre as it is often found embedded in the narrative discourse type.

FIGURE 19.2

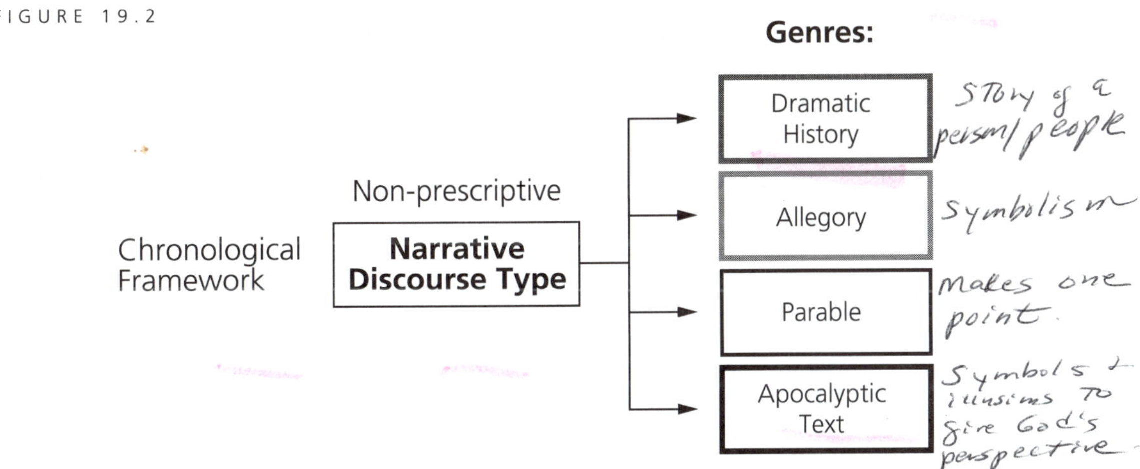

The distinctive feature of the genre of **dramatic history** is a focus on the activity of an individual and/or certain groups of people, their interaction with one another and with God. The features of narrative are also present - the events described occur in chronological order and no particular instructions are given to the reader (it is non-prescriptive). The story of Gideon (Judg 6-8) is cast in the genre of dramatic history. It focuses primarily on Gideon and his interaction with God and unfolds as one event follows another.

An example of an **allegory** is found in Judg 9:8-15. The distinctive feature of the allegorical genre is that the characters and events symbolise something else. Sometimes the events and participants in an allegory correspond with the people being addressed. This is the case in the allegory of the trees. The trees are identified with the people of Shechem and the thorn-bush with Abimelech. The enthronement of the thorn-bush as king of the trees is likened to Abimelech's enthronement, and the fire as God's judgment for the crime Abimelech and the people of Shechem committed against Gideon's family. The features of the narrative discourse type are also present. The events occur in sequence (chronological framework) and the allegory does not contain instructions to the reader (non-prescriptive).

The story of the good Samaritan (Lk 10:30-35) is an example of a **parable**. Its events take place in sequence (chronological framework) and there are no explicit instructions (non-prescriptive). The distinctive feature of a parable is that it usually makes one main point. The point (teaching) of this parable has to be understood in the light of two questions: firstly, the teacher's question (v29) and secondly, Jesus' question (v36) which broadens the issue from 'who is my neighbour?' meaning "whom should I love?" to 'which... was a neighbour to the man' meaning "who... really loved the man?". The issue now is, not only *whom* we love, but *what it means to love* one's neighbour. The main point of the parable would seem to be that true neighbourly love is not limited to only certain people, *and* involves doing good to others.

The categories of parable and allegory have much in common. For example, both are based on comparisons like the metaphor or simile. We will actually often find a mixture of features from parables and allegories in a text. An example of this is the allegorical parable of the weeds (Mt 13:24-30). Parables have one overriding point, in this case that at the end of the age those who do evil will be punished and those who are in a right relationship with God exalted. Its allegorical features are seen in the heavy use of symbolism. For example, the harvest is a symbol for the end of the age, the weeds symbolise people who have rejected Christ, the enemy is a symbol for the devil, etc (Mt 13:36-43).

Apocalyptic text is found in Revelation, the latter chapters of Daniel (chs 7-12) and in parts of Zechariah (eg 1:7-6:8). It is loaded with symbolic events and allusions that give God's perspective on what is happening in the world (past, present and future). The features of narrative discourse are also present. The events described take place in sequence and no explicit instructions are given to the reader.

The genre of **conversation** is a special type which often involves characteristics of a mixture of other discourse types. It is mentioned here because it is frequently embedded in narrative but should not be mistaken for pure narrative. Kathleen Callow (1974:17) says this about conversational genre: 'Conversation differs from the other types in that more than one speaker is involved; it is very varied, in that it may have the characteristics of any other type...or may be more informal than all of these'. Nevertheless, the features of narrative are also present. People are reported to converse one after another (chronological sequence) and, although the speakers may tell each other what to do, the reader is not directly addressed (non-prescriptive) as in exhortation. The conclusion has to be that conversational genre has to be treated with special care. An example of conversation embedded in narrative discourse type is found in the book of Ruth ch 2.

STUDY TIP

Chapters 19 and 20 focus primarily on how to interpret the genre of dramatic history. Nevertheless many of the principles mentioned here will also apply to the other genres mentioned above. When interpreting other genres, we need to be aware of their distinctive features and fine-tune our approach accordingly. When we deal with how to interpret the Gospels (ch 27) and Revelation (ch 30) we will look at some of these other genres.

Exercises

3. What are the distinctive features of the following genres in the narrative discourse type?
   a) dramatic history
   b) allegory
   c) parable
   d) apocalyptic text

4. What are the genres of the following passages?
   a) 2 Sam 12:1-4
   b) 2 Chr 32
   c) Dan 8:1-12
   d) 2 Kgs 14:9

19.3 How different genres of narrative influence interpretation

The fact that the Bible was written in different types of literature will influence and guide our approach to exegesis. Making a mistake in determining what kind of literature we are dealing with, or ignoring it altogether, can have a major influence on the message. Such exegetical approaches have lead to some creative interpretation, and make for interesting reading, but are not based on a sound understanding of how the Bible came into being, or of communication or linguistic principles.

A case in point is some of the work done by Origen (exegete and philosopher from Alexandria, 185-254). He interpreted the genre of dramatic history as if it had been written as an allegory. This allegorical approach was a method adopted from the Greeks who had used it to interpret their own mythology. It was a search for the hidden and more spiritual meanings behind simple statements and the plain meaning of a text. The result of Origen's work on Ex 1:22 to 2:10 is discussed by Kaiser (1987:199) as follows:

> With bold strokes he proclaimed that Pharaoh, the king of Egypt, represented the devil while the male and female children of the Hebrews represented the rational and animal faculties of mankind. Pharaoh wished to destroy all the males, that is the seeds of rationality and spiritual science through which the soul tends to and seeks heavenly things. However, he wished to preserve all the females alive, that is all those animal propensities of man, through which he becomes carnal and devilish. Thus, wherever men live in luxury, banquetings, pleasures, and sensual gratifications, one can be assured that there the king of Egypt has slain all the males and preserved all the females alive.
>
> This silliness can be carried one step further. Pharaoh's daughter might represent the Church which was gathered from among the Gentiles. Although she had an impious and iniquitous father, the psalmist said of her, "Harken, O daughter, and consider, incline thine ear: forget also thine own people, and thy father's house; so shall the king greatly desire thy beauty" (Ps 45.10-11). Her coming to the waters to bathe was tantamount to coming to the baptismal font that she might be washed from the sins which she had contracted in her father's house. But this has gone far enough. Wouldn't Moses have been thrilled if he had known how much was going on when he wrote the narrative?

This example hardly needs further comment. It is clear that the genre of dramatic history was ignored and the writer's intention completely twisted. Moreover, this example illustrates that the message is profoundly changed when a text is interpreted without due care and attention given to the kind of literature. Such an approach opens the door to all kinds of fanciful interpretations, with each student arriving at a vastly different understanding of the message. To avoid this bottomless pit of subjectivity, our approach to exegesis will need to be based on the correct identification of the type of literature involved.

Exercise

5. Explain why it is important to correctly identify the genre of a text.

19.4 The plot structure of narrative

Why is it that people always enjoy a good story? It is because a well-written story will usually catch our attention immediately with some daring plan to be pursued, unusual or mysterious events to be explained, or a tricky problem to be solved. Once our attention has been captured, we are kept in tension until, towards the end of the story the plan is achieved, the mystery revealed or the problem solved.

This brings us to another important characteristic of the narrative discourse type and its genres: the plot structure. Although not all narratives are based around a plot structure, many do exhibit this characteristic. The plot structure in narrative arises from the need to arouse the reader's interest - in other words, the author needs to capture the interest of the reader so that he will actually read the story. This means that the author structures his narrative in a certain way in order to create interest and keep the reader's attention to the end.

For example, the initial chapters of a detective novel often describe some mysterious events. For instance, a novel could begin by describing the mysterious disappearance of several million francs in gold bars from a high security Swiss bank. This grabs the reader's interest, creates tension and an expectation in him that the rest of the novel will explain who the thieves were and how they committed the crime.

Apart from creating interest and certain expectations in the reader, the plot structure helps us to discover the message of a narrative. It helps us to recognise the significant events of a narrative from the author's point of view, and this in turn helps us to arrive at the intended message (more will be said in 19.4.3 about how the plot structure helps us find the author's purpose).

Just as the plot structure helps us to recognise the significant events in a narrative, it could also help us to make a good summary of the story. For example, in a detective novel the two main elements of a summary would be the mysterious events happening at the beginning of the story (the disappearance of the gold bars from the Swiss bank) and the explanation of these mysterious events near the end of the story (who did it and how the robbery was done). Therefore, recognising the plot of a narrative really helps us to understand the central and important content of a narrative, which is of course an important step in arriving at the message of any narrative.

When we analyse the plot structure in step 3.2 (mark the significant meaning indicators), the most significant elements to look for are those which create some kind of tension. Elements that create significant tension in the reader or in a character are usually those which describe something that is difficult to attain (eg the plan to climb the highest mountain in the world), something unexplained (eg an unknown cause of a sickness) or something undesirable (eg the exploitation of poor people) (Callow 1989:106). When such tensions are present, they raise the expectation in the reader that later on in the narrative these tensions will be resolved. So the main elements in a plot are those which create and resolve some kind of tension. All other events in a story relate to these main elements and support them. We will first look at the main elements, and later in the chapter at the supportive elements.

According to Callow (1989:112), there are three general areas where tension is created for the reader or in a character in the narrative.

Firstly, in the area of the **will** (if the plan is to climb the highest mountain, will it succeed?). Secondly, in the area of the **known/unknown** (is the unknown cause of the sickness going to be discovered?). Thirdly, in the area of **need/distress** (what will be done about the exploitation of the poor?).

Tension in these areas gives rise to different kinds of main elements in the plot structure, as shown in figure 19.3.

FIGURE 19.3
Three general types of plot structures

The area of tension for the reader or in the character of the narrative	PLOT STRUCTURE	
	Element which creates tension	Element which resolves tension
Will (something be attained)	Plan	Execution
Known/unknown (something is unknown)	Mystery	Explanation
Need/distress (something is undesirable)	Problem	Resolution

An example of a **plan-execution** structure is found in the plot structure of Acts. In the first chapter of Acts, Jesus instructs his disciples to be his witnesses to the ends of the earth (the plan) and the rest of the book describes how this plan was carried out (the execution).

A **mystery-explanation** structure is found in our example of the Swiss bank robbery. The mystery is the robbery and the explanation is the disclosure of who committed the crime and how it was done. A biblical example of this structure is the riddle that Samson tells his thirty wedding companions (the mystery), and after the story takes a few unexpected turns, they find the answer to the riddle (the explanation) (Judg 14:12-18).

The **problem-resolution** structure is the most commonly found plot structure in biblical narratives. Many Bible stories are built around this framework, eg the healing of the cripple (Acts 3:1-10). The following illustration is a simplified analysis of the story's plot structure, outlining the main tension-creating and resolving elements.

v2a	the problem:	'a man crippled from birth'
v7c	the resolution:	'the man's feet and ankles became strong'

When analysing the plot structure, we should do it in the light of these three tension areas.

19.4.1 Combinations of plot structures

A narrative may well combine some of the above patterns of creating and resolving tension. We may find a combination of these: a mystery may create a problem which gives rise to a plan, etc.

It must be added that in real life a problem may, of course, not be solved, a mystery not explained and a plan abandoned or unfulfilled. This does not mean the absence of a plot structure, but instead of a resolution, a story may end by stating the failure to resolve the problem, in other words a counter-resolution. For example, our mystery story of the Swiss bank robbery could have ended like this: After many months of slow progress and painstaking detective work, the investigating squad from Scotland Yard finally conceded its defeat. The culprit was still as elusive as ever and little hope was expressed of ever solving this mystery (counter-explanation).

19.4.2 Combination of the main and supportive elements

Figure 19.4 serves to illustrate a combination of the main tension creating and resolving elements (listed below the time line) and possible supportive elements (above the time line).

FIGURE 19.4

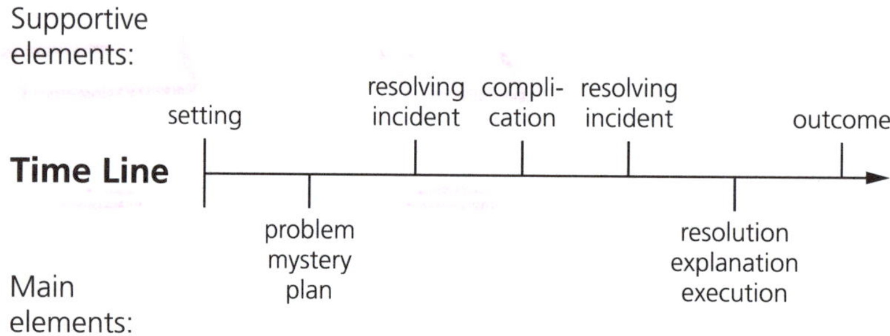

We will now briefly note some of the supportive elements which may be found in the problem-resolution framework. It is important to understand that the supportive elements purposefully relate to the problem and the resolution. Particularly note what is said about the **outcome**.

The **setting** introduces the story, giving us the necessary and important background information in order to make sense of the story.

A **resolving incident** moves the story closer to the resolution of the problem.

A **complication** hinders progress towards the solution, or it may even create a new problem to be solved, before further progress towards solving the main problem can be made. It is often there to create further tension and leave the reader in suspense.

The **outcome** is an event which happens as a result of the resolution of a problem, the explanation of a mystery or the execution of a plan. In real life there may be a number of outcomes resulting from the resolution of a problem, but a writer may often select one specific outcome that he considers significant. It is significantly related to the writer's purpose and the question must be asked why a specific outcome is mentioned. The outcome then usually becomes the most important element as far as the author's purpose is concerned. If there is no outcome, the tension-resolving element (resolution, explanation or execution) often becomes most significant (see 20.6 where the outcome of the Dorcas narrative is discussed).

For our purpose it will often be sufficient to identify only two supportive elements, namely the setting and outcome together with the two main elements (problem-resolution, mystery-explanation, plan-execution).

19.4.3 An analysis of the plot structure and the author's purpose

An analysis of the four important elements and the author's purpose for Acts 3:1-10 follows below (figure 19.5).

FIGURE 19.5
The healing of the cripple (Acts 3:1-10)

v1 setting:	Peter and John on their way to the temple
v2a problem:	a man crippled from birth
v7c resolution:	the man's feet and ankles became strong

Now that the problem has been resolved, what significance does the rest of the story have?

v10b outcome:	crowd's response is amazement and wonder

Now, we must ask why Luke mentions this specific outcome? He wants his readers to be absolutely certain that a very great and true miracle was performed by the followers of Jesus and moreover, one that was publicly witnessed. He wants his readers to consider his records as trustworthy. This conclusion fits in with one of Luke's main purposes for his two volume work; to give careful evidence in support of the events surrounding Jesus' and the early church's ministry (Lk 1:1-4; Acts 1:1).

This conclusion also fits in with the immediate context. The narrative continues until a definite break in the chain of events occurs (Acts 4:31). The healing of the cripple (3:1-10) gives rise to the events that follow. And so, our evaluation of Luke's purpose for this part of the narrative must be tested in the context of the whole narrative (3:1-4:31). Several events which Luke carefully notes, confirm his concern for the truthfulness of his records. For example, on account of Peter's explanation of the miracle and its relationship to the risen Christ (3:16; 4:10), many people believed (4:4) and the religious leaders had to acknowledge the miracle as true. In both these events the affirmative response of people to the miracle (albeit indirectly through Peter's sermon and defence) fits in with Luke's purpose and strengthens his testimony.

19.4.4 Narratives without plot structures

Some narratives may not exhibit tension elements and therefore no plot structure will be found. Such narrative units may simply be held together by their content and events that are chronologically and/or causally related. See for example Mk 1:14-20.

Mk 1:14-20 is simply held together by the following features:

1. Location: Area of Galilee (1:14,16,19)
2. Main participant: Jesus
3. Main events: Jesus calling people to follow him (1:17;20)
4. Relationships within the passage: V14-15 provide the setting in which Jesus' call to his future disciples comes. It provides background information for the reader's frame of reference. V16-18 and 19-20 are related by sequence.

Exercises

6. Why are narratives formed around a plot structure?
7. List the three types of plot structures (you could draw a table to do so).
8. How can the plot structure help us to identify the author's purpose?

9. Do all narratives have a plot structure?
10. Mark the setting, problem, resolution and outcome in Acts 9:32-35. Explain what Luke's purpose is, and how he emphasises it.

19.5 The problem of finding the message in dramatic history

As we have seen in chapter 1, God desired to communicate with mankind and he made sure that his communication was recorded. Much of his communication was written down in the form of dramatic history. These stories contain real history, but are nevertheless part of God's message for all people of all times. Being in the form of dramatic history, this part of God's message is not always as easy to understand as one might think. A variety of reasons account for this. There is an immense time and cultural gap between us and (especially) the Old Testament times. Also, there's our odd habit of reading the Bible in little bits and therefore, never really gaining a good overview of the whole Bible. But maybe another fundamental reason for our difficulty is often overlooked. This reason can be found in the distinctive features of the dramatic history genre.

When we compare the narrative discourse type with exposition, we find that both present us with facts related to specific topics, and both are non-prescriptive. Generally speaking, exposition deals primarily with explaining an idea, theory or argument. Narrative often deals with the past and uses concrete terms. Specific people, their actions, places and objects are the primary focus.

In Paul's letters (genre of letters), usually *both* exposition and exhortation discourse types are present. He moves from explaining certain facts (exposition) to stating how those facts should change the thinking and behaviour (exhortation) of his receivers. So, both non-prescriptive and prescriptive characteristics are present. There was therefore little need for the original receiver to figure out how the facts applied to his or her life, because the message was understood quite easily. Besides, Paul usually knew the readers of his letters, so what he wrote was specifically addressed to them and relevant to their problems and circumstances.

The following is a list of the ways in which dramatic history in the Bible is in general different from Paul's letters:

- The writer and reader are not in a direct, personal relationship with one another.
- The writer and reader are not usually part of the communication. There is no first or second person reference to writer or reader within the narrative.(One notable exception to this is the 'we' sections in the book of Acts which point to the fact that Luke was Paul's travelling companion (Acts 16:10-17; 20:5-21:18; 27:1-28:16). Often if the writer was involved in the narrative he was writing, he would use the third person to refer to himself.)
- Dramatic history is non-prescriptive.
- Although both kinds of writings present facts, the writer of dramatic history does not relate these facts directly to the original receiver. This means that the content of the stories do not directly and specifically address the reader's life in the same way as Paul's letters did.
- Although the Biblical writer certainly wanted to communicate a specific message, it may seem to the casual reader that the writer simply recounts a story about people and events of the past.

The result of these differences is that the reader has to form his own conclusions about the message of a narrative. Once the narrative has been carefully read, and the clues towards the author's purpose have been understood, the reader then has to decide what the writer wanted to express in terms of absolute truths. Also how this should influence his thoughts and actions.

As far as this process of forming a conclusion is concerned, the difference between dramatic history and NT letters (exposition/exhortation) could be illustrated with the following examples:

Message in form 1:

Grandma and family are sitting in the lounge. One of the children has just come in and left the door open. She shivers and says, 'Don't you feel a draft?'The family would immediately conclude that she is not just asking for an opinion but would like the door to be shut.

Message in form 2:

In the same setting grandma could just as easily have said, 'Please shut the door, it's drafty!'

In the first message, the process of conclusion is involved. The family, due to the context of communication and the facts, have to conclude what grandma wants them to do. This of course, comes quite naturally, and the family would hardly be aware of the mental process of conclusion.

In the second message, grandma expresses her purpose explicitly, so the family members do not engage in the mental process of conclusion.

Figure 19.6 illustrates the different processes required to arrive at the messages of NT letters (exposition/exhortation) and dramatic history.

FIGURE 19.6

NT letters

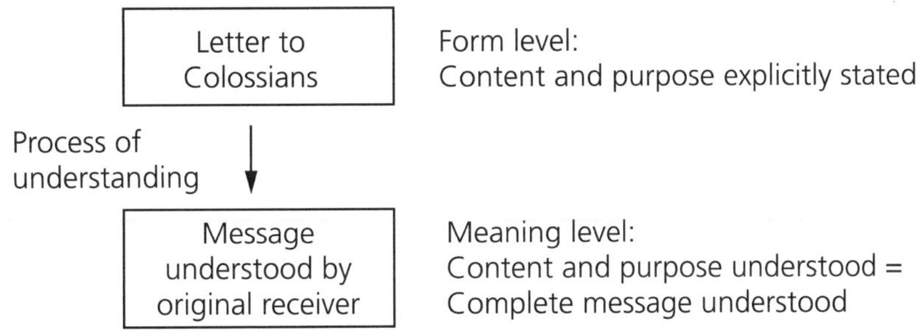

Dramatic history

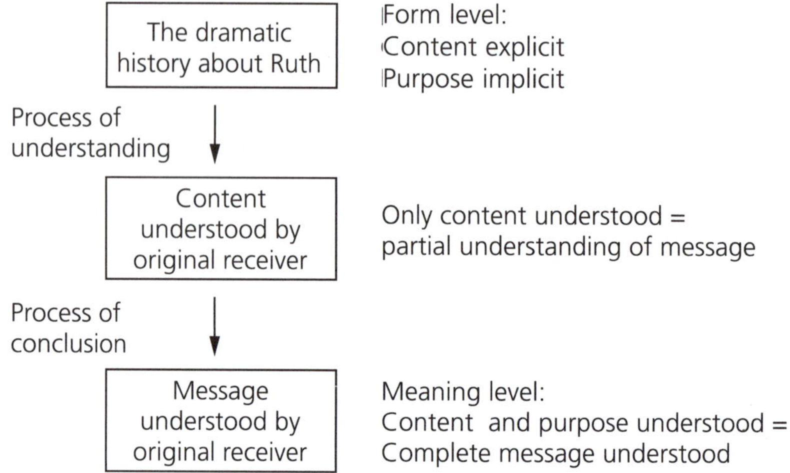

It is evident that the processes of understanding and conclusion cannot really be separated. Rather, they merge into one another and have fuzzy borders. It would be difficult, if not impossible, to separate these mental processes. The fact is, that in understanding messages, we always grapple with both content and purpose, or else we do not fully understand the message. When the purpose of a message is explicitly stated, as is generally the case in NT letters, the original reader would not have found it difficult to understand. When the purpose is left implicit, as is the case of dramatic histories, understanding the message is just that much more difficult. Therefore, to understand the message the writer wanted to communicate, careful consideration must be given to any signposts which help us understand both the content and purpose of a story.

STUDY TIP

It takes practice to develop sensitivity and understanding when exegeting narrative. So don't be discouraged when you find narrative difficult.

Exercises

11. One of the main characteristics of narrative is that it is 'non-prescriptive'. Describe what that means.
12. What makes it difficult to discover the message to the original receiver in dramatic history? List four reasons.
13. What is required of the reader after careful exegesis, in order to arrive at the message to the original receiver?

19.6 The structure of a narrative book

In chapter 9.8 we explained how to discover the structure of a book. We will now highlight some of the main structural features of narrative. We will also explain that the basic unit for analysis in narrative is the episode.

A Time + culture gap; not readin whole Bible; narrative deals with concrete details of people in the past; and the writer's purpose is implicit, not explicit as in exposition

Figure 19.7 illustrates how the blocks of thought in narrative could be grouped and labelled within the hierarchical structure of a book. Beginning with the whole book, it may be divided into 'parts', and in turn each 'part' into several 'acts' and each 'act' into several 'scenes', etc.

FIGURE 19.7
Structure of a narrative book

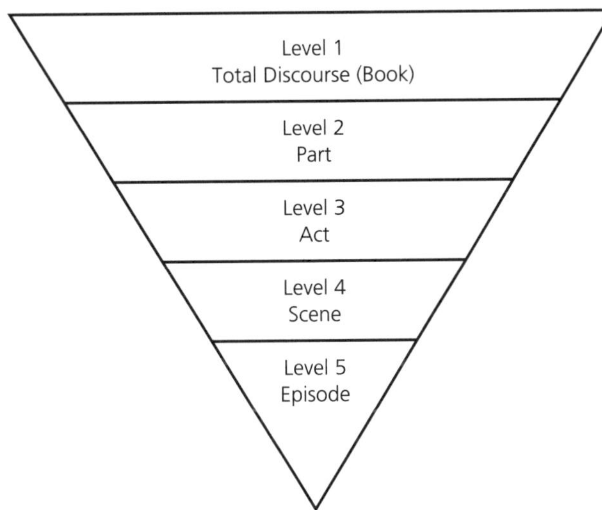

Since each book has its own structure, the number of levels required will differ according to how many blocks of thought are found. So, no preconceived structure should be imposed on a book. Rather, the structure and number of levels should become apparent after the analysis has been completed, and the blocks of thought have been identified. Although it is important to understand the structure of a book and how the various parts relate to one another, the specific labels given to each level in figure 19.7 are only to be viewed as a practical means of reference.

The following structure shows how the major blocks of thought are grouped together to form a hierachical structure within the book of Acts. It also describes how the main plot develops and what events are central to it. This provides us with a useful starting point for the exegesis of individual passages in the book.

The following structure of Acts has been adapted from Blood & Blood (1979).

Introduction to Parts 1 and 2 (1:1-11)
As recorded in the gospel of Luke, the risen Jesus commands his disciples to await the Spirit's empowering to be his witnesses, and then he ascends to heaven.

Part 1 (1:12-19:20)
Against adversity, the disciples' Spirit-empowered witness about Jesus expands from Jerusalem, Judea, and Samaria to Asia Minor and the Aegean area.
Act 1 (1:12-6:7)
In spite of opposition and problems, the apostles' Spirit-empowered witness continues in Jerusalem, as miracles are done, resulting in a multitude of unified believers.
Act 2 (6:8-9:31)
Scattered by persecution, the disciples witness about Jesus effectively in Samaria and Judea, and Saul, witnessing boldly as a new convert, is rescued from opposition.

Act 3 (9:32-12:24)
Through Peter, salvation comes to Gentiles in Caesarea and, through Barnabas and Saul, growth to Gentile believers in Antioch, and the Lord removes a threat to the witness.
Act 4 (12:25-16:5)
Churches are established and strengthened in Asia Minor, as Paul and his company expand the witness to Gentiles in spite of opposition from the Jews.
Act 5 (16:6-19:20)
In spite of opposition and problems, the witness through Paul and his company extends to both sides of the Aegean Sea, and Gentile believers show decided growth.

Part 2 (19:21-28:31)
Against adversity, the witness about Jesus Christ, through Paul's trial, extends to Jews at Jerusalem, to Roman authorities at Caesarea and to all at Rome.

Introduction to Part 2 (19:21-22)
Paul purposes to go to Jerusalem via Macedonia and Achaia, and then on to visit Rome, but remains in Asia for a time.

Act 1 (19:23-21:16)
Travelling to Jerusalem, Paul brings believers comfort, bids farewell to leaders, is advised against going to Jerusalem, is informed of imprisonment there, and finally reaches Jerusalem.
Act 2 (21:17-23:11)
After Paul has been accused and arrested and has given his testimony before the Jews in Jerusalem, the Lord tells him he must similarly testify in Rome.
Act 3 (23:12-26:32)
Paul, transferred to Caesarea, gives his defence and testimony before Felix, and then, Festus and Agrippa, who conclude he is innocent but must stand before Caesar.
Act 4 (27:1-28:16)
Paul, along with other prisoners, is transferred to Rome, being providentially spared and given respect in crucial situations enroute.
Act 5 (28:17-31)
Paul, although a prisoner, witnesses about Jesus Christ to the Jews and to all who come to him in Rome.

The above-mentioned acts could be further subdivided, and the relationship between the blocks of thought described. The following is an example of how this could be done, using act 1 of part 1 to illustrate this. Observe how the content and purpose determine which basic narrative units group together as blocks of thought.

Part 1, Act 1 (1:12-6:7)

Scene 1 (1:12-26) (preliminary events)

The apostles and believers prayerfully pick Judas' successor, Matthias.

Scene 2 (2:1-4) (events that trigger other events)

The Holy Spirit comes visibly and fills the disciples who are enabled to speak in other languages.
The events in this scene set off a chain of events reported in the remaining scenes in act 1.

Scene 3 (2:5-47) (result of scene 2)

After Peter's empowered witness, the Lord adds many new believers and they continue in fellowship with one another.

Episode 1 (2:5-41) After Peter's witness, many believe.

Episode 2 (2:42-47) United believers continue in fellowship with one another.

Scene 4 (3:1-4:31) (result of scene 2)
After the cripple's healing, many believe. Peter and John remain firm in their witness in spite of opposition, and the believers experience God's power.

Episode 1 (3:1-10) The cripple is healed.

Episode 2 (3:11-4:4) After Peter's witness, many believe and opposition arises. These events result from the previous episode.

Episode 3 (4:5-22) Peter and John remain firm in their witness despite opposition. These events result from the previous episode.

Episode 4 (4:23-31) The believers pray for boldness and experience God's power. These events result from the previous episode.

Figure 19.7 also illustrates a hierarchical arrangement of the structure of the book (graphically illustrated by the inverted triangle). This hierarchy of blocks of thought implies that the meaning of a block of text is influenced not only by the adjacent units but by the total structure. The structure of Acts given above illustrates this:

The events that take place in scene 2 (Acts 2:1-4) empower the disciples to witness. The following scenes are related to it and can be seen as a result of the Holy Spirit's work through the disciples. Thus, scene 2 (Acts 2:1-4) greatly influences how we understand the following scenes. There is a clear emphasis on the Holy Spirit's dominant role in transforming people's lives and in building the church.

A different approach to the structure of Acts is explained in 'True to the Faith' (Gooding 1990). It is a useful approach and complements the aforementioned structure. Gooding's focus is on tracing how the themes in Acts are emphasised by parallel arrangements of events in the six sections of his structure:

Section 1 (1:1-6:7) Christianity and the Restoration of All Things
Section 2 (6:8-9:31) Christianity's Worship and Witness
Section 3 (9:32-12:24) The Christian Theory and Practice of Holiness
Section 4 (12:25-16:5) The Christian Doctrine of Salvation
Section 5 (16:6-19:20) Christianity and the Pagan World
Section 6 (19:21-28:31) Christianity and the Defence and Confirmation of the Gospel

In most of these sections, Gooding sees a parallelism in events which highlights and emphasises the themes of the book. For example, his description of parallel events in section 4 is as follows (Gooding 1990:206):

Section 4: The Christian Doctrine of Salvation (12:25-16:5)	
Movement 1: The Preaching of the Good News of Salvation (12:25-14:28)	**Movement 2:** The Discussion of the Terms of Salvation (15:1-16:5)
1. Antioch to Paphos (12:25-13:12) The false prophet Bar-Jesus (13:6) tries to turn a Gentile from the faith (13:8) Paul smites the false prophet with blindness (13:9-11)	1. Antioch to Jerusalem (15:1-5) False teachers from Judea (15:1) teach that Gentiles must be circumcised in order to be saved Paul and Barnabas have sharp dispute and debate with the false teachers (15:2)
2. Pisidian Antioch (13:13-52) 'From this man's descendants God has brought... the Saviour Jesus' (13:23); '...it is to us that this message of salvation has been sent' (13:26); '...a light for the Gentiles... salvation to the ends of the earth' (13:47) David (13:22, 34-37) and Moses (13:39) Old Testament quotation regarding the Gentiles (13:46-48)	6. The conference (15:6-21) 'We believe it is through the grace of our Lord Jesus that we (Jews) are saved, just as they (Gentiles) are' (15:11) David (15:16) and Moses (15:21) Old Testament quotation regarding the Gentiles (15:14-19)
3. Iconium to Derbe (14:1-20) 'Jews... stirred up the minds of the Gentiles' (14:2) Paul and Barnabas restrain Gentiles from idolatry (14:11-18)	7. The letter (15:22-35) 'some (men) disturbed you, troubling your minds' (15:24) '... abstain from food sacrificed to idols...' (15:29)
4. The Return (14:21-28) 'remain true to the faith... We must go through many hardships to enter the kingdom...' (14:22) 'they... reported... how (God) had opened the door of faith to the Gentiles' (14:27)	8. The Return (15:36-16:5) Paul and Barnabas have a sharp disagreement and separate. Paul circumcises Timothy! (15:36-16:3) 'So the churches were strengthened in the faith...' (16:5)

STUDY TIP

How the structure of a book is discovered, and how a block of thought is influenced by other blocks, is explained in depth in chapter 9.8.

19.6.1 The episode as the smallest unit for analysis in narrative

In 4.5 and 10.2 the paragraph is introduced as the smallest unit for analysis. In narrative, we will work with the episode as the smallest unit for analysis. An episode has a similar function in narrative to the paragraph in exposition/exhortation and the strophe in poetry. So, just as we analyse one paragraph at a time in exposition/exhortation we will analyse an episode at a time in narrative.

Exposition	⟶	paragraph
Poetry	⟶	strophe
Narrative	⟶	episode

We will find that in dramatic history, as for example the Samson story (Judg 13-16), the text is often not broken down into episodes. The text needs to be grouped into episodes for us to analyse. Practically, this means that in step 3.1 (write the passage out in smaller units) one should read the whole story and roughly divide it up into episodes. This is not necessarily an accurate division but will provide a practical framework for step three. Your divisions however will need to be evaluated and possibly changed when continuing through step three of exegesis (analyse the passage). The following criteria will help you to divide up the text into episodes.

An episode may be defined as a chain of events which are related (often one event leading to another), having the same location, time and major participants. A break in the events, a change of participant, location or time often indicates the beginning of a new building block within the structure of a narrative. An exception to this definition is an episode describing a journey. The location will constantly change but this alone will not indicate a new episode.

The episode can be compared with a play in which intervals indicate the change from one part of the play to another. The set of characters changes, the backdrop is different and time has elapsed.

The definition of an episode will be your guide in grouping a portion of text together. In addition, the following indicators may help you to do this. It should be noted that these indicators may also be used to signal larger blocks of thought (eg a group of episodes making up a scene). One has to evaluate the function of each indicator within the larger context.

19.6.2 Indicators which help to determine the structure

The content:
If you can reduce the content of a block of text to a brief summary (conceptualise it), it indicates that it belongs together. Its parts relate closely to each other.

For example, Acts 3:1-10 is about the cripple who is healed after Peter prays for him. We have been able to conceptualise what this episode is about.

The purpose:
Here we ask how a block of text functions within the context of the whole book or part of a book.

For example, Acts 3:1-10 relates to the events of scene 2 (Acts 2:1-4) as a specific result but it also brings about the chain of events narrated in the following episode (Acts 3:11-4:4). Its clear purpose within the structure of the larger narrative helps us to see that this block of text belongs together.

The boundary markers:
Boundary markers are words, phrases or even whole paragraphs that mark the beginning or end of a unit. Therefore they may help you decide when a new unit begins or ends. Some examples of boundary markers follow:

GRAMMATICAL MARKERS:

'When'	Acts 2:1
'Then'	Acts 12:19b
'Now'	Acts 5:1

Notice that 'now' does not always mean "at this time" but in a specific context it alerts the reader to a change in the story line or flow of thought. In Acts 5:1 it shows that a new episode begins.

CHANGE IN PARTICIPANTS, TIME AND PLACE:
Participants:
It may be either a participant who is completely new or one that has been out of the text for a while and is brought back into the narrative. For example look up Acts 5:1; 6:8; 9:32; Ruth 2:1.

Time:

One day....	Acts 3:1; Judg 16:1; Ruth 3:1
In those days...	Acts 6:1
Meanwhile.....	Acts 9:1; Ruth 4:1
Later on......	Judg 15:1

Place (location):

When they had passed through ...	Acts 17:1
When we arrived at Jerusalem....	Acts 21:17

Summary statements:
These may occur either at the beginning or end of a unit. For examples see Judg 13:1; 15:20; Acts 6:7; 9:31

Exercises:

14. What is the smallest unit for analysis in dramatic history? episode
15. Mark the indicators that make Acts 9:32-35 such a unit.

STUDY TIP
Look at the immediate context of the episode (the episodes before and after) and observe the changes as you move from one episode to the next.

CHAPTER TWENTY

The steps of exegesis applied to narrative

Objectives:

1. To be able to adapt and apply the steps of exegesis to narrative, in particular the genre of dramatic history

Contents:

STUDY TIP
To maximise your learning and to benefit most from this chapter, it is recommended that, before you continue, to have completed the exercises of the previous chapter.

For the purpose of illustrating how the steps of exegesis are applied to narrative and in particular to the genre of dramatic history, the miracle story of Acts 9:36-43 will be our main example.

20.1 Step 1: Research the communication situation

STUDY TIP
Complete this exercise before reading on. Do the same with all of the exercises in this chapter. At the end, you will have exegeted Acts 9:36-43, applied the skills you've learnt, and evaluated your own work.

Exercise

1. Research the communication situation of Acts 9:36-43.

The communication situation is researched according to the principles described in chapter eight.

Who was the author?

The following information about the communication context is found in the book of Acts itself:

Although the name of the author is not mentioned, careful examination renders some clues:

- The book is dedicated to Theophilus (1:1).
- There is reference to a former book, which implies that this is the second volume of a book which he has written (1:1).
- Acts 1:1-11 repeats and overlaps with what was said in Lk 24 and thus ties the two books together.
- Some terminology indicates a writer with medical experience (both in Luke and Acts).
- The 'we' sections infer that the writer was present at certain stages of the narrative (16:10-17; 20:5-15; 21:1-18; 27-28).

Information from other Bible books which help complete the picture of the communication situation:

- The similar language of Luke and Acts indicates a common author.
- The Gospel of Luke is also addressed to Theophilus.
- Luke, a physician by profession and Gentile by birth is a fellow-worker of Paul and was with him during his imprisonment in Rome (Col 4:14, Phlm 24).

Information from other sources:

- Early church tradition (eg the Muratorian Canon (AD 170), Irenaeus (AD 180) and Eusebius (AD 325)) ascribe authorship to Paul's companion, Luke.
- The language in both Luke and Acts is sophisticated in the tradition of the Hellenistic historians and so reflects a writer with a good educational and cultural background.

Therefore, Luke who is Paul's 'dear friend and doctor' (Col 4:14; Phlm 24) becomes the most likely candidate for authorship.

Who are the recipients?

- Theophilus, of whom we know nothing else (1:1). He is addressed as 'most excellent' in Lk 1:3.
- Probably not only Christians as there is a strong element of defending the truth of the message.

Information from other sources:

- It was customary for an author to dedicate his book to a person who may have contributed towards the cost, or who was in other ways closely related. Theophilus may have been a Roman official or someone with considerable wealth and status.

What are the circumstances?

- Rome is the likely place where the book was written although we cannot be very certain about this. It seems likely that Luke was with Paul (Col 4:14) during his first imprisonment, as the account of Acts ends with Paul under arrest in Rome.
- Paul's first imprisonment is often dated about 60-62 AD.

What was Luke's main purpose for writing?

If we take the Gospel of Luke and the book of Acts as a two volume book, the purpose is clearly stated in the prologue of the Gospel.

- To present a well-researched and attested account of the life and ministry of Jesus in order to strengthen the faith of believers (Lk 1:1-4). And, by implication in Acts 1:1, to give his readers a well-researched account of the things that Jesus continued to do through his followers.

It is important to note, that it is possible to say more about the circumstances, Luke's purposes, etc, but we can return to this step at any stage during our exegesis if it seems necessary.

20.2 Step 2.1: Establish the type of literature

STUDY TIP
Refer to ch 9.6 and 19.1-2 if you are uncertain about this step.

Exercise

2. What type of literature is Acts 9:36-43?

- The form of discourse in Acts 9:36-43 is prose.
- The discourse type is narrative.
- The genre is dramatic history - a miracle story.

20.3 Step 2.2: Establish the position in the book

STUDY TIP
You may find a review of chapter 9.7-8 and 19.6 helpful before you proceed.

Exercise

3. How does Acts 9:36-43 fit into the immediate context, ie Acts 9:32-35 and Acts 10:1-47?

The position in the book of Acts 9:36-43

The general context:
This is the second episode in the third act (9:32-12:24) (see the structure of Acts in 19.6). In this block of thought (act 3), the gospel is spread by Peter to the Jews in Judea and the Gentiles in Caesarea. And by the scattered believers. And by Barnabas and Paul to the Gentiles in Antioch. Luke begins to show one of his concerns - that the gospel is not only for the Jews but also for the Gentiles.

The whole episode functions as an 'execution' in the overall plot structure 'plan-execution' (see 19.3) - the plan being Jesus' command, '...and you shall be my witnesses in Jerusalem, and in all Judea and Samaria and to the ends of the earth' (Acts 1:8). Like the previous episode, this is a fulfilment of the plan, in that the gospel is spread from Jerusalem and more people become believers.

The immediate context:
9:32-35: The healing of Aeneas confirms the truthfulness of the gospel and the church grows beyond Jerusalem - a sign of the kingdom.

10:1-47: Cornelius, as a Gentile, is included in the church and thus the church grows across ethnic barriers. It unites Jews and Gentiles into the new people of God - a sign of the kingdom.

Apart from their function in the overall plot structure of Acts, the two miracle stories (9:32-35 and 9:36-43) set the stage for Peter's witness to the Gentiles.

20.4 Step 3.1: Write out the passage in smaller units

Characteristically, narrative exhibits less complex syntactical structures than the other discourse types. The words and phrases usually refer to simple concepts like people, animals and objects. Because of this, dramatic history is easy to comprehend without having to write out each episode in smaller units. So, in most cases this step becomes optional. There may be exceptions when we will find it helpful to write out an episode in smaller units. This is the case when a passage is difficult to understand, or if one desires to get a clearer idea of the structure. This happens in Acts 2:42-47, where a pattern in the repetition of events becomes clearer when it is written out in smaller units.

STUDY TIP

Review section 10.2 if you do not remember the reasons for writing a paragraph out in smaller units.

In the case of Acts 9:36-43, it is not necessary to write it out in smaller units since the passage is not written in complex language. Therefore, we only need to indentify the boundaries of the episode.

Exercise

4. Describe what makes Acts 9:36-43 an episode.

The following evidence suggests that Acts 9:36-43 is an episode:

- The problem of the previous episode (paralysed Aeneas) has been solved and the outcome stated in v35.
- A new cycle in the plot structure begins. A new problem (Dorcas' death) which is not related to the previous events is introduced .
- There is a change of location from the previous events. This is emphasised by putting the new location (Joppa) at the beginning of the new sentence.
- A new participant is introduced, namely Dorcas.

20.5 Step 3.2: Mark the significant meaning indicators

In chapter eleven (11.1) three basic types of significant meaning indicators are described:

- indicators of events, people, things and attributes
- stylistic feature indicators
- syntactic relation indicators

The emphasis in narrative is on the first two types of meaning indicators. Meaning indicators that signal relationships between different syntactic parts are present, but greater importance should be given to the development of the plot structure.

Note: The following are general guidelines in marking meaning indicators. Narratives may differ from each other in the selection, manner and frequency with which such indicators are used. In historical books of the Bible, such indicators will often only be recognised and their significance understood when seen in the context of a whole book. This understanding can only be gained by reading the whole or large parts of a book, or good secondary literature (eg an introduction to a Bible book's literary features).

We've grouped the principal meaning indicators in narrative together according to the basic types described in chapter eleven.

20.5.1 The indicators of events, people, things and attributes

Participants:
In marking the people involved in a narrative we roughly distinguish between principal and non-principal participants. This simply means that some participants are more important (principal) in the flow of a story than others. The words and actions of the principal participants are those that usually cause movement and development, or change the direction of the plot or sequence of events. As we move through a narrative, principal and non-principal participants may change and we may also find that several participants have a dominant role. For example, the Dorcas episode focuses on Peter's actions and Dorcas' situation - they are the principal participants in this episode. Dorcas disappears immediately after this episode and later on in Acts, Paul replaces Peter as the principal participant.

In looking for the intended message of the narrative, special attention must be given to the principal participants' words and actions. We must observe carefully their decisions, purposes, desires, intentions, emotions and evaluations. It is primarily in these elements, and the development of the plot, that we find important clues which help us to arrive at the message.

An example of important words spoken by one of the principal participants is found in Ruth (1:16-18). Ruth, in a deeply emotive manner, expresses her firm commitment to Naomi. This decision significantly influences the rest of the story's plot development and reveals much about Ruth's character and faith. As each scene develops, the writer continues to build on this and his sympathies become evident. Moreover, her positive statements contrast sharply with Naomi's emotionally charged evaluations of her misfortune, which she attributes to God (Ruth 1). A significant contrast of attitudes begins to show. Such contrasts should be carefully noted and their significance evaluated.

Another example of how words and actions influence the development of a narrative is Acts 9:36-43. Peter and Dorcas are the principal participants. What Peter says and does, and what happens to Dorcas, determine the story's events and outcome (9:42). The disciples, the widows and the new believers influence the development of the story's plot to a much lesser extent and Simon the tanner is mentioned only to provide the setting for the following episode.

God as the decisive participant:
God is the overall decisive participant in biblical stories. His involvement in the events of a narrative is often explicitly reported. At other times his actions are only understood from the larger context of the book or the Bible.

His explicit involvement is particularly evident when reading through the Pentateuch. For example, the book of Exodus paints a wonderfully vivid picture of God's involvement in people's lives. His words and actions are described as he delivers Israel from the terrible hardships suffered in Egypt. All along, his involvement is seen as he takes the initiative, raises up Moses as Israel's leader and brings about the defeat of the Egyptian army. Thus he reveals himself to Israel as their God.

In other narratives God's decisive involvement is found only implicitly - for example, in statements evaluating past events, as in the story of Joseph. The statement '... and the Lord was with Joseph...and gave him success...' is repeated several times (Gen 39:2-5, 39:21,23). Then there are the passages where even such statements are lacking and little is said about God's involvement. This is the case in the stories of Ruth and Esther. There, understanding God's implicit involvement does not mean that we read something into the story. It is through the words and actions of the human participants, the development of the narrative and its larger context, that we come to understand God's participation in it.

Places and change of location:
At times places and change of location are important. Consideration should be given to their historical and cultural significance in relation to the events of the story.

'Joppa' in Acts 9:36 is a new location in the passage. It is significant in two ways. Firstly, it is one of the clues indicating the beginning of a new episode. Secondly, it shows how the disciples' witness reaches beyond Jerusalem and how the church grew as a result of it. This shows the further fulfilment of the plan set out in Acts 1:8.

Time and change in time:
A change in time is often one of the indicators signalling the beginning of a new episode. In Acts 9:36-43 Dorcas' illness and death happen simultaneously with the events of the previous episode. This is indicated by the phrase 'About that time...'. In this case it is not a time change but the focus on a set of different events during the same time that indicate that we are dealing with a different episode.

An example where a lapse in time indicates the beginning of a new episode is Acts 2:1. The change of time is indicated by the phrase 'When the day of Pentecost came,...'.

Objects:
Look also for those objects which seem to be significant or express some symbolic meaning. An example is found in the story of the prodigal son. The father, on the son's return, requested three things to be brought - sandals, robe and a ring. The ring certainly went far beyond the physical needs of the son and seems to emphasise the father's acceptance of his repentant son as a full member of the family.

In the Dorcas narrative (figure 22.4) the 'robes and other clothing' made by Dorcas give us an idea of how she cared for others, emphasising and elaborating on Dorcas' caring and commendable life (Acts 9:36).

20.5.2 Indicators of stylistic features

Author's remarks and summary statements:
These are a kind of commentary on the events of a story and stand apart from the story line.

They do not contribute to the development of the plot, but evaluate and emphasise certain facts which may otherwise not be obvious to the reader. Thus, these remarks or summary statements are important pointers to the purpose of the narrative. Examples of such remarks are found in the Joseph narrative (Gen 39:2-5, 39:21,23) or in Judges (17:6; 18:1; 19:1; 21:25). Acts is well-known for its repetitive summary statements (eg 6:7; 9:31; 12:24; 16:5; 19:20).

Repetitive structures:
In 11.6 the two main patterns mentioned are parallelism and chiasm. These can also be found in narrative. For instance, in Judg 6-8 the narrative starts by describing Israel's apostasy and ends with Israel's renewed apostasy. This is a sandwich structure (inclusion). This kind of feature often helps us to determine the boundaries of an episode or larger blocks in a narrative. A similar stylistic feature is the repetition of the basic plot structure in many of the episodes in Judges (see figure 23.2).

20.5.3 Indicators of relationships

In narrative, we primarily look for the main features of the plot structure. The importance of the plot structure was demonstrated in the previous chapter (19.4). It helps us not only to see how the events relate to one another but it often helps us bettter understand the author's purpose and message.

STUDY TIP
Reviewing figure 19.5 may help you in completing the following exercise.

Exercise

5. Mark the meaning indicators of Acts 9:36-43. Make sure you also mark the main elements of the plot structure.

The following figure (figure 20.1) illustrates the important elements of the plot structure.

FIGURE 20.1
Plot structure of Acts 9:36-43

v36	setting: Dorcas is introduced
v37	problem: Dorcas died
v40	resolution: Dorcas raised to life
v42	outcome: many people believed in Jesus

In figure 20.2, the main meaning indicators have been marked. It may not always be necessary to mark all the repetitions of indicators as this could produce a mass of colours or symbols and may be more confusing then helpful. Nevertheless, a recognition of the significant meaning indicators is still important.

FIGURE 20.2
Marking meaning indicators in Acts 9:36-43

setting
36] **In Joppa there was a disciple named**
∠∠∠ ∩∩∩∩ αααα
Tabitha (which, when translated, is
ααααα
Dorcas), who was always doing good and
ααααα αα
helping the poor. 37] About that time **she**
==== αα
problem
became sick and died, and her body was
⊥⊥⊥⊥⊥⊥⊥⊥⊥ ααααααα
washed and placed in an upstairs room. 38]

Lydda was near Joppa; so when the disciples
∠∠∠ ∩∩∩∩∩
heard that Peter was in Lydda, they sent two
>>>>> ∩∩
men to him and urged him, "Please come at
>>> >>>
once!"

39] Peter went with them, and when he
>>>>> >>
arrived he was taken upstairs to the room.
>>
All the widows stood around him, crying and
===== >>>
showing him the robes and other clothing
>>>
that Dorcas had made while she was still
αααα αα
with them.

40] Peter sent them all out of the room;
>>>>
then he got down on his knees and prayed.
>> >>>
Turning toward the dead woman, he said,
αααααααα >>
solution
"Tabitha, get up." **She opened her eyes, and**
ααααα αα ⊥⊥⊥⊥⊥ αα ⊥⊥
seeing Peter she sat up. 41] He took her by
>>>> αα ⊥⊥⊥⊥ >> αα
the hand and helped her to her feet. Then
αα αα
he called the believers and the widows and
>> ∩∩∩∩ =====
presented her to them alive. 42] This
αα ∩∩∩ === ⊥⊥⊥⊥

25	outcome	became known all over Joppa, **and many**
		∠∠∠ xxxxx
26		**people believed in the Lord**. 43] Peter
		xxxx —— >>>>
27		stayed in Joppa for some time with a tanner
		∠∠∠
28		named Simon.

20.6 Step 3.3: Explain words and phrases

In step 3.2 we marked the significant meaning indicators. In this step we try to explain them. Here it is especially important to understand the words and actions of the participants in their cultural and religious context as well as in the context of the episode and the whole book. We are aiming to understand the contextual meaning of words (see 12.1). A thorough and broad knowledge of the Bible will be of invaluable help here. Other literature such as Bible dictionaries also provide us with valuable insights into the religious and cultural context of the time.

The book of Ruth illustrates how understanding the flow of thought in the episode and the cultural and religious context, help us to interpret words and actions.

The context of the episode and the cultural situation:
What is the meaning of Ruth's statement, '...and there I will be buried' (Ruth 1:17)? The content of her statement is quite easily understood: She wants to be buried in the same place (country) where Naomi will be buried. But to understand the full meaning of Ruth's statement we must also understand its significance. Both the context of the episode (ch 1:3-22) and the cultural context will help us to understand its significance. The context of the episode helps us understand that Ruth is determined not to leave Naomi under any circumstance. From the cultural context we understand that in the ancient Near East, the burial place was very important. People moved away but they usually wanted to be buried in their home land (see Gen 47:29f; 50:5). In this context, this statement emphasises her strong and unlimited loyalty to Naomi and unwillingness to forsake her.

The religious context:
An understanding of Old Testament civil law will help us evaluate the significance of Boaz's words and actions. In chapter two Ruth goes gleaning. There was a provision made in the law for the poor to pick up what was left over from the harvest (Lev 19:9-10; Deut 24:19-21). When Boaz instructs his workers to let Ruth glean where she would normally not be allowed to glean, he goes beyond the requirements of the law (Ruth 2:15). This is significant as it reveals to us something about Boaz's character and faith. We come to understand that he is an Israelite who really cares for the poor. This in turn shows his respect for God and obedience to the law.

Exercise

6. Explain the meaning indicators of Acts 9:36-43.

The meaning indicators of Acts 9:36-43 explained:
Plot structure - setting: 9:36 provides us with background information so that we can understand the narrative. It introduces a new participant (Dorcas) and gives us some information about her.

Joppa: a town about 35 miles from Jerusalem on the coast of Palestine. It often served as the main sea port for Jerusalem and Judea.

a disciple named Tabitha: a woman called Tabitha who is a committed follower of Jesus Christ.

(which, when translated, is Dorcas): both Tabitha (Aramaic) and Dorcas (Greek) mean gazelle (NIV Study Bible 1987:1629). The author's comment gives us a clue that he was writing for Greek speaking people who did not know Aramaic.

who was always doing good and helping the poor: this description of Dorcas provides us with background information necessary to help us understand the narrative, and who she is. Note that the writer could have said a variety of things about Dorcas (eg whether she was single or married, young or old etc) But all he says is that which the reader needs to know in order to make sense of the story.

About that time: refers to the time of the events of the previous episode (9:32-35) and so marks the relationship of the episode within the larger structure of the book.

she became sick and died: In the plot structure this is the problem to which all the following events are related in some way.

her body was washed and placed in an upstairs room: in accordance with Jewish custom, the body was washed and placed in the upstairs room until burial time, which usually took place within twenty-four hours after death.

Lydda was near Joppa: a town a little distance north of the road connecting Jerusalem with Joppa and about 12 miles from Joppa. (It also shows that the author or his source is familiar with the geography of Palestine.)

disciples: the group of people who are followers of Jesus Christ and who live in Joppa.

heard that Peter was in Lydda: considering that the disciples sent for Peter, it seems likely that they had also heard about the miracle in Lydda.

they sent two men to him and urged him, "Please come at once!": This shows their expectation that Peter will help solve the problem (because of what God had done through him previously).

he was taken upstairs to the room: up until this point the events of the story follow in quick succession, creating a kind of urgency and expectation to resolve the problem.

All the widows stood around him, crying...: highlights the problem by showing the kind of caring woman Dorcas was, and so her death was a great loss to those who benefited from her care.

he said, "Tabitha, get up.": Shows Peter's trust in God to solve the problem and raise Dorcas from the dead.

She opened her eyes, and seeing Peter she sat up: The miracle makes visible God's rule in the present. (It is also a sign of Peter's apostleship - 2 Cor 12:12)

'She opened her eyes' is the resolution part of the plot structure. The problem has been resolved. Dorcas is alive again. Now that the problem has been solved, what is the significance of the following events? Note that Luke repeatedly includes certain similar patterns of events throughout the book of Acts; miracle story - witness - outcome (9:32-35; 3:1-4:4).

and presented her to them alive: It is significant that Luke mentions that the miracle was witnessed by others. (The testimony of others to the factual truth of the miracle would have been important to the original receiver or inquirer.)

This became known..., and many people believed in the Lord: The outcome of the miracle, that many believed must be explained as a result of Peter's witness. That he shared the gospel verbally is implied from the context as well as it being a logical conclusion, since the event of the miracle itself could be interpreted in various ways and would not necessarily have led to people becoming believers. Peter's mission was to make disciples which is impossible without verbal communication. Peter is seen to be fully aware of this. Therefore he speaks to the onlookers at Pentecost (Acts 2:14-40) and to the crowd astonished by the healing of the cripple (Acts 3:11-26). In these two settings he explains how the miracles are possible and the consequences of this to the listeners. Therefore, the miracles repeatedly function as a confirmation of the spoken message, convincing people to put their trust in this message and become believers.

We explained in 19.4 and step 3.2 that the plot structure may give us some clues as to the author's purpose and message. Let us see how Luke provides some clues in the **outcome** of this episode.

Firstly, the story could have ended with the resolution of the problem. In which case the emphasis of the message would have been on how the problem was solved and on the miracle itself.

Secondly, in real life this story might have had many different 'outcomes' eg Dorcas continues to provide for the poor, but Luke selected this very specific outcome 'many people believed'. In doing so, he has selected the result he considers significant. This enables us to understand something of his purpose and message; that the reader should also believe on account of this story, and that the church, empowered by the Holy Spirit, should grow and spread.

Confirmation of this conclusion may be sought by comparing the structure of other episodes, scenes or acts (the bigger blocks) in the book of Acts which frequently exhibit the pattern of problem - resolution - outcome, eg Acts 3:1-4:4; 6:1-7. The following references are outcomes: 2:47b; 4:31b; 5:11, 42; 9:31; 12:24.

20.7 Step 3.4: Establish the meaning structure

The principles explained in chapter 13 apply in general, but need to be adapted somewhat to suit narrative:

1. What is said in general about the paragraph should, in narrative, be applied to the episode.
2. The episode is often one meaning block within a larger block of narrative. It may or may not be necessary to break it down into smaller meaning blocks.
3. It is at this stage that we take into consideration all our findings from the previous steps (steps 1 to 3.3) to summarise the meaning or content of the episode. As we

move from this step into the next step (3.5), we also have to answer the question, what did the author want the reader to learn from this? In answering this question we are engaging in the process of conclusion.

Exercise

7. Establish the meaning structure of Acts 9:36-43. It is not necessary to divide this episode into smaller meaning blocks. It can be seen as one meaning block.

Acts 9:36-43 has only one meaning block that can be stated as:

> As a result of the miracle many believe in Christ and the church grows beyond Jerusalem into the borders of Judea.

A summary of how each step helped us to arrive at this meaning block will now be given.

Step 1 — Luke's overall concern is to confirm the message about Jesus by means of a well-researched account - an apologetic.

Step 2 — We noticed an overall plot structure in Acts:
plan - execution: 'you will receive power when the Holy Spirit comes on you; and **you will be my witnesses... to the ends of the earth**' (Acts 1:8)

Position in the book: This episode is part of the block of thought, Acts 9:32-12:24 (act 3) - the witness for Christ across Jewish territory and national barriers; Gentiles become Christians (Cornelius in Samaria and Gentiles in Antioch)

The preceding episode (9:32-35) is very similar in structure and content.

Step 3.2 — We observed the plot structure which has common elements and repetitive patterns similar to other episodes in Acts.

Step 3.3 — We noticed that the author has included specific events to give emphasis to certain parts, eg Luke selects the event of many people believing as the specific outcome of the episode. This helps us to understand his purpose.

Therefore, the emphasis is on Peter's empowered witness, confirmed by the miracle which results in new believers beyond Jerusalem.

20.8 Step 3.5: Conclude and summarise the message

The principles of this step are described in chapter 14. The following adaptations need to be made for narrative:

1. As explained in 19.5, a process of conclusion helps us to arrive at the message of the narrative. This is not always easy, but considering all the findings of the previous steps should help us.
2. It is important here not to confuse the message with a summary of the story! The message must tell us what the story wants to teach its reader.

Exercise

8. Summarise the message of Acts 9:36-43 to the original receiver.

The message to the original receiver could be described as follows:

Firstly, just as the people in Joppa who heard about the miracle came to believe in Christ, so the reader is urged to believe in Christ. (This emphasises one of Luke's main purposes, to confirm the gospel message about Christ).

Secondly, just as the Holy Spirit empowered the church to grow and spread beyond Jerusalem, so the reader should understand that God intends the church, empowered by the Holy Spirit, to grow and spread.

We would be hard pressed to say that it is Luke's intention to urge the reader to pray for the resurrection of the dead and expect it every time he prays. Although we have not explicitly included the resurrection miracle in our message, the recurring theme of miracles in the book of Acts shows that the Holy Spirit does sovereignly work miracles through believers. These are signs to confirm the gospel, and anticipate the renewal and restoration of all things at Christ's second coming. So, by looking at the book of Acts as a whole, we can surely conclude that it is Luke's intention for the reader to understand that God will continue to break into this present age with signs and wonders to bring healing and restoration and point towards our future hope. The significance of signs and wonders in Acts is further discussed in 28.5.

We have arrived at what we see as Luke's intended message by considering all the evidence of the previous steps. In particular, Luke seems to furnish us with evidence of his purpose in the outcome of this episode (see explanation of meaning indicators). As we read through Acts, it becomes obvious that the message of this episode is not unique but is repeated more than once. By repetition, Luke is emphasising some of his main concerns as he traces the geographical and historical growth of the church.

20.9 Step 4: Relate message to broader biblical and theological framework

Firstly, the message that people should believe the gospel on account of miracles performed and explained as supernatural deeds of God is repeated several times in Acts. For example, the miracle of the languages (2:1-13) and Peter's explanation (2:14-41); the healing of the cripple (3:1-10) and Peter's explanation (3:11-26). It can further be said that Luke is calling those who accepted the truthfulness of the gospel because of the miracles as his witnesses. This substantiates his claim to be writing an accurate account of Jesus and his work through the early church. On this basis of a trustworthy written account, people should come to trust in Christ (Lk 1:1-4; Acts 1:1).

Secondly, the fact that God empowers the church to witness, and that he intends it to grow and spread, is part of the great commission (Mt 28:19-20; Lk 24:46-49).

20.10 Step 5: Read interpretations of others

See chapter sixteen for an explanation of this step.

part six

HOW TO INTERPRET DIFFERENT TYPES OF BIBLE BOOKS

CHAPTER TWENTY ONE

How to practise biblical theology and hermeneutics

Objectives

1. To understand that one discovers who God is by seeing how he revealed himself throughout history and not by limiting him to certain attributes
2. To grasp that one should not expect answers to questions that a passage does not ask
3. To realise the importance of knowing the situation of your target group in the process of hermeneutics
4. To understand the dynamic interaction between the Bible and practice
5. To understand the sufficiency of the biblical message

Contents

STUDY TIP
This chapter serves as a general introduction to part six.

We have explained the method of exegesis as applied to exposition/exhortation (part three), poetry (part four) and narrative (part five). In this part (part six) we are going to look at how to interpret (exegesis and hermeneutics) certain groups of Bible books. These groups are the Pentateuch, OT historical books, Psalms, wisdom literature, the Prophets, the Gospels, Acts, the epistles and Revelation. These groups cover all of the Bible books, and the reason for grouping them in this way is because of their shared characteristics. These characteristics will become obvious as each group is described. There is an overlap between some of these groups. For instance, while Genesis falls within the Pentateuch, it can be argued that it is an OT historical book. Some of the guidelines on how to approach the OT historical books will indeed be applicable to parts of Genesis.

In looking at how to interpret these groups of books, we will present some guidelines for exegesis and hermeneutics, and highlight the contribution these books make to the overall message of the Bible.

The rest of this chapter serves as an introduction to part six of this book and deals with a few important issues on how to practise biblical theology and hermeneutics.

21.1 The starting point makes all the difference

I was told of a young boy from a believing family who went to his mother with a deep theological question: 'God knows everything, why then did he create Adam and Eve if he knew beforehand that they would sin?'

Many other such questions concern an apparent conflict between who God is and his actions. For instance, why does God require repentance from everyone if salvation is only for those that he has already chosen to be saved?

This type of conflict between who God is and his actions, is found when our thinking about God is dominated from the perspective of his attributes. Certain attributes are attached to God. All his actions in history and in saving people are then related to these attributes. This is due to the influence of Greek thinking that saw the world shaped by a principle that was immaterial (having no physical substance), impassive (not feeling or showing emotion), immobile (immovable), immutable (unchangeable) and timeless.

By looking at God in this way, some conflicting theologies have arisen. Some Christians will describe God as omnipotent (having all power), omniscient (knowing everything), omnipresent (present everywhere) and unchangeable. These characteristics are then applied to God's relationship with people. The logical consequence for some is that they don't have to carry responsibility for their own decisions, either to accept or reject God, because it was decided beforehand by God which way each individual would choose.

Other Christians argue against such a view of how God saves people and ask why then does God keep a person responsible for his choice? What is the sense of praying to a God who has already decided what he is going to do? They will continue to argue that this doctrine of who God is cannot be correct. He is certainly not omnipotent, omniscient, omnipresent and unchangeable. For these Christians, God becomes very small and the world a very frightening place! We have to pray more! If we do not pray enough the angels will become weak and their swords will drop from their hands and the battle will be lost!

I need to stress that I am describing opposite extremes in order to illustrate the problems one can end up with if one views God's deeds of salvation from the perspective of rigid attributes ascribed to him.

21.2 God revealed himself throughout history

Where, then, should one start in order to build up a biblical view of who God is? One should start with the Bible itself and see how God reveals himself in his interaction with people. Firstly in the time of the Old Testament and ultimately in Jesus and the life of the early church. In other words, how did God reveal himself through history?

When God appeared to Moses in the desert and gave him the task of leading the Israelites out of Egypt, Moses wanted to know God's name. Is he dealing with the god of the sun, the god of war, the god of fertility...? Won't God tell him his name so that it's easy to put God in a box and know how to deal with him and try to manipulate him?

God's answer is very different (Ex 3:14): 'I AM WHO I AM'. God is saying that he is much bigger than any one name can describe. He does not fit into human definitions or categories. He is who he is!

This is very unfair on Moses and the Israelites, isn't it? No, certainly not. Before Moses asked for God's name, God had already revealed himself to Moses (Ex 3:6):

> I am the God of your father, the God of Abraham, the God of Isaac and the God of Jacob.

God preferred to reveal himself as the God who committed himself in the past (history) to Abraham, Isaac and Jacob. He is the God who made certain promises to Moses' ancestors and who will fulfil those promises. At the same time he is a God who is dynamically involved with what is happening at that particular time in history (Ex 3:7-10):

> I have indeed seen the misery of my people in Egypt. I have heard them crying out because of their slave drivers, and I am concerned about their suffering. So I have come down to rescue them from the hand of the Egyptians and to bring them up out of the land into a good and spacious land, a land flowing with milk and honey...And now the cry of the Israelites has reached me, and I have seen the way the Egyptians are oppressing them. So now, go. I am sending you to Pharaoh to bring my people the Israelites out of Egypt.

As we continue to follow God's revelation of himself through the pages of the Bible, we find him in dynamic interaction with people. He listens to Moses' complaints about his inability to speak and although he is angry about it, he is willing to meet Moses in his objections by sending his brother Aaron to meet him on his way back to Egypt (Ex 4:10-16).

Similarly, Moses pleads for the Israelites when they have made the golden calf, and it is said: 'Then the Lord relented and did not bring on his people the disaster he had threatened' (Ex 32:14).

At other times we see God announce what he was going to do and then doing it: He announces beforehand that he will harden Pharaoh's heart (Ex 4:21) and that he will make the Egyptians favourable towards the Israelites (Ex 3:21), both of which were fulfilled (Ex 9:35 and 12:36).

As we study the Bible and see how God reveals himself, we find a picture of God limiting himself at certain times in order to interact with human beings and at other times overruling human behaviour in a powerful way. God is indeed the great 'I AM WHO I AM'.

I believe that we cannot understand God completely and neither should we try to, because he is infinite. However, we should grow in our understanding of him as he revealed himself to us throughout history. He does not reveal himself in concepts or in philosophical abstracts, but as a God who is intensely involved with us and who cares for us.

As a God who is certainly able to know everything, to do anything, to be everywhere and who is faithful to his promises, he is in dynamic interaction with us. Sometimes he limits himself in order to watch with expectancy what we are going to choose or decide. At other times he breaks forth in great power in order to direct us clearly in a specific direction, or even to overrule our decisions.

We see God limiting himself to the extreme when Jesus is hanging on the cross. Jesus is powerless, although twelve legions of angels are available to him (Mt 26:53). He decided to limit himself and to give himself over into the hands of his torturers because of his love for us!

We see God using his power mightily when he raised Jesus from the dead and seated him at his right hand 'far above all rule and authority, power and dominion, and every title that can be given, not only in the present age but also in the one to come' (Eph 1:21). He decided to use his power because of his love for us!

21.3 Don't ask what a passage doesn't answer

When exegeting a specific passage, you must ask the questions that are addressed by the author, since they were relevant to the people for whom the book was originally written. The Bible was not intended (for example) as a scientific handbook that would answer all the scientific questions that we may have today.

The Bible was written long before Darwin, so when it addresses creation, the authors of the Bible did not approach it with the questions in mind that we have because of our exposure to theories of evolution. When we want to know what Gen 1 teaches us about creation, we need to restrict ourselves to the communication context in order to do proper exegesis: What are the issues that are relevant to the original receivers? How does the author address these issues? Only when we have discovered the answers to these questions will we be able to formulate the absolutes and see what contribution they make to the debate on evolution.

Let us look at the communication context of Gen 1. The Israelites had been living for more than four hundred years in Egypt. They were oppressed by the Egyptians and did not have complete freedom of religion. At the same time they were influenced by the religious thinking of the Egyptians. They are now in the wilderness outside of Egypt and God has to get Egypt out of their system by teaching them who he is and what it means to follow him.

The Egyptians (and also the Babylonians) had many creation myths. In these stories there was not a clear distinction between the gods, nature and human beings. Some gods were created just like human beings were created, others were created from other gods and ultimately, human beings were created from gods. Some animals were held to be sacred, or even worshipped as deities in their own right. In the Egyptian religion, these included bulls, dogs, jackals, cats, baboons, crocodiles and snakes. The sun, moon and stars were worshipped as gods.

The most widespread Egyptian creation myth is that the sun god Re appeared from the watery chaos on a dry mound and created the deities Shu and Tefenet by masturbation or by spitting. These two gods in turn produced the earth (Geb) and the sky (Nut).

From this background, the questions of the Israelites would never have been whether the earth was created by a god or not. Every one believed it was created by a god. No-one would even have considered evolution as a possibility. For the people of ancient times, the issue was which god was the creator, and what is the relationship between him, nature and human beings.

We should read the creation story of Gen 1 against this background. It addresses the questions and the popularly held answers of the time, and comes up with a completely different answer than the Egyptian and other religions offered! The God of the Bible created everything. There is a clear distinction between him and nature. There are no deities in the created world. He even created light on the first day, independent of the sun and the moon that were made on the fourth day! Human beings do not come forth from God but are different from him and created by him. They are also different from the rest of creation, with a special calling to rule over it. Because it is the Creator who gives them this calling, they are not allowed to exploit nature, but they have to fulfil their calling in the context of the unique and intimate relationship they have with God himself.

As Gen 1 says a great deal about who created everything and the relationship between God, nature and human beings, it does not give a scientific explanation of exactly how God created: Sometimes he speaks something into existence (v3), sometimes he gives a command and then does what he has commanded (v6-7), sometimes he commands the earth to bring something forth (v11-12) and sometimes he separates things that have been created by him (v4).

Once we have established what a passage does say about a particular issue, we can take our questions to that passage and see what it answers and what it does not. From the message of Gen 1 it is very clear that God is the creator and that the physical world did not come into being by chance. At the same time, the passage does not rule out that God could have used evolution in certain ways as a means by which to create.

If we try to make a biblical passage say what it doesn't say, the results could be devastating. Think how long ancient scientists maintained, because of the wrong exegesis of the church, that the earth was the centre of our universe and that the sun circled the earth. People were even executed when they questioned this assumption. At the same time, if we ignore the message of the Bible, it could for example, lead to fruitless efforts developing scientific theories that will never be able to explain the origin of man because it does not bring God into the picture.

When approaching a passage we do not always have a clear understanding of what its communication situation is, and therefore there has to be interaction between what we believe it to be and the content of the passage. This means that the known facts about the communication situation may help us to understand the passage, while the message of the passage will in turn help us to understand the communication context. There should be a correlation between what we find from the analysis of the passage and the communication context that we work from. From the analysis of Gen 1, it can be seen that it was not the intention of the author to tell us exactly how God created everything. This confirms a communication situation which did not ask for a scientific explanation.

When our understanding of the communication situation is challenged, we need to ask how the message will change if the communication situation was different. For example, our interpretation of Gen 1 was based on an understanding that it was written just after the exodus. If it is challenged by the possibility that it came into being during the time of the patriarchs, or was written during the time of the exile, what difference will it make to the message we arrived at? The answer is nothing, because even if the background is that of the Mesopotamian or Canaanite gods, these were - as far as the issues that we took into consideration - not very different from the Egyptian gods. There is still a great correlation between our established communication situation and the end product of our analysis. The message arrived at is also in line with what other passages teach on creation.

To summarise: If we have a question that is not addressed by the passage we are exegeting, we will not find the answer in that passage (figure 21.1). In such a case one should look for a passage or a few passages that do address the issue (figure 21.2).

FIGURE 21.1

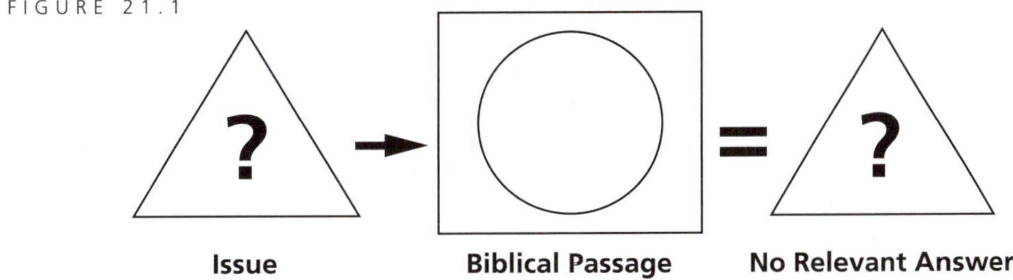

If a biblical passage does not address the issue in question, then it is NOT a suitable passage

FIGURE 21.2

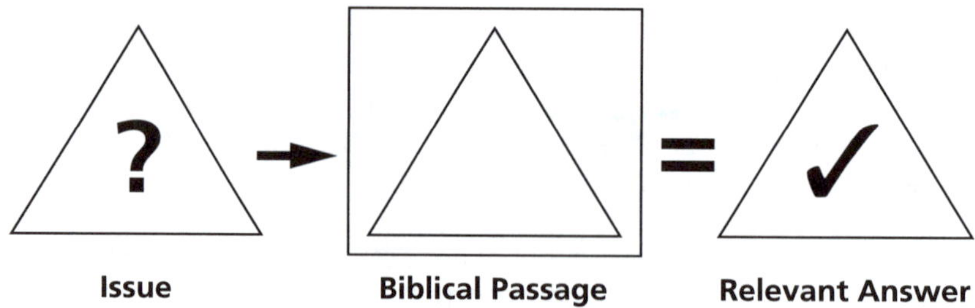

Find a biblical passage which addresses the particular issue

21.4 Know your target group

For successful hermeneutics, it is not only necessary to understand the biblical passage properly, but also the situation of the target group to whom the absolutes are applicable. The better one's understanding of the situation, the better one will be able to apply the absolutes in a relevant way.

If the target group is church members, then the state of the church as well as the broader society of which they are part, should be studied. This should involve an understanding of the social, spiritual, economic, judicial, educational, moral and theological values of society and how they influence the church in its thinking and lifestyle.

It is not always easy to know what these values are for a particular target group and its surrounding society. A way to find out what they are, is to observe and analyse them in the daily lives of people. If one's target group is a group of Christian businessmen, one can research their values and that of their specific world by looking at one's own experience of it, other people's experiences and views, its traditions and cultural heritage, and events that are taking place in that world.

We do not only find this information through our relationships with others, but also through the media - the kind of media will obviously differ according to the specific target group. Media to analyse include newspapers, magazines, books, television documentaries and dramas, films, music, paintings and sculpture.

We do not only need to have a knowledge of the values of the world in which the target group moves, but also of the circumstances in which they are operating. Do the businessmen operate in a time of recession or of economic prosperity? This may make a difference to the type of message that they need to receive.

This knowledge can be gained through observation or through a systematic scientific study of a particular target group eg, research projects on the views of teenagers that are done with the help of questionnaires. In the social sciences, research projects have been done on a large spectrum of issues related to human views and behaviour. The findings of these scientific projects can be very helpful.

However, a word of caution is needed. A number of researchers (Shepherd Scale 1981) conducted an extensive study of measuring instruments available to make a distinction between Christians and non-Christians. They found that not one of these instruments used the Bible to define Christianity, except to summarise a few Bible stories to test factual knowledge of the Bible! Their opinion of ignoring the Bible as source for a definition of a Christian, is as follows:

> ...to ignore such a resource when developing an instrument designed to distinguish Christians from non-Christians seems similar to describing a car without looking at the owner's manual.

This lack of biblical definition in the social sciences means that the Christian researcher may have specific research questions and interests that are not dealt with by, for instance, psychology and sociology (Wolvaardt 1984:25). If more scientific research into the state of society and the church is done from a biblical perspective, it will make a tremendous contribution to the process of hermeneutics and will lead to a clearer proclamation of the biblical message.

21.5 Dynamic interaction between exegesis and hermeneutics

There should always be dynamic interaction between the message of the Bible and the situation. One's theological understanding is formed through this process of interaction. This means that while we acknowledge that the biblical message is infallible, we cannot say the same of our theology, as it depends on both our ability to exegete, as well as on our understanding of how the biblical message bears on the situation.

In this dynamic interaction, the situation does not only provide us with the questions, but it may also challenge our theology (see fig 21.3). Say, for example, someone believes that every person who is filled with the Holy Spirit will speak in tongues. When this theology is tested in the Christian world (3), it will not take a long time to discover that there are many who are clearly filled with the Spirit who do not speak in tongues, while there are many who may be speaking in tongues who appear not to be filled by the Spirit (4). This finding should send one to the Bible to find out what it says on the subject (1) and be brought in dynamic interaction with the product of one's exegesis (2). Through this process one's theology develops (5) by being confirmed or changed.

FIGURE 21.3

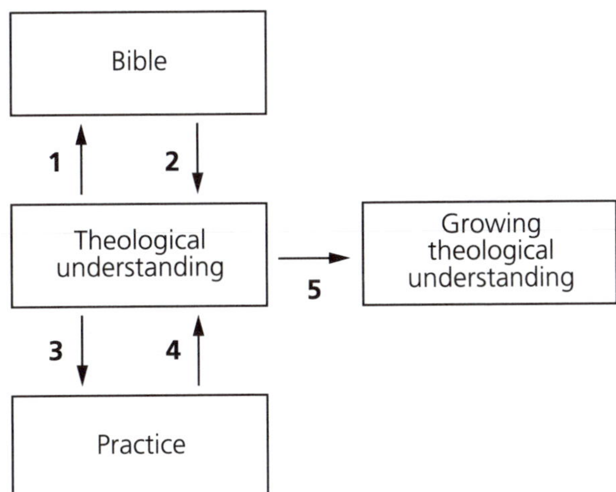

In the above example, dynamic interaction began by testing our understanding against practice (in the Christian world). It can also be started by testing our understanding against the Bible. We might find that a specific new practice becomes very important in the Christian world, like the practice of spiritual warfare by which territorial spirits are addressed in specific ways. This practice takes place because of our specific understanding. When this understanding is tested against the Bible (1), it will soon be found that it says very little about territorial spirits and that there is no exhortation to address them directly (2). This biblical message should be used to ask questions about the practice of spiritual warfare (3) and then to compare the answers to the biblical message (4). The result of this is a growing theological understanding (5).

In this process the Bible is authoritative. Through the dynamic interactive process, one is challenged to constantly make sure that one's theology is both biblical and relevant. This process should continue in the life of the individual believer as well as in that of the church.

When involved in this process of dynamic interaction between the situation and the Bible, it is important to know what the general view of society is. This is to make sure that it does not influence us negatively in how we view the Bible and how we go about interpreting it. For example, if one reads the history of biblical interpretation as practised in some of the world's most influential seminaries, it looks more like a history of the views and methods of society than a prophetic biblical response to the apostasy of society!

21.6 Issues not directly addressed in the Bible

The Bible does not deal directly with all the issues that are relevant to us in today's society. The growth in technology has brought questions that were not possible to ask at the time when the Bible was written, (eg the use of contraceptives and abortion). In cases like these, the first step is to identify the different elements that relate to the issue (see step 1 in figure 21.4). For example, in the case of the use of contraceptives, related elements are those of the meaning of the sexual act in marriage, the importance of human responsibility and the cultural commands given to Adam and Eve to fill the earth and to subdue it.

Once the related elements have been identified, the second step is to find the biblical principles of these elements (see step 2 in figure 21.4).

The third step is to apply the biblical principles found in step 2 to the original issue that was not directly addressed (see step 3 in figure 21.4)

FIGURE 21.4

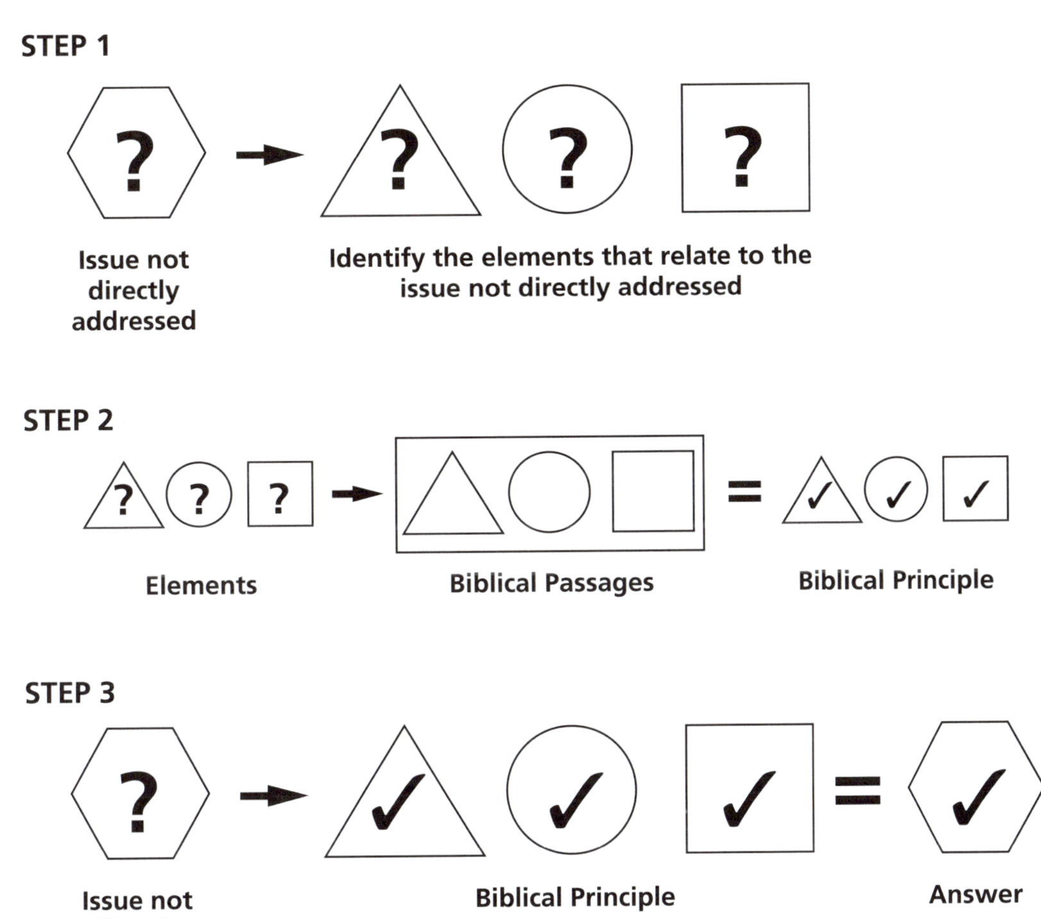

When viewed in this way, we will find that all ethical issues are related to biblical absolutes.

The Bible gives us a clear framework for understanding God's message to us, so that we can be reconciled to him, know him and live a life that is pleasing to him. We can therefore know that all the issues that are important for our spiritual well-being are covered in the Bible. As we grow in our understanding of the framework of truths that the Bible presents, it will become easier to discern what is right and what is wrong, as stated in Rom 12:2:

> Do not conform any longer to the pattern of this world, but be transformed by the renewing of your mind. Then you will be able to test and approve what God's will is - his good, pleasing and perfect will.

If we are dealing with issues of church practice, where some new experience is introduced into the life of the church, we need to submit it to the dynamic process of interaction with the Bible (see 21.5). If it is not even to be found in the New Testament then one should ask serious questions as to its right of existence. A further step should be to fit it into the broader framework of the biblical message: How does it relate to what Jesus did for us on the cross? This will safeguard the church against experiences that subtract from the absolute truths of the Bible.

CHAPTER TWENTY TWO

How to interpret the Pentateuch

Objectives

1. To be able to exegete the Pentateuch
2. To understand the contribution of the Pentateuch to the broader biblical message
3. To be able to do hermeneutics of the Pentateuch

Contents

STUDY TIP
When exegeting the Pentateuch, the skills of working with exposition/exhortation, poetry and narrative are required. In chapter 21 there are references to the Pentateuch that should be read with this chapter.

The purpose of this chapter is to orientate ourselves with the exegesis of the Pentateuch. This will be done under the headings of the steps of exegesis and hermeneutics.

22.1 The communication situation

We saw in the previous chapter how important it is to take the communication context of a book into consideration when exegeting a passage (21.3). It protects us from asking questions that the passage never intended to answer. We also pointed out that we will not always know exactly what the communication situation was, and therefore we need to check that there is a correlation between the results of our analysis and the assumed communication situation. In some cases we may even need to keep an open mind to the possibility of a different communication context.

The Pentateuch has provoked more debate about the communication situation than any other group of Bible books. This is particularly true concerning authorship. Opinions vary, some seeing Moses as the sole author, others believing that a redactor compiled it from different sources a long time after the exodus, the 'source theory'.

With the source theory, it is believed that the compiler used different sources, cut them into pieces and then put them together again. Almost like taking extracts from several different films and then editing them into a new film. While some believe there were two main sources, others believe there were four. The weakness of these theories is that they are largely based on speculation. They also have some drastic and unacceptable effects on the interpretation of the Pentateuch. This will be shown by quoting from the commentary on

Genesis by Gerhard von Rad who followed the source theory. Von Rad (1984:25) works with four sources, Yahwist (J) (circa 950 BC), Elohist (E) (circa 850-750BC), Deuteronomy (D) and the latest source, the Priestly document (P) (circa 538-450 BC).

Concerning the message of the Pentateuch, von Rad (1984:39) states:

> Any scholarly commentary must attempt to understand the narrative material of Genesis primarily in the way in which it was understood in the context of the great narrative works of J, E, and P, that is, as it was understood in Israel between the ninth and the fifth centuries BC. This is difficult, because the narrators do not interpret the events directly, but are quite restrained in their judgements. They do not hand over an explanation to the reader, but take him through the events without assessing men's actions and experiences, evidently on the presupposition that these events are able to speak for themselves to the reader or hearer. For this reason, the interpreter has to give up from the start any search for one meaning which is the only meaning that the narrator can have intended.

Von Rad bases his whole exegesis of the Pentateuch on this speculative communication situation. His presuppositions make it impossible to find only one meaning, in spite of the fact that he (1984:40) pleads for a careful analysis and the right of the exegete to reject 'interpretations which are inappropriate to the narrative or to the understanding of the reader'.

As far as the historicity of Genesis is concerned, we can clearly see von Rad's presuppositions from his following statement (von Rad 1984:40):

> What we have said so far has already suggested one thing: the old naive idea of the historicity of these narratives as being biographically reliable stories from the life of the patriarchs must be abandoned. If the narratives of Gen., chs. 18; 22; 28; 32 were once very early Palestinian cult legends (and therefore pre-Israelite and pre-Canaanite), and if the tradition of the patriarchs was only interwoven with these narratives after the Israelite incursion, we can no longer accept them as documents from the life of the patriarchs. The same is true of most of the patriarchal narratives.

The NIVSB (1987:4) says the following on the evidence of the source theory:

> ...this view is not supported by conclusive evidence, and intensive archaeological and literary research had tended to undermine many of the arguments used to challenge Mosaic authorship.

The source theories in general should be seen as a product of the influence of reductionism during the Enlightenment. Reductionism is essentially based on the belief that if one takes a thing apart, you understand what it means. Reductionism had an enormous influence on biblical scholarship. John Drane (1994:211) states in this regard, that one needs

> ...only select at random any commentary on any book of the Bible written in the last couple of centuries, to discover that they all start from the assumption that we can best understand things by taking them to pieces. Theories on source documents and ultimate origins of the biblical materials all feature prominently in the basic tool-kit of today's Bible interpreter. We have convinced ourselves that, once you can discover what a piece of literature is made of, you also know what it means. You don't, of course: if you are very lucky, you might just manage to come up with some approximate idea of what it is made of. But such is our love affair with the reductionist model that very few stop to make that observation.

We will deal in more depth with the unity of the different books of the Pentateuch and its historicity under the heading of the literary context (22.2).

As far as the authorship of Moses is concerned, neither the Pentateuch nor the rest of the Bible gives a direct statement that Moses was the author of the whole Pentateuch. However, there are many references that link it directly or indirectly to Moses:

- In Ex 17:14 the LORD told Moses to write the story of the defeat of the Amalekites on a scroll;
- In Num 33:2 it is stated that Moses recorded at the LORD's command the stages in their journey;
- In Ex 24:4 it is said that Moses wrote down everything the LORD had said;
- In Ex 34:27 Moses is told by the LORD to write down 'these words';
- We read about Moses writing things down and the command to do so in Deut 31:9, 19, 22, 24;
- Moses received the two tablets with the Ten Commandments written by God (Ex 31:18);
- Moses wrote the Ten Commandments down (Ex 34:27-28);
- The instructions for the building of the tabernacle is received by Moses during the 40 days and nights on mount Sinai (Ex 21:1-31:17);
- In Num, the same references to God's communication with Moses is found;
- In Ex 15 we find the song of Moses of which he is most probably the author;
- Deut is written in the form of a speech delivered by Moses

In addition to this, we find references in other places in the Old Testament where at least parts of the Pentateuch are attributed to Moses:

- Josh 8:31; 1 Kgs 2:3; 8:53; 2 Kgs 14:6; 18:12.

In the New Testament Jesus bears testimony that at least certain parts of the Pentateuch were written by Moses:

- Mt 19:7-8; Mk 10:3-5; Jn 5:46-47.

Other New Testament authors do the same:

- Acts 3:22-23; 7:37-38; Rom 10:19.

If the whole Pentateuch, with the exception of short sections, was written by Moses, it was most probably done during the 40 years in the wilderness.

The dates of the events described in the Pentateuch can be grouped into three main time periods:

- Pre-history (Gen 1:1-11:26): This covers the period from the creation to the first Semitic history;
- Patriarchal history (Gen 11:27-50:26): This covers the period from the life of Abraham to Joseph's last days;
- History of deliverance from Egypt and travelling to the Promised Land (Ex - Deut).

To understand the Pentateuch, it is important to understand the history, customs and religions of the peoples of the specific times and places that feature in these books. If one knows, for example, that Baal worship in Canaan led to extreme evil, including child sacrifice, it will be easier to understand the Lord's strict commands to the Israelites not to inter-marry with the Canaanites, but to destroy them completely (Deut 18:9-13).

All the rituals like the religious feasts, worship in the tabernacle and sacrifices had a rich symbolism that was obvious to the worshipper. This is because of the general understanding of the people of that time. With this we do not say that the worship of the idols of Canaan, Mesopotamia or Egypt is the same as the worship of Yahweh or that the latter evolved out of the former. The worship of Yahweh was completely different as he revealed himself as a holy God that can only be approached through the forgiveness of sins. He is invisible and cannot be worshipped through idols. However, the external rituals that he gave to the Israelites, were clear ways of communicating to them who he is in their context - they were able to understand the meaning of the rituals clearly.

In understanding the communication context of the Pentateuch, it is helpful to have some knowledge of the three main types of covenants that were made during that time, because many of the Lord's dealings with the patriarchs and the Israelites took place in the form of covenants.

The first type of covenant is the parity covenant. It is made between equals binding them to mutual friendship or at least respect (eg the covenant between Abraham and Abimelech in Gen 21:22-34). God does not make this type of covenant with his people.

The second type of covenant is the Suzerain-vassal covenant. The ruler initiates it from his position of authority and makes certain promises, eg promises of protection. In return he demands loyalty and sets certain conditions (eg taxes that must be paid to him). God frequently uses this type of covenant (eg when he deals with Abraham in Gen 17:1-14). God initiates this from his position of authority and he promises Abraham many descendants and the possession of the land for all generations (v1-8). God requires Abraham and his descendants to keep the conditions of the covenant (v9ff).

The third type of covenant is a Royal Grant covenant. A promise is made without any conditions attached to it. An example is God's promise (Gen 9:8-17) to Noah, his descendants and all living creatures, that all life will never again be destroyed by a flood. God gives the rainbow as the sign of the covenant and he does not state any conditions.

What should we do with literary parallels of the non-Israelite literature of that time? The existence of parallels on subjects such as creation and the flood can be understood from the perspective that Israel shared their early history, from creation to the calling of Abraham, with all other nations. However, the parallel biblical stories reveal Yahweh to us as very different from the gods of the other nations, eg the message of the creation story of Gen 1 (see 21.3). Another example is the genealogies in the Bible that are very different from the ones in the pagan religions that usually start with gods from whom human beings are born.

22.2 The literary context

The Pentateuch is mainly written in prose with a few passages of poetry in between (eg Jacob blessing his sons in Gen 49:2-27, and the song of Moses and Miriam in Ex 15:1-18). The prose can be divided into the major discourse types of exposition, exhortation, narrative and procedure.

A lot of procedure (see 9.3) is found in the Pentateuch (eg Ex 40:1-16 where Moses is instructed by God how to set up the tabernacle). It is prescriptive and the instructions have to be followed in a chronological framework. Although we have not dealt directly with the interpretation of procedure, it should be pretty straight forward if one has mastered the methods of interpreting exposition/exhortation and narrative, as it shares characteristics with exhortation and narrative.

The narrative in the Pentateuch is written with the author's purpose of communicating a specific message. We should approach it with the purpose of discovering that message. Even though this message, as tends to happen with narrative, may not be stated explicitly, it does not take away from the fact that there is a clear message.

The fact that the author intended to communicate a specific message and arranges his material accordingly, does not take anything away from the historicity of the events. The events did take place. However, they are selected and ordered in such a way as to achieve the author's purpose and should be read as such and not as bare facts.

The importance of always reading in the context of the whole book cannot be overemphasised in the case of the Pentateuch. When objectively and scientifically analysed, it should be clear that each book of the Pentateuch has a wonderful structure of its own. Deuteronomy, for example, seems to have a chiastic structure, starting with a look at the past (Deut 1-3) (A) and ending with a look at the future (Deut 31-34) (A*). We find Moses' farewell speech from chapters 4-11 (B) balanced by the covenant ceremony covered by chapters 27-30 (B*). The middle part is the covenant stipulations as found in chapters 12 to 26 (C). Each one of these five parts seems to have a well-organised structure.

Whether or not the author borrowed some material from other sources is not really relevant. The end product should be seen as a unit that has been arranged in a particular way to serve the purpose of the author. There is no convincing evidence to break a book up into smaller sections according to assumed sources (see 21.1), and such an action would be arbitrary and violate the unity of the book.

The overall and immediate context can be very helpful in analysing a passage. In Gen 6 verses 2 and 4, we read about the 'sons of God' that married the 'daughters of men'. What is meant by these terms? The Translator's Guide (1982:45) suggests 'supernatural beings', 'divine creatures' or even 'angels'. Linguistically, it can't be said that 'sons of God' must mean "divine creatures". Therefore, we should focus more on the context to help us to find the contextual meaning. Directly before Gen 6:2 we find two genealogies, of Cain and then of Seth. Cain's genealogy (Gen 4:17-24) ends with Lamech, who claims to be master of his own destiny. Seth's genealogy (Gen 5:1-32) stands in sharp contrast with that of Cain, with the description of his descendant Enoch who 'walked with God' and ending with Noah and his three sons.

After these contrasting family lines, we find the contrasting 'sons of God' and 'daughters of men' who intermarried. In this context, it seems that 'sons of God' are the descendants of Seth who married the daughters descended from Cain and thereby ended the separation between the two groups. The immediate context tells us that from then on, everyone was wicked and only Noah found favour in God's sight (Gen 6:5-8).

This interpretation also fits in with the message of Gen 1 (see 21.3), that there are clear distinctions and differences between God, nature and man in the creation. If 'sons of God' is read as 'supernatural beings', that principle is violated.

Another example of the importance of the immediate and wider context is the story of the death of Aaron's sons, Nadab and Abihu, in Lev 10. They offered 'unauthorised fire before the LORD, contrary to his command'. The result is that God consumed them with fire. Read in isolation, this story seems to present God as heartless. However, if we read this in context, it makes perfect sense and does not take anything from who God is. Lev 1-7 deals with the five main offerings and God gives clear instructions on how and when they should be brought. Through these offerings, spiritual holiness is symbolised by physical perfection and the offerings cannot be brought without the proper ordination of Aaron and his sons and atonement for them (Lev 8-9). Against this background we find the casual and disobedient behaviour of Nadab and Abihu. God's holiness was ridiculed as we can see from Moses' response after their death when he said to Aaron (Lev 10:3):

This is what the LORD spoke of when he said:

'Among those who approach me
  I will show myself holy;
in the sight of all the people
  I will be honoured.'

22.3 Analysis of the passage

The value of proper semantic discourse analysis cannot be overestimated when analysing a passage from the Pentateuch. In Gen 1, a proper analysis will reveal the use of repetitive features (step 3.2). Each one of the eight creation acts is described according to a set formula with the repetition of the following phrases (see fig 22.1):

And God said...
There was... (It was so...)
God saw that it was good
And there was evening and there was morning...

One of these creation acts takes place on each of the six days with the exception of the third and sixth days when two creation acts take place. For the sake of effect, and to keep the structure from becoming monotonous, one of the repetitive phrases is dropped in describing days 2 and 5.

These different creation acts are, according to form (two creation acts on both day three and six) placed in a beautiful parallel arrangement, starting at the beginning of the week and repeated in the second half of the week as shown in figure 22.1.

FIGURE 22.1
Structure of the days of creation

Day	Act	Day	Act
1	1 a God said v3 b there was v3 c God saw... good v4 d evening... morning v5 **Light**	**4**	5 a God said v14 b it was so v15 c God saw... good v18 d evening... morning v19 **Sun, moon and stars**
2	2 a God said v6 b it was so v6 c --- d evening... morning v6 **Expanse – water in air, on earth**	**5**	6 a God said v20 b --- c God saw... good v21 d evening... morning v23 **Birds, fish**
3	3 a God said v9 b it was so v9 c God saw... good v10 d --- **Dry ground**	**6**	7 a God said v24 b it was so v24 c God saw... good v25 d --- **Animals**
	4 a God said v11 b it was so v11 c God saw... good v12 d evening... morning v13 **Plants**		8 a God said v26 b it was so v30 c God saw... good v31 d evening... morning v31 **Man**

The structure in which the author arranged his material, highlights the message of the passage. The fact that God first created light, and that he only created the sun, moon and stars on the fourth day, has a strong message in the context of the religions of those days where the sun, moon and stars were worshipped and seen as gods or were directly related to gods. The systematic arrangement points to the orderliness of God's creative activities.

Some parts of the Pentateuch are stated in extremely condensed forms, eg the Ten Commandments. This presents a problem as far as the analysis of each commandment is concerned: What does it mean to commit adultery? What does it mean to covet? The passage itself does not elaborate much on each of the commands. The result is that we need to discover the meaning of the terms (step 3.3) largely from the context of the rest of the Pentateuch, and the rest of the Bible, where the principles of these commands are elaborated.

22.4 The broader biblical framework

It is an understatement to say that the Pentateuch makes an extremely important contribution to the message of the whole Bible. The rest of the Bible, and in particular all the books of the Old Testament, have to be read in the context of the calling of Israel and how God revealed himself to them, as described in the Pentateuch. The New Testament is the fulfilment of the promises of the Pentateuch when Jesus comes as the perfect high priest.

A brief explanation of the significant contribution that the Pentateuch makes to the message of the Bible:

In Gen 1 and 2 we find two creation stories which tell us that Yahweh created the whole world and that there is a clear distinction between God, nature and man. Man is created in the image of God and he has a special task to look after and rule over nature. He must do this in relationship and in obedience to God. In Gen 3, man's disobedience and its consequences are described - but, a promise is also given. The promise that the offspring of the woman will bring deliverance over Satan - a theme that is described in similar imagery in Rev 12.

From Gen 4 to 6 we find the contrast between those who were following Yahweh and those who were not, until even that distinction has been erased. God destroyed the whole human race and began again with one family who served him, Noah's family. However, when the people increased in number, they collectively rebelled against God - they built a city and a tower in order not be scattered over the earth. How will God now fulfil his promise when the whole of humanity is united in rebellion against him?

God decided to start a new nation and he called Abraham as the patriarch, giving him certain promises (Gen 12:2-3):

"I will make you into a great nation and I will bless you; I will make your name great,	A
and you will be a blessing.	B
I will bless those who bless you, and whoever curses you I will curse;	A
and all people on earth will be blessed through you."	B

From the very start of Abraham's calling, it is stated that God will bless his descendants (A), but they will have the obligation to be a blessing to all nations (B). They will do this by obeying God and by being an example to all nations of what it means to follow Yahweh and to experience his blessings. The missionary calling of Israel is established. From now on, the focus of the whole Old Testament is on Israel and God's dealings with them.

As God deals with the patriarchs, he makes covenants with them. And in spite of their failings, we see God's faithfulness to them. He will fulfil his promise of deliverance to humankind and will do it through the descendants of Abraham. At the same time, he reveals himself as a holy God who requires obedience (Gen 18:18, 19).

The greatest event in the OT history of Israel is when God delivers them from bondage in Egypt. He reveals himself as the God who cares, and as the one who cannot be kept captive by our small theologies (see 21.2). When God gives the Ten Commandments to his people, he reveals himself:

> I am the LORD your God, who brought you out of Egypt, out of the land of slavery.

So, in his relationship with Israel, God makes covenants through which he commits himself to them. At the same time he requires obedience and punishes rebellion.

God reveals himself and his purpose to fulfil the promise of Gen 3 through the laws he gives the Israelites. The significance of these laws will be discussed under the next heading 'hermeneutics'.

22.5 Hermeneutics

Once we have arrived at the message for the original receivers through the process of exegesis, we must now apply it to the target group in our time. This presents us with the problem of transferring the message from the Old Covenant to the new one. The death and resurrection of Jesus marks the end of the Old Covenant and the beginning of the new. For this reason any absolute for the Old Covenant should be interpreted in the light of what Jesus achieved on the cross.

This will now be illustrated by discussing the process of hermeneutics for the three different types of laws that are found in the Old Testament; ceremonial, civil and moral laws.

22.5.1 Ceremonial laws

The ceremonial or ritual laws related specifically to Israel's worship (eg instructions for the tabernacle, priestly duties, types of offerings, religious feasts, etc). While these laws revealed Yahweh's holiness, his grace to forgive and his goodness, they also pointed forward to Christ. In Heb 7, Christ is depicted as the eternal High Priest whose work far surpassed that of Aaron and his successors. In his death, Jesus fulfilled the levitical concept of the sin offering (Rom 8:1-4; 2 Cor 5:18-21; Heb 9:11-28; 10:11-12; 13:10-15). Just as the tabernacle symbolised God's presence in the midst of Israel, so the incarnation of Christ is an assurance that God is present continuously in human society.

The ceremonial laws are no longer necessary after Jesus' death and resurrection. However, the principles behind them still apply. This is illustrated in figure 22.2 which shows the hermeneutics of Ex 30:17-21. The message to the original receivers was an absolute in the time of the Old Covenant and therefore no relatives are to be found. When applying the message to our time, it has to be seen in the light of what Christ achieved.

FIGURE 22.2
Hermeneutics of the the ceremonial laws, eg Ex 30:17-21

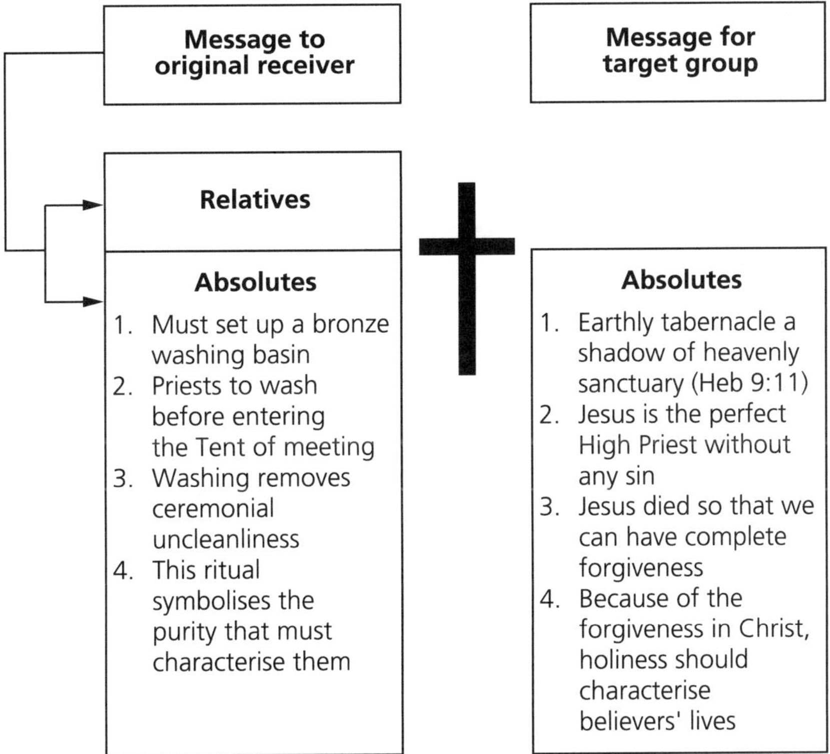

22.5.2 Civil laws

The civil laws applied God's norms to daily living in Israel. They include criminal, hygiene, medical, economic and social laws. Because it was Israel's law and applied to them in their specific setting and in their covenant relation with God, we cannot apply the laws today. But many of the principles behind the commands are timeless and should guide our conduct. An example of one is the command in Deut 22:8 to put a railing around the roof of one's house. As shown in figure 22.3, the message was an absolute in the time of the Old Covenant. Although the message is not absolute for our time, there is a principle behind it that is applicable to us.

FIGURE 22.3
Hermeneutics of the civil laws, eg Deut 22:8

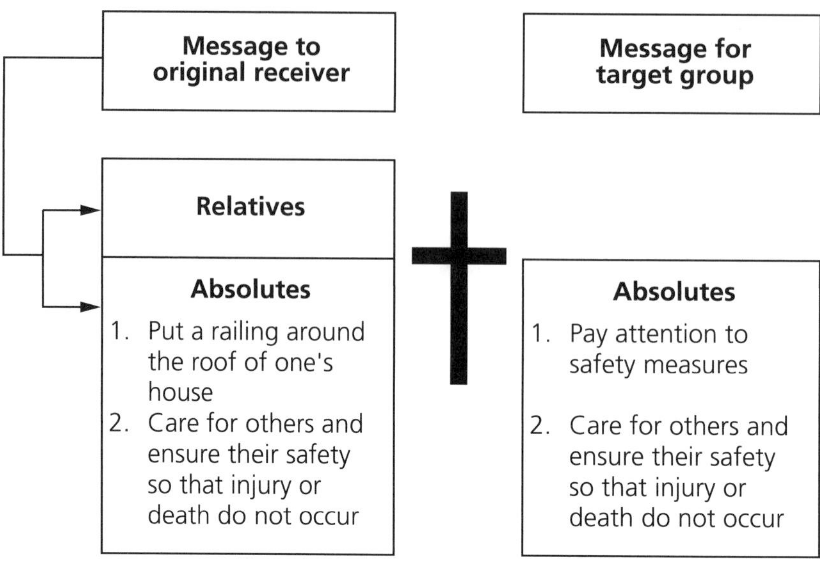

22.5.3 Moral laws

The moral laws (such as the Ten Commandments) are commands from God and need to be obeyed. Jesus himself kept the moral law (Mt 5:17-20). These laws are applicable not only to one's acts, but also to one's words, attitudes and thought life (Mt 5:21-22; 27-39). The moral laws are repeated in one or other form in the New Testament. An example of one is the prohibition of homosexual acts as stated in Lev 18:22. It was an absolute in the time of the Old Covenant and still is in the time of the new one, as illustrated in figure 22.4.

FIGURE 22.4
Hermeneutics of the moral laws, eg Lev 18:22

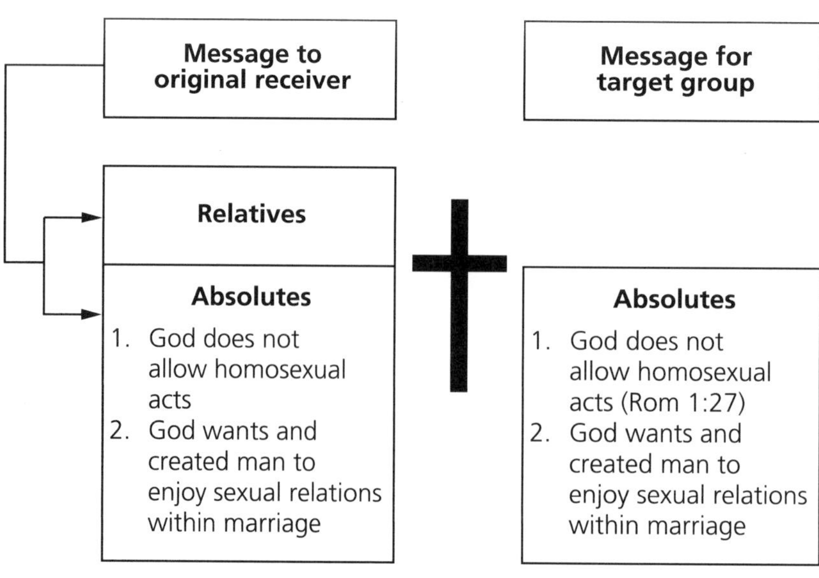

CHAPTER TWENTY THREE

How to interpret the OT historical books

Objectives

1. To be able to exegete stories from the Old Testament historical books
2. To understand the process of hermeneutics for stories from the Old Testament
3. To understand the contribution of the historical books to the broader biblical message

Content

23.1 The communication situation
23.2 The literary context
23.3 Analysis of the passage
23.4 The broader biblical framework
23.5 Hermeneutics

The aim of this chapter is to help you to improve your skills of interpreting narrative, particularly the stories (dramatic history) of the OT historical books (Joshua to Esther). In order to illustrate how the steps of exegesis and hermeneutics are applied to these books, we will use the story of Samson (Judg 13-16). The principles explained in this chapter are of course also applicable to the narratives found in other sections of the OT (eg the Pentateuch).

STUDY TIP
You will benefit more from this chapter if you complete each step of exegesis yourself before working through each section. Use the principles of exegesis learnt in previous chapters, especially chapters 19 and 20.

23.1 The communication situation

Who was the author?
The book itself does not provide us with any clues. Hebrew tradition ascribes it to Samuel with whom the period of the 'judges' ends.

When was it written?
It is not our intention to discuss the various theories of how the book was compiled as there is much scholarly work that can be consulted on this issue. Suffice to note a couple of scholars' comments that support the antiquity of the book. Harrison (1969:689) remarks as follows: 'Viewed holistically it furnishes a remarkably coherent picture of a specific age in Hebrew history, the general political, cultural, geographical, and religious aspects of which are consistent with what is now known of Palestine between 1200 and 1000 BC'. Cundall et

al (1968:27) in their discussion about a date suggest that 'a date for the book of Judges about 980 BC seems not unreasonable'.

Who were the recipients?
No mention is made of any particular person or group of people for whom it might have been written. If we are content with what we have noted above, we may assume that the people of Israel, particularly during the early period of the kings, were the target group.

What is the primary purpose for writing?
There is no explicit statement made about the book's main purpose. This leaves us with two ways of finding out. We may survey the book (as illustrated in section 23.2). Alternatively, we may use any secondary literature available. This is especially useful if you are pressed for time.

We will consider the main purpose of Judges in the following section, the literary context (see especially 23.2.3).

23.2 The literary context

In chapter twenty we took note of the fact that an author usually purposefully selects and arranges his material in order to communicate a message. Several elements point to the fact that the narrative material of the book has been selected and arranged, for example, the structure of the book (fig 23.1) and the repetitive plot structure (fig 23.2). The selection and arrangement of narrative material can also be seen in the major judges narratives. Many of these individual narratives seem to indicate that the events take place in small geographical pockets of the land (eg the Samson narrative in the western foothills and Philistine territory, 13-16) and involve just a few of Israel's tribes (eg the Ehud narrative involves the tribes of Benjamin and Ephraim, 3:12-30). However, the author makes sure that these narratives are understood as representative of the social, moral and spiritual climate affecting the whole nation during this historical period (eg Judg 2:6-3:6; 3:11,30; 8:27; 15:20; 21:25).

23.2.1 Step 2.1: The type of literature

The book of Judges and the Samson narrative

The events and actions narrated in Judges and the Samson story are presented along a time line and no explicit instructions are given to the reader. The focus is on the actions of individuals and groups of characters. This is consistent with the characteristics of the narrative discourse type and the genre of dramatic history.

23.2.2 Step 2.2: The position in the book

A good structure will provide us with clues to help us understand the purpose and message of the book and the individual narratives. Figure 23.1 gives an overview of the structure of the book and is followed by a brief discussion, showing how we arrived at this.

FIGURE 23.1

Major parts of the book (Narrative units)	Introduction:		Part 1	Part 2
	Part A 1:1-2:5	**Part B** 2:6-3:6	3:7-16:31	17-21
Plot structure of book	**Problem:** (this triggers events of part 1 and 2) Israel is unfaithful to God by making covenants with people of the land instead of driving them out completely.	**Problem repeated and elaborated:** (intensifies problem and previews part 1) Israel is unfaithful to God by worshipping other gods. This results in God's discipline. When they repent, God delivers them through a judge and gives them peace.	**Outcome 1:** (events triggered by the problem) Israel is unfaithful to God by worshipping other gods. This results in God's discipline. When they repent, God delivers them through a judge and gives them peace.	**Outcome 2:** (events triggered by the problem) Israel's social, moral and religious chaos.

Explanation of plot structure:
Although this is a brief explanation, we trust that it will provide a useful starting point for exegesis and further research.

Introduction: Part A (1:1-2:5)
Problem: Israel is unfaithful to God by making covenants with people of the land instead of driving them out completely.

> This part of the introduction provides the reader with essential background to the unfolding narrative, especially describing the basic problem which triggers subsequent events to which all the remaining parts of the book are related. The basic problem (disobedience, by making covenants with the Canaanites and not conquering the land) is introduced in 1:1-36 and described specifically in 2:2-3 with its results: Israel broke God's covenant resulting in his discipline. Here the recurring plot structure of Israel's sin and God's discipline is already hinted at.

Introduction: Part B (2:6-3:6)
Problem repeated and elaborated: Israel is unfaithful to God by worshipping other gods. This results in God's discipline. When they repent, God uses a judge to deliver them and gives them peace.

> By repetition and elaboration, this part emphasises and intensifies the problem of unfaithfulness to the covenant. The link between introductory parts A and B is highlighted by the following indicators: Part B repeats the recurring plot structure 'sin - discipline' (2:2-3) noted in part A and elaborates on it. It assumes that the reader is aware of the basic problem narrated there and at the same time previews - in general terms - the same events described in detail in part 1 of the book.

Part 1 (3:7-16:31)
Outcome 1: Israel is unfaithful to God by worshipping other gods. This results in God's discipline. When they repent, God delivers them using a judge and gives them peace.

This is the main part of the book and its link as the 'outcome' to the introduction (parts A and B) can be seen by its repetition and elaboration on the recurring plot structure 'sin - discipline' (see figure 23.2 below) and the fulfilment of the anticipated consequences of Israel's disobedience (2:3, 22-23).

Part 2 of book (17-21)
Outcome 2: Israel's social, moral and religious chaos

Part 2 (17-21) has been described as appendices by commentators (Cundall et al, 1968:50). Where this part fits into the chronological history of judges is a debatable matter. But rather than simply describing this part of the book as appendices, it may be more useful to search for its relationship to the overall plot structure. In part 2 (17-21) we find Israel's national life described from a different point of view than in part 1 of the book (3:7-16:31).

How does part 2 of the book (outcome 2) relate to the introduction (A and B)? Part of the answer can be found by the repeated ideas the narrative deals with, and in the fact that these ideas are the resulting events (outcome) arising from the basic problem, namely Israel's disobedience (2:2). For example, the worship of idols (17:5), sexual immorality (19:25) and general disobedience to God and his law (17:6; 21:25) can be linked with and seen as the resulting events (outcome) of the original problems, namely disobedience to the covenant (2:2,11) and worship of idols which often involved sexual immorality (2:3,11-13) found in part 1.

Plot structure of major judges narratives:
The repetitive plot structure referred to above is illustrated in figure 23.2.

FIGURE 23.2
The plot structure of the major judges

		Intro PART B	PART 1						
				A	B	C	C*	B*	A*
	Repeated Pattern	Intro 2:6-3:6	Othniel 3:7-11	Ehud 3:12-30	Deborah Barak 4:1-5:31	Gideon 6:1-8:35	Abime-lech 9:1-57	Jephthah 10:6-12:7	Samson 13:1-16:31
X	Sin (problem)	2:11-13	3:7	3:12a	4:1	6:1a	The anti-judge No pattern	10:6	13:1a
Y	Discipline (resolving action)	2:14-15	3:8	3:12b-14	4:2-3a	6:1b-6a		10:7-9	13:1b
X*	Repentance (resolution)	implied	3:9a	3:15a	4:3b	6:6b		10:10-16	implied
Y*	Deliverance (removes discipline)	2:16	3:9b-10	3:15b-29	4:4-24	6:7-8:27		10:17-11:33	13:2-16:30
Z*	Peace (outcome)	2:18	3:11	3:30	5:31	8:28		11:33	lacking

Chiastic arrangement of part 1 - the major judges:
Further analysis of the structure of the book aids us in understanding its message, particularly recognising the chiastic arrangement as described by the NIVSB (1987:323). It notes a chiastic arrangement of the major judges as follows:

Introduction: Othniel - The framework 'sin-discipline-repentance-deliverance-peace' is introduced
A: Ehud - the lone hero
B: Deborah - a woman
C: Gideon - the ideal judge
C*: Abimelech - the anti-judge
B*: Jephthah - an outcast
A*: Samson - the lone hero

The NIVSB (1987:322) makes the following comment about this arrangement:

> The arrangement of these narrative units is significant. The central accounts of Gideon (the Lord's ideal judge) and Abimelech (the anti-judge) are bracketed by the parallel narratives of the woman Deborah and the social outcast Jephthah - which in turn are framed by the stories of the lone heroes Ehud and Samson. In this way even the structure focuses attention on the crucial issue of the period of the judges: Israel's attraction to the Baals of Canaan (shown by Abimelech) versus the Lord's kingship over his people (encouraged by Gideon).

The chiastic arrangement of the major judges is a repetitive feature used to highlight the crucial issue of the period. Therefore the description of Gideon as the 'ideal judge' should be seen with this in mind and is not meant to say that he was perfect. He was far from it, as the end of the narrative only too vividly describes.

23.2.3 The message of the book

There are four significant elements which help us to find the main message of the book:

1. The overall structure: see 23.2.2

2. The repeated plot structure: Because of Israel's idolatry (problem [X]), God handed them over to their enemies who severely oppressed them (resolving action [Y]). When Israel repented and turned (resolution [X*]) to God for help, he graciously saved them (removed discipline [Y*]) and they had peace for as long as they followed him (outcome [Z]) (see also figure 23.2). The letters in square brackets mark a parallelism which is typical of the development of a problem-resolution type structure. The deviation from the pattern in the outcome [Z], highlights its significance (see also the discussion on the significance of the outcome in the Samson narrative later on in this chapter).

3. The chiastic arrangement of the major judges: see 23.2.2

4. Author's commentary: Significant comments are found in part 2 of the book and they are likely to provide further evidence that the main message of the book is to make clear to the reader that loyalty to God as their king alone secures Israel's existence, national unity and well-being. These comments are found in the context of some of the most abhorrent and gruesome stories in the Bible. With his commentary, 'In those days Israel had no king; everyone did as he saw fit' (Judg 17:6; 21:25), the author wants the reader to understand that the mayhem in Israel is due to the absence of unity or leadership under a king (Judg 18:1; 19:1). But is this commentary simply drawing a contrast with the better times had under a human king during the early days of the monarchy? We think not. Rather, a double meaning could have been intended which is in line with the main message of the book and the reader should discover that Israel had rejected God, so was like a nation without a king. This is at the heart of Israel's chaotic state of affairs (see also 1 Sam 12:6-25).

Having researched the literary context, we may conclude that the main message of the book is:

The readers (people and king) are urged to remain loyal to Yahweh and accept him as the true king of Israel because:

- The rejection of Yahweh as Israel's king and ruler through disobedience and idolatry leads to:
  God's discipline (the covenant curses Deut 28);
  the loss of the promised land, political unity and social well-being;
  a spiritually and morally corrupt life.
- Through repentance and faithfulness to God as their king, Israel will experience the covenant blessings as he graciously and mercifully gives them peace and order in the land.

23.3 Analysis of the passage

The work done in the previous step provides us with solid boundaries within which to interpret the Samson narrative. The importance of a good understanding of the overall structure and message the OT historical books cannot be overemphasised, particularly when interpreting an individual narrative.

STUDY TIP

Not all the steps of exegesis that follow will explain every detail of the Samson narrative. We have concentrated on those elements that make a significant contribution to the message. It is important to keep your Bible open at the Samson narrative during the following explanation of the text.

23.3.1 Step 3.1: Write out the passage in smaller units

As we are dealing with narrative, it is not necessary to write the passage out in smaller units. But to be able to start our analysis, we need to divide the story into units we can easily handle. This will usually mean looking for episodes (see 19.6.1,2) by reading through the story and roughly dividing it up.

We can divide the Samson narrative into episodes as shown in figure 23.3.

FIGURE 23.3
The episodes of the Samson narrative

Episode (1) 13:1	Episode (2) 13:2-25	Episode (3) 14:1-20	Episode (4) 15:1-20	Episode (5) 16:1-3	Episode (6) 16:4-22	Episode (7) 16:23-31
God disciplines unfaithful Israel through Philistine oppression	Because of his covenant with Israel, God raises up Samson to deliver Israel from the Philistine oppression	Samson's marriage to a Philistine woman leads to his first conflict with the Philistines	The loss and murder of Samson's wife leads to further conflicts with the Philistines	Samson and the Philistine prostitute	Samson and Delilah – his downfall	Samson's last conflict with the Philistines and his death

Once we have divided the story up into episodes, we can continue with the next step. In each of the steps of exegesis, we may review our divisions if necessary, as at this stage they are only a practical way to enable us to carry on with the steps of exegesis.

23.3.2 Steps 3.2 and 3.3: Mark and explain the significant meaning indicators

In this section we are going to combine steps 3.2 and 3.3 by listing and explaining the most significant meaning indicators. No illustration of marking the text will be given but this could be done as explained in previous chapters.

It may be helpful if we begin by looking for one of the most common stylistic features of narrative, the overall plot structure. We will do this by reading the whole narrative and marking the main features of the plot. We may adjust our findings later on as we proceed with our analysis.

The plot structure:
The recognition of the plot development helps us not only to appreciate the artistic and literary skill of the author, but provides us with clues that give us a better grasp of the message. Analysis of the recurring plot structure in the major judges narratives (see figure 23.2) helps us to draw conclusions about the main message of the book. It also helps us to see the significant events from the author's point of view in the Samson narrative. This in turn will help us draw conclusions about the narrative's message. For the basic plot structure of the Samson narrative refer to figure 23.2 and the explanation there.

Look for the overall plot structure when marking a narrative with more than one episode. Individual episodes may also have their own sub-plots, which is the case with Samson, but to analyse those would usually go beyond what is necessary for our analysis.

The significant meaning indicators explained:

Episode 1 (13:1)
v1 did evil: (problem) the repetitious pattern begins. Israel's disobedience and idolatry is noted in the familiar formula.

v1 the LORD delivered them...: God's punishment is noted in the familiar formula, indicating his sovereign involvement in Israel's history. This is the 'resolving action' in the main plot.

This formula in Judg 13:1 emphasises that God is dealing with Israel's unfaithfulness (the problem) according to his covenant agreements with them (see eg Lev 26; Deut 28). As noted in figure 23.2, Israel's repentance is not mentioned, but the author assumes the reader's familiarity with the conditional covenant and the repetitive plot structure of the preceding narratives where Israel's repentance is explicitly mentioned. The plot development of the next episode makes clear that God responds to this repentance and plans to remove his means of discipline from Israel.

Episode 2 (13:2-25)
v5 the boy is to be a Nazirite: A Nazirite is someone who makes a voluntary vow to set aside a period of time to serve God in a special way. One's total devotion and commitment to God during this time is expressed by strict obedience to a special set of rules. These stipulations are recorded in Num 6:1-21 and govern three areas of life that distinguish a Nazirite from contemporary culture and customs: (1) diet - abstain from eating and drinking anything that comes from the grapevine, therefore denying oneself the common adult beverage of fermented drinks and becoming distinct in an environment were alcoholism was a serious problem; (2) appearance - no hair cut or shaved as a public sign and in contrast to those who shaved their head in service to pagan gods; (3) association - must remain ritually clean just like the high priest (Lev 21:1) to serve as an example of God's perfection and holiness. Strict obedience was demanded by the covenant. For Samson this was not a voluntary vow but God's call - not for a limited period, but for all his life.

Contrasts:
Manoah's wife's inability to bear children: God's ability to give her a child (13:3,24). This shows and emphasises God's sovereign action and his power to deliver Israel.

Repetitions:
The requirements for a Nazirite to express total devotion to God is emphasised by repetition (see 13:4,5,7,8,12,13,14). This illustrates that Samson was to be a man who would lead

Israel as a spiritual as well as a military leader. Military strength and spiritual devotion were to be two sides of the same coin. That this was God's intention for all of Israel's leaders is evident from 2:17 (disobedience to the leader is tantamount to being unfaithful to God - this presupposes a devout leader).

Important words and actions:
God's sovereign initiative and power to raise up a deliverer for Israel (13:3,5,24,25): This shows his mercy and compassion and his faithfulness to the covenant.
The revelation of the angel's identity to Manoah and his wife: God intended to leave the parents in no doubt of their calling to bring Samson up as someone who is devoted to God.

Episode 3 (14:1-20)
Contrasts:
Samson's self-willed action and disobedience to the law in wanting to marry a Philistine woman (14:2) contrasted with his parents' disapproval (14:3) and the expectation raised in episode 2 of a devoted leader for Israel. This shows that his parents had some kind of awareness of the law which forbids marriage with the original inhabitants of the land (see Deut 7:1-3). Consequently, through Samson's words and actions, the reader understands that Samson's character is consistent with the people of his time, who drifted relentlessly into moral decay and idolatry as they intermarried with the original inhabitants of the land (see 3:5-6). This is confirmed by the word play which links Samson with later parts of the book.

Author's comment:
Verse 4 (14:4) has to be seen in the light of God's sovereign ability to use people's sinful desires and actions to achieve his purposes (see eg Gen 45:8 or 50:20). Just like the people of his time, Samson is portrayed to be so self-willed that any direct command from God would probably have been ignored. In these circumstances God is using Samson's sinful action for his own purposes. The author is emphasising God's sovereign power to work through sinful man.

Scripture makes it clear that God does not cause anyone to sin (Jas 1:13-15). This would be contradicting the general biblical teaching on God's holiness. Another example indicating the fact that the biblical writers understood God to be totally sovereign both over people's sinful actions and Satan's work is found when comparing the two accounts of king David's sin in counting his fighting men (2 Sam 24:1 and 1 Chr 21:1). The ultimate example of God's sovereignty is seen in Christ's death. God allowed the sinful actions of the Jewish religious leaders and the Roman authorities to murder God's son and at the same time fulfil his purposes to put people right with himself through the death of Christ.

Important words and actions / Repetition:
God's sovereign activity in using a sinful man (14:6) to deliver Israel becomes apparent. The events in 14:19 indicate a repetition of this idea.

Episode 4 (15:1-20)
Important words and actions / Repetition:
v7 I won't stop until I get my revenge: Samson fights his own battles (see also 15:3,11b,16 - events here indicate repetition of the same idea), indicating a total lack of concern for God's will and plan for his life.

v14 The Spirit of the LORD came upon him in power: God sovereignly works to deliver Israel through a sinful and proud man who fights his own battles.

v16 Then Samson said, "With a donkey's jawbone I ...": Samson's song of triumph completely lacks praise for God, the true source of victory, indicating arrogance and pride.

Summary statement:
15:20 indicates a major division in the Samson narrative, and shows how the author has carefully selected significant events in order to communicate his message. The summary statement in v20 could be understood in two ways. Firstly, it seems to contradict the narrative, since Israel did not recognise Samson's leadership (see 15:11) and moreover, the narrative lacks any description of real leadership. Thus the statement could be taken as a sarcastic remark, indicating the failure of Samson's leadership and highlighting the fact that God is the real leader of Israel who uses Samson's own battles to achieve his purposes. Secondly, it could mean simply that Samson led Israel in physical victory over the Philistines but not in devotion to Yahweh. This would indicate Samson's failure to fulfil his calling. Either interpretation would strengthen the main message of the narrative.

Review of plot development to end of episode 4:
Episode 2 raises high hopes for the reader as God plans to remove his means of discipline from Israel by raising up a deliverer who is to be completely devoted to him and who would lead Israel in faithfulness to God. In episodes 3-4 this hope turns into despair as Samson's character becomes known. Yet rays of light shine through as the true hero becomes evident: it is God who sovereignly fulfils his plan and delivers Israel through someone who fights his own battles.

Having arrived at a stage where a narrative plot could have ended we must now ask the question: Why did the author add the final episodes?

Episode 5 (16:1-3)
Important words and actions:
v1 ...saw a prostitute...He went in to spend the night with her: This highlights the problem (Samson's selfish lifestyle and his morally low standards in contrast with what God intended him to be) which eventually leads to the loss of Samson's calling.

Episode 6 (16:4-22)
Important words and actions / Repetition:
v4 ...he fell in love with a woman...: Repeats and emphasises the problem of the previous episode, namely to show Samson as immoral and unfaithful to God.

v19 shave off the seven braids of his hair...his strength left him...: the public sign of a Nazirite was cut off, the Nazirite vow finally and completely broken. Consequently, God withdraws his power from Samson, indicating that sin limits God's beneficial acts through a person.

v20 But he did not know that the Lord had left him: The message already carried by the plot development of this episode is made explicit by the author's sad commentary: Samson's sinful lifestyle has left him ignorant of God's actions and finally God no longer uses him, indicating God's sovereignty and power as well as man's responsibility in fulfilling God's purposes.

v21 ...the Philistines seized him, gouged out his eyes...: The consequences of his sinful lifestyle are humiliation and defeat.

Episode 7 (16:23-31)
Important words and actions:
v28...let me with one blow get revenge...for my two eyes: Samson still fights his own battles through which the Lord sovereignly brings deliverance to Israel (16:30).

Author's commentary:
v30 Thus he killed many more when he died than when he lived: This seems to be the author's sarcastic evaluation of Samson's life: Samson achieves more through his death than through his life! In this victory over the Philistines God fulfils his plan by delivering Israel from his means of discipline. This indicates that Israel's existence and well-being is based on God's sovereign will and power to carry out the promises he made, based on his covenant.

Summary statement:
v 31 He had led Israel for twenty years: The closing formula notes the period of leadership. The other part of the formula that denotes peace is missing. We will consider the significance of this under 'plot structure').

Review of plot development to end of episode 7:
Having worked through episodes 5-7, we will now return to the question we asked at the end of episode 4. Why has the author added episodes 5-7? The narrative could have ended at 15:20, where the author notes a fulfilment of God's plan; the start of the removal of Philistine oppression. The answer would seem to be that, in parallel with the overall message of Judges, (unfaithfulness to God eventually brings about his punishment), episodes 5-7 focus on and emphasise Samson's immoral and sinful lifestyle which leads to the termination of God's calling on his life as sin's consequences finally catch up with him.

What happens to Samson parallels that which happened to the nation of Israel time and again during the dark ages of the judges - sin leads to punishment and destruction. This leaves no doubt in the reader's mind that it never pays to live sinfully as Samson did. At the same time, episodes 5-7 emphasise and repeat the message of episodes 2-4. Samson's weakness and death is contrasted with God's sovereign power to achieve his purposes for Israel. This shows that Israel's existence and well-being is absolutely dependant on their God (see also 'parallel arrangements of events' below).

The stylistic features of the Samson narrative:
We have noted many stylistic features in the above explanation of the plot structure, significant meaning indicators and literary context. The explanation that follows focuses on those features not yet discussed that will further aid us in our search for the message.

It is important to note that you need to mark and compare the meaning indicators within an episode and across episodes, and even across major individual narratives. Recognising such rhetorical and stylistic features as contrasts in words and actions, structures and repetitions of ideas, will help us arrive at the message.

Contrast between the main parts of the narrative:
Episode 2 (ch 13:2-25) raises the hope for an ideal leader who is completely devoted to God. He is to be a Nazirite who would lead the people by example to show them what it means to be faithful to God.

In contrast to this, the remaining episodes show a leader who is completely the opposite. He lives a sinful life, doing what he wants and therefore fits the general description of the people of his time (see 21:25b). This contrast is emphasised by the parallel arrangement of events (see table below):

Parallel arrangements of events:

A
14:1-9

- Samson wants to marry a Philistine woman in disobedience to the law
- God is sovereignly involved and begins to deliver Israel through a sinful deliverer
- Samson saves himself from a lion by a display of power as the Spirit of God comes upon him

A*
16:1-3

- Sleeps with Philistine prostitute in disobedience to the law
- Lacks explicit reference to God and no progress delivering Israel is made
- Samson saves himself from Philistines by a display of power (city gates removed)

B
14:10-20

- Samson reveals the secret of his riddle to his nagging wife
- God is sovereignly involved in starting to bring deliverance for Israel
- Samson kills thirty Philistines as God's Spirit gives him the power

B*
16:4-22

- Samson reveals the secret of his stength to his nagging lover, Delilah
- God's desire to deliver Israel is temporarily hindered by a sinful deliverer
- Samson is defeated and captured by the Philistines as God's Spirit leaves him

C
15:1-20

- Samson takes personal revenge for the loss of his bride and her death
- God is sovereignly involved in bringing deliverance to Israel
- Samson kills many Philistines as God's Spirit gives him the power
- Samson cried out to God for water – God saves his life
- Samson led Israel for twenty years

C*
16:23-31

- Samson seeks personal revenge for the loss of his eyes
- God is sovereignly involved in bringing deliverance to Israel
- Samson achieves his major victory over Philistines and their rulers
- Samson prays to God for power to revenge himself – he loses his life
- Samson led Israel for twenty years

This parallel arrangement of events strengthens our conclusions reached in 'review of plot development to end of episode 7', as well as under 'the stylistic features of the Samson narrative'. It seems to emphasise the message that those who live contrary to God's law will eventually experience the consequences of such a lifestyle and forfeit God's purposes for them. On the other hand, the true hero of the story is emphasised - it is God, who despite human selfishness, overrules and carries out his plan for Israel.

As was mentioned in 20.5.2, sometimes the recognition of parallelism or other arrangements can help us to decide on the boundaries of an episode. So, the above parallel arrangement may lead us to revise our episode divisions in figure 23.3. However, in this case, the message doesn't change if we change the episode divisions. It is possible that parallel arrangements could form different blocks from the episode structure and not exactly match it, just as it is the case with the formal structure of Paul's letters and the arrangements of meaning blocks. In such a case, we have an overlap of structures (see 29.2).

Contrast across major judges' narrative:
Another contrast becomes apparent when comparing the Gideon narrative with Samson: Judges relates (explicitly) how Gideon exercises his spiritual responsibility to lead people to be faithful to their God by standing against idolatry (ch 6). This highlights Samson's total lack of it, indicating failure in his call to be a spiritual leader.

Plot structure:
How the plot structure of the Samson narrative helps us has already been discussed. Further clues to the message may be found by comparing the plot structure of the major judges narratives:

In figure 23.2 we noted the basic (common to all the major judges narrative) plot structure. Comparing these structures, it becomes apparent that the story of Samson lacks an element, the outcome '...the land had peace...' which is an idea repeatedly found in the other major stories. Although it is mentioned twice that he led Israel for twenty years (see comments under 'summary statement' of episode 4, earlier), there is no mention of a major victory over the Philistines comparable with the victories of the other major judges. Major victory over the rulers of the Philistines only comes through Samson's death. So, it would seem that real peace during Samson's time as judge was elusive. This helps the reader understand that he not only failed to lead Israel according to its covenant relationship with God, but - at least in his lifetime - did not deliver Israel to the extent God intended him to. The author's (probably) sarcastic remark at the end of Samson's life seems to emphasis this (see 16:30).

23.3.3 Step 3.4: Establish the meaning structure

In both this and the following step we integrate all the previous findings and begin to draw conclusions about the message. A typical feature of dramatic history is that the meaning blocks can be quite big and even span several episodes. This is also the case in the Samson narrative.

In most parts of the narrative, God's sovereign will and power to bring about his purposes for Israel, according to his covenant, is a major meaning element - even in spite of and through a sinful man.

13:1: God punishes disobedience and idolatry according to the covenant.

13:2-25: God is compassionate and forgives Israel according to his covenant. This is seen by his sovereign act of raising up a leader through whom he intends to restore peace in the land and faithfulness in his people.

14:1-15:20: God is sovereignly beginning to restore peace and order in the land through an unfaithful and sinful leader.

16:1-31: God sovereignly uses an unfaithful leader. But the leader suffers the consequences of his sin, loses God's calling and fails to lead people in faithfulness to God.

23.3.4 Step 3.5: Conclude and summarise the message

The reader is urged to learn that:

- Above all God is their true king and ruler who is faithful to his covenant commitments
- God will discipline Israel's persistent unfaithfulness according to his covenant with them
- God is compassionate and forgiving. The nation's existence, well-being and peace depend primarily on him
- God wants faithful leaders to lead his people
- God is sovereign to carry out his plan despite human sinfulness
- Those who persist in sin will suffer the consequences of their sin, lose their calling and limit God's beneficial acts through them

23.4 The broader biblical framework

23.4.1 The broader biblical framework of the Samson narrative

It is clear that God's ideal for Israel was that they should serve him as their king and ruler without a human monarch. Israel was meant to be a theocracy (a nation ruled by God) and not a monarchy. Although provision is made for a human king in Deuteronomy (17:14-20), the events surrounding Israel's request for a king make it utterly plain that it was not God's plan for Israel (1 Sam 8:6ff; 12:17,19). It would seem that just as God allowed divorce because of their hard hearts, so he would also allow them to have a king.

It is part of God's covenant with Israel that faithfulness to him is rewarded with political stability as well as social and material well-being (Deut 28:1-14). Unfaithfulness to him inevitably brings God's discipline on them, as described in the covenant (eg Deut 28:15-68).

God wants his people and their leaders to be faithful to him (Deut 17:19; Josh 1:7; 1 Sam 12:24,25). Unfaithful leaders will experience God's punishment and will eventually be removed (Deut 28:36; 1 Sam 12:25; 13:13,14).

23.4.2 The contribution of the OT historical books to the broader biblical message

These historical books follow on from the Pentateuch and take us right into the history of ancient Israel. Joshua, Judges, the two books of Samuel and the two books of Kings lead us right up to the time when the whole of Israel is overrun by the Babylonians and carried away into exile. Ezra and Nehemiah together tell of the return of some of the people of Israel and the rebuilding of the nation.

As we have seen in chapter 22 (Gen 12.2-3), God raises a new nation in order to fulfil his promise made in Gen 3:15. This new nation is to live in a specific location which God will give them and in which they are to live out their specific calling among the nations. As the books of Exodus through to Deuteronomy make abundantly clear, this calling to live in obedience to God's covenant is a must if they are to remain in the land and fulfil their calling to be a blessing to the nations.

So, the historical books relate and focus on Israel's covenant relationship with God. This relationship continues in the same stormy fashion in which it began during the time in the wilderness. After a period of faithfulness under Joshua's leadership, Israel is quick to forget Yahweh and turn to other gods. The fickleness of their commitment to God is vividly portrayed in Judges and continues on to the exile, with periods of faithfulness in between. Although God's salvation plan seems to make no progress during Judges, there are a faithful few through whom he continues to work out his promise. Ruth, the Moabitess, and Boaz, an upright Israelite, become the ancestors of king David (Ruth 4:17-22). Throughout this period, God's patience, mercy and his sovereign power to work out his plan, shines through, creating hope and anticipation.

The next ray of hope that God's promise is going to be fulfilled, comes at an all time high in Israel's history, during which king David leads Israel in covenant faithfulness to God. To him God makes the promise of an eternal kingdom and a royal line through which God's promise will eventually be fulfilled (2 Sam 7).

After Solomon's death, Israel is divided into two kingdoms as the northern tribes reject Solomon's son, Rehoboam, as their king. Thus, the northern kingdom puts itself on a slippery slope where king after king defies God, and the nation's religious and moral life is desperately corrupted. After God's many unheeded warnings and threats through the prophets, their fate is inevitable. Less than two and a half centuries have passed since the division of the kingdom, and the Israelites find themselves deported from the promised land by the Assyrians (2 Kgs 17).

As for the southern kingdom, a few faithful kings give reason for hope. But just over a century after the fall of its northern neighbour, the same fate overtakes it. God's patient pleading and his firm warnings did not find many receptive hearts, and the covenant curse - the exile - becomes reality (2 Kgs 25).

Has God's promise to Abraham and David failed? How is he now going to work out his plan? Words of hope were added to the prophets' warnings and visions of doom (Jer 29:10-14). God would continue to work out his plan through Israel. The seventy years in exile were to purify Israel once and for all from its promiscuous relationship with foreign gods and idolatrous ways. Then, being wonderfully consistent with his covenant promises, God would demonstrate his mercy and sovereignly return them to the promised land using Cyrus, the pagan ruler of Persia as his servant (Is 44:28; Ezra 1).

The books of Ezra and Nehemiah with which the biblical account of ancient Israel ends, leaves the reader with a note of hope and expectation. The exile seems to have achieved its purpose to purify Israel from idolatry. Almighty God is faithful to his covenant and brings his people back to the promised land under the leadership of Zerubbabel (Ezra 2:2; 3:2) who is of Davidic descent (Mt 1:13). And so, God's promise to David continues to be fulfilled. The temple and the city are rebuilt and Yahweh is worshipped once again.

Finally, any survey of the OT historical books shows above all that Israel's history is fashioned and guided according to the covenant relationship established at Sinai. Throughout this period God uses unlikely Israel to reveal himself and to continue to work out his plan. Until, at the turning point of history, we meet Jesus Christ, the completion and fulfilment of God's wonderful promises.

23.5 Hermeneutics

23.5.1 Pitfalls

Events narrated in Old Testament stories are often used as precedents for all kinds of practices in the church today. Take for example, the battle of Jericho. To possess the promised land, God commanded the Israelites to walk around the city of Jericho (Josh 5:13-6:27). This biblical event is sometimes copied in prayer. It may be a building or a community which is the object of a 'prayer walk' today and somehow it is thought that this kind of prayer will be more effective in achieving the desired results. Several things may be said about this:

Firstly, there are great inconsistencies in chosing this event as a precedent for a practice in prayer today. For example, if we should walk, why do we not have people blowing ram's horns in front of us? That was God's command, just as much as his instructions to walk around the city walls (Josh 6:4). He certainly expected the Israelites to obey both of these instructions. And have we noticed that the Israelites were not even asked to pray as they walked? The fact is, they were asked to remain silent until the seventh day and even then no prayer was offered!

Secondly, biblical teaching on prayer nowhere encourages the use of certain methods to achieve results. This would seem to go against the general principle that prayer should be based on simple trust in God, offered in accordance to his will and with perseverance. If walking around our object of prayer helps us to concentrate and to pray more fervently, then it should be encouraged. But if we think that because we walk our prayer will be more effective, we are in the danger of fooling ourselves and reducing our relationship with God to mere mechanics.

Thirdly, by practising this kind of application, we go against the generally agreed principle that the message (absolutes) from a story should be consistent with the author's intention. This brings us back to the issue of exegesis. Only through applying proper exegetic principles can the message for the original receiver be established. And only once this has been done, can we continue with the process of hermeneutics.

STUDY TIP
More will be said about how to avoid such pitfalls in ch 28.5. The principles explained there apply also to the Old Testament historical books.

23.5.2 Hermeneutics of the Samson narrative

In chapter twenty two we have seen that the absolutes of the message of the Old Testament books can only be applied to us today once we have considered them in the light of what Christ has achieved for us as explained in the New Testament.

Absolutes for the Old Testament	Absolutes for Today
Above all, God is Israel's true king and ruler who is faithful to his covenant commitments	Above all, God is the king and ruler of the church (Acts 2:36; Rom 14:9; Eph 1:22) who is faithful to the New Covenant
God will discipline Israel's persistent unfaithfulness according to his covenant	God will discipline any persistent unfaithfulness (Heb 12:1-13; see also hermeneutics of ch 26)
(a) God is compassionate and forgiving (b) The nation's existence, well-being and peace depend primarily on him	(a) God is compassionate and will forgive those who confess their sins and believe in Jesus (1 Jn 1:9; Acts 10:43) (b) This part does not apply in the same way to the church today (see note (b) below for explanation)
God wants faithful leaders to lead his people	God wants faithful leaders to lead his church (1 Tim 3:1-13; 1 Pet 5:1-4)
God is sovereign to carry out his plan despite human sinfulness	God is sovereign to carry out his plan despite human sinfulness (This can be seen supremely in the death and resurrection of Jesus)
Those who persist in sin will suffer the consequences of their sin, lose their calling and limit God's beneficial acts through them	Those who persist in sin will suffer the consequences of their sin (Acts 5:1-11; Heb 2:2-3; 10:26-31; Tit 3:10-11). Leaders and members who persist in sin should be disciplined by the church. This could result in a limitation of their ministry. (Gal 2:11ff; Paul's charge to Timothy and Titus to correct and rebuke false teachers eg Tit 1:13; 1 Tim 1:3-6).

Note (b): For the people of the Old Covenant, God promised and secured their national well-being, including material wealth, and physical peace. They were a political nation as well as God's people. The church is not a nation, nor is any nation today God's people like Israel was under the Old Covenant. Therefore, this absolute does not apply in the same way to people in the New Covenant. In his New Covenant, God makes clear that he will preserve the Church world-wide (Mt 16:18) and care for its spiritual well-being as well as look after the believers' physical needs as they live in faithfulness to God (Mt 6:25-34). But this has to be held in tension with the fact that local and national churches may be severely oppressed by antichristian governments. They may cause believers to suffer materially and physically for their faith. Moreover, believers, as citizens of a secular nation, may of course also experience the material suffering of a nation in economic depression. And finally, how God deals with secular states is not an issue that is addressed by this narrative, or the main message of the book. Therefore, evaluating OT absolutes in the light of the NT is absolutely vital, as this will really help us to avoid pitfalls when applying these absolutes today.

CHAPTER TWENTY FOUR

How to interpret the Psalms

Objectives

1. To understand how to do exegesis on the Psalms
2. To understand the process of hermeneutics for the Psalms

Contents

STUDY TIP

It is important to have mastered the content of chapters seventeen and eighteen before commencing this chapter.

In chapter 17, we discussed the characteristics of biblical poetry and looked at the stylistic features typically found in it. In chapter 18 we discussed and applied the steps of exegesis to biblical poetry. The largest collection of Hebrew songs is the Book of Psalms (or the Psalter), and it is here that we have the richest source for the study of biblical poetry.

The aim of this chapter is to show how the steps of exegesis and hermeneutics can be applied to the Book of Psalms by analysing Psalm 100, a song of praise. This additional example of the analysis of a psalm (Ps 1 was done in chapter 18) will help us to see that the method of interpreting biblical poetry is the same, regardless of the type of psalm one analyses.

24.1 The communication situation

The psalms were written over a period of at least seven centuries, stretching from before or during the time of the exodus until the Israelites returned from exile.

24.1.1 Function of psalms: a part of Israel's worship

The psalms were used on specific and significant occasions like David's successful attempt to bring the ark to Jerusalem (2 Sam 6:5; 1 Chr 15:16, 27). Another example is Jehoshaphat's wonderful deliverance by God from his enemies, the Moabites and Ammonites, which led to hymns of praise and thanksgiving (2 Chr 20:21, 28). The Old Testament psalms were used in Israel's worship, and in 2 Chr 29:25, 30 we see king Hezekiah committing himself to restore the temple worship and provide for the musical celebration of its services. During his reign, the use of ancient sacred music was revived, and he commanded that the psalms of David and of Ashaph should be sung in the temple as of old. Additionally, as Ps 150 illustrates, instrumental music was closely linked with the psalms.

24.1.2 Authorship and editing

The Psalter is an anthology of collections. It represents the final stage in the long process of canonically ordering the psalms. It was probably put into its final form in the post-exilic period. There is no certainty regarding the date and reliability of the titles (superscriptions). However, the practice of attaching titles, including the name of the author, is an ancient custom, well-known and conventional in Old Testament times.

Regarding authorship, opinions are even more divided. The notations themselves are vague, since some scholars believe that the Hebrew expression used, meaning in general "belonging to", can also be taken to mean "for the use of" or "dedicated to". That means 'a psalm of David' may have been written by him, it may concern him or one of the later Davidic kings, or it may have been written in the manner of those he composed (NIVSB:765). We do know, however, that David was a musician (1 Sam 16:18) and a poet (2 Sam 1:17-27, 3:33-34). In addition, the NT not only accepts, but bases arguments upon Davidic authorship of material bearing his name.

24.1.3 The communication situation of Psalm 100

Like most of the psalms, the historical context of Psalm 100 is not totally clear, and theories speculate as to the function, author and purpose of this psalm. However, the text itself gives us some indication of the communication situation of this psalm.

Purpose:

- The religious context in which worship took place for the Israelites should be taken into account here. Worshippers are again invited to enter the gates of the temple. The worshipping community worshipped in the courts and in the temple itself, because God was present in the inner sanctuary (1 Kgs 6:16, 19; 7:49). From there he communicated his word to his people (Ps 60:6; 108:7). Important components of Israel's worship in the sanctuary, include the gates of the holy area (Ps 9:14, 87:2) and the outer courts (84:2,10; 96:8). The worshipping community assembled in the outer courts, and on the festival days, participants in the religious ceremonies entered the temple itself.
- According to verse 4, this psalm was most probably used in a service of worship in the temple and forecourt, where God was praised by singers, musicians and believing Israelites.
- So Ps 100 is a song of praise (vs 1-2,5) in which God was praised by singers and musicians.

Authorship and title:

The psalm does not state who the author is, and there is no clarity from secondary sources.

24.2 The literary context

24.2.1 The classification of the Psalms

In chapter 18 (see 18.2.1) we stated that the psalmist's circumstances determined his mood and helped him to choose a suitable poetic genre, such as a lament for a sorrowful occasion or personal trauma or a song of praise for a joyful occasion. To help us further in determining which kind of psalm we are dealing with, we can classify psalms according to four main criteria, namely:

1 The theme of the psalms
2 The worship situation from which they had sprung
3 Thoughts and moods which are held in common
4 Features of style, form and imagery

Figure 24.1 gives an idea of how a number of psalms could be classified. The ideal is that you learn to use the content of a psalm itself to arrive at your own classification in exegesis. With practice this skill will impove.

FIGURE 24.1
Classification of types of Psalms (adapted from NIVSB)

Laments	Individual laments	3, 22, 31, 39, 42, 57, 71
	Corporate laments	12, 44, 80, 94, 137
Thanksgiving psalms	Community psalms	65, 67, 75, 107, 124, 136
Hymns of praise	Individual Psalms	18, 30, 32, 34, 40, 66, 92
	God as Creator	8, 19, 104, 148
	God as Protector	66, 100, 111, 114, 149
Salvation history psalms	God of history	33, 103, 113, 117, 145-147
	Focus on the history of God's saving works	78, 105, 106, 135, 136
Psalms of celebration and affirmation	Covenant renewal liturgies	50, 81, 89, 132
	Royal psalms	2, 18, 20, 21, 45, 72, 101, 144
	God's universal reign	24, 29, 47, 93, 95-99
	Songs of Zion	46, 48, 76, 84, 87, 122
Wisdom psalms	Wisdom psalms	36, 37, 49, 73, 112, 119, 127, 128
Songs of trust	Songs of trust	11, 16, 23, 27, 62, 63, 91, 121

24.2.2 The position in the Psalter

The book of Psalms consists of five books. The division goes back as early as the third century BC. Every section is easily recognisable, because a short doxology (praise to God) closes each book. The divisions are:

Book I :	Ps 1-41
Book II :	Ps 42-72
Book III:	Ps 73-89
Book IV :	Ps 90-106
Book V :	Ps 107-150.

Many have seen in this fivefold division an attempt to imitate the division of the Torah (New Bible Dictionary 1980:993).

24.2.3 The literary context of Psalm 100

Type of psalm:

- Psalm 100 is a song of praise. In chapter eighteen (18.2.1), we discussed the textual organisation of a song of praise. In fig 24.2 we apply this to Ps 100.

FIGURE 24.2

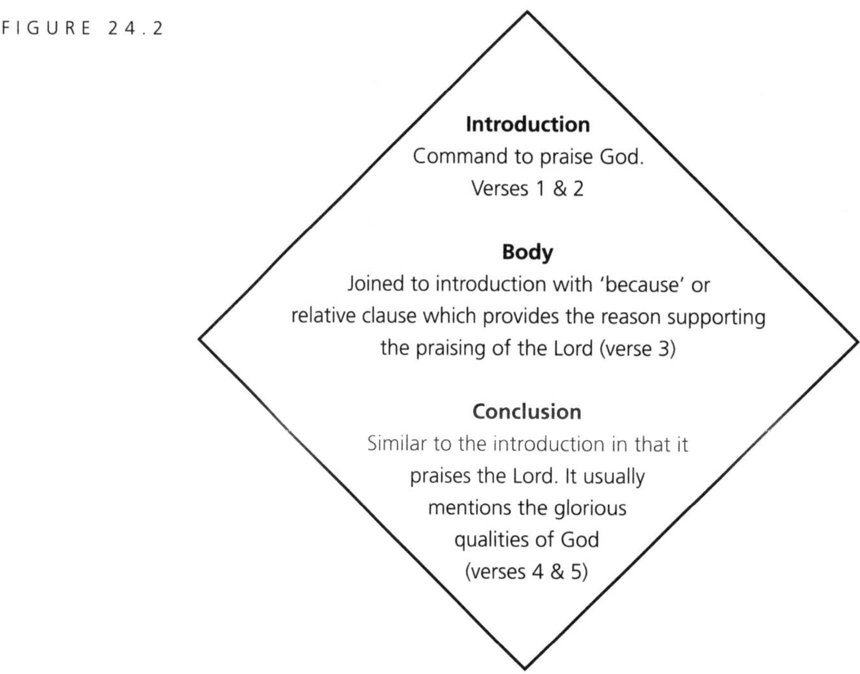

- More examples of praise hymns are: Ps 8, 19, 29, 33, 47, 65-67, 100, 103-105, 111, 114, 145-150.

Position in the psalter:

- This psalm is found in Book IV (Ps 90-106).
- The final editors of the psalter used Ps 100 to close the series that begins with Ps 93. It has special affinity with 95:1-2,6-7 and shares the theme of Ps 94 - 99; praise to the eternal, universal, and invincible reign of the Lord, stating his kingship above 'all gods' (95:3).

24.3 Analysis of the passage

The theory and method for analysing biblical poetry is discussed in chapter 18 (18:3). The different steps will therefore not be discussed in such detail here.

Step 3.2: Mark the significant meaning indicators

FIGURE 24.3

Psalm 100

A psalm. For giving thanks.

similar parallelism in which line 1 is general/ hyperbole:

1 Shout for joy to the LORD, all the earth.
a b
2 [Worship the LORD] [with gladness];
a b
3 [come before him] [with joyful songs].

4 Know that the LORD is God.

developing parallelism

a b
5 [It is he who made us], [and we are his];
b c **metaphor**
6 [we are his people], [the sheep of his pasture].

similar parallelism:

a b
7 [Enter his gates] [with thanksgiving] A
a b
8 [and his courts] [with praise]; B
b b
9 [give thanks to him] [and praise his name]. A + B

similar parallelism:

a b c
10 [For the LORD] [is good and his love] [endures for ever];
a b c
11 [his] [faithfulness] [continues through all generations].

In this psalm, God and Israel are the main actors, and the themes of praise, thanks and joy can be marked.

The syntactic elements (eg parallelisms) and figurative expressions (eg metaphors) are marked as indicated in figure 24.3.

The marking of all these types of significant meaning indicators leads us to identify the following relationships in Ps 100:

L1-3 form a unit, in which L1 functions as an introductory statement.
L4 is a transitional sentence , in which the psalm moves from an invitation to praise God in a

specific way, to the reason for praise. It is strategically placed to introduce the metaphor in L6.
L7-9 form a unit and correspond closely with L1-3 as an invitation to worship God.
The word 'for' in L10 introduces the reason why the Lord is worthy of praise and links closely with L11.

Step 3.3: Explain words and phrases

STUDY TIP
As mentioned in 18.6, not only the words and phrases, but the stylistic features need to be explained properly in order to understand the meaning of the psalm.

LINES 1-3
The first line is a general introduction to the whole psalm, giving a call to all people to praise God. We find similar parallelism in L2-3, describing the manner in which God should be praised.

The utterances 'shout for joy', 'gladness' and 'joyful songs' have a strong emotive quality which accentuate the invitation to joyously praise God. Joy should characterise worship among God's people.

all the earth: This hyperbole emphasises the invitation.

This invitation clearly shows the psalmist's desire that everyone should come and worship God. Hans-Joachim Kraus (1979:73) amplifies this thought in an excellent way:

> The blessing for which Israel prays and which has been promised to the nation is not a power restricted to the boundaries of God's people and actively only there, but it is a light shining on Israel which is to shine forth into the world of the nations and move all the ends of the earth to fear Yahweh and to praise him. The religion of Israel is set within a universal framework, in its beginning, in all its festivals and observances, and in its conclusion. God's people never celebrate their own glorification, but understand it as the consequence of divine election, destiny and mission in the world.

L2-3: The event words, 'worship' and 'come before Him', mean that the worshipper, along with others from the community, came into the temple where God was to be worshipped.

LINE 4
L4 is the transitional line between L1-3 and L5-6.

know that the LORD is God: 'know' means "acknowledge" (GNB). This phrase completes the theme of L1-3 and forms the introduction to the reason for worshipping God in L5-6.

LINES 5 - 6
L5-6 describe the reason for praising God.

it is he who made us, and we are his: The psalmist emphasises God as their creator and therefore his ownership of them.

we are his people, the sheep of his pasture: This is a significant metaphor commonly applied in Hebrew poetry. It underlines the concept of belonging to and being rooted in God.

The topic is	Israel
The illustration is	sheep
Point of similarity is	being looked after and taken care of
Non-figurative language:	Just as a Middle Eastern shepherd takes care of his flock with tenderness, so the Lord takes care of Israel because they belong to him.

These two lines therefore compliment one another, using imagery to convey the message that God, who made them, is the shepherd who tends them.

LINES 7-9
Now the psalmist bursts into another call to worship.

L7-9 form a beautiful pattern in which the effect of the parallelism can clearly be observed. L7 and L8 are synonomous, stressing the call to and manner of praise. The two themes of worshipping God thankfully (L7) and worshipping him joyfully (L8) are combined in L9, emphasising the fact that Israel's worship is to be joyful simply because it is based on gratitude.

LINE 10-11
As in the first strophe, the call to praise is followed by a declaration of the reasons for praising God.

for the Lord is good; his faithfulness: these two phrases emphasise God's covenant love and faithfulness.

endures forever; continues through all generations: these two phrases mean "unlimited and continuous goodness and trustworthiness". God is the covenant God of Israel and his goodness can be seen in his love that endures forever. Kraus (1979:104) explains this theme of God's covenant love, which is a constant refrain throughout the psalms, as follows:

> ...there is a constantly new manifestation of his grace, and that he appears again and again, and thus demonstrates his living presence, is the proof of his faithfulness. Manifestation of his grace and proof of his faithfulness are based on Yahweh's actions in history by which he chose his people and made himself accessible to them. The entire cultus in Jerusalem harked back to these actions and drew from them God's assurance and promises.

Step 3.4: Establish the meaning structure
As discussed in chapter 18 (18.7), a psalm should be seen as an integrated and whole unit. Concepts and themes in the psalms are therefore closely related and build up towards a central integrated meaning structure. Ps 100 is an excellent example, illustrating the way in which the psalmist used content and stylistic features to develop his line of thought.

FIGURE 24.4
Psalm 100
A psalm. For giving thanks.

1	Shout for joy to the LORD, all the earth.	A
2	Worship the LORD with gladness;	
3	come before him with joyful songs.	
4	Know that the LORD is God.	
5	It is he who made us, and we are his;	B
6	we are his people, the sheep of his pasture .	

7	Enter his gates with thanksgiving	
8	and his courts with praise;	A*
9	give thanks to him and praise his name.	
10	For the LORD is good and his love endures for ever;	B*
11	his faithfulness continues through all generations.	

It can be seen that there are two main parts to both strophes:

1. a call to praise (A: L1-3, A*:L7-9) followed by a declaration of
2. why the Lord is worthy of praise (B: L5-6, B*: L10-11).

Block A: The first block (L1-3) gives the invitation for everyone to joyously worship and praise God.

Block B: The second block (L5-6) gives the reason for praising God, namely an acknowledgement that he created them, chose them as his own and that he cares for them.

L4: This is the transitional line that links blocks A and B. The people's worship is based on their acknowledgement of the LORD as God.

Block A*: The third block (L7-9) corresponds with block A, in that there is again an invitation and call to come into God's presence with joy, gratitude and praise.

Block B*: The fourth block (L10-11) gives the reason for praising God, that he is faithful and loving to his covenant people.

Step 3.5: Conclude and summarise the message
This step in the psalms has been discussed in chapter 18.8. We can conclude the message of Ps 100 as follows:

The people of God are called to praise and worship him. Their worship should be marked by joy and gratitude.

Their worship is based on their acknowledgement of the LORD as God.

The reasons for praising and thanking God are not only because he created, chose and cared for them as his own people, but also for who he is; a faithful, trustworthy, covenant-keeping God.

24.4 The broader biblical framework

24.4.1 The theology of the Book of Psalms

Introduction:

The 'theology' of the book of Psalms is spread over a large collection of independent pieces of many kinds, serving different purposes and written and edited over a period of at least seven centuries. A great variety of experiences and events in the lives of the Israelites come to the fore in this collection. However, because the different psalms are bound to the worship of Yahweh, they show certain common theological features. Let us look at a number of these theological themes.

Knowledge of God is central:
At the core of the theology of the Psalter is the conviction that God is at the centre of the believer's life (his understanding, trust, hope, service, morality, adoration), and also of history and of the whole creation (heaven and earth). He is the great king over all, the one to whom all things are subject. As seen in the hymns of praise (24.2.1), the Israelites never grew tired of singing of God's majesty in creation, through which he has made himself known as good (wise, righteous, faithful, merciful - evoking trust) and great (his knowledge, thoughts and works are beyond human comprehension - evoking reverent awe). He created all things and preserves them.

But, as seen in 'salvation history psalms' (24.2.1) God is also uniquely the God of Israel who revealed himself to Abraham, Isaac and Jacob. Who, through Moses, delivered Israel from Egypt, entered into a covenant with them and gave them the promised land.

It is with this concept of God that the psalmists found delight in prayer to God. In their prayers they praise, plead and commune with God, and find refuge from sickness, pestilence, slander and attack. In the life of the Israelite community, their behaviour is marked by loyalty to God, reverent obedience to the law, kindness to the oppressed and joy in the worship of God's people.

Prayers for punishment:
It can be difficult for us to understand theologically the prayers of retaliation, bitterness and anger that are found in some of the psalms. There are no simple answers to this. Fee and Stuart (1988:182,183) state that these psalms guide our anger to and through God verbally, rather than to anyone else. It invites us to 'be angry but not to sin' (Ps 4:4). In this way we fulfil the New Testament teaching 'Do not let the sun go down while you are still angry, and do not give the devil a foothold' (Eph 4:26-27). Most prayers for vengeance are found in laments, and some are lengthy and harsh (see Ps 12, 35, 58, 59, 69, 70, 83, 109, 137, 140). It should be remembered that people in the OT used strong language (hyperboles).

These psalms are not oracles of God, but they are Israel's response to God's revelation emerging from the painful realities of human life. They therefore give us insight into the inner life of the psalmists. In the plea for vengeance, the psalmists are motivated by their zeal for the God of Israel who must exercise retribution in the present world. Right and wrong are important to God, and therefore judgment as well as grace must function in God's moral order for this world. It was natural, then, for men living under the dispensation of the law, to pray for the destruction of God's enemies through judgment. Heeding God's word 'It is mine to avenge, I will repay' (Deut 32:35, cf Rom 12:19), the psalmists call for judgment according to the covenant curses.

In Ps 137:7-9, the psalmist tells God about the feelings of the suffering Israelites, using hyperbolic language of the same extreme sort found in the covenant curses themselves. The fact that he is addressing the Babylonians directly is simply a feature of the style of the psalm - he also addresses Jerusalem directly in verse 5. It is God who hears our angry words. Understood in this context, as part of the language of the laments, and used rightly to channel and control our potentially sinful anger, these psalms can indeed help keep us from sinning.

These psalms do not contradict Jesus' teaching to love our enemies. The psalmists in ancient times were bound to the same commitment of love for enemies as Christians are (cf Lev 19:17-18; Ex 23:4-5; Prov 25:21). His teachings define love actively, and it is not so much how you feel about a certain person, but what you do for that person that shows love

(Lk 10:25-37). These psalms teach us to express honestly our anger to God, no matter how bitterly and hatefully we feel it, and let God take care of the justice against those who abuse us.

Messianic psalms:
An important factor in the national survival of Israel has been the Messianic hope (2 Sam 7:4-16). This hope centres on the return of the period of David, whose reign marked the golden age in Israel's history. It is against this background that the Messianic psalms should be viewed (New Bible Dictionary 1988:995).

The perspective of the Messiah that springs from the Psalms is a twofold one:
He is to be king of the Messianic age. The Psalms foresee the coming of a divine Messianic king who will reign universally, and against whom the nations will rebel in vain (Ps 2). In Ps 110 the Messiah is king, priest and victor who sits in glory at God's right hand. Ps 45 speaks of his eternal dominion, while Ps 72 emphasises his universal rule.

Secondly the Psalms also prepare people's minds for a suffering Messiah. The anointed Son of Yahweh, the Priest-King whose reign is eternal, is to yield himself to dreadful suffering (Ps 22, 69).

24.4.2 The broader theological perspective of Psalm 100

The message we find in Psalm 100 is clearly in line with the rest of Scripture. Worship in the Old Testament, as well as in the New, was a response to God's revelation. Worship is therefore not a spark and motivation for ecstatic behaviour in itself, but because of the way God revealed himself in history. We can rejoice for the exact reasons that the psalmist rejoices, that God has created and called us, and recreated and restored our relationship with him through Jesus Christ (Heb 10:1-4).

24.5 Hermeneutics

As stated in chapter 22, when one arrives at the message to the original OT receivers through the process of exegesis, the application to a target group in our time needs to be seen in the light of the redemptive work of Christ and the message of the New Testament.

From the use of the psalms both in ancient Israel and in the New Testament church, there are certain ways in which we as Christians can use them. They are an effective guide to worshipping God individually and communally. The worshipper who seeks to praise God, or appeals to God, or remembers God's blessings, can use the Psalms as a formal means of expressing his or her thoughts and feelings. When a psalm touches upon a topic or theme that we wish to express to the Lord, we can use it to help us with our expression.

The Psalms demonstrate the importance of reflection upon things that God has done for us. They invite prayer, reflection upon God's Word, and reflective fellowship with other believers, as Fee & Stuart (1988:185) explains :

> The Psalms, like no other literature, lift us to a position where we can commune with God, capturing a sense of the greatness of His Kingdom and a sense of what living with Him for eternity will be like. Even in our darkest moments, when life has become so painful as to seem unendurable, God is with us.

We can study the principles expressed in the various psalms and apply them to ourselves, our church and society as Kaiser (1993:9) writes:

> They are so intensely practical, so wide-ranging in their scope of topics and so eminently

down to earth in what they have to teach us about our walk with God, whether that walk takes us to the marketplace, the home, or the nation.

How then, do we apply the message of Psalm 100 to a church today? This psalm contains some principles which are applicable to us today.

The first principle is that the psalmist, as one of God's people, expresses a command and desire that worship and praise to God should be universal and marked with exuberance and joy.

This principle for our time should be interpreted in the light of what Jesus achieved on the cross and in the context of the New Testament. We see clearly in the NT that its writers expressed this desire and command as believers, that all people should come to worship and praise God in Christ Jesus (Rev 4, 5). Phil 2:10-11 states that God's design is that all people everywhere should worship and serve Jesus as Lord. The NT also expressed that ultimately all will have to acknowledge Christ's Lordship which arises from of his death and resurrection (Rom 14:9-11).

The other principles derived from this psalm can similarly be applied, by looking at them in the context of the Old and New Testament.

Absolutes for Old Testament	**Absolutes for Today**
The people of God are called to praise and worship him. Their worship should be marked by joy and gratitude.	Church members are called to praise and worship God. Their worship should be marked by joy and gratitude (Col 3:16, 17).
Their worship is based on their acknowledgement of the LORD as God.	The church's worship is based on her acknowledgement of the LORD as God.
The reasons for God's people praising and thanking God are not only because he created, chose and cared for them, but also for who he is, namely a faithful, trustworthy, covenant-keeping God.	The reasons for the church praising and thanking God are not only because he creates, chooses and cares for her as his body through Jesus Christ, but also for who he is, namely a faithful, trustworthy, covenant-keeping God (Heb 10:1-4; 12:28; Col 3:16, 17).

One should avoid the trap of trying to apply the form of Israel's worship directly to our situation today. When the worshippers are called upon in the first line of Ps 100 to 'shout for joy', the message is not that we must shout when we worship God. The author is using strong metaphorical language. We have already seen this when we discussing exegesis of the first line.

CHAPTER TWENTY FIVE

How to interpret wisdom literature

Objectives

1. To be able to exegete wisdom literature
2. To understand the contribution of wisdom literature to the broader biblical message
3. To understand the process of hermeneutics for wisdom literature

Contents

STUDY TIP
As wisdom literature is mainly written in poetry, it would be helpful to revise the characteristics of poetry (chapter 17) and the methodology of the exegesis of poetry (chapter 18) before proceeding with this chapter.

The purpose of this chapter is to familiarise ourselves with the exegesis of wisdom literature. This will be done under the headings of the different steps of exegesis and hermeneutics. Passages from Proverbs will be used as examples.

25.1 The communication situation

When we speak of wisdom literature, we refer especially to the Old Testament books Proverbs, Ecclesiastes and Job. Wisdom literature as found in the Psalms has already been dealt with in chapter 24.

Whereas David is seen as the father of biblical poetry, Solomon is seen as the father of the so-called wisdom movement in ancient Israel. In 1 Kgs 4:29-34 we read of his outstanding wisdom, including the fact that he spoke three thousand proverbs and that his songs numbered a thousand and five (v32).

Wisdom was highly valued in most of the nations of that time. We read in the Bible of the wisdom and wise men of Egypt (Acts 7:22; 1 Kgs 4:30; Is 19:11-12), Babylon (Is 47:10; Dan 1:4, 20), Phoenicia (Ezek 28:3), Edom (Jer 49:7), Mesopotamia and Arabia (1 Kgs 4:30). Referring to the thinking of the wise men (sages) of these other nations, Kidner (1964:17) points out that 'while the Old Testament scorns the magic and superstition which debased much of this thought (Is 47:12-13), and the pride which inflated it (Job 5:13), it can speak of the gentile sages with a respect it never shows towards their priests and prophets.'

It is stated that Solomon's 'wisdom was greater than the wisdom of all the men of the East, and greater than all the wisdom of Egypt' (1 Kgs 4:30). His 'fame spread to all the surrounding nations' (1 Kgs 4:31). 'Men of all nations came to listen to Solomon's wisdom, sent by all the kings of the world, who had heard of his wisdom' (1 Kgs 4:34). The queen of Sheba is one of those who came to listen to Solomon's wisdom and to test him with questions (1 Kgs 10:1-13). Jesus used her as an example to condemn the people of his day for not recognising his wisdom since he is greater than Solomon (Lk 11:31).

As far as Egyptian wisdom is concerned, we read in the Bible that Moses was educated in 'all the wisdom of the Egyptians' (Acts 7:22). According to Jewish tradition, this included subjects like mathematics, geometry, poetry, music and astronomy. So, wisdom was not isolated from other disciplines. When Solomon's wisdom is described in 1 Kgs 4 it states that he described 'plant life, from the cedar of Lebanon to the hyssop that grows out of walls. He also taught about animals and birds, reptiles and fish' (v33).

The same integrated approach is true of Babylonian education. When Daniel and his three friends were recruited to be trained for three years, they had to fulfil a number of requirements, ie 'young men without any physical defect, handsome, showing aptitude for every kind of learning, well informed, quick to understand, and qualified to serve in the king's palace' (Dan 1:4). When they were tested by the king at the end of their training, he found Daniel and his friends ten times better than all the magicians and enchanters in his kingdom 'in every matter of wisdom and understanding' (Dan 1:20).

When the queen of Sheba was impressed by Solomon's wisdom, it was not only by his words (1 Kgs 10:4-5):

> When the queen of Sheba saw all the wisdom of Solomon and the palace he had built, the food on his table, the seating of his officials, the attending servants in their robes, his cupbearers, and the burnt offerings he made at the temple of the LORD, she was overwhelmed.

By looking at Egyptian and Babylonian wisdom, and the wisdom of Solomon, we see that the wisdom of biblical times was not isolated from the rest of life. It was very much about life, the questions of life and also everyday living. The wise observed life and generalised their observations into proverbs. Therefore, it is not surprising that there are some remarkable parallels between biblical and non-biblical wisdom literature. The following is an example (Bruce 1981:48):

First saying:
> Even a fool is thought wise if he keeps silent,
> and discerning when he holds his tongue.

Second saying:
> Even a fool, covered with fine clothes,
> is fair in the assembly up to a point;
> yea a fool is fair so long as he utters no word.

The first saying is from Proverbs 17:28 and the second from Sanskrit literature (the classical literature of India written in the Sanskrit language).

There was a time when there was much discussion in scholarly circles about the relationship between the Egyptian proverbs of Amenemope and Prov 22:17-23:11. Which influenced which? Was Amenemope the original, or is it a translation of a Hebrew document? In his book on the scholarly study of Proverbs during the past century, Whybray (1995:15) states that the debate has now moved on to the relationship between Egyptian and Israelite ideas on a much wider base. This is as a result of the discovery of more documents of wisdom literature in the Middle East and the realisation that it was a generally used genre. The result is that 'most recent writers, while admitting a general affinity between Proverbs and the foreign wisdom traditions, have been less convinced than their predecessors of the existence of direct links with particular Egyptian texts' (Whybray 1995:147).

Because wisdom is about the whole of life, it functions in the context of the god or gods that one serves. In biblical times no distinction was made between 'religious' and 'secular' as understood today. The schools in Egypt were governed in close relation with the temples and were often controlled by priests. When Daniel and his friends were examined by Nebuchadnezzar, they were compared to the magicians and enchanters who functioned in the power of the Babylonian gods. When the queen of Sheba came to visit Solomon she did so because she had heard about his fame 'and his relation to the name of the LORD' (1 Kgs 10:1). She recognised that Solomon's wisdom was a gift from Yahweh (1 Kgs 10:8-9): '"...Praise be to the LORD your God, who has delighted in you and placed you on the throne of Israel. Because of the LORD's eternal love for Israel, he has made you king, to maintain justice and righteousness."'

Biblical wisdom makes it clear that Yahweh's acts are wise and that gaining wisdom starts with 'the fear of the LORD', ie an attitude of awe and respect towards God (Prov 1:7; Ecc 12:13; Job 28:28). God is the one who gives wisdom.

The fact that wisdom literature is relevant to everyday-living can be seen clearly when we look at the theme of the wisdom books. It could be said that Proverbs focuses on the question of how to master life, Job on how to master pain and suffering, and Ecclesiastes on how to master death.

Other background information on the wisdom books, such as author, time of writing, etc will not be dealt with in this chapter because of a lack of space. The introductions to the wisdom books in the NIVSB are recommended for basic background information.

As far as the specific historical background to Proverbs is concerned, we do not possess much information to help us understand individual sayings in the book. Therefore, we will have to lean heavily on the literary context (Van Leeuwen 1988:2).

25.2 The literary context

When we look at the type of literature of the OT wisdom books, we find that the form of discourse is mainly poetry. An exception is the narrative at the beginning of Job (ch 1-2) and the end (Job 42:7-17). The main genre is wisdom literature. There are also various subgenres. In Proverbs, the most common subgenre is the proverb. In Job we find primarily the subgenre of dialogue. In Ecclesiastes we deal with monologue and we find a very fine example of allegory in 12:2-5.

If the issue of the structure of the book has been important in biblical interpretation in general, it is even more true in the case of the OT wisdom books.

For example, in the case of Job, much of the book takes the form of argument. Job's friends argue about what they believe to be the reason for his suffering. This takes the form of three cycles of dialogue (see figure 25.1) in which Job has to state his case against his friends' accusations (chs 3-27). A wisdom poem follows in ch 28 which some commentators believe to be the words of the author 'who sees the failure of the dispute as evidence of a lack of wisdom' (NIVSB 1987:717). Three monologues follow (chs 29-42:6), namely Job's, Elihu's and God's. In his monologue, Job turns to God to vindicate his innocence against the accusations brought by his friends. Elihu rebukes Job and brings another human perspective on the reason for suffering. God's monologue gives the divine perspective that Job does not suffer because of sin, but it does not present Job or the reader with an answer to the question of why Job has to suffer.

FIGURE 25.1

Structure of Job

A	Prologue (chs 1-2)
B	Three cycles of dialogues (chs 3-27)
C	Wisdom poem (ch 28)
B	Three monologues (29:1-42:6)
A	Epilogue (42:7-17)

So, where does one find the reason for suffering that has been debated so strongly in Job? The literary structure leads us to the answer. The reader has the background of the prologue (chs 1-2) that provides a heavenly perspective on Job's suffering. The whole book is framed by this prologue and the epilogue which presents us with Job's restoration. Both these passages are written in prose and it is only through them that the lengthy argument of the rest of the book is brought into perspective. Therefore, any attempt to make sense of Job without taking the literary context of the whole book into consideration would be futile.

Ecclesiastes has never been an easy book to interpret. The existence of tensions within the book has been recognised as a problem for interpretation from the earliest times. From the middle of the second century, some rabbis even questioned the canonicity of the book, mainly because of what they perceived to be the contradictions within it. An example of such a perceived contradiction is 2:2 where laughter and pleasure are called senseless and 8:15 where laughter and therefore pleasure are praised. This has led some commentators to think that the book consists of a number of separate pieces, while others have tried to identify different sources in the book.

Loader (1979) subjected Ecclesiastes to a literary analysis of its form and contents, and the relationship between the two. Loader's (1979:132) conclusion is that its 'form and contents fit each other in delicate detail as well as in general' and he (1979:133) sees Ecclesiastes as 'one of the most delicate and complex literary products of the ancient Near East'. He believes that the literary structure of the book is determined by what he calls 'polar structures'. The contradictions can be accounted for as intended ways of building these polar structures. (I am afraid that I would not do justice to his findings by trying to describe it in detail within the limitations of this chapter).

Loader (1986:7) states in his 'practical commentary' on Ecclesiastes that 'the style of the author is so consistently uniform, and the basic theme so consistently pursued, that there can be no question of different sources.' This research by Loader again proves the importance of dealing with the text as we have it in front of us. If we cannot find the structure, it doesn't mean it's not there, just that more research may be needed to unearth it!

When we turn to Proverbs we see that it starts with a short prologue stating its purpose and theme (1:1-7) and it ends with a longer epilogue (31:10-31). The epilogue is identifiable by its subject matter and its alphabetic form in Hebrew. The rest of the book is made up of seven main parts to which the NIVSB (1987:927) gives the following headings:

Part 1:	1:8-9:18	The Superiority of the Way of Wisdom
Part 2:	10:1-22:16	The Main Collection of Solomon's Proverbs
Part 3:	22:17-24:22	The Thirty Sayings of the Wise
Part 4:	24:23-34	Additional Sayings of the Wise
Part 5:	chs 25-29	Hezekiah's Collection of Solomon's Proverbs
Part 6:	ch 30	The Words of Agur
Part 7:	31:1-9	The Words of King Lemuel

Five of these parts are fairly well organised, while the second (10:1-22:16) and fifth (25-29) have traditionally been seen as lists of individual proverbs that are separate and unconnected. Whybray (1995) traces more recent research about the deliberate arrangement of the proverbs in Prov 10-29. Whybray (1994) also carried out a detailed investigation of the whole of parts 2 and 5 of Proverbs, and he (1995:60) finds that:

> There are few completely isolated proverbs, at least as far as the modern reader can discern; but even when no common theme can be found in a sequence of verses there are sometimes verbal or sound links between them.

Whybray (1995:61) sees an increasing number of discoveries of the deliberate arrangement of proverbs in recent research. This has been made possible by 'an increased perception of the part played by various formal features - assonance, alliteration, word pairs, word play, repetition and the like - and also by the development of a broader understanding of what is meant by theme.'

What are the implications of a deliberate arrangement of proverbs? It means that the original receivers would have perceived the related proverbs as such and would have interpreted them together. Each proverb is therefore understood in the context of the others in the same group with the result that the whole grouping presents a coherent message.

If groupings of sayings are identified and interpreted, it could add tremendously to our understanding of Proverbs, and in turn lead to more preaching and teaching from Proverbs in the church. Heim (1993) did an analysis and discovered that Prov 10:1-5 forms a coherent grouping. Seen from this perspective Heim (1993:203) summarises the content of these five verses as follows:

> The wise son who delights the father (v. 1) is the competent son who works in summer (v. 5), so becoming rich through his diligent hand (v. 4). He does not need wicked tricks in order to make a living, so his righteousness saves him from death in a (financial?) crises (v. 2) because Yahweh will fulfil his expectations (v. 3). The foolish son who is his mother's sorrow (v. 1) is the disgraceful son who sleeps during harvest time (v. 5), becomes poor because of his laziness (v. 4), and has to use tricks to gain wealth (v. 2). So the Lord will reject his desires (v. 3).

Heim (1993:203) continues to summarise the teaching and instruction in this passage as follows:

> Be a wise son and be diligent, because then you will not have to gain money through unrighteous practices, so your parents can be proud of you and the Lord will bless you!

This example illustrates that viewing a passage in Proverbs from a coherent perspective could be revolutionary to say the least.

In the next section (analysis of the passage), we will show how you can establish whether there is coherence between apparently unrelated proverbs and how to analyse such a group of sayings.

However, before we can do this, we need to find out how to identify a number of proverbs on which to perform detailed analysis for coherence. Let us take Prov 16:3 as an example: 'Commit to the LORD whatever you do, and your plans will succeed.' In order to identify a related pattern, one starts by reading the neighbouring proverbs while looking for a central theme (perhaps more than one), change of the central theme, repetitions, summarising phrases and sentences that introduce a new theme.

In 16:3 a central theme is "plans", ie things that a person wants to do. By scanning the preceding and following proverbs one comes across words and phrases with related meanings, eg 'plans of the heart' in v1 and 'a man plans his course' in v9. In v4-5 there are references to God's judgement. 'LORD' is repeatedly used in 16:1-9, in contrast to the preceding and following verses. In 16:10 a new subject 'king' is introduced and the following verses deal with this subject. It seems that the group of sayings ends at 16:9 and that the grouping starts with 16:1 as 15:33 appears to be a summary statement of the preceding proverbs.

It should be emphasised that this process of identifying a group of sayings is only a preliminary exercise, as the analysis of the identified sayings will show whether there is indeed coherence between them. The idea is that one studies the whole book and then identifies groupings. However, if this is not practical, the first step will be to identify a group of sayings through methods of observance, as just described.

FIGURE 25.2
Prov 16:1-9

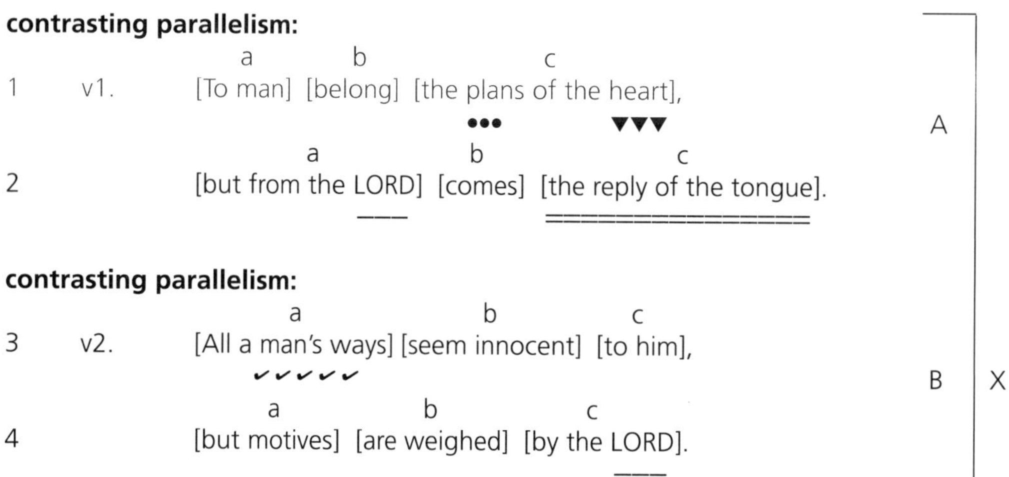

developing parallelism:

a b
5 v3. [Commit to the LORD] [whatever you do],
XXXXXXXXXX ——
b c
6 [and your plans] [will succeed]. C
••• ^^^^^

developing parallelism:

a b c
7 v4. [The LORD] [works out everything] [for his own ends] -
——
d e
8 [even the wicked] [for a day of disaster]. D
∪∪∪∪ ♦♦♦♦♦♦♦

developing parallelism:

a b c
9 v5. [The LORD] [detests] [all the proud of heart].
—— ∪∪∪∪∪∪∪
d
10 [Be sure of this: They will not go unpunished]. E Y
∪∪ ♦♦♦♦♦♦♦♦♦♦♦

developing parallelism:

a b
11 v6. [Through love and faithfulness] [sin is atoned for];
a c
12 [through the fear of the LORD] [a man avoids evil]. F
——

developing parallelism:

a b c
13 v7. [When a man's ways] [are pleasing] [to the LORD],
✓✓✓✓✓ XXXXXXXXXX ——
c d
14 [he] [makes even his enemies live at peace with him]. C*
— ^^^^^^^^^^^^^^^^^^^^^^

contrasting parallelism:

a b
15 v8. [Better a little] [with righteousness]
a b
16 [than much gain] [with injustice]. B* X*

contrasting parallelism:

a b c
17 v9. [In his heart] [a man] [plans his course]
▼▼▼ •••
b c
18 [but the LORD] [determines his steps]. A*
—— ==========

25.3 Analysis of the passage

25.3.1 Step 3.1: Write out the passage in smaller units

The NIV already provides us with lines. Each proverb consists of two lines. For the purpose of reference, we can number the lines as done in figure 25.2. Please refer to figure 25.2 when each one of the steps of exegesis is discussed.

25.3.2 Step 3.2: Mark the significant meaning indicators

The first two and last two proverbs display contrasting parallelism. The rest of the proverbs display developing parallelism. As the different types of parallelisms have been explained and shown in detail in chapters 17 and 18, it is not necessary to discuss the parallelisms in this passage.

The name LORD is found in all the proverbs, except in L15 and L16.

The word *'plans'* is found in L1, L6 and L17.

The word *'heart'* in L1 and L17. It refers to one's desires.

The phrase *'reply of the tongue'* (L2) is similar in meaning to *'determines his steps'* (L18). The translation of the GNB makes this clear with its translation of L2 as 'but God has the last word.'

The phrase *'man's ways'* in L3 and L13 refers to how a person lives.

'Succeed' in L6 and *'enemies live at peace with him'* in L14 both express being successful.

'Commit to the LORD' in L5 and *'pleasing to the LORD'* in L13 both refer to God's involvement in a person's actions. In the first case, one's actions are submitted to God and in the second case, one's actions are approved by God.

References to people whose actions are not acceptable to God are *'the wicked'* of L8, *'proud of heart'* of L9 and *'they'* (proud of heart) of L10.

'Day of disaster' in L8 and *'not go unpunished'* in L10 refer to the certainty of the LORD's judgement

25.3.3 Step 3.3: Explain words and phrases

To man belong the plans of the heart (L1): a person decides what to do out of his own desires

but from the LORD comes the reply of the tongue (L2): but God has the last word (GNB)

All a man's ways seem innocent to him (L3): a person may think that everything he does is right

but motives are weighed by the LORD (L4): but the LORD evaluates his motives

Commit to the LORD whatever you do (L5): submit everything that you do to God

and your plans will succeed (L6): and you will have success in what you do

The LORD works out everything for his own ends (L7): the LORD is ultimately in control of everything

even the wicked for a day of disaster (L8): God will bring disaster on the wicked

The LORD detests all the proud of heart (L9): The LORD hates people who are arrogant

Be sure of this: They will not go unpunished (L10): God will certainly punish the arrogant

Through love and faithfulness sin is atoned for (L11): God will forgive the sins of those who live in love and who are faithful. This line speaks about moral qualities that will accompany the behaviour of those who are forgiven.

through the fear of the LORD a man avoids evil (L12): if a person has reverence for the LORD he will refrain from sinning

When a man's ways are pleasing to the LORD (L13): if the LORD approves of how a person lives

he makes even his enemies live at peace with him (L14): the LORD makes it possible to live at peace with one's enemies

Better a little with righteousness (L15): it is better to earn a little honestly

than much gain with injustice (L16): than gaining a large income dishonestly

In his heart a man plans his course (L17): a person decides what to do out of his own desires

but the LORD determines his steps (L18): but the LORD decides what will happen to him

25.3.4 Step 3.4: Establish the meaning structure

The whole passage can be divided into three main meaning blocks, of which the first (X) and last (X*) express a similar meaning (see figure 25.2). The proverbs (A, B, C) of the first block are in a chiastic arrangement with the proverbs (C*, B*, A*) of the last block.

Let us first look at this chiastic arrangement of the proverbs in the first and last blocks. Proverbs A and A* are almost synonymous, as both express the fact that God controls a person's life. Proverb B states the moral requirement of pure motives and proverb B* the moral requirement of honesty (even if it means not having much). Proverb C states submission to God, and proverb C* states God's approval of a person's life as requirements for success.

The chiastic arrangement of the first three and last three proverbs is undergirded by the contrasting parallelism of the first two and last two proverbs that form a frame around the whole passage.

The middle block (Y) starts with the same theme that is found in A and A*, that God is in control (L7). This is then applied to judgment (L8-10) and salvation (L11-12). God will judge and he provides forgiveness and the ability to avoid evil.

25.3.5 Step 3.5: Conclude and summarise the message

The content of the passage can be summarised as follows:

> As God determines the direction of people's lives (A,A*), he gives success to those who submit their plans to him (C) and of whose lives he approves (C*). Their motives are pure (B) and they are honest (even if it means not having much) (B*). As God is in control of everything he will punish the wicked and arrogant (D,E), but he forgives the sin of those who are faithful and live according to his laws (love). Those who have reverence for God refrain from sinning (F).

In the context of the instructional character of Proverbs, this passage should be seen as an exhortation to live and plan in such a way as to have God's blessing in one's life. This could be summarised as follows:

> Son, if you want the success that the LORD gives, you must submit your plans and life to him for approval. Your motives must be pure and you must be honest (even if it means not having much). You must not be wicked and arrogant because the LORD will punish those who are like that. You must ask God to forgive your sins and be faithful to him, living according to his laws. Have reverence for God and this will keep you from sinning.

25.4 The broader biblical framework

We will first look at the contribution of the different wisdom books to the message of the whole Bible, and then at that of the passage in Proverbs we have exegeted.

The message of Job can be seen as a correction of the dogma that there is a direct correlation between a person's holiness and his prosperity. The implication of this dogma is that when a person suffers it is because of his sin (dogma of retribution). That is precisely what Job's friends believed was the cause for his suffering.

The message of Job is that the righteousness of the believer is of cardinal importance in the sight of God. Satan challenges the righteousness of Job, the believer, and states that Job's relationship with God is dependent on the prosperity with which God has blessed him. In other words, Job has been bribed to serve God. In his suffering, Job is tempted by his wife (2:9): ' "Are you still holding on to your integrity? Curse God and die!" ' Job's reply speaks of his commitment to God (2:10): '"You are talking like a foolish woman. Shall we accept good from God, and not trouble?"' Although Job never knew the reason for his suffering, he had to put his trust in God and live a life of true commitment in spite of his circumstances.

To summarise: The main contribution that Job makes to the overall message of the Bible is to show clearly that on earth there is no direct correlation between sin and suffering, also that the righteousness of the believer should not be assessed by whether he is prosperous or understands his circumstances.

The message of Ecclesiastes can also be seen as a correction of the dogma of retribution. In addition to this fundamental message, some commentators see a declaration of meaninglessness. The more the readers see the meaninglessness of life, the more they realise their own helplessness. 'We can view the Preacher as a painter who offers a realistic portrayal of human life as it looks apart from Christ.' (Loader 1986:15). If viewed like this, Ecclesiastes makes the contribution of preparing the reader of the Old Testament for the revelation of Jesus Christ as mediator.

However, other commentators who also see the theme of meaninglessness functioning in Ecclesiastes, nevertheless also see a positive message presented in the book, especially in the epilogue. If one sees Ecclesiastes from this perspective, the contribution of the book to the overall message of the Bible is mainly to correct the dogma of retribution and, by majoring on the meaninglessness of life, to emphasise the importance of fearing God, keeping his commandments and knowing that he will ultimately judge (12:13-14).

As we have already seen, the message of Proverbs is very practical. It gives clear instructions to fear the LORD and to live in a right relationship with him. It also gives general instructions on how to live morally, eg not to commit adultery (ch 5), to be hard working (10:5), to serve the king wisely (14:35) and to be honest in business dealings (16:11). In addition, it gives instructions on how to conduct oneself in different situations, for instance, during a meal with an important person (23:1-3). These wide applications of wisdom underline the fact that when one is in a relationship with Yahweh, it influences every part of your life. This is certainly in line with the message of the Pentateuch, that following God means loving and obeying him (Deut 6).

The sayings of Proverbs that make statements about certain effects and results (eg the righteous have abundant food (10:3), but the wicked will go hungry (13:25)), should not be seen as literal promises. To interpret it as such takes you into the dogma of retribution that Job and Ecclesiastes refute in very clear terms. They are general truths that hold true for many situations and are often the ideal. However, we live in a fallen world and therefore, these proverbs do not always work out as absolutes.

If we turn to the results of our exegesis of Prov 16:1-9, we see that this interpretation is not in conflict with the overall message of the Bible. Ps 37, for example, could almost be read as a commentary on Prov 16:1-9.

Absolutes for Old Testament	**Absolutes for Today**
Son, if you want the success that the LORD gives, you must submit your plans and life to him for approval.	Identical, eg Jas 4:7, 13-16
Your motives must be pure and you must be honest (even if it means not having much). You must not be wicked and arrogant because the LORD will punish those who are like that.	Identical, eg Jas 4:3-6
You must ask God to forgive your sins, be faithful to him and live according to his laws.	Identical, eg 1 Jn 1:5-10
Have reverence for God and that will keep you from sinning.	Identical, eg Acts 5:1-11

25.5 Hermeneutics

As we have looked at the specific contribution that the wisdom books make to the message of the Bible (25.4), it should be clear that most of it is applicable to our time.

Job is saying to people of our time, that they should not be enticed by those who teach a direct correlation between righteousness and material blessings, or between faith and miracles. Does it not have a tremendous message of encouragement to the Christian who is going through a time of suffering? The Preacher of **Ecclesiastes** is saying (in the context of the NT) to people of our time, that without Christ everything is meaningless. When we analyse the instructions of the **Proverbs** we find that many of them should be treated as applicable to our time. Either because they state truths about our relationship with God or because they give commands that are similar to the moral laws of the Pentateuch (see 22.5.3). Others are more cultural, such as how to behave yourself when having a meal with an important person, etc. However, although they are not absolutes, even most of these have a message for our time, similar to the civil laws of the Pentateuch (see 22.5.2).

We will now look at how the message of Prov 16:1-9 is applicable to our time. Although the Proverbs were originally intended as instruction to young men, it goes without saying, that the message is applicable to all.

CHAPTER TWENTY SIX

How to interpret the Prophets

Objectives

1. To be able to exegete OT prophetic books
2. To understand the process of hermeneutics for the OT prophetic books

Contents

STUDY TIP
Due to the poetic format and the employment of rich metaphorical language in most prophetic books, an understanding of the skills of analysing poetry is needed for exegeting the Prophets.

The exegesis and hermeneutics of the Old Testament prophetic books will be discussed and illustrated with a passage from the book Amos.

26.1 The communication situation

More prophets are mentioned in the Old Testament than just those dealt with in what is known as the Prophets, or the prophetic books. In the historical books of the Old Testament like Kings, Chronicles and Samuel, we read about prophets like Nathan (1 Sam 7,12) and Gad (1 Sam 22) of whom there are no specific books. In these historical books, except for a few passages, we don't find a great deal of any of the prophets' messages, whereas in the prophetic books (eg Amos, Isaiah and Jeremiah) we read the prophets' messages in detail.

The main activity of the prophet was not prediction of future events, but to call the Israelites back to follow God according to the principles and stipulations of the covenant. This means that the prophet had to be relevant to the religious, social, economic and political life of his time by speaking God's message in those particular circumstances. In the light of this message, the prophets did some times predict the future, mainly announcing God's judgment or deliverance. The call to repentance features prominently, and God's faithfulness in fulfilling his promises is a central theme. It is because of his covenant faithfulness that God will send the Messiah. A true prophet was called and appointed by God (Ex 3:4, 1 Sam 3:4, Is 6:8, Jer 1:4,5) and was God's spokesperson or messenger (Is 44:26; Hag 1:13).

The prophetic books of the Old Testament span a rather short period of approximately 300 years in the history of Israel, with Amos as the first prophetic book (c 760 BC) and Malachi (c 460 BC) as the last one. At this time Israel had already been divided into the Northern

Kingdom (Israel) and the Southern Kingdom (Judah). The fall of Israel took place in 722 BC and the fall of Jerusalem (Judah) in 586 BC. This period in the history of the two kingdoms was characterised by the rejection of God's covenant and rebellion against his laws. One king after another (especially in Israel) broke God's laws, and even worshipped the idols of the nations the Israelites were supposed to have destroyed because of their idolatry.

When we interpret the prophetic books, it is essential to understand the communication situation well. This includes understanding the theological background of the covenant by which the prophets evaluated the political, social, economic, moral and religious life of the Israelites (more about this in 26.4).

When reading the prophetic books, one realises that there is often little background information of the historical setting of the books. In this regard, the OT historical books can be very helpful, as they provide much of the historical setting in which the prophets functioned. For example, in Amos, the prophet spells out eight oracles against eight different nations. In order to understand them, one has to research the historical, social, economic and political setting of Israel, as well as of these nations (Aram, Philistia, Phoenicia, etc). As the ministry of Amos took place in the time of King Jeroboam II, it could be helpful to read 2 Kings 13-15. In addition to the text itself and OT historical books, dictionaries and other secondary literature could be used to get more information

It would be useful for you to draw up your own chronological chart showing dates of main events in Israelite history, the reigning kings and the periods in which the prophets ministered. This will help you to develop an integrated, more comprehensive understanding of each prophet and the whole OT. As well as God's specific and overall message and purpose regarding mankind. A time line could also be found in secondary literature.

We will now discuss the communication situation of Amos 6:1-14 to show which information is relevant for exegesis. Information has been drawn from the book of Amos itself, from the rest of the Bible (especially the OT historical books) and from biblical encyclopaedias and dictionaries.

Author:
Amos came from Judah (Southern Kingdom) to minister in Israel (Northern Kingdom). He came from a small town called Tekoa near Bethlehem/Jerusalem (Amos 1:1; 7:12). He was a shepherd and fig-grower (Amos 1:1, 7:14). The term used for shepherd suggests that he was not a mere shepherd but a sheep-owner or breeder, who had other shepherds under him. His general knowledge of history, and the excellence of his literary style (note the brilliant use of metaphorical features) show that he wasn't an ignorant man.

Original receiver:
Israel, the Northern Kingdom. However, Judah is also addressed (Amos 2:4-16).

Time:
Amos' ministry most probably took place around 760-750 BC. Jeroboam II is the king of Israel (793-753). Uzziah reigns in Judah (792-740). A great earthquake is mentioned in 1:1 two years after Amos started his ministry. This was apparently a major and long-remembered event which is archaeologically confirmed. Zech 14:5 may also refer to it.

Location:
Amos probably ministered for the most part in Bethel, Israel's main religious centre (Amos 7:10-13). Jacob named the place Bethel when he had a dream with a vision and the call of

God (Gen 28:10-22). The ark was also kept there during the time of the judges. It was Jeroboam who finally established Bethel as one of the centres of worship in the Northern Kingdom (1 Kgs 12:25-30). Amos had a confrontation there with Amaziah, the priest (Amos 7:10-17) who opposed Amos' uncompromising message. Amos was the first prophet whose prophecies were in writing.

Historical context:
It was a time of prosperity for Israel, which is seen in the economic revival with its commercial activities (8:5), flourishing agriculture (5:11) and architecture in extensive building projects (3:15). This was accompanied by a cultural revival with its new developments in music (6:5).

Unfortunately this period was also marked by social and economic injustice. The powerful rich gained wealth by exploiting the poor (8:4) and lived in excessive luxury (6:4-7). They sold those who could not pay their debts into slavery (2:6) and were totally corrupt (5:12). This was completely in contravention of the law (Ex 22:21-27; 23:6-9; Lev 19:35,36). It was a time of religious and moral decline. Idolatry was widely practised with the characteristics of drunkenness, violence, immorality, prostitution (2:7) and Canaanite Baal worship. As far as the worship of God was concerned, many thought they could please God and secure his protection with elaborate religious activities and costly offerings and rituals (4:4,5; 5:5).

This national prosperity led to a false sense of security. In spite of their sin, they did not realise the need to repent and do the will of God. Even 'the day of the Lord' that Amos presented as a time of judgment was viewed by the Israelites as a time when God would exalt them above the other nations.

Purpose:
Amos announces God's judgment on the people of Israel, because of their sin (unfaithfulness, disobedience, breaking of the covenant, pride). Through this he appealed to them to repent and to return to the Lord. There is hope of a future blessing for a faithful few.

26.2 The literary context

26.2.1 Step 2.1: Type of literature
In the prophets, poetry is frequently used since it was a good way of learning and remembering. Narrative is also used and to a lesser degree exposition. The genres of visions, parables and allegories are employed and to a lesser extent apocalyptic literature. Ezekiel 40-48 and Daniel 7-12 contain portions written in apocalyptic form. Because of the highly symbolic language used in this form, one must be careful not to misinterpret these prophecies (see chapter 30 for how to interpret the apocalyptic).

Oracles (speech used by prophets to prophesy usually starting and concluding with 'the LORD says') are the key genre used in prophetic books. We shall now discuss the three most common types of oracles; the lawsuit, song of lament and the promise.
In the lawsuit, God is portrayed imaginatively as the prosecuting attorney and judge in a court case against the defendant. The full lawsuit form contains four parts - orator, summons, accusation, verdict (punishment for disobedience in breaking the covenant). However, some of these elements may sometimes be implied rather than stated explicitly (eg Amos 1:3-2:16; Is 3:13-26; Hos 3:3-17; 4:1-19). The figurative style (comparison of God's judgment with a court case) is a dramatic and effective way of communicating to Israel and

Judah that they are going to be punished because of their disobedience, and that the punishment will be severe. The special structure of lawsuits helps get the message across. Figure 26.1 shows the parts of a lawsuit against Damascus as found in Amos 1:3-5.

FIGURE 26.1
The Lawsuit
Amos 1:3-5

This is what the LORD says:	Orator
"For three sins of Damascus, even for four, I will not turn back my wrath.	Summons
Because she threshed Gilead with sledges having iron teeth,	Accusation
I will send fire upon the house of Hazael that will consume the fortresses of Ben-Hadad. I will break down the gate of Damascus; I will destroy the king who is in the Valley of Aven and the one who holds the sceptre in Beth Eden. The people of Aram will go into exile to Kir,	Verdict (punishment)
says the LORD.	Orator

The second type of oracle is the song of lament or 'woe oracle'. 'Woe' was the word ancient Israelites cried out when facing disaster, death or in mourning at a funeral. Through the prophets, when God made predictions of approaching doom using the woe oracle, no Israelite could miss the significance of that word. The woe oracle usually first announces the doom, then gives the reason for the judgment and finally predicts the judgment. Figure 26.2 shows the parts of a woe oracle found in Amos 5:18-27.

FIGURE 26.2
Woe Oracle
Amos 5:18-27

Woe to you who long for the day of the LORD! Why do you long for the day of the LORD? That day will be darkness, not light. It will be as though a man fled from a lion only to meet a bear, as though he entered his house and rested his hand on the wall only to have a snake bite him. Will not the day of the LORD be darkness, not light - pitch-dark, without a ray of brightness?	Announcement of doom

"I hate, I despise your religious feasts; I cannot stand your assemblies. Even though you bring me burnt offerings and grain offerings, I will not accept them. Though you bring choice fellowship offerings, I will have no regard for them. Away with the noise of your songs! I will not listen to the music of your harps. But let justice roll on like a river, righteousness like a never-failing stream! "Did you bring me sacrifices and offerings for forty years in the desert, O house of Israel? You have lifted up the shrine of your king, the pedestal of your idols, the star of your god-- which you made for yourselves.	Reasons for judgment
Therefore I will send you into exile beyond Damascus,"	Prediction of judgment
says the LORD, whose name is God Almighty.	Orator

The third most common type of oracle is the promise or salvation oracle. The elements in this form are references to the future, mentioning of radical change and restoration, and announcement of blessing. Figure 26.3 shows the parts of a promise oracle as found in Amos 9:11-15.

FIGURE 26.3
Promise Oracle
Amos 9:11-15

"In that day I will restore David's fallen tent.	Future introduced
I will repair its broken places, restore its ruins, and build it as it used to be, so that they may possess the remnant of Edom and all the nations that bear my name,"	Radical change and restoration
declares the LORD, who will do these things.	Orator

"The days are coming," declares the LORD,	Orator
"when the reaper will be overtaken by the ploughman and the planter by the one treading grapes. New wine will drip from the mountains and flow from all the hills. I will bring back my exiled people Israel; they will rebuild the ruined cities and live in them. They will plant vineyards and drink their wine; they will make gardens and eat their fruit. I will plant Israel in their own land, never again to be uprooted from the land I have given them,"	Blessings
says the LORD your God.	Orator

26.2.2 Step 2.2: Position in the book

A good understanding of the overall structure is very helpful when analysing a passage in the prophetic books, because it shows the flow of the prophet's argument. It also indicates the smaller parts that should be analysed together. This is illustrated by looking at the structure of Amos.

De Waard and Smalley (1979:192) suggest a fascinating chiastic structure for Amos, shown in a slightly simplified form in figure 26.4. When we look at this structure, we see that 1:3 - 3:2 forms a unit (C). In that unit we find a series of oracles depicting God's judgment against different nations. After Amos had pronounced judgments on Israel's neighbours for various atrocities, setting a mood with judgments that Israel would naturally applaud, he suddenly and dramatically announces God's condemnation of his own two kingdoms for despising his laws. His listing of Israel's sins under the same form of indictment (lawsuit) used against the other nations, shockingly pictures Israel's sins alongside those of her pagan neighbours, and the oracle against Israel is significantly longer than the previous ones. These oracles were therefore skilfully employed to convey Israel's special guilt among the nations before God, because she stood in a special covenant relationship with him. In order to understand the significance and impact of the message, the entire unit (1:3-3:2) should be analysed as a whole, highlighting not the other nation's, but Israel's guilt. This illustrates the importance of exegeting passages together which belong together.

FIGURE 26.4
Structure of Amos

A Prologue: The prophet	1:1-2a
B The power of God to punish [hymn]	1:2b
C Israel's special guilt among the nations	1:3-3:2
D The prophet's role and commission	3:3-4:3
E Israel doesn't learn God's lessons	4:4-12
(B* The power of God to create [hymn])	4:13
F Lament for Israel	5:1-3
G Seek God and avoid destruction	5:4-6
H Warning to sinners	5:7
I The power of God to create [hymn]	5:8
J THE LORD IS HIS NAME	

I* The power of God to punish [hymn]	5:9
H* Warning to sinners and righteous	5:10-13
G* Seek good and obtain mercy	5:14-15
F* Lament for Israel	5:16-17
E* Israel relies on false security	5:18-6:14
D* The prophet's experiences	7:1-8:3
C* The punishment of Israel	8:4-9:4
B* The power of God to punish and create [hymn]	9:5-6
A* Epilogue: punishment and re-creation	9:7-15

De Waard and Smalley (1979:195) suggest that the overall structure can further be divided into three balanced parts, 1:1-5:3, 5:4-15 and 5:16-9:15. The basic structure of the third part is shown in figure 26.5 in slightly simplified form. The hymn (9:5-6) does not balance with anything in this specific part but balances in the overall structure as we have seen in figure 26.4.

FIGURE 26.5
Structure of Part 3 of Amos

ISRAEL'S GUILT AND PUNISHMENT: THE PROPHET'S INVOLVEMENT (5:16-9:15)

a Introduction: Lament for Israel	5:16-17
b Israel relies on false security	5:18-6:14
c The prophet's experiences: visions	7:1-9
d The prophet's role and commission	7:10-17
c* The prophet's experiences: visions	8:1-3
b* Punishment of Israel	8:4-9:4
(B* the power of God to punish and create [hymn]]	9:5-6
a* Epilogue: Punishment and re-creation of Israel	9:7-15

When reading through Amos for the first time, it may appear that the book is not always organised with a smooth, logical flow from one passage to the next. The reason is that the prophetic books contain many collections of spoken oracles that are not always presented in their original chronological sequence. For example, why does the meeting between Amaziah and Amos (7:10-17) come between two visions which seem to belong together (7:7-9 and 8:1-3)? In answering this, a good understanding of the structure is essential. If we look at the chiastic structure of the third part (figure 26.5) we can see that although the two visions were 'interrupted' by the meeting (d), they are actually kept together by the way in which they are balanced in the structure (c and c*).

In the context of the third part of Amos (figure 26.5), 5:18-6:14 is balanced by 8:4-9:4.

26.3 Analysis of the passage

Because Amos 6:1-14 is poetry it will be analysed accordingly.

FIGURE 26.6

similar parallelism: **metonomy:**

a b c d
1 [Woe] [to you] [who are complacent] [in Zion],
b c d
[and to you] [who feel secure] [on Mount Samaria],
sarcasm/ irony:
you notable men of the foremost nation,

to whom the people of Israel come!

developing parallelism:

a b
2 [Go to Calneh] [and look at it];
b c
[go from there] [to great Hamath],
d
[and then go down to Gath in Philistia].

similar parallelism: **rhetorical questions:**

a b
[Are they better off] [than your two kingdoms]?
a b
[Is their land] [larger than yours]?
personification:
3 You put off the evil day

and bring near a reign of terror.

A: Israel's sins of complacency and pride (trusting in her own strength) fill the whole land

similar parallelism:

a b
4 [You lie] [on beds inlaid with ivory]
a b
[and lounge] [on your couches].
a b
[You dine] [on choice lambs]
b
[and fattened calves].

similar parallelism: **simile:**

a b
5 [You strum away] [on your harps like David]
a b
[and improvise] [on musical instruments].
hyperbole:
6 You drink wine by the bowlful

and use the finest lotions,
contrast/ metonomy:
but you do not grieve over the ruin of Joseph.

B: Israel lives in excessive luxury and self-indulgence, ignoring the coming judgment

7 Therefore you will be among the first to go into exile;
your feasting and lounging will end.

C: Consequence is God's judgment of deportation

8 The Sovereign LORD has sworn by himself -
the LORD God Almighty declares:

Orator

similar parallelism: **metaphor:**

a b
"[I abhor] [the pride of Jacob]
a b
[and detest] [his fortresses];

similar parallelism:

a b
[I will deliver up] [the city]
b
[and everything in it]."

D: God hates Israel's self-confidence and pride

9 If ten men are left in one house, they too will die.
10 And if a relative who is to burn the bodies comes to carry
them out of the house and asks anyone still hiding there, "Is
anyone with you?" and he says, "No," then he will say,
"Hush! We must not mention the name of the LORD."

11 For the LORD has given the command,

similar parallelism:

a b c
[and he will smash] [the great house] [into pieces]
b c
[and the small house] [into bits].

C*: God's judgment: total destruction

rhetorical questions:

12 Do horses run on the rocky crags?
Does one plow there with oxen?

metaphor:

But you have turned justice into poison
and the fruit of righteousness into bitterness -

developing parallelism:

a b
13 [you who rejoice] [in the conquest of Lo Debar]
a b c
[and say], "[Did we not take Karnaim] [by our own strength]?"

B*: Israel's sin of perverted justice and pride

14 For the LORD God Almighty declares,

climactic parallelism:

a b c
"[I will stir up a nation] [against you], [O house of Israel],
d
[that will oppress you all the way]
e
[from Lebo Hamath to the valley of the Arabah]."

A*: God will judge Israel with total defeat and break her pride completely

Explain words and phrases:

VERSES 6:1-7

The introduction of the word 'woe' indicates the beginning of a new unit.
Woe: meaning "how terrible".

Zion: Metonymy (see 17.3.4) - Zion represents the southern kingdom of Judah. Amos prophesied primarily in the northern kingdom and this reference to Zion revealed a similar condition in Judah.

You notable men of the foremost nation: The rich ruling class in Israel. Through sarcasm, Amos is highlighting their pride and complacency. This final woe is directed at the nation's leaders. The influential men of the day considered Israel the most prominent among all nations, a position occupied only because of the temporary weaknesses of the surrounding nations.

Sarcasm and irony (meaning the opposite of what you say) are used in these verses. Amos talks about the men to whom the people of Israel come for justice and religious guidance.

Calneh/Hamath: Hamath, a city-state in the north of Syria (Aram). It was recovered by Jeroboam II (2 Kgs 14:28). Calneh, an unidentified place north of Hamath.

Gath: One of the five main cities in Philistine. Subdued by Uzziah, king of Judah (2 Chr 26:6).

Are they better off/ their land larger than yours?: Israel is complacent and proud, relying on her own strength. In verse 2 Amos is most likely quoting, in the form of rhetorical questions, the self-assured and proud statements of Israel's ruling class to highlight their pride. According to facts about the city-states mentioned, none was larger than Israel, which highlights that Amos used these rhetorical questions to emphasise the unlimited boasting of the prominent leaders of Israel.

You put off the evil day: Israel ignores the coming judgment, refusing to admit that it is coming.

bring near a reign of terror: means "because of the way you live, you bring the judgment of God closer".

lie/lounge - ivory/couches: The parallelism in v4 highlights their excessive luxury. Many of these expensive carving and inlays of ivory (1 Kgs 22:39) have been found in ruined palaces in Samaria and other cities.

wine by the bowlful/ finest lotion: Israel lives in self-indulgence and for its own pleasure.

but you do not grieve over the ruins of Joseph: Metonymy - the ruins of Joseph represents the nation Israel. 1) The rich in Israel do not care about the terrible judgement of God that is coming soon. 2) Possibly it could also refer to a lack of concern for the present moral state of Israel (including the oppressed poor).

VERSES 8-11

The Sovereign LORD has sworn by himself: The verdict of judgment is final; it will not be changed. God cannot swear by anyone greater than himself (Gen 22:16).

detest his fortresses: Strong emotive language is used to demonstrate that God hates Israel's reliance on her own strength and her arrogant and proud self-confidence.

who is to burn the bodies: The burning of the bodies underlines death in this eerie scene just after the judgment.

"Hush! We must not mention the name of the LORD": The person uttering these words seems afraid that if the name of the Lord is mentioned again, God might bring more destruction on them (cf Deut 5:11).

Verses 9-10 paint a picture of terrible destruction and death, and the last quotation communicates a deep reverence and fear of God, which stands in stark contrast to the self-reliance and pride of Israel. It is implied that God will break the pride of Israel.

great and small house: God's judgment will be total. This could refer to the rich and poor, therefore the whole of Israel, or possibly to the 'summer house' and the 'winter house' in Amos 3:15, which would more emphasise the destruction of wealth and luxury.

Note the theme of destruction right through verses 8-11.

VERSES 12-14
Do horses run on the rocky crags?: Rhetorical question. An illustration of something illogical, something going against the order of things.

Does one plough there with oxen?: Rhetorical question, echoing the previous one. It again illustrates the illogical and impossible. The function of the rhetorical questions (see 17.3.3) in this section is to force the readers to examine and change their wrong attitudes.

you have turned justice into poison/ and the fruit of righteousness into bitterness: Justice has been totally and utterly corrupted. Israel's perversion of justice goes completely against common sense - wrong has been made into right (metaphor).

conquest of Lo Debar/take Karnaim: Here Amos is stressing that the pride Israel takes in her own military strength is worth nothing before God. Israel's pride has resulted in self-deception.

oppress you/ from Lebo Hamath to the valley of the Arabah: The entire land will be occupied and defeated. Lebo Hamath, north of Syria (Aram) and Arabah, south of the Dead Sea. It climactically stresses the total defeat and oppression of Israel that is coming.

Conclude and summarise the message:

1. God hates Israel's pride and total reliance on their own strength, which leads to false security and self-deception. He warns that he will judge these sins by destroying the entire land. (A, A*)

2. God condemns Israel's excessive luxury, self-gratification, utter self-indulgence as well as their perverted justice. (B, B*)

3. Israel must never ignore God if he warns of judgment. They must repent, since it is their sins that bring God's judgment on them. The persistence in sin (and transgression of the covenant) results in God applying the covenant curses, where the final judgment is total destruction of their entire land as well as exile. (C, C*)

4. God warns that he hates pride and will humble Israel when she is proud. (D)

26.4 The broader biblical framework

The message of the prophets was not a new message, as they applied the principles of the covenant to the specific circumstances of their time. They did this by:

- declaring God's hatred of Israel's idolatry (Jer 2:23-25), empty ritualistic worship (Amos 5:21-27), social injustice (Amos 2:6-8; 4:1; 5:10-13; 8:4-6) and immorality.
- announcing the punishment for Israel's rebellion (curse). In doing so they functioned as watchmen who warned the people of God's coming judgement (Jer 6:17; Ezek 3:17).
- a call to repentance, to avoid judgment (Amos 5:4; 6:14).

Therefore, one must always bear in mind that the prophets did not invent the blessings and curses they announced, but only worded these blessings and curses in a captivating way as they were inspired to do so.

The Messianic prophecies uttered by the prophets were also not new. The prophets perhaps wrote about the life and role of the Messiah in more detail (eg Is 42, 49, 50 and 53), but the belief of a Messiah originated in Gen 3:15, and also clearly from the law (Deut 18:18).

The prophets had a future hope in spite of Israel's failure, because of their awareness that God is faithful to his promises given to Abraham (Gen 12:1-3), David (2 Sam 7) and his people:

- the New Covenant for the returning and faithful remnant (Hos 1:10) which includes the Gentiles, who 'call on the name of the Lord', with the accompanying blessings (Amos 9:13-15).
- the coming Messiah, who will reign eternally as King of a new kingdom (Amos 9:11-15).
- the age to come with a new heaven and earth (Is 65:17; 66:22).

We shall now look specifically at the message of Amos 6:1-14 in the wider biblical and theological context.

God's hatred of pride and arrogant self-confidence in man is a theme that runs throughout the Bible: 1 Sam 15:23; Jer 17:5-8; Jas 4:6.

Wealth and health is seen as part of the covenant blessing from God in the OT (Deut 6:10-12; 12:1-10). Alongside this, however, are detailed instructions on how to care for the poor, which command the rich to be generous (Deut 15:7-11; 24:12-13,17; Ex 22:26-27). In the NT, Jesus promises that God will care for our basic needs, Mt 6:25-34, but also clearly warns against love of wealth (Mt 6:24, Mk 10:17-31 and 1 Tim 6:6-10). The themes of contentment and self-denial (Phil 2:1-11) clearly oppose self-indulgence, and to care for and be generous towards the poor is clearly taught in the NT (Acts 6:1-7; Gal 2:10). In the OT there are clear commandments to deal justly (Ex 23:6) as Jesus also states in the NT (Lk 11:42).

God's judgment of total destruction of the land and exile is clearly set out in the curses in Deut 28. God eventually applied the curses of the covenant because of Israel's persistent sin. The NT also warns that Christians who persist in sin will be disciplined by God in order to purify their lives (Heb 12:4-11; Rev 2:20-23). God has commanded his church to exercise discipline to purify the church from sin (1 Cor 5:1-13). The NT also warns against apostasy, where the consequence is God's judgment (Heb 6:4-6). Then there is clearly the final day of judgment when all people will be judged.

26.5 Hermeneutics

If the task of exegesis is to place the prophets within their own historical context and to hear what God was saying to Israel through them, then the task of hermeneutics is to discover God's Word to us through them. Before we discuss this process, we shall first look at the chronological fulfilment of the prophetic predictions.

The prophets predicted the future, although this was not their primary task. Generally speaking, the future which they predicted is already past for us. They spoke of the coming judgment or salvation in the relatively immediate future, not our own future. Therefore to see their prophecies fulfilled, we must look back upon times that for them were still future, but for us are past. For example, there are various oracles in Amos concerning the judgment of different nations surrounding Israel, as well as of Israel and Judah. The fulfilment of some of these oracles came within decades of when the prophecies were delivered (in 722 BC the Northern Kingdom fell, not even 30 years after Amos' prophecies). Indeed, most of the prophecies concerned Old Testament times and events.

We should also note that some of the prophecies of the near future were set against the background of the great eschatological future (God's final plan for human history). This means that as prophecies referred to the near future, they were fulfilled relatively soon. Where they referred to the eschatological future, they were only fulfilled, for example in Christ or will be fulfilled when Christ comes again. An example of this is Amos 9:11-15 where we read of Israel's restoration. It was fulfilled in the relatively near future, when the first group of Israelites returned under Zerubbabel (538 BC), the second group in 458 BC under Ezra, and the last group returning in 432 BC, under Nehemiah. The eschatological fulfilment comes in the time of the New Testament, with Christ as King and in him there is restoration for both Jew and Gentile (Acts 15, Rom 9-12).

As stated in Chapter 22, when one arrives at the message to the original receivers through the process of exegesis, the application to the target group in our time needs to be seen in the light of the redemptive work of Christ. The transfer process from the Old Testament prophetic books needs to be done in the light of what Christ achieved on the cross; principles that are stated explicitly in the New Covenant itself. Most of the sins that the prophets addressed in Israel's life in the Old Covenant, are addressed in the New Covenant as well.

The hermeneutics of the message of Amos 6:1-14 can be found at the end of this chapter. We shall now look at the principle of God's judgment found in this passage, to see why and how it is applicable to our time.
Throughout the Bible we see God evaluating Israel according to his covenant conditions with them. This leads to either earthly blessings or punishment (Deut 28). An example of earthly blessing is king Hezekiah in Is 37 experiencing God's help for him and his nation against the Assyrians. An example of punishment is the exile of Israel announced by Amos.

When we apply the absolutes of God's judgment in the light of the NT we see that:

a) All people will be judged when Christ comes (Mk 8:38, 1 Cor 4:5; 2 Thes 1:5-10), both the living and the dead (Acts 10:42), both Christian and non-Christian (Rom 14:10-12). This final judgment will reveal who truly belongs to Christ and who does not. By the choices people make and by the way in which they respond when confronted by Christ and his gospel, they bring judgment on themselves (Jn 3:19-20; Mt 10:32-33; Rom 1:18-32).

b) We need to understand Christ's atonement for sin to understand God's judgment for disobedience. Through his atonement, Christ has turned the wrath of God and his judgment away from sinners (1 Thes 1:10; 5:9).

c) It is clearly stated in Mt 18:15-20 that people are called not only to receive forgiveness, but to live a holy life. The purpose of God's warnings and discipline in the church is that honour would be given to Christ by its members. True discipline is therefore an expression of Christian concern and encourages real distinction between the church and the world.

Absolutes for Old Testament	Absolutes for Today
1. God hates Israel's pride and total reliance on their own strength, which leads to false security and self-deception. He warns that he will judge these sins by destroying the entire land. (A, A*)	1. God hates it when his church is proud and totally reliant on it's own strength, which leads to false security and self-deception. God warns that he will judge these sins. (1 Cor 4:6-7, 18-21; 1 Cor 5:2; Rom 12:16-20)
2. God condemns Israel's excessive luxury, self-gratification, self-indulgence as well as their perverted justice. (B, B*)	2. God condemns his church if they live in excessive luxury, gratification and self-indulgence. God condemns the perversion of justice. (2 Cor 8; Mk 12:41-43; Lk 12:13-21)
3. Israel must never ignore God if he warns of judgment. They must repent, since it is their sins that bring God's judgment on them. The persistence of sin (and transgression of the covenant) results in God applying the covenant curses, where the final judgment is total destruction of their entire land as well as exile. (C, C*)	3. Christians must never ignore the final day of judgment, but live responsibly and in gratitude for Christ's salvation. Therefore they must respond to any conviction of sin by repenting. (Acts 17:30-31; Rom 6:1-2; Heb 12:1-12)
4. God warns that he hates pride and will humble Israel when she is proud. (D)	4. God warns and humbles the proud. (Rom 14:10-12)

CHAPTER TWENTY SEVEN

How to interpret the Gospels

Objectives

1. To be able to exegete the Gospels
2. To understand the contribution of the Gospels to the broader biblical message
3. To understand the process of hermeneutics for the Gospels

Contents

STUDY TIP
To interpret the Gospels one needs the skills of exegesis for exposition/exhortation as well as narrative.

The main message of the Gospels is 'God with us' (Mt 1:23) - the glorious message that God chose to become a human being, to leave the glory of heaven, to experience humanity in its best and worst forms, to die for us so that we can be free from sin, to return to heaven to prepare a place for us so that we can be with Him forever, and imparting his power to us through his Holy Spirit so that we can live as his witnesses. No wonder that Satan and the world do their best to destroy the validity of the truth of the Gospels!

27.1 The communication situation

We need to differentiate between the Synoptic Gospels and the Gospel of John. Matthew, Mark and Luke are known as the Synoptic Gospels because if one compares them, they are noticeably similar in terms of the language they use, the material they cover and the order in which events and sayings of Jesus are arranged. In comparison, John's Gospel is different in many of these areas. In this chapter, only the Synoptic Gospels will be discussed.

Many arguments, theories and questions have been raised in terms of the Synoptic Gospels - questions such as, did the authors use a common source, were they inter-dependant on one another, and so on. Many books have been written trying to resolve the so-called synoptic problem. One of the theories is that two major sources - the Gospel of Mark and a hypothetical document called 'Q' (*Quelle* - German for 'source') - were used by Matthew and Luke as sources for most of the content included in their Gospels. One should remember that these are only theories and the following should be borne in mind:

- The Gospels were written to announce Christ. Although all of what he said and did is written down in a time line, the primary purpose of the Gospels is not historical sequence, but proclamation. The history merely serves as a bearer for the proclamation.
- We must also keep in mind that each author had a specific point of view, target group and purpose for writing his Gospel, eg:

Matthew portrays Jesus as the Messiah, the Old Testament prophesies being fulfilled in him. He also emphasises how Jesus differs in his approach to the law from the Pharisees and experts in the law.

Mark describes Jesus as the Son of God (see Mk 1:1; 15:39b), mighty in word and deed, but who paradoxically must suffer as the servant of God.

Luke also shows Jesus as the Son of God, but places emphasis on the fact that Jesus is a universal Redeemer, for all peoples, not only for the Jews. We must bear in mind that Luke was a Gentile (said to be from Antioch in Syria) and consequently connects the history of Jesus with the broader world history. He also shows Jesus as compassionate especially to socially unacceptable people. Whereas Matthew and Mark probably had a broad target group in mind, Luke very definitely writes to prove to someone called Theophilus that the story of Jesus is true (Lk 1:1-4). Luke frequently mentions the work of the Holy Spirit in his Gospel which forms a strong link with his book of Acts.

In the light of the specific emphasis of each author, each Gospel should be read as an individual book and interpreted as such.

The question also often arises: How do we know that Matthew, Mark and John were really the authors of the books that bear their names? In the case of Matthew and Luke there is external evidence from the Church fathers that these writers were truly the authors of the Gospels. In the case of Mark, the Church father Papias said that Mark was the apostle Peter's expositor and carefully wrote down everything that Jesus said and did. 1 Pet 5:13 also shows that there was a close relationship between Peter and Mark. There is also evidence in the Gospels themselves indicating who the authors are:

Matthew: He was a Jew and his Gospel clearly shows that the author was of Jewish descent - typical Jewish customs and idioms are not explained (15:2; 23:5; 23:24); emphasis on Jesus' commission to Israel (10:5,23; 15:24); emphasis on Jesus' words concerning the law (5:19; 23:2).

Mark: Jewish customs are explained in a way which suggests that they were unfamiliar to the recipients; there are some Latin terms which suggest that this Gospel originated in a part of the Roman empire where Latin was spoken (15:16); Mk 15:21 mentions Rufus, as does Rom 16:13.

Luke: We know that Luke was a doctor and there is medical interest shown in this Gospel, eg healings are described in greater detail. In the original Greek text, the correct medical terms are used in certain instances eg 'convulsions' in 9:39. Mk 5:25 describes the failure of the doctors to heal a woman whereas Lk 8:43 does not mention the doctors.

Many excellent books have been written in which the socio-political and religious climate of the world into which Jesus was born is described, eg Bruce (1982), Parker (1982) and Harrison (1970). The NIV Study Bible also has a helpful section. Suffice it to say that Israel was under the dominion of a cruel Roman empire and the Jews were constantly rebelling - this often resulted in the slaughter of many by the Romans and the poor ordinary Jewish citizens were weighed down by the legalistic laws which the Jewish religious leaders had thought up. How true are the words written on a poster - We did not enter his light, he came crashing into our darkness. The world into which Jesus entered was very dark indeed. One positive element however, was the great expectation amongst the Jews for a coming Messiah. For 400 years God had not spoken to his people - there had been no prophets - but now people were eagerly waiting for someone sent from God who would free them from their oppression. Unfortunately their expectations and God's plan did not have much in common, with the inevitable result that only some recognised Jesus as the Messiah.

There are certain concepts which are often repeated in the Gospels and it is important to know what they mean as this will help us in our interpretation. They are 'Messiah', 'Son of God', 'Son of Man', 'the Suffering Servant' theme and the 'Kingdom of God' (or 'Heaven' as found in the Gospel of Matthew). These concepts are discussed in some detail in Appendix B.

27.2 The literary context

The form of discourse used in the Synoptic Gospels is prose with a few poetic parts, which are mainly quotations from the Prophets. The major discourse type is narrative containing many embedded passages of differing genres. (It would be very helpful to review 19.2 at this point.) The genres which can be found in the Gospels are allegory, as in the story of the sower (Mt 13:3-23), dramatic history where the stories of Jesus' birth and death are told (eg Lk 1:26-45; Mk 15), parables (Mt 13) and conversation (Jn 3). Many of the conversations which take place are actually situations where Jesus is asked a question and then his answer becomes a teaching session. While narrative is non-prescriptive (see 19.1), in the Gospels we find embedded portions of exposition and exhortation such as the sermon on the mount (Mt 5:1-7:29) where direct prescription is given. In this situation no conversation takes place - Jesus is giving certain instructions to those who will listen. The important thing to remember is that narrative is the vehicle in which the Gospels are driven, but when doing exegesis of a particular passage, we need to ask the following question: is this exposition/exhortation, a parable, dramatic history (be it a miracle or an incident in the life of someone), allegory or conversation? Only when we have answered this question, can we decide which is the best method for exegeting a particular passage.

When exegeting, it is also helpful to remember the following when working on passages which contain miracles and parables:

Miracles

- In the Gospels, miracles do not exist for their own sake, but as part of Jesus' teaching/message or to solve the problems of others.
- The purpose of miracles can helpfully be compared to parables. To those who are willing to trust God, they are a vehicle of revelation. But to those whose minds are closed, not even a miracle will bring understanding (Jn 10:25-26; 12:37).
- Faith in Christ and repentance are often keys to experiencing/ understanding miracles (and parables).

In the Gospels, the type of miracles covered are: driving out of demons, healing of various illnesses, the raising of the dead, miracles affecting nature (eg Jesus calming the storm).

Parables

- They usually contain a single truth. They are a means of jolting people into decision-making. Jesus used familiar imagery to bring new and unfamiliar insights to people.
- At times, allegory is also used in parables, like the parable of the sower. Allegories are usually more elaborate stories in which almost all the details are symbols of something else. However, a single truth is still communicated through the various symbols. In the case of the sower (Mt 13:1-23) the single truth is that we have to respond to the Gospel in the correct way. Each one of the parables could be placed on a continuum (see figure 27.1) to the extent that they use allegory or not.

FIGURE 27.1

parable ———————————————— allegory

- The meaning of the parable is not always obvious (Mt 13:10-13). John Drane (1986:134) makes the following point: 'Though they (parables) do not require great mental effort, a certain degree of commitment is called for in order to understand what Jesus is saying'.
- We don't always know the exact communication situation in which the parables were told.
- Different authors have the same parable in a different setting because they want to emphasise a different point.
- It is quite possible that Jesus told his parables more than once.
- Remember that the original receivers of the Gospels were Christians, whereas Jesus told his parables to a mainly Jewish audience. We need to ask whether this affects their interpretation in any way.

A very helpful book on the interpretation of parables and the Middle-Eastern way of thinking is 'Poet and Peasant' by Kenneth E. Bailey (1980).

As in the case of other Bible books, structure can also be found in the Gospels. The structures given below have been found to be helpful when exegeting passages and are given as examples - not as the final word on each Gospel structure!

The structure of Matthew:
There are five discourses in Matthew. Stories and discourses follow one another in a chiastic arrangement, around the central theme of the kingdom of heaven.

A	1-4	Narrative	Genealogy, birth, baptism, temptation
B	5-7	Discourse	Sermon on the mount
C	8-9	Narrative	10 miracles - Jesus' authority in action
D	10	Discourse	Sending out of the 12
E	11-12	Narrative	Jesus rejected by the Jews
F	13	Discourse	Kingdom parables
E*	14-17	Narrative	Disciples accept Jesus' authority
D*	18	Discourse	Authority and forgiveness in the church
C*	19-22	Narrative	Authority and invitations
B*	23-25	Discourse	Judgment and coming of the Kingdom
A*	26-28	Narrative	Passion, death and resurrection

Note the ending of the discourses:
7:28 When Jesus had finished saying ...
11:1 After Jesus had finished instructing ...
13:53 When Jesus had finished these parables ...
19:1 When Jesus had finished saying ...
26:1 When Jesus had finished saying all ...

The structure of Mark:
The literary form of Mark is essentially narrative and has the following sections:

Introduction	1:1-15
Exposition	1:16-14:42
Ending	14:43-16:8

This Gospel traces Jesus' life in a line from Galilee to Jerusalem. From ministry to resurrection with the confession of Jesus as Messiah as the turning point of the narrative (see figure 27.2).

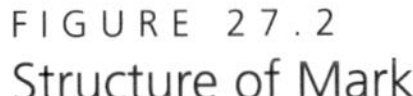
FIGURE 27.2
Structure of Mark

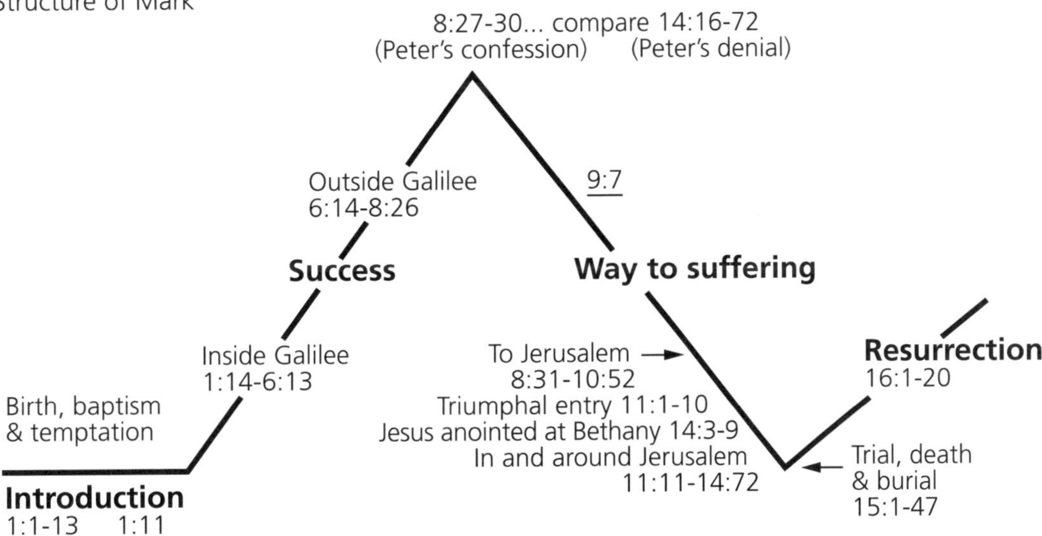

The underlined verses indicate those parts where Jesus is identified as God's Son, along with Mk 14:61-62 and 15:39.

The structure of Luke:
As with Matthew, there is also a type of chiastic structure to be found in Luke, with the turning point, Peter's confession of Jesus as Messiah (9:18-36):

A	1:1-4	Introduction - certainty of salvation
B	1:5-4:13	Birth, baptism, temptation
C	4:14-9:17	Narrative - words and deeds of Jesus, lots of miracles, few parables
D	9:18-36	MESSIAH - PETER'S CONFESSION
C'	9:37-21:36	Narrative - words and deeds of Jesus, lots of parables, few miracles
B'	21:37-23:56	Passion of Christ, betrayal, trial and crucifixion.
A'	24:1-53	Resurrection - ascension

Luke also uses parallelism at times, such as in the events concerning the births of John the Baptist and Jesus (Gooding 1987:71).

JOHN THE BAPTIST		JESUS
1:5-7	Parents introduced	1:26-27
1:8-11	Angel	1:28
1:12	Zacharia/ Mary upset	1:29
1:18	Zacharia doubts/ Mary believes	1:34
1:19-20	Angel's reaction	1:35-37
1:24-25	Mothers' reaction	1:38
Mothers meet 1:39-56		
1:57	Mothers give birth	2:1-7
1:58	Joy about birth	2:8-20
1:65-66	Reaction to birth	2:17-18
1:59-64	Circumcision and naming	2:21-24
1:67-79	Praise	2:25-38
1:80a	Child grows up	2:39-40
1:80b	Abode	2:41-52

27.3 Analysis of the passage

The important thing to remember when analysing the Gospels, is that one must analyse according to the genre of the specific passage. For example, when analysing dramatic history such as the crucifixion, one uses the method of narrative analysis. In the two examples exegeted below (see 27.6 and 27.7), conversation and a parable are present in the good Samaritan whereas conversation and exposition/exhortation are found in Peter's confession of Christ. Consequently, the two passages will be analysed using different methods.

27.4 The broader biblical framework

The Gospels form an important connection between the Old and New Testament. Many of the prophets pointed to the coming of Christ and the Gospels often refer to them and to other Old Testament authors (Mt 4:15-16; 8:17; Mk 1:2). Jesus also said that he did not come to abolish the Law and the Prophets but to fulfil them (Mt 5:17). The New Testament then goes on to build on that which Jesus taught, lived and achieved for us. (Rom 3:21-26; Phil 2:5-11). All of the principles which are found in the Gospels are reiterated in one or more places in the Bible.

27.5 Hermeneutics

Jesus introduced a new and better covenant. So most of what he taught is directly applicable to us living as Christians today. Some of Jesus' teaching (eg his more prophetic statements such as the destruction of Jerusalem), only came to have meaning in later times. Also, Paul in particular has helped us to understand more fully some of Jesus' teaching, as he repeats or explains what Jesus said or meant, (Rom 2:1-4; 7:1-3). The book of James also has many passages which relate directly to teaching found in the Gospels, (Jas 1:19-20; 2:5).

27.6 Exegesis and hermeneutics of The Good Samaritan

FIGURE 27.3
The Good Samaritan
Luke 10:25-37

25] On one occasion an expert in the law stood up to test Jesus. "Teacher," he asked, "what must I do to inherit eternal life? "	a	setting question
26] "What is written in the Law?" he replied. "How do you read it?"	b/c	answer/question
27] He answered: " 'Love the Lord your God with all your heart and with all your soul and with all your strength and with all your mind'; and, 'Love your neighbour as yourself.' "	d	answer
28] "You have answered correctly," Jesus replied. "Do this and you will live."	e	command
29] But he wanted to justify himself, so he asked Jesus, "And who is my neighbour?"	a	question
30] In reply Jesus said: "A man was going down from Jerusalem to Jericho, when he fell into the hands of robbers. They stripped him of his clothes, beat him and went away, leaving him half-dead. 31] A priest happened to be going down the same road, and when he saw the man, he passed by on the other side. 32] So too, a Levite, when he came to the place and saw him, passed by on the other side. 33] But a Samaritan, as he travelled, came where the man was; and when he saw him, he took pity on him. 34] He went to him and bandaged his wounds, pouring on oil and wine. Then he put the man on his own donkey, brought him to an inn and took care of him. 35] The next day he took out two silver coins and gave them to the innkeeper. 'Look after him,' he said, 'and when I return, I will reimburse you for any extra expense you may have.'	b	answer in the form of a parable
36] "Which of these three do you think was a neighbour to the man who fell into the hands of robbers?"	c	question
37] The expert in the law replied, "The one who had mercy on him."	d	answer
Jesus told him, "Go and do likewise."	e	command

Step 1: Research the communication situation
When researching the communication situation, one must always take the author of the Gospel into account and see if this makes any contribution to the context. For example, Luke

is the only one who tells the story of the good Samaritan and, as a Gentile author, his Gospel is the most universal of all. Thus one understands why he is the only one to tell this story.

Other significant information on the communication context of Luke has been discussed in 27.1.

Step 2: Literary context
Genre: Narrative with some conversation and an embedded parable.

Position in the book: This incident takes place shortly after Jesus 'resolutely set out for Jerusalem' (Lk 9:51), knowing that he must endure suffering and death. As the expert in the law in this passage is Jewish, Jesus is probably already in Judea. The position of the passage does not seem to have any significance.

Step 3: Analysis of the passage

Step 3.1: Write out the passage in smaller units
It is not necessary to write this passage out as it is not so complex and the layout in the NIV translation is helpful for analysing the passage.

Step 3.2: Mark the significant meaning indicators
In v25a we find the setting for the passage (see also communication situation above). V25b has the expert asking a question which Jesus answers in the form of a question ("What is written in the Law") in v26a. Jesus then asks another question in v26b to which the expert replies (v27). Jesus then gives the expert a command to obey in v28. Therefore, we have a structure looking like this (see figure 27.3):

	25a:	setting
a	25b:	question (Expert)
b	26a:	answer in the form of a question (Jesus)
c	26b:	question (Jesus)
d	27:	answer (Expert)
e	28:	command (Jesus)

In v29 we again have the expert asking a question to which Jesus replies (in v30-35) by telling a parable. At the end of the parable Jesus asks a question (v36) and the expert answers in v37a. Jesus again gives the expert a command. The structure looks like this:

a	29:	question (Expert)
b	30-35:	answer in the form of a parable (Jesus)
c	36:	question (Jesus)
d	37a:	answer (Expert)
e	37b:	command (Jesus)

So, we've found a parallel structure in this passage. The structure itself emphasises the message, as we will see later on.

Step 3.3: Explain words and phrases
v25: on one occasion: This introduces a new episode.

expert in the law: A term for the so-called teachers of the law, most of whom were Pharisees. As this expert addresses Jesus as 'Teacher', one wonders if there is sarcasm in his use of the title. David Gooding (1988:231) says that the 'Pharisees and lawyers had not deliberately set out to become perverse and wicked, but moral judgment had become so distorted by religious pride and mere academic theology that they had become perverse'.

stood up: It appears that the people are sitting around Jesus, perhaps for a teaching session, when the expert stands up. Bailey (1980:35) refers to the Arabic commentator Ibrahim Sa'id, who observes that there is a basic contradiction in the actions of the expert in the law. While standing up was a social courtesy and a sign of respect, the purpose was 'to test him'. This is an inner deception coming from a corrupt heart.

test: Taking issue with Jesus or wanting to see what kind of teacher he is. This kind of testing took place at other times as well (Mt 22:15-22; Mt 22:35). The GNB translates this as 'to trap'.

what must I do: The wrong notion that eternal life could be obtained by one's own efforts.

inherit eternal life: This was synonymous with entering the kingdom of God and being saved (NIVSB footnote Mt 19:16).

v26 law: This is a reference to the law of Moses (the Pentateuch) and points to the covenant relationship that believing Jews had with God. Jesus understood this but the experts in the law and the Pharisees had added to this their own oral law with its legalism. The oral law consisted of the man-made rules of the teachers of the law which they then passed down to the people.

v27: The expert answers by quoting Deut 6:5 and Lev 18:5. The point made by this law is that total devotion to God is required.

heart: This was the governing centre of a person in Hebrew thinking.

heart, soul, strength, mind: Man in his totality

neighbour: This refers to one's fellow-man, not only Jews. The law had included foreigners from the time it was given to Moses (Num 15:13-16; Lev 19:33-34).

v28 live: In this context it refers to eternal life. 'The law was the way of life for the redeemed, not a way of salvation for the lost (NIVSB footnote on Lev 18:5).

v29 justify: Two possibilities, ie to prove himself an expert or to justify his lack of love for certain people. The parallel structure of the passage seems to indicate the latter option.

v30 down from Jerusalem to Jericho: A distance of 17 miles and a descent from 2500 feet above sea level to 800 feet below sea level.

v31 priest: Descended from Aaron (tribe of Levi).

Levite: Also descended from Levi but not allowed to be priests. They did other tasks in the temple.

Samaritan: A mixed-blood race resulting from the intermarriage of two groups; the Israelites who were left behind when the people of the northern kingdom were taken away into exile by the Assyrians, and the Gentiles who the Assyrians placed in Israel. There was bitter enmity between the Jews and the Samaritans in the days of Jesus. The fact that Jesus commends an 'enemy' of the Jews seems to support the fact that the expert wanted to justify his lack of love for certain people.

v34 oil and wine: A medical remedy known to the Greek and Jewish world.

v35 silver coins: Two days' wages.

v36: In v29 the expert asked 'who is my neighbour?' Now Jesus turns this around by asking who was a neighbour to the robbed man. In other words, he asks the expert 'are you a neighbour to those around you?'

v37 the one: The expert doesn't even use the word Samaritan

go and do: A command

Step 3.4: Establish the meaning structure
Where narrative is found in the Gospels, one will need to establish the meaning structure as discussed in 20.7. There is no hidden meaning that needs to be discovered. The interpretation of the parable is straight forward - be willing to serve those who are in need. Jesus commands the expert to do this. We don't know whether he obeyed. The question is, will we?

Step 3.5: Conclude and summarise the message
1. Those who live in a covenant relationship with God and in obedience to him, will receive eternal life.
2. Jesus commands to love God and others with total commitment.
3. Jesus commands that love for others should be made practical by caring sacrificially for anyone in need, without making excuses or excluding anyone.

Step 4: Broader biblical and theological framework
The message which is contained in this passage will be found in many other parts of the Bible, and the three points made above can now be linked with the following passages:
1. Rom 6:20-23; Gal 2:20-21; 3:14.
2. Gal 5:13-14; Mk 12:28-34.
3. Mt 5:43-48; Lk 6:27-36; 1 Cor 13; Rom 12:9-21.

Hermeneutics
We are now in a covenant relationship with God through the death of Jesus on the cross. All the points mentioned above are relevant for all Christians of all times.

27.7 Exegesis and hermeneutics of Peter's Confession (Luke 9:18-27)

Step 1: Research the communication situation
See 27.1 for more information on the communication context of Luke.

Step 2: Literary context
Discourse type: Conversational narrative (dialogue) and some exposition/ exhortation.

Position in book:
If we look at the overall chiastic structure of the book of Luke (see 27.2), we find that Peter's confession forms the middle, or turning point, of the book. Contained in this passage are all the main elements of the second part of the book: Christ's suffering, death and resurrection.

- The twelve have been sent out - preaching the kingdom of God and healing the sick (9:1-2).
- Herod has heard about Jesus, wondering if he is perhaps John the Baptist raised to life or Elijah or another prophet as some were saying (9:7-8).
- The disciples were unable to feed the 5000 but see Jesus do it (9:10-17).
- With all this evidence in place, Jesus now confronts his disciples and asks 'who do you say I am?'
- As Peter recognises Jesus as the Christ, Jesus confronts them with the reality of what it actually means to follow him.

It is interesting to note that the Gospels of Mark and Matthew which also recount this incident, mention that it happened in the region of Caesarea Philippi, which was an especially pagan region. It could be significant that Jesus was identified as the Christ there.

FIGURE 27.4
Peter's confession of Christ   Luke 9:18-27

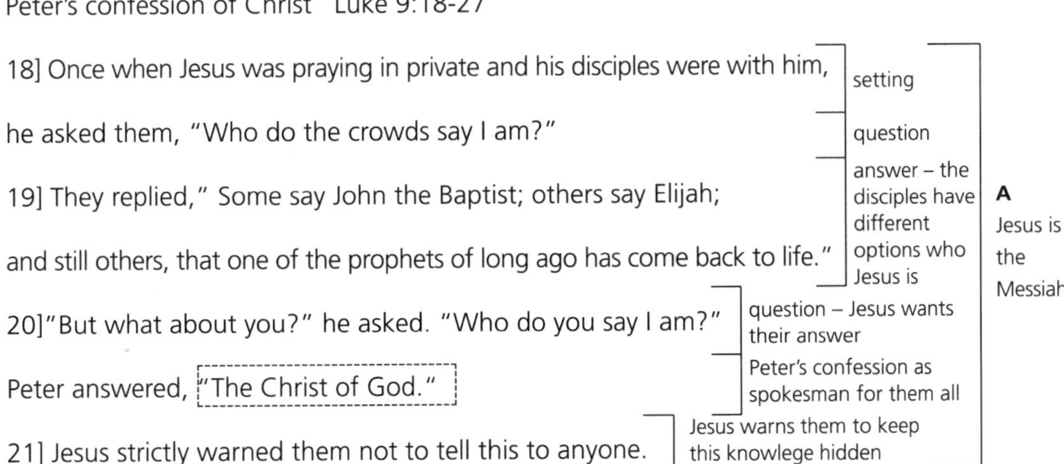

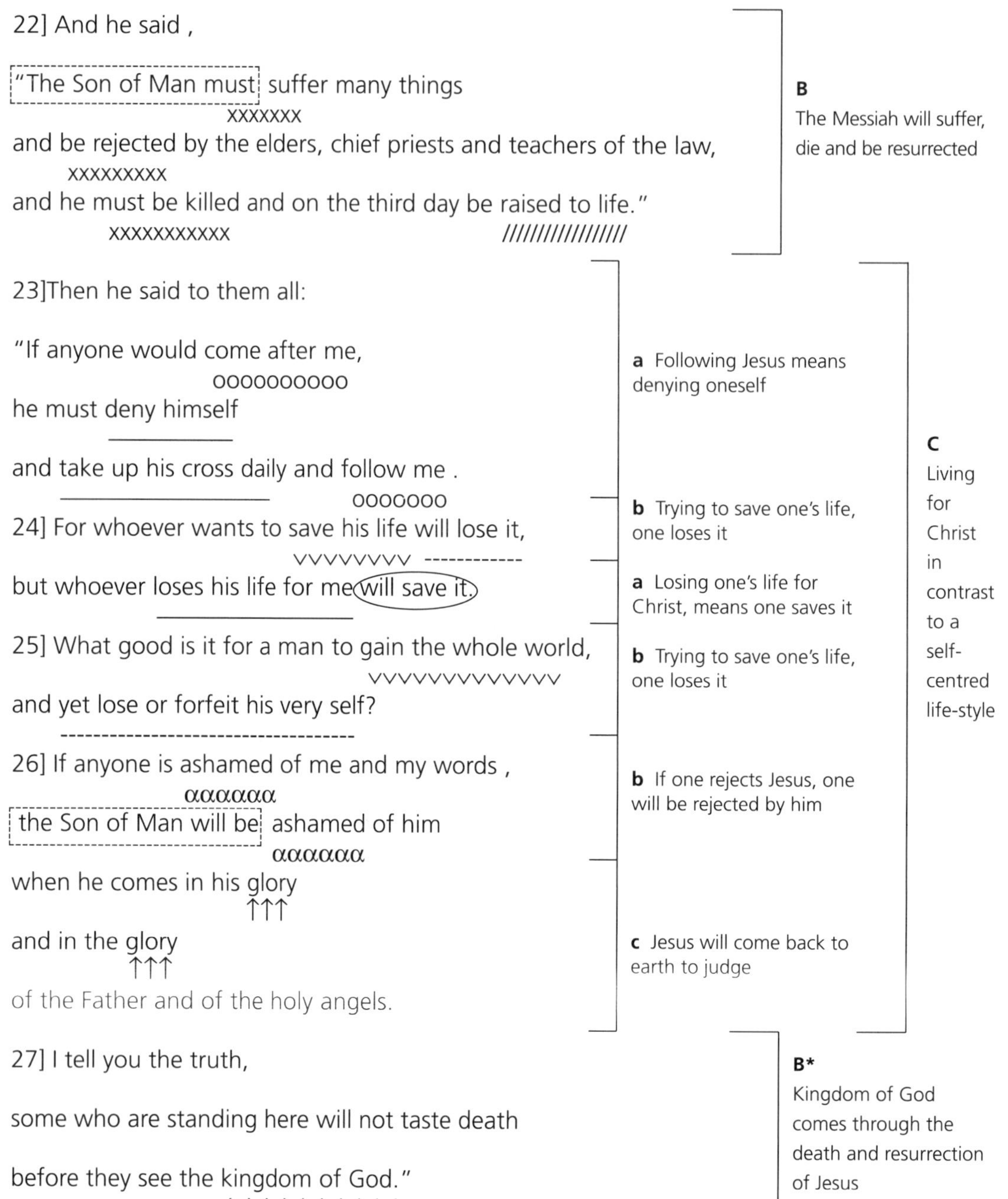
22] And he said ,
"The Son of Man must suffer many things
and be rejected by the elders, chief priests and teachers of the law,
and he must be killed and on the third day be raised to life."
B
The Messiah will suffer, die and be resurrected
23]Then he said to them all:
"If anyone would come after me,
he must deny himself
and take up his cross daily and follow me .
24] For whoever wants to save his life will lose it,
but whoever loses his life for me will save it.
25] What good is it for a man to gain the whole world,
and yet lose or forfeit his very self?
26] If anyone is ashamed of me and my words ,
the Son of Man will be ashamed of him
when he comes in his glory
and in the glory
of the Father and of the holy angels.
a Following Jesus means denying oneself
b Trying to save one's life, one loses it
a Losing one's life for Christ, means one saves it
b Trying to save one's life, one loses it
b If one rejects Jesus, one will be rejected by him
c Jesus will come back to earth to judge
C
Living for Christ in contrast to a self-centred life-style
27] I tell you the truth,
some who are standing here will not taste death
before they see the kingdom of God."
B*
Kingdom of God comes through the death and resurrection of Jesus

Step 3: Analysis of the passage

Refer to figure 27.4 for the following steps.

Step 3.1: Write out the passage in smaller units

This is particularly helpful for v 22-27.

Step 3.2: Mark the significant meaning indicators

In v18a we have the setting. Then Jesus asks his disciples a question in v18b to which they respond in v19. Again Jesus asks a question in v20a and Peter responds with the marvellous confession 'the Christ of God' in 20b. Jesus then gives them a warning in v21 and follows it with teaching in the form of exhortation/exposition in vv 22-27.

The following meaning indicators have been marked from v20:

'Christ of God' (v20), 'Son of Man' (v22), 'Son of Man' (v26) - all of these terms refer to Jesus. Peter proclaims Jesus as the 'Christ of God' and Jesus speaks of himself as the 'Son of Man'. In v22 the 'Son of Man' title is used in the context of the suffering that Jesus is about to enter into. In v26 the title is used in the context of Jesus as the one who will come to judge at the second coming (see notes in appendix B).

References to the suffering of Jesus: 'must suffer', 'be rejected', 'must be killed' (v22) and in v27 'kingdom of God' which refers to the fact that some of his disciples will not die before they have seen the coming of the kingdom of God brought about by the suffering of Jesus.

References to the exaltation of Jesus: 'raised to life' (v22) and 'kingdom of God' (v27) which will be brought about not only by the suffering and death of Jesus, but also by his resurrection.

References to following Jesus in v23: 'come after me', 'follow me'.

References to the denial of self that Jesus requires of his disciples in v 23-24: 'must deny himself', 'take up his cross daily', 'loses his life for me'.

Reference to the result of denying self in v24: 'will save it'.

References to human attempts to save one's life in v24-25: 'save his life', 'gain the whole world'.

References to the results of human attempts to save one's life in v24-25: 'will lose it', 'lose or forfeit his very self'.

Repetition of 'ashamed' in v26.

Repetition of 'glory' in v26.

The meaning indicators of self-denial help us identify the repetition of this theme (a) in vv 23 and 24b.

The meaning indicators of human attempts to save one's life, help us identify the repetion of this theme (b) in vv 24a, 25 and 26.

The themes of self-denial and human attempts to save one's life are followed by the theme of the glorious second coming of Jesus (c) in v26b.

Step 3.3: Explain words and phrases
v18: It appears that Jesus is praying on his own but his disciples are near by or with him. He then asks his disciples a question (see literary context above).

v19: The response that the disciples give shows that they have other options in deciding who they think Jesus is.

Elijah: People were thinking that Jesus could either be Elijah (who never really died, see 2 Kgs 2:1-12) or one of the prophets or John the Baptist brought back to life.

v20: Jesus repeats the word 'you' twice - really confronting the disciples into making a choice.

v20b: Peter answers for all of the disciples. See notes on Messiah in appendix B. The people were divided over whether Jesus was the Messiah or not. Throughout the Gospels we see this division.

v21: Jesus strictly warns the disciples not to share this knowledge with anyone for the following possible reasons:

- As the people had a wrong and inadequate understanding of who the Messiah was, a political movement or even a revolution could have been started if it was publicly acclaimed that the Messiah had come.
- As shown in v22, Jesus had to suffer and die. If the people knew that he was the Messiah, they may have tried to prevent his death.

v22: This is such a contrast and paradox to the statement in 20b. How can the Messiah go through such suffering? Here Jesus destroys any possible idea of a political national leader. He tells the disciples that it will mainly be the religious leaders of that time who will reject him but he also shows them hope in saying that he will be raised on the third day.

Son of Man: See notes in appendix B.

elders, chief priests and teachers of the law (NIVSB footnote Mk 14:55):

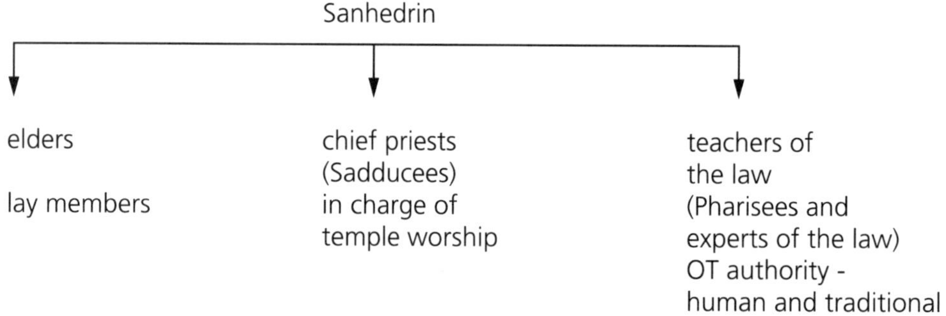

v23: deny himself/ take up his cross: Similar in meaning. This means to put Christ and his commands and demands above one's own selfish interests. The cross was a very clear symbol of death because hundreds of men had been crucified in that region.

v24: save his life: a self-centred life-style.
loses his life for me: a life lived completely for Christ.
save it: this refers not only to eternal life but also to the quality of life that we can have from now until eternity.

v25: This is a rhetorical question.
the whole world: This refers to all those things which could be achieved or acquired in this life.

v26: ashamed of Christ and his words: Christ and his words are distinguishable but not to be separated. Being more concerned about fitting into and pleasing this sinful world rather than following and pleasing Christ.
Son of Man: See previous references. Here we have a combination of the Son of Man, Suffering Servant and Messiah (see appendix B).
comes in his glory: Comes with majesty and to judge.

v27: some who are standing here: Referring to those who are present at this discussion. Jesus appears to be saying that some of the disciples present will experience the kingdom of God before they die.
kingdom of God: See notes in appendix B and the following discussion.

It seems that the reference to seeing the kingdom of God before the death of some of the disciples, refers to the suffering and resurrection of Jesus as mentioned by him in v22. God's kingdom was inaugurated on earth by Christ's suffering, death and resurrection.

Step 3.4: Establish the meaning structure
Vv 18-21 form the first meaning block (A). The message is that Jesus is the Messiah.

V 22 forms the second meaning block (B). The message is that the Messiah will suffer, die and be resurrected.

Vv 23 to 26 form the third meaning block (C). Here we find the contrasting themes of a life lived completely for Christ (a) and a self-centred life-style (b). The message is that living for Christ results in quality of life here (a) and in eternity (c) whereas a self-centred life results in death here (b) and in eternity (c).

V27 forms the fourth meaning block (B*). The message is that the disciples will see the coming of the kingdom of God through the death and resurrection of Jesus. This meaning block relates to B as the themes of the death and resurrection of Jesus are found in both.

Step 3.5: Conclude and summarise the message
Jesus is the Messiah (A)
Jesus will suffer, die and be raised to life (B), and through this the kingdom of God comes (B*). Living for Christ results in quality of life here and in eternity. Whereas a self-centred life results in death here and in eternity (C).

Step 4: Broader biblical and theological framework
Jesus saying that one should lose one's life for him is found in all four Gospels and no other saying of Jesus is given more emphasis (NIVSB, footnote on Lk 9:24). There are also many other references to Jesus being the Messiah in the Gospels (see notes on Messiah in appendix B). It is beautifully described in Phil 2:5-11 that the exaltation of Jesus came about

through his suffering and death. References to Jesus coming as judge can be found, amongst others, in 2 Tim 4:1, Heb 10:13, Rev 20:4.

Hermeneutics

All the elements of the message are applicable to our time, except that the suffering, death and resurrection of Jesus, and through this the coming of the kingdom of God, are not predictions any more, but have been fulfilled in history.

CHAPTER TWENTY EIGHT

How to interpret Acts

Objectives

1. To be able to exegete Acts
2. To understand the process of hermeneutics for Acts
3. To understand the contribution of Acts to the broader biblical message

Contents

The main purpose of this chapter is to give general guidelines on how to approach the exegesis and hermeneutics of Acts. We have already looked at how the steps of exegesis are applied to narrative and several examples have been given in previous chapters, including one from Acts.

STUDY TIP
For a review of the steps of exegesis as applied to narrative, refer to chs 19, 20, 23.

The book of Acts is always of great interest to Christians because it lets us catch a glimpse of what is was like to be part of the exciting early days of the new community of believers, the church. And because Luke's 'subject' is the church, we Christians often take Acts as the blueprint for our church life. In other words, if it happened in the church then, it should also happen today. But it is not quite as simple as this. Differing views on church structure, baptism in the Holy Spirit, and miracles are some of the thorny issues which have beset us and in some cases have caused much hurt, misunderstanding and disunity. We may ask why there are so many different interpretations of Acts if it is so easy to read. This brings us back to the fact that the way in which we interpret Scripture is crucial and absolutely essential for a common understanding of the message of the Bible - our unity as Christians depends on it. Much has already been said in previous chapters about exegesis. And we believe that in applying those principles with humility, undergirded by a strong trust in the Holy Spirit's help, greater unity will be found in our understanding and application of the message of Acts.

28.1 The communication situation

In chapter 20 we discussed the communication situation of Acts. It is significant that Acts is 'part two' of Luke's account addressed to Theophilus (Lk 1:1-4; Acts 1:1). We don't know who Theophilus was, and whether or not he was a believer. What we do know, is that Luke's main purpose for writing is to persuade Theophilus that what he has already learnt about

Jesus' life and ministry is consistent with the historical facts Luke now presents (having carried out careful investigations - Lk 1:3-4). Because of this, we may assume that Theophilus was either a seeking non-believer or possibly a new believer. Whatever the case may be, Luke's writings were meant to bring people to Christ and affirm their faith.

Luke also leaves us in no doubt about the content of his two volume work. He says 'In my former book, Theophilus, I wrote about all that Jesus began to do and to teach until the day he was taken up to heaven,...' (Acts 1:1). Therefore, the content of the gospel is summed up and the content of Acts is implied, saying that his latter work describes what Jesus continues to do from his heavenly position, sending the Holy Spirit to work through the apostles and believers.

The general purpose of Luke will help us only to a certain extent in our interpretation of individual passages. Nevertheless, it may just be the clue that tips the balance in coming to understand a passage better.

To grasp the message of Acts, a good understanding of the literary context is vital.

28.2 The literary context

Acts has the characteristics of the narrative discourse type in the genre of dramatic history. We also find many embedded genres such as conversations, sermons, miracle stories and we will need to adjust our approach to exegesis accordingly.

In our approach to Acts, it is (for example) an interesting and useful pursuit to study all the sermons and speeches recorded in Acts. But we must never forget that they are carefully interwoven into the narrative for a purpose. As is characteristic of narrative, Luke wants to communicate a specific message through a series of events and interactions between characters within the purposefully arranged structure of the whole narrative. However, the message for the reader is never explicitly stated. It is this non-prescriptive characteristic of narrative that is at the root of the different interpretations and lessons people have drawn from the events recorded in Acts. Therefore, in order to find unity in our understanding and arrive at Luke's intended message, we must try to understand how and why Luke has arranged his narrative in a certain way and make sense of any other clues he left for us.

Therefore, in our attempt to understand what Luke, as the inspired writer, wanted us to learn, we must neither come to Acts as a text to prove our practice (because we may be asking questions that Luke never intended to answer), nor ignore the basic characteristics of narrative.

Previous chapters have explained the importance of understanding the plot structure and the relationships between episodes and larger sections of a narrative. They help us arrive at the meaning structure, which in turn helps us arrive at the message.

To our knowledge, there are two works which concentrate on outlining the meaning structure of Acts based on semantic discourse analysis. These are extremely useful for us in coming to understand the message of Acts.

The first of these works attempts to give an outline of the plot structure (see Blood and Blood's structure in 19.6) and shows how the narrative develops and the sections relate to one another. This is formally described and is of tremendous help in getting to grips with the message of the book. It is a much more comprehensive study than many of the over-simplified structures which we may find in some commentaries or introductions in Bibles. It is described as a 'literary-semantic analysis' and the authors, Blood and Blood (1979:2) say about their work:

> it is hoped that both the approach and the results of this study of Acts will make some contribution to Biblical scholarship, since the type of analysis represented in this paper has not traditionally been used.

Their work does not attempt to give the message of the book but provides us with a significant tool for further study.

Another recent and very interesting study of the semantic structure and message of Acts is the work of Gooding entitled 'True to the faith'. Gooding (1990:425) says that the purpose of his work is:

> a study of the material which Luke has selected for inclusion in his history; of the way he has put together the items he has selected; of the thought-flow which his arrangement of the narrative creates; and of what that can tell us about the book's major themes.

Gooding's emphasis is on seeing how Luke has arranged his material purposefully in order to explain certain themes and communicate the message as it unfolds through the development of the narrative. By doing this, the author provides us with valuable insights into the meaning structure of Acts and arrives at its message in a way that has not traditionally been done.

Both of these works make clear that the importance of understanding the structure of a book based on semantic discourse analysis cannot be overestimated and will be of invaluable help when approaching an individual passage.

Luke's view of God's plan in history:
When considering the literary context of Acts, we must also have an understanding of Luke's view of how God develops his plan of salvation in history. Therefore we need to understand how Acts fits in with this.

For Luke, history as we know it, will come to an end at Christ's second coming when he will restore and liberate the whole of creation (Acts 3:21; Rom 8:21) and everything will have to submit to his rule (Lk 21:27,36; Acts 10:42; 17:31). Running up to this event, history can be divided into three major periods:

The first period - the Law and the prophets: This is the period which is covered by the Old Testament. God's promise (eg Gen 3:15; 12:2-3) to bring deliverance from Satan and the consequences of the fall is waiting for its fulfilment. This promise runs like a thread right through the Old Testament and is fulfilled during the second period through Jesus Christ's birth, death and resurrection (Lk 24:27; Acts 3:17-18; 24-26; Jn 1:45). Luke's narrative makes clear that the first period came to an end with the ministry of John the Baptist:

> 'I tell you, among those born of women there is no-one greater than John; yet the one who is least in the kingdom of God is greater than he.' (Lk 7:28)

John is 'greater' because he had the privilege of introducing Jesus and preparing people for the long awaited Messiah (Lk 1:14-17). But at the same time 'the least...is greater' than John because with him the first period, the Old Covenant ends.

The second period - Christ's work on earth: This is the central period and turning point in God's plan. For Luke, Christ's arrival and mission fulfil promises made long ago:

- the promise made to King David of an eternal kingdom (Lk 1:32-33)
- the promise of a deliverer (Lk 2:11, 4:18-19)
- the promise that God will give the Holy Spirit to those who believe in Christ (Lk 3:16)

Therefore, this period marks the beginning of God's kingdom rule in and through individuals who accept Christ (Lk 17:21, Jn 1:12).

The second period, encompassing Christ's birth, death and resurrection was only completed when Christ had taken up his position of power at his Father's side and given the glorious gift, the Holy Spirit, to all who believe in him (Acts 2:32-36). So, the first two chapters of Acts are a record of the wonderful events connected with the end of the second period which at the same time ushers in the third period.

The third period - Christ's work on earth through the church by means of the Holy Spirit: It is of course no coincidence that the third period was ushered in on the day of Pentecost. The disciples had not yet received the Holy Spirit which John the Baptist and Jesus had promised them (Lk 3:16, 24:49, Acts 1:4-5,8). They were to wait for this before getting on with their mission. God chose the day of Pentecost to fulfil the promise in order to leave no doubt in people's minds that they were now entering a new period. Many things would be different during this time and the day itself had symbolic significance.

Pentecost was a joyous feast rooted in the Old Covenant when the Israelites brought the first-fruits of the wheat harvest to the temple and offered them to God (Ex 23:16; Deut 16:9-11). Therefore, just as the feast of Pentecost was a time of giving the first-fruits of the harvest to God, so God gave the Holy Spirit as the first-fruit on the day of Pentecost - only a part of that which Christ has achieved for God's creation. God assures the believers by giving them the Holy Spirit, that at Christ's second coming they will be given all that Christ has achieved for them (Eph 1:13-14; Rom 8:23; 2 Cor 1:22; 5:5).

So then, Acts is a record of the beginning of the third period - the day of Pentecost has happened and human history has once and for all entered this period. Just as Jesus' birth, death and resurrection fulfilled in a unique way, promises made during the first period, so the day of Pentecost fulfilled in a unique way promises made in the first and second period. So we need to interpret Acts in its context - the beginning of the third period of God's plan. This context helps us to understand, for instance, the significance of audible and visible phenomena. In particular the gift of tongues, or languages, that accompanied the arrival of the Holy Spirit on the day of Pentecost.

Three things may be pointed out in this regard. Firstly, God made sure that the believers would not miss the coming of the Holy Spirit and that the reader should understand that we have entered a new era - an era anticipated by the promises made in the first and second periods. Secondly, absolute certainty of the Holy Spirit's arrival was necessary as it was the sign for the believers that they must now embark on their mission to make disciples. Naturally, the audible and visible phenomenona were important signs. Thirdly, the ability to communicate the gospel with people whose languages the disciples did not speak, stands in stark contrast to what happened at Babel (Gen 11:1-9). There, the people were divided because of their united rebellion against God. Now, through the gospel which is proclaimed in their own language, God is restoring their unity based on repentance and faith in Christ. This should impress upon the reader that these are the glorious beginnings of the restoration of all things.

The third era will end with the wondrous renewal of all creation! The gift of tongues in this context has a different and greater significance than the gift of tongues given to believers in other parts of Acts. Whether or not it is the same gift, surely has no significance for church practice today and was a question which Luke most probably never intended to answer.

28.3 Analysis of the passage

Previous chapters have already covered the foundational principles of applying this step to narrative. This section will therefore contain a certain amount of repetition, but we will limit this to the central issue of grappling with the author's intended message. This will naturally lead to a discussion on hermeneutics of narrative.

In the previous two steps of exegesis, we concentrated on getting a broad understanding of the structure and message of Acts, something that is absolutely vital in the study of narrative. In this step, our focus is on understanding the contribution a particular episode makes to the overall message. This will help safeguard against using certain isolated events as proof for our experience or doctrine.

A case in point is Acts 8:14-17 which has been taken in some parts of the church today, as the proof text for establishing the 'absolute' that 'baptism in the Holy Spirit' is separate from and subsequent to conversion.

That it happened to the Samaritans is one thing, but whether Luke intended to establish such a doctrine seems at least debatable if not mistaken. Other events in Acts like the conversion of Paul (Acts 9) and the household of Cornelius (Acts 10:44-46; 11:14-16; 15:7-9) are also quoted to support this position.

What is Luke's intended message through the Samaritan episode? In order to understand Luke's intended message we must carefully observe the clues which he has left for his readers:

The structure and relationships between the episodes (the macro level) in this part of Acts provide us with some clues. It is generally agreed by commentators that this section of Acts begins at 6:8 and ends at 9:31. The relationship between the first three episodes in this section could be seen as follows:

Episode 1: (6:8-8:1a) Stephen's death leads to wide-spread persecution. The events in this episode set the scene for the events that follow in the coming episodes.

Episode 2: (8:1b-3) A great persecution against the Jerusalem church led by Saul begins. This episode results from Stephen's persecution and at the same time is the problem and leads to the following episodes.

Episode 3: (8:4-25) Samaritans become believers through Philip's preaching. The problem is not resolved but this episode is related to episodes 1 and 2 as an outcome.

Through this arrangement of episodes, Luke seems to emphasise that opposition to God's plan to build the church is sovereignly overcome. The very thing that the persecutors set out to do - to destroy the church - is turned around by God and used to accelerate the spread of the gospel (Acts 8:4). The summary statement with which this section of Acts concludes, emphasises this message: 'Then the church throughout all Judea, Galilee, and Samaria enjoyed a time of peace. It was strengthened; and encouraged by the Holy Spirit, it grew in numbers, living in the fear of the Lord' (Acts 9:31).

Focusing on episode 3 itself (the micro level), Luke makes his intention clear with the following:

There is an overwhelmingly strong focus on Simon throughout the episode. He is mentioned more than any other character. The people of Samaria take second place in the number of references. The narrative becomes much more detailed when Simon is directly referred to, and direct speech is only employed in interaction with him. In contrast, when Simon remains in the background, events follow each other quickly. Little detail and no direct speech or conversation is recorded (eg v14-17). This evidence alone should alert us to the fact that Luke's intended message revolves around the main character Simon and the people of Samaria.

Luke omits any specific mention of visible signs when the Samaritans receive the Holy Spirit (although the context may imply it). The narrative immediately switches back to Simon. This contrasts with all the other instances in Luke's narrative where the Holy Spirit is given to converts and visible signs are explicitly mentioned. A further contrast seems to be that those who believed Philip's message, received the Holy Spirit when the apostles prayed for them. Simon does not seem to be part of this group but is seen to be an onlooker and spectator, particularly fascinated by the visible demonstration and work of the Holy Spirit (v13,18). His fascination and preoccupation with the signs come as no surprise, since supernatural activities were the very means for him to gain status and create a following for himself (v9-11). To him, the Holy Spirit is another magic trick to add to his repertoire and vital to prevent the loss of followers as they turned away from him and false religion to Christ (v12). His motives are clearly wrong, as Peter's response indicates (v20-23).

In contrast to Simon, the Holy Spirit is given to the Samaritans, who like him, had also believed in false religion. We don't know exactly what the beliefs of this group were, but the Samaritans generally held to the Pentateuch but rejected the rest of the Jewish Scripture and the teaching that salvation was promised to come through the Jewish nation. By submitting themselves to the apostles, they accept that salvation comes through the Jews, and they embrace the whole of the Old Testament. Thus their act of submission to the apostles was a vital demonstration of their break with their own traditional beliefs. God is now able to give the Holy Spirit and thus demonstrates that he has made the Samaritans part of the church with its historical roots in the whole of the Old Testament.

So then, through the larger structure, and its emphasis and contrasts, we must understand and conclude Luke's intended message. Let us try to summarise our findings and formulate what seems most likely to have been Luke's message:

- The growth of the church is God's sovereign work and will happen despite opposition.
- God shows by his gift of the Holy Spirit, that he includes in the church everyone who believes in Christ, not just the Jews.
- In contrast, God does not give the Holy Spirit to those who do not truly forsake their false beliefs and want the Holy Spirit (just like occult power) as a means for personal gain. For such people, there is no salvation and they have no part in the new community of believers.

28.4 The broader biblical framework

The main issues for interpreting Acts in the context of the broader biblical framework have already been discussed under 28.2. You may refer to that section to help you with this step.

28.5 Hermeneutics

We started this chapter by saying that the book of Acts has always been of great interest because it relates the experiences of the early church. We also noted the wide variety of interpretations that exist because we are dealing with narrative literature. Narrative may be more open to misuse than other types of literature in the Bible because it characteristically does not address the reader directly and does not give him direct instructions. This has led to different and conflicting ways in which narrative is used in preaching and teaching (eg often single events are turned into absolutes). This leaves us with the inadequate situation of different standards for different believers. Let us consider a few examples which illustrate the point.

We may ask: Should we select church leaders through prayer and drawing lots (Acts 1:26) even though later on we find a variety of ways in which church leaders are selected? Should we live in the kind of communal setting seen in Jerusalem even though there is scarce evidence of this happening later on in Acts? Is there a particular sequence in the elements of conversion in Luke's thinking even though the events lack consistency? Should we always expect miracles to happen before we preach the gospel while (again) no consistent pattern can be found? To use such inconsistent and irregular patterns of events to establish an absolute pattern for today would surely be going against common sense. If Luke had intended for us to use such patterns would he not have been more consistent in his narrative?

What then, are the hermeneutical principles that should guide us to a more unified interpretation of Acts? We believe the answer is found in our approach to exegesis. The purpose of exegesis is 'to arrive at the message the original receiver understood' (see 2.2). This could also be expressed by saying that the purpose of our exegesis is to understand the message that Luke intended to communicate to Theophilus. Although it is not always easy to discover Luke's intended message, a consistent and linguistically informed approach to exegesis will help to find it. We believe that if we pursue this together, it could result in genuine progress towards unity in the church today.

This leads us to formulate some guiding principles for approaching hermeneutics of Acts:

1. We cannot view a historical event (some call it historical precedent) as an absolute, unless it was the author's intention that it should be seen as an absolute. This is found through the steps of exegesis.

2. An event which is not part of the author's intended message should be seen as a relative. By this we do not mean to say that such events have nothing to teach us, but isolated and by themselves, they should not be turned into an absolute truth.

3. When it is difficult to decide what the author's intended message is, we should not turn biblical events into absolutes when they change from situation to situation or when they are only partially described.

The following examples illustrate these principles. See also 28.3 for a further example.

We would be hard pressed to conclude that Luke's intention was to say that the gift of tongues and prophetic messages should be an absolute for Christian conversion just because it happened in Acts 19:6. A careful look at all the references in Acts reveal that there is no consistent pattern of conversion to be found in the various episodes in which people become Christians and are filled with the Holy Spirit.

This is the case when comparing Acts 8:4-25 with 10:44-47. In the first passage, belief in the gospel message is followed by water baptism and later the Samaritans receive the Holy Spirit. In Acts 10:44-47 the pattern of events is different: belief in the gospel is not mentioned, the Gentiles receive the Holy Spirit and then water baptism follows.

Conversions are also often only partially described. For example, Luke records what Peter said about conversion - he mentions repentance, water baptism and the gift of the Holy Spirit (Acts 2:38). In Acts 8:4-25, there is no mention of repentance, the gift of tongues or prophesy. However, tongues and prophesy are mentioned in Acts 19:6, and often all that is said in other passages is that people 'turned to the Lord', 'believed', 'were persuaded', eg Acts 9:35, 42; 14:1; 17:4.

This should alert us to the fact that Luke's intended message was not to give us a particular pattern of conversion. However, when we look at Acts as a whole (and this is how we must read Luke's narrative), what Luke seems to be saying (and what seems to be consistent with the rest of the New Testament) is that there is no genuine Christian conversion which does not involve the renewing and empowering work of the Holy Spirit. Such a conversion results in a life lived in the power of the Holy Spirit, as can be seen in a growing understanding of who Christ is, deep love for fellow believers, boldness to witness and an openness to the gifts of the Holy Spirit.

Another example that illustrates the principles for hermeneutics mentioned above, is the idea that evangelism should always include healing or other kinds of miracles. It's clear that this often happened, but again no consistent pattern is found. On quite a few occasions, no miracles are recorded, but people nevertheless responded to the gospel (Acts 13:13-52; 16:11-15; 17:1-4). Miracles are recorded less frequently (although there are still quite a few) after the initial reports in Acts (chs 1-6).

Let us look at a specific example before we try to summarise Luke's intention for the frequent recording of miracles in Acts.

We looked at Acts 9:36-43 in chapter 20. A great miracle takes place and Dorcas is raised back to life. Having exegeted this passage, we came to understand that it was Luke's intention to bring the reader to faith in Christ, just as those people in Joppa who heard about the miracle, received the gospel, and as a result became Christians. So, how does the miracle function within Luke's intended message for his readers? For them, the miracle is a historical fact which confirms the good news about the risen Christ and thus convinces them to accept the gospel as truth for themselves. The trustworthiness of Luke's account - from the reader's point of view - is supported by the fact that the miracle was witnessed by others. So, to say that miracles should always form part of evangelism would seem to be going beyond what Luke intended to communicate.

Let us now try to summarise Luke's intention for his frequent recording of miracles. Firstly, they are not an absolute for evangelism. Different patterns can be observed. Secondly, they are signs which confirm that Christ was indeed who he claimed to be (Acts 2:22) and thus they confirm the gospel message which the disciples proclaimed (3:11-16). Thirdly, they are signs of God's rule breaking into the present age and thus anticipating and giving us a foretaste of the renewal of all things (Acts 3:21). Lastly, miracles also affirmed the apostles in their ministry (2 Cor 12:12). This fact is of importance as the church was founded on their ministry (Mt 16:18; Eph 2:20).

Having summarised all this, does it mean miracles stopped with the completion of the Bible? No, Luke's account as a whole shows that we live in a period which anticipates the final coming of God's kingdom - a period in which people are invited to turn to God to prepare themselves for his final coming (Acts 3:19-21). Moreover, this period begins and continues to be marked by 'tasters' of his kingdom - miracles breaking into this present age to encourage and show us that we are heading towards the final stage of history, culminating in Christ's return, when God's plan will be completed and creation restored from the havoc wrought by sin. Thus we may still pray for, and expect, this dynamic and supernatural work of God in our lives today.

CHAPTER TWENTY NINE

How to interpret the NT letters

Objectives

1. To be able to exegete NT letters
2. To understand the contribution of the NT letters to the broader biblical message
3. To understand the process of hermeneutics for the NT letters

Contents

STUDY TIP
Read this chapter together with Part Three, the steps of exegesis, where all the exegetical steps of exposition and exhortation were explained and applied to Col 1:21-23.

So much has been written on exegesis of the NT letters and much more can still be written. Therefore, in this short chapter, I can only touch on the essential issues that will be a practical help when applying exegesis and hermeneutics to the letters. Different examples will be used to illustrate the issues.

29.1 The communication situation

The first letters by Paul were written no more than two decades after the formation of the earliest congregation in Jerusalem. Because of their early dates, they are valuable resources for information on the life of the early church regarding its beliefs, victories, questions and problems.

It was the particular concern of the apostles for the churches that led to the writing of most of the letters. Paul even wrote letters to churches that he had not met, because of this concern for them and because he believed that his apostolic authority also extended to them (Col 2:1-5).

The letters were not theological dissertations, but letters written at a particular time to address the particular needs of a church or churches in particular places. This emphasises the importance of knowing the communication situation of the letters and interpreting them accordingly, as Du Toit (1992:3) illustrates:

> Just how important the specific situation is may be illustrated by the letter to the Galatians and James. Suppose that these two writings were penned at the same time, and that en route to their respective destinations they were accidentally interchanged. It does not take much imagination to reflect on the catastrophic results: the Galatians

would have all the more earnestly concentrated on 'works', while those addressed by James would have grown even more lax in living out their religion. But the science of introduction makes clear why the writer of Galatians finds it necessary to emphasise faith for his readers, and why James has to stress works.

A few brief remarks on the authorship of the letters follow:

- Of the 21 NT letters, 13 have traditionally been ascribed to the apostle Paul as he is identified in them as the author. These letters are Rom, 1&2 Cor, Gal, Eph, Phil, Col, 1&2 Thes, 1&2 Tim, Tit, Philemon.
- The author of James identified himself by that name and it is traditionally accepted that it was the James who was the brother of Jesus.
- The author of 1 Peter identifies himself as the apostle Peter, and that of 2 Peter as the apostle Simon Peter - both thus ascribed to the apostle Peter.
- The author of 1 John does not identify himself, while the author of 2&3 John identifies himself as 'the elder'. Church fathers ascribed these letters to John the apostle.
- The author of Jude identifies himself as 'a servant of Jesus Christ and a brother of James' and is most likely the brother of Jesus.
- The writer of Hebrews does not identify himself and the letter was ascribed to Paul roughly between the years 400 and 1600. Since the Reformation it has been widely believed that Paul could not have been the author, and either Barnabas or Apollos is thought to have been the author.

Volumes have been written on the question of the authorship of the letters. In the case of the Pauline letters, various arguments have been brought in against the likelihood of Paul writing all of the letters. These arguments tend to concentrate on differences in language and style between different letters, and on issues addressed in the letters that are supposedly not relevant to the circumstances of the church of the first century.

Various quasi-statistical methods have been employed in the past, eg the counting of words and phrases used in a particular letter that are not found in other Pauline letters and vice versa. On that basis, it is then decided that the particular letter could not have been written by the apostle Paul. Prof Louw, editor of the Greek-English Lexicon (1988), tells of how he requested the Department of Statistics at the University of Pretoria to do a similar analysis on two different books by a contemporary author. The result was that the books could not have been written by the same author!

Based on speculation of the first century church's situation, it is sometimes concluded that particular letters could not have been written by Paul, but that they belong to a post-Pauline era. Colossians and the pastoral letters (1&2 Timothy and Titus) are examples where it is felt that the false teaching addressed must have belonged to a later era. However, no conclusive evidence can be produced to support this.

As I have read numerous arguments against Pauline authorship of the letters ascribed to him, I have not once come across an argument that I have felt could be used as convincing evidence against his authorship. In most cases, the arguments can be refuted by the understanding that the communication situation of each letter was in some way different from that of any other letter. Differences in language and style between Pauline letters could, for example, be ascribed to different issues addressed, different target groups, and the development and change in the style of the author as the letters were written at different time periods.

Throughout the process of exegesis it may be necessary to relate one's findings to the communication situation as it can help to determine whether a specific exposition is feasible or not. The interpretation of Eph 1:3-14 is a good example. Paul wrote this letter to the church in Ephesus, and because of the influence of the Ephesian church on surrounding churches, it would also have been relevant to the needs of those churches. Ephesians should therefore not be seen as an isolated theological dissertation, but as an occasional letter addressing the needs of the church in Ephesus and the surrounding churches.

When interpreting Eph 1:3-14, the question arises of exactly what issue Paul is addressing. Is he dealing with predestination (that God selected some people to be saved and others to be lost), or is he dealing with God's intention to make salvation available to every one, Jew and Gentile alike, through Christ. Obviously the answer to this should be discovered through the steps of exegesis. The communication situation functions as one of the pointers to help us decide which is the most likely interpretation.

From the rest of Ephesians we see that Paul addresses the issue of salvation for Jews and Gentiles in detail. So that was certainly a contemporary issue. As far as personal predestination is concerned, we do not find any hints from the book itself, or from what we know about the church in Ephesus that it was an issue in the church. Therefore, we can conclude from the communication situation that Paul probably addressed the fact that God had a plan to make salvation available to Jews and Gentiles alike, through Christ.

29.2 The literary context

Of the 27 books in the NT, 21 can be regarded as belonging to the literary genre of the letter. In contrast, no single writing in the OT belongs to this genre. In certain OT books, letters are found as embedded literature (eg 2 Sam 11:15; 1 Kgs 21:9f; Ezra 4:9-16, 17-22). This occasionally happens in the NT, (Acts 15:23-29; 23:25-30; Rev 2-3).

If one realises that the letter was in general use in the Roman empire of that time, it is not so difficult to understand why so many books were written in the form of letters in the New Testament. It was a useful medium for the leaders of the early church to communicate with the churches that were spread out over such a vast area. Of the different contemporary types of letters, the biblical letters were nearer in form to the personal than the business or official letter.

The Greek letter had a particular standard form which was in use for centuries before and after Christ. Not all letters kept strictly to this form and some of the elements could be left out or some could be intermixed in such a way that it is difficult to identify them. In using the standard form, the biblical authors also intermixed some elements and certainly employed this to serve their purposes. For example, when Paul wishes the churches well in his letters, he does so by applying the well-wishes to their relationship to God and not to their physical health as was customary. In 3 John 2 the author trusts that the health of the receiver will be as good as his spiritual well-being.

The six main elements of the Greek letter are the opening, well-wishes, introduction to body, body, conclusion of body and closing. Each one of these elements will be discussed as they are found in Colossians and Romans.

The **opening** of Col is found in 1:1-2. Paul states that he and Timothy are the senders, that the Colossian believers are the recipients and he presents a greeting. The opening of Rom is found in 1:1-7 where there is an extensive elaboration on the different parts of the opening.

The **well-wishes** of Col are found in 1:3-14. It takes the form of thanksgiving (1:3-8) and of a prayer (1:9-14) for the well-being of the Colossian believers. The well-wishes element in Rom is found in 1:8-10 and contains a short thanksgiving and prayer for the believers in Rome.

The **introduction to the body** of Col can be seen in 1:21-2:5 where Paul states his own relationship to the Colossian believers very clearly, inter-twined with the same themes that are addressed in 1:3-14. Between the well-wishes and the body we find the wonderful passage on the supremacy of Christ (1:15-20), that was most probably a hymn in the early church. By placing the hymn between these two elements and putting it in the centre of the chiastic arrangement, its contents are emphasised. The rich content of Col 1:3-2:5 serves as an expositional base for the direct and specific exhortations that are to follow from 2:6 onwards.

For Rom, the introduction to the body is found in 1:11-17 where Paul expresses his wish to see them (v11-12), states that he has planned many times to visit them (v13), explains that he wants to visit them because he is called to both Gentiles and non-Gentiles (v14-15), writes about the power of the gospel (v16) and presents the theme of the letter (v17).

The **body** usually consists of an expositional part followed by an exhortational part. In Colossians this is not the case as the well-wishes and introduction to the body fulfil the expositional function. In Romans, the expositional part is 1:18-11:36 and the exhortational one is 12:1-15:13. It should always be kept in mind that although a particular part of a book may be written in expositional style, it does not rule out that it may contain strong, embedded exhortational appeals. For example, when Paul writes in Rom 6 about dying to the sinful nature, he includes a few exhortations:

> "...count yourselves dead to sin but alive to God..."(v11)
> "...do not let sin reign..."(v12)
> "Do not offer the parts of your body to sin...but rather offer yourselves to God..."(v13)

Even if something is not written in exhortational form, its end purpose may be to motivate the listeners to action. This can even be achieved by asking a question, like the rhetorical question in Rom 6:16 through which the believers are exhorted to serve God:

> Don't you know that when you offer yourselves to someone to obey him as slaves, you are slaves to the one whom you obey - whether you are slaves to sin, which leads to death, or to obedience, which leads to righteousness?

The **conclusion of the body** is not always easy to distinguish from the closing of the letter or from the body. For instance, in Col it is clear that 4:7-9 is part of the conclusion, with Paul stating that he is sending Tychicus and Onesimus (they were probably delivering the letter) who will tell them about Paul and actually compensate for his absence. However, it is not easy to decide whether 4:2-6 is part of the body or of the conclusion of the body. It could be seen as part of the body because of the various instructions that it contains. At the same time, it could be seen as part of the conclusion of the body because of the reference to Paul's ministry and his request for prayer. If the former is the case, 4:2-6 is part of the body and 4:7-9 forms the conclusion of the body.

In Romans the conclusion is 15:14-33 where Paul expresses his trust in the believers in Rome (v14), refers to his letter to them in the context of his calling to minister to the Gentiles (v15-21), explains why he has not been able to visit them before (v22), sets out his future plans that include visiting them (v23-29) and requests them to pray for him.

The **closing** keeps the balance with the opening by again sending personal greetings and bestowing a blessing. Sometimes the names of quite a few people are listed as the senders of greetings (Col 4:10-14) while the greetings can also be addressed to quite a few people (Rom 16:3-16). The closing of Col is 4:10-18 and that of Rom is 16:1-27. The closing in Romans contains, in addition to the greetings also commendations, exhortations and praise of God for Christ (doxology).

When comparing the six elements as found in Colossians and Romans, we can clearly see similarities and differences in how the letters are constructed. They are similar in that both of them contain all six the elements. At the same time they are different, as we saw in the case of Col where a hymn is found between the well-wishes and introduction to the body and these three parts together fulfil the expositional function for the body.

When identifying the elements of a letter, it is important to remember that there are not only differences between letters in how the elements are organised, but that some elements may even be absent. In Galatians, for example, we do not find the customary well-wishes, but in its place, astonishment about the acceptance of false doctrine by the Galatians and very severe condemnation of the preachers of it. It seems that Paul may have done this in order to shock his hearers - not only by what he says, but also by the position of these statements in the overall structure of the book.

We now come to the question of the relationship between the elements of the letter and the meaning structure of the book (the relationship between paragraphs and groups of paragraphs according to meaning, as shown in figure 9.2 and discussed in 9.8). There is not always a direct correlation between the elements of the letter and the meaning structures, and in such cases a letter could be viewed from the perspective of the overlap of structures. Let us look at the element of well-wishes in Col that is found in 1:3-14. When we look at these paragraphs in the context of the structure of Colossians (figure 9.2), they don't form a separate meaning group. The reason for this is that Paul fills them with content in such a way that they cannot be separated from what follows and they form part of a chiastic structure that includes everything up to the end of Col 2:5.

When doing exegesis on a passage, the overall meaning structure will in some cases be the most important factor to take into consideration. In other cases, the emphasis will be on the element of the letter that a passage belongs to, and in other cases, the emphasis will be equal. The best way to approach a passage is from both perspectives, and looking at what influence each and both perspectives together have on the meaning of the passage.

29.3 Analysis of the passage

When we analyse passages from the letters, we should make maximum use of the fact that the message is not only communicated by the meaning of the words and sentences, but also by the form of the passages. In other words, by the way in which words and phrases are arranged. One thinks of how rich in stylistic features, like parallelism and chiasm, the letters are (see 11.6). These features not only serve the purpose of emphasis, but can also help us to discover the meaning of single words and phrases. This will now be illustrated by looking at the question of what Eph 5:23 means when it says that 'the husband is the head of the wife'.

One sometimes hears people say that the meaning expressed by 'head' in this context is to be the source of something, and that it does not refer to authority. A different view is held by Louw and Nida (1988:739) when they give the meaning of the Greek word as "one who is of supreme or pre-eminent status, in view of authority to order or command". Let us look at the form of the passage, Eph 5:22-24 (figure 29.1), to see how the structure may shed light on the meaning of 'head'.

FIGURE 29.1
Eph 5:22-24

1	Wives, submit to your husbands as to the Lord.	A
2	For the husband is the head of the wife	B
3	as Christ is the head of the church,	
4	his body, of which he is the Saviour.	C
5	Now as the church submits to Christ,	B*
6	so also wives should submit to their husbands in everything.	A*

The relationship between the lines will now be discussed with the help of figure 29.1.

Line 4 (C) is an elaboration of 'church' in L3. It describes the intimate relationship between Christ and his church and the fact that Christ is the one who saved the church. With this, the theme of the following passage (5:25-33) (that the husband should love and care for his wife in the same way as Christ does for the church), is introduced.

In L1 (A) wives are told to submit to their husbands. (Although the verb 'to submit' is not found in the Greek text, it is assumed by the translators of the NIV, because it is found at the end of the previous paragraph. This is typical of Greek sentence construction.) The fact that wives should submit to their husbands is motivated by L2 and L3 (B). The husband is the 'head' of his wife (L2), in the same way that Christ is 'head' of the church (L3).

Line 6 (A*) is parallel to L1 (A) in form and meaning. (Although the verb 'to submit' is again not found in the Greek text, it is assumed by the NIV translators because of its relationship to L5 where the verb is found.) Wives should submit to their husbands (L6) in the same way as the church submits to Christ (L5).

We therefore see that the parallelism between L1 and L6 with the meaning "to submit" clearly supports the interpretation that we are dealing with authority in this passage. This is emphasised by the comparison with L5 where 'submit' is used again. As L5 serves to qualify L6, similarly L2 and L3 qualify L1. This chiastic structure of the whole passage makes the element of authority the most likely focus of the meaning of 'head'.

In our analysis we should look for meaning blocks that are arranged according to particular patterns (see chapter 13). An example is 2 Tim 1:3-18. The five paragraphs have been divided in figure 29.2 into nine meaning blocks. We can see from this example that the chiastic structure serves to emphasise that the salvation of the Christian is based on the content of the gospel. The repetition of the themes serves to highlight the meaning of some of the passages that one could have read over easily without realising their significance. The identification of these meaning blocks is extremely helpful when preparing a sermon or Bible study.

FIGURE 29.2
2 Tim 1:3-18

3] I thank God, whom I serve, as my forefathers did, with a clear conscience, as night and day I constantly remember you in my prayers. 4] Recalling your tears, I long to see you, so that I may be filled with joy.	A Personal relationship
5] I have been reminded of your sincere faith, which first lived in your grandmother Lois and in your mother Eunice and, I am persuaded now lives in you also.	B Discipleship in family
6] For this reason I remind you to fan into flame the gift of God, which is in you through the laying on of my hands. 7] For God did not give us a spirit of timidity, but a spirit of power, of love and of self-discipline.	C Press ahead in God's power
8] So do not be ashamed to testify about our Lord, or ashamed of me his prisoner. But join with me in suffering for the gospel, by the power of God,	D Suffering
9] who has saved us and called us to a holy life – not because of anything we have done but because of his own purpose and grace. This grace was given us in Christ Jesus before the beginning of time, 10] but it has now been revealed through the appearing of our Saviour, Christ Jesus, who has destroyed death and has brought life and immortaliy to light through the gospel. 11] And of this gospel I was appointed a herald and an apostle and a teacher.	E Content of the Gospel
12] That is why I am suffering as I am.	D* Suffering
And yet I am not ashamed, but I know whom I have believed, and am convinced that he is able to guard what I have entrusted to him for that day.	C* Press ahead in God's power
13] What you have heard from me, keep as the pattern of sound teaching, with faith and love in Christ Jesus. 14] Guard the good deposit that was entrusted to you – guard it with the help of the Holy Spirit who lives in us.	B* Discipleship
15] You know that everyone in the province of Asia has deserted me, including Phygelus and Hermogenes. 16] May the Lord show mercy to the household of Onesiphorus, because he often refreshed me and was not ashamed of my chains. 17] On the contrary, when he was in Rome, he searched hard for me until he found me. 18] May the Lord grant that he will find mercy from the Lord on that day! You know very well in how many ways he helped me in Ephesus.	A* Personal relationship

29.4 The broader biblical framework

Without the NT letters, it would have been difficult for us to comprehend the full meaning of the fact that Jesus Christ became a human being, died for us, was raised from the dead and is seated at the right hand of the Father. As the letters were written after Jesus' life on earth, they majored on that in order to apply the inheritance that the believers have in Christ to the life and ministry of the church.

To do justice to the message of Paul and the other letters within a short section like this, is completely impossible. However, an attempt will be made to explain something of the central concept of the believer's identification with Christ as it features in particularly Paul's writings.

The terms 'in Christ' and 'with Christ' are found in most of the letters. In most of those cases (and also in some cases where these specific terms are not used) the concept of the identification of the believer with Christ is expressed. It can be summarised as follows. Through Christ's life, death and resurrection, he achieved certain things: he paid for people's sins; he was victorious over the binding power of the world with its temptations and rebellious lifestyle; he conquered the power of Satan and his demonic forces; and he had victory over man's sinful nature. Together with all of these, he showed that he was stronger than the power of death. The believer shares in all of this because of his relationship with Christ.

This fact of the believers' identification with Christ has many implications for their lives and for that of the church. Because of their relationship with Christ, the focus of their lives should be completely different - they will be motivated to live a morally pure life. In order to do so, power is needed. The relationship with Christ means that believers do not have to live such a life in their own power, but in the power of Christ. They are able to say 'no' to the sinful world, Satan and the sinful nature, because they share Christ's victory over these forces (died with him). They are able to say 'yes' to the life that God has called them to live, because they share Christ's victory to live according to God's calling (raised with him and seated at the right hand of the Father with him).

The fact that believers have this victory does not mean that they are perfect in their behaviour. That will only happen when they are with God in heaven. In the meantime, they are acutely aware of their own sin and sinfulness, and live constantly in dependence on Christ, receiving forgiveness and accepting victory by faith. This is illustrated in figure 29.3.

FIGURE 29.3

TEMPTATION → SIN → CONFESS → ACCEPT FORGIVENESS BY FAITH

Refuse to do it – count yourselves dead to sin (Rom 6:11)	Choose to do God's will – count yourselves alive (Rom 6:11)	Step out and act by faith
1. Recognise it as sin 2. Make a choice 3. Put faith in God's power through the Holy Spirit because of what Christ did for us	1. Know what God's norm is. 2. Make a choice 3. Put faith in God's power through the Holy Spirit because of what Christ did for us	DON'T LIVE ACCORDING TO FEELINGS

When looking at this wonderful and exciting message that is there to be discovered by everyone, it is sad that so many of the interpretations of the NT letters (in particular of Paul's as the major author of the letters) have not been done from an objective literary interpretation of the letters themselves, but from contemporary philosophical presuppositions. It is therefore quite understandable that one interpretation was soon replaced by the next, as the newest philosophical fad came to replace the previous one. The effect of this on interpretation over the last two centuries, is illustrated when Ridderbos (1975:15) refers to the 'Hegelian Paul' of the Tubingen school, the 'liberal Paul' of liberal theology, the 'mystical Paul' of the history of religions school, and the 'existentialist Paul' of the school of Bultman.

It does not fall within the scope of this chapter to discuss all these major trends in the interpretation of Paul. Only the Tubingen School will be discussed briefly as an example of these 'trendy' ways of biblical interpretation. This school of thought was extremely influential as far as the course of theology of the nineteenth century was concerned, and every theological direction was forced to take issue with it one way or another, even if only to establish its own position against it.

Ironically, Baur (the head of the school) attempted to set up an objective method of interpreting the Bible - a purely historical interpretation. However, for him such an historical interpretation meant that there could be no miraculous or supernatural events in history. Therefore, the origin of Christianity could not be seen as supernatural. Harris (1990: 252) evaluates Baur's views as follows:

> ...even if there were a God who had created the world, this God would be unable to break into history; he would be locked out of his world. But in actuality Baur did not believe that such a God existed, and consequently there could be no miraculous intervention into the history of the world. This, in fact, was the one presupposition which determined the whole of Baur's historical investigation and also that of the Tubingen School. On this point all the members of the School were agreed, and it is just here that the whole on-going critical investigation must give account of itself. **The acceptance or rejection of a transcendent personal God determined Baur's dogmatic and historical investigations.**

Those Pauline books which did not fit Baur's theological framework, were rejected as not being genuine and most of them seen as written in the second century. The result was that of all the New Testament books, he only accepted Romans, Galatians, 1 and 2 Corinthians and Revelation as authentic.

29.5 Hermeneutics

The letters were written after the death and resurrection of Jesus, after the outpouring of the Holy Spirit at Pentecost, when a number of churches had already been established. Therefore, one would have expected the hermeneutics of the letters to be very straightforward. Unfortunately, this is not the case! There are quite a few issues in the letters on which Christians are divided. One thinks, for example, of women in ministry and the gifts of the Holy Spirit.

Having said this, the message on the essentials of the gospel, like the Christian's identification with Christ, is crystal clear. These essentials also form the main framework of most of the letters. The key for us in doing the hermeneutics of the letters is that we should see all the less clear issues in the light of the overall message of the letters and therefore, the whole Bible, as the letters present a wonderful exposition of the essentials of the gospel.

When the letters address moral issues (such as the lists of sins that Paul gives), these issues are always of an absolute nature and not culturally determined. The ban on homosexual activities is an example of such an absolute as we see it in 1 Cor 1:18-32, addressed in the context of idolatry and a list of other very obvious sins.

It seems that hermeneutics becomes more difficult with instructions about practice in the church, eg greeting with a kiss, lifting up of holy hands, wearing of head coverings, role of women in the meetings, etc. In such cases, we are challenged in our exegesis to find in that particular culture the principle that is concerned. For example, in the case of Rom 16:16 (see 2.2) it was not enough to see that the Christians in Rome had to greet one another with a kiss, but the principle or purpose behind it also had to be discovered (ie to show love and respect in the Lord to one another). Once this was discovered, it was not difficult to make the decision as to what was absolute and what was relative. Another example is the requirement of women to have their heads covered during worship (1 Cor 11:3-10). One first has to find out exactly what this instruction meant in the culture of that time. The discovery that it refers to the relationship between husband and wife and the public expression of the nature of that relationship, is invaluable in finding the message and therefore, the absolutes.

When we are in doubt as to whether something is culturally relative or absolute, it is helpful to place it in the context of the wider biblical message. Think of the issue of the role of women in worship services. It could be argued that 1 Cor 14:33-35 and 1 Tim 2:11-15 are highly dependent on the particular circumstances in those churches, with the result that we cannot derive any instructions for the public ministry of women from them. However, through careful exegesis, we find that in both cases, the role of the woman in the church is linked to her role in marriage or in the family.

This brings us to the wider question of what the woman's role is in marriage as we find it defined in the Bible. When we exegete two key passages, Eph 5:22-6:4 and Col 3:18-21, we find that Paul is certainly not dealing with issues that are purely dependent on the particular local circumstances of these two churches. He is dealing with relationships within the godly institution of the family, relationships that are grounded in creation order and rooted in the whole of Scripture. These relationships are defined according to the roles of each member of the family and are absolutes that can be established from a broader reading of the Bible.

I believe that exegesis of Eph 5:22-6:4 and Col 3:18-21 reveals that the husband does have an ultimate responsibility of leadership in the family. This authority is clearly defined by his responsibilities that rule out the right to abuse it in any way. The role of the wife is that of submission to her husband (see 29.3 for discussion of Eph 5:22-24). This does not mean that she is of less value than her husband.

In each culture, these principles of leadership and submission will be worked out in different ways, according to cultural taboos and customs. It seems that this is exactly what Paul is doing in 1 Cor 14:33-35 and in 1 Tim 2:11-15. He applies the absolute of the submission of the wife to her own husband to the particular circumstances addressed in these two passages, and then comes up with instructions that were relevant to those different situations. Therefore the instructions of these two passages are not necessarily relevant today.

However, we need to do exactly the same as Paul and look at the public role of women in the church today, from the viewpoint of maintaining biblical roles in the family. Indeed, the main battle-field is the family in many cultures. For example, in the Western world the family is under severe threat, especially because of a confusion of roles. Even families within the church have not escaped. Roles in the church should be defined in such a way that they will set role models for the family.

This strong link between roles (and therefore leadership) in the family and in the church is illustrated by the strong requirements for elders (overseers) to be people who manage their own families well (1 Tim 3:4-5):

> He must manage his own family well and see that his children obey him with proper respect. (If anyone does not know how to manage his own family, how can he take care of God's church?)

Unfortunately, the West is gripped by an individualism that certainly does not put the well-being of children and the family at the top of its agenda. In the light of this it is a tremendous challenge for our time to know 'how people ought to conduct themselves in God's household, which is the church of the living God, the pillar and foundation of the truth.' (1 Tim 3:15).

This all illustrates the point mentioned above: we should always work towards a broader biblical understanding in order to determine the absolutes. Once we have established them, we can then use that framework as we make applications to the particular circumstances of our time.

CHAPTER THIRTY

How to interpret the book of Revelation

Objectives

1. To be able to exegete Revelation
2. To understand the contribution of Revelation to the broader biblical message
3. To understand the process of hermeneutics for Revelation

Contents

STUDY TIP

It may seem daunting to interpret Revelation. However, if you accept the challenge, the reward will follow, and you will be tremendously blessed by its message!

When I was in confirmation class as a teenager, our local minister, the Rev Slabbert, said to us more than once: 'When you read the newspaper, do it with your Bible next to you in order to find the biblical perspective on the news.' If this is true of the Bible in general, it is especially true of Revelation. It is a very exciting book that gives us a wonderful framework of understanding about what is happening in the world as seen from God's perspective.

Whereas in previous chapters the reader was encouraged to use commentaries only in the last step of exegesis, the case will be different here. It is strongly recommended that one makes use of a commentary while acquiring the skills of interpreting Revelation. The reason for this is that apocalyptic literature is not that easy to interpret. Although a number of good commentaries can be recommended, I want to suggest one in particular that is a pleasure to read and that does excellent exegesis (and to a certain extent hermeneutics) of Revelation. It is written by W Hendriksen (1976) with the title 'More than Conquerors'.

It was decided not to enter into an explanation of and discussion on the different theological views held on the teaching of the last days (eschatology), but to present an approach for the interpretation of Revelation that is believed not only to be scientific, but extremely helpful in applying it to our time. This will be done by discussing how to apply the principles of interpretation to Revelation and by illustrating it from a passage. Quite a bit of what is going to be said is similar to what is contained in Hendriksen's book, and the reader will find that it is in line with the principles of exegesis and hermeneutics that have already been stated in this book.

30.1 The communication situation

When reading many of the popular books on the interpretation of Revelation, one cannot be blamed for having the impression that this book is only meant for Western Christians living at the particular time that the interpretation was written. As one vision after another is applied, the impression is that Revelation did not have any message for Christians of all the previous centuries, nor for Christians from other parts of the world. In the 1970's for example, Revelation told us everything about the coming world war between the United States and the Soviet Union! But the comfortable Western Christians did not have to fear anything. Before they could suffer in the 'great persecution', God would intervene and take them with him to heaven. Just think what the unfortunate Christians who were suffering in the Communist countries at that time must have thought of the idea that their persecution was not 'great' enough for God to rescue them!

This brings us to an extremely important, and very logical principle for the interpretation of Revelation: It was written for the Christians to whom it was addressed. It is set in a particular cultural and historical setting with a message applicable to the situation and needs of its original receivers. It does have a wonderful message for us today, but this can only be applied to our situation after we have gone through the steps of exegesis in order to find the message to the original receivers.

The author identifies himself as John four times (1:1,4,9; 22:8), but it is not clear which John it was. However, it must have been a church leader with influence writing to the seven churches of Asia Minor.

The purpose of Revelation is to give comfort to the persecuted believers in their battle against demonic forces: God sees their tears (7:17; 21:4); their prayers rule the world (8:3-4); their death is precious (14:3; 20:4); their final victory is assured (15:2) and their blood will be avenged (6:9-10; 8:3-5).

The book was most probably written around the year 95 AD while the author was living in exile on the island of Patmos. The Christians had already witnessed and experienced severe persecution for their faith. The main reason for the persecution at the end of the first century, during the reign of Domitian (81-96), was the enforcement of emperor worship. Christians who refused to worship Caesar as Lord were severely persecuted.

Persecution was reality for most of the seven churches of Revelation: 2:3; 2:9-10; 2:13; 3:10. False teachers tried to deceive the churches: 2:2; 2:14-15; 2:20. The seduction that was typical of the life-style of Rome was also a temptation for churches: 2:6; 2:14-15; 2:20.

30.2 The literary context

The form of discourse used in Revelation is prose with embedded poetic parts. The major discourse type of the book is narrative and the specific genre is apocalyptic (see 19.2). Parts of it also contain exposition and exhortation. The whole book is presented in the form of a letter. We will firstly look at the letter format of the book, and then discuss the characteristics of the apocalyptic genre. After that, the overall structure of Revelation will be discussed, with the help of a brief overview of the message.

Although Revelation was written as a letter, it is not generally treated as one for the purpose of interpretation because of its apocalyptic nature. John uses the format of a letter to communicate the content of the visions that he saw. We find five of the six main elements of a letter (see 29.2) in it: After a prologue, the opening starts in 1:4; this is followed by a doxology; an introduction to the body starts in 1:9; the body begins with the seven letters in chapters 2 and 3; the conclusion of the body starts in 22:7; the closing most probably starts in 22:18.

An Old Testament book that uses the apocalyptic genre extensively, in order to show God's purposes in history, is Daniel. Apocalyptic text was popular in Jewish culture during the two centuries before and the one after Christ's birth, especially to relate world events to the coming of the day of the Lord. It was used in such a way as to present a kind of philosophy of history that could be used to understand what was happening in the world.

In addition to Dan 7-12, we also find apocalyptic text in parts of Zechariah (eg 1:7-6:8) and obviously in most of Revelation. Because it was a form of literature that was known to the recipients, it was not that difficult to understand at the time that it was used. This could be illustrated by looking at a modern parallel, as described by Beasley-Murray (1974:16-17):

> The closest modern parallel to this mode of communication is the political cartoon, which has gained an established place in the popular press all over the world. The purpose of a cartoon is to embody a message relating to a contemporary situation, whether it be of a local, national, or international import. Many of the symbols employed by cartoonists are stereotyped. Some of their representative figures are human (like John Bull and Uncle Sam), others are animal (eg, the lion for Britain, the bear for Russia, the eagle for the USA)...Now it would be overpressing the parallel to suggest that the apocalyptists were religious cartoonists, for much of their writing is not in picture form. But it would not be misleading to compare their works with writings frequently illustrated by drawings, and at times containing whole chapters of strip cartoon. The book of Revelation uses the cartoon method more consistently than any other work of this order.

The political cartoon can only really be understood by those who are familiar with the symbolism and the situation that it refers to. A political cartoon featuring Uncle Sam, a bear and a dragon at the time of the war in Vietnam, would mean nothing to a person who does not know that Uncle Sam represents the USA, the bear the USSR, and the dragon China. Similarly, Revelation can only be interpreted by discovering what the symbolism stands for and what situation it refers to. This will be further addressed in 30.3.

Revelation can be divided into seven main parts, each one covering the same part of history, but from a different perspective each time. The period of history that is covered in each part or cycle, runs from the first coming (incarnation) of Christ until his second coming when the final judgment will take place and the new heaven and earth will be established. We therefore find a structure of parallelism in the overall structure of Revelation.

Although there are differences of opinion on where each one of these parts exactly starts and ends (see Wendland (1990) for a detailed structure), it is sufficient here to indicate the boundaries of the parts according to the chapter divisions. The message of each part will be described very briefly:

Ch 1-3: Christ among the seven lampstands: Christ has a specific message for each one of the seven churches. Seven is symbolic of completeness and although applicable to the specific situation and state of each church at that time, these conditions are representative of churches in all times and therefore, the message is applicable to churches of all times.

Ch 4-7: The seven seals: Christ as the Lamb is the only one who can give meaning to history (opens the seals). In history there will be trials and persecution (the seals) for the believers.

However, the church is protected (seal on forehead) and the believers will be with Christ for all eternity.

Ch 8-11: The seven trumpets: The unbelievers are warned and punished by God in order to lead them to repentance. The church witnesses faithfully to the world in spite of the fact that it is persecuted because of its message. God judges the unbelievers and rewards the believers at the end of time.

Ch 12-14: The woman and her son persecuted by the dragon and his helpers: Satan (dragon) tries to keep Christ (child) from being born, and when he fails, attempts to destroy him. Christ overcame Satan through his death and resurrection and obtained victory for the believers. Satan concentrates on persecuting the church (woman) and calls on his three allies to help him; antichristian government and political power (beast out of the sea); false religion and philosophy (beast out of the earth); and antichristian culture and seduction (Babylon, the prostitute that is introduced here but described in chapter 17). The believers spend eternity with God and Christ, and the unbelievers are judged at the end of time.

Ch 15-16: The seven bowls: The unbelievers are judged throughout history through the same type of events that are found when the trumpets are blown as a warning (chs 8-11). However, the seven bowls also introduce the final judgment for the unbelievers, as well as for Babylon the prostitute (antichristian culture and seduction).

Ch 17-19: The fall of the prostitute and the beasts: antichristian culture and seduction (the prostitute) are introduced with the announcement of God's judgment. This is something that happens throughout history, as cultures with their accompanying economies rise and fall, one after another. However, there will also be a final judgment that will put a final end to antichristian culture (prostitute), antichristian government and false religion (the beasts).

Ch 20-22: The judgment of the dragon and the new heaven and earth: The dragon (Satan) cannot do what he wants to because he is bound, except at the end of time when he deceives the nations to oppose the believers. This sets the stage for God's final judgment over Satan and all the dead. God will create a new heaven and earth where there will be no evil, and where he will be in control of everything and will provide for the needs of everyone.

This parallel structure of the seven parts (cycles) of Revelation is supported by the following:

- The time period that is covered in each part: In each case it is the whole period, since the first coming of Christ until his second coming.
- The direct parallel references to the same time period in the third and fourth parts:
  Third part: forty-two months; 1260 days.
  Fourth part: 1260 days; a time, times and half a time (three and a half years).
- The direct parallel between the third (trumpets) and fifth (bowls) parts as far as the areas of warning and judgment are concerned: Land, sea, water, heavenly bodies, psychological agony, deception of the nations to make war, and final judgment.

Although the seven parts cover the same time period, there is progression as far as the focus is concerned. The latter parts focus progressively more on the final judgment and the new heaven and earth.

It seems that the seven parts themselves are chiastically arranged:

A	Ch 1-3:	Christ and his battling and suffering church on earth
B	Ch 4-7:	Persecution and trials of the church
C	Ch 8-11:	Unbelievers are warned and punished
D	Ch 12-14:	The church is victorious because of Christ's victory over Satan
C*	Ch 15-16:	Unbelievers are judged
B*	Ch 17-19:	Those who persecuted the church are judged
A*	Ch 20-22:	Christ and his victorious church in the new earth and heaven

This arrangement highlights the centrality of the role of Christ in the history of the world and in the well-being of his church. It also brings out the difference in emphasis between the first three parts and the last three. In the first three, the emphasis is on the suffering of the church. In the last three it is on the judgment of the church's enemies and Satan.

The example that we want to look at in this chapter is Rev 12:1-6. It is the first episode of the fourth part of the book, Rev 12-14. It links together with the next two episodes (12:7-12 and 12:13-17) to form a scene. Therefore, when preaching, it is recommended that these three episodes are used together. The three episodes relate in the following way to one another:

12:1-6: Satan tries unsuccessfully to destroy Christ who has victory over him.
12:7-12: What Christ's victory over Satan accomplishes for the church.
12:13-17: Although defeated Satan attacks the church.

30.3 Analysis of the passage

The apocalyptic genre belongs to the narrative discourse type. Many of the principles and methods of the exegesis of dramatic history (described in chapters 19-20) are also applicable to it. However, because of its distinctive character, apocalyptic passages will require an adaptation of those principles and methods. This will now be discussed and illustrated for our example, Rev 12:1-6. The example will only be done in such detail that is needed for illustrative purposes.

Step 3.1: Write out the passage in smaller units

The first step is to find out what the boundaries of the episodes are (see 20.4). As we are dealing with only one episode, as discussed under 30.2, no further discussion is required.

Step 3.2: Mark the significant meaning indicators

Let us start with the plot structure. After the introduction of the woman who is about to give birth (v1-2), the awful sight of an enormous dragon is introduced (3-4a). The setting is in place for the introduction of the problem in verse 4b: the dragon wants to devour the child as soon as it is born. The resolution follows immediately (verse 5-6): The child, who will rule all the nations, is taken up to heaven to be with God. The outcome is that the woman flees into the desert where God takes care of her.

Let us now look for any literary devices of repetition. It is easy to observe that the focus is on the woman at the beginning and also at the end of the passage. This should alert us to the possibility of a chiastic structure. There is indeed a chiastic arrangement as illustrated in figure 30.1 where the paragraph is divided into five different blocks. A and A* relate to one another as both refer to the woman, in the first case before the child was born and in the second case after the birth of the child. B focuses on the picture of the enormous dragon who is about to devour the child when it is born. B* stands in very sharp contrast to this picture with the emphasis on the real authority of the child. He is the one who will rule the nations with power and who shares God's authority. In spite of the appearances of the dragon, the child is the one with the authority and power. C is just a short remark that the woman gave birth to a son, a male child. The position of this remark within the chiastic structure serves to emphasise its importance. It is indeed the turning (pivotal) point of the episode as the tension was on the threat of the dragon to the child and the woman in the first half, while the emphasis in the second half is on the authority of the child and the protection of the woman.

The influence of the plot structure, as well as the chiasm in the message will be examined in step 3.4 ('establish the meaning structure').

FIGURE 30.1
Rev 12:1-6

1] A great and wondrous sign appeared in heaven: a woman clothed with the sun, with the moon under her feet and a crown of twelve stars on her head. 2] She was pregnant and cried out in pain as she was about to give birth.	A
3] Then another sign appeared in heaven: an enormous red dragon with seven heads and ten horns and seven crowns on his heads. 4] His tail swept a third of the stars out of the sky and flung them to the earth. The dragon stood in front of the woman who was about to give birth, so that he might devour her child the moment it was born.	B
5] She gave birth to a son, a male child,	C
who will rule all the nations with an iron sceptre. And her child was snatched up to God and to his throne.	B*
6] The woman fled into the desert to a place prepared for her by God, where she might be taken care of for 1,260 days.	A*

Step 3.3: Explain words and phrases

When one compares the episode of our example with the examples of dramatic history in Acts 20 (the Dorcas story) and in Judges 23 (Samson), it can clearly be seen how apocalyptic literature is different from dramatic history. In describing the visions, extensive use is made of symbolism and figurative language and events are sketched in cosmic terms with sharp and vivid contrasts. It certainly does not describe the acts of human beings with whom we can relate, as is the case with dramatic history.

This is the real challenge of finding the message of Revelation. What do the symbols that feature in the visions represent? What message does the complete vision communicate? As the example is discussed, some guidelines as to how to go about discovering the meaning of the symbols, will become clearer.

In general, it could be said that one should always start with the part of the overall picture that is the clearest and from there work to the more obscure and less known. Clues as to the meaning of the symbols may come from a number of sources: the passage itself, other passages in Revelation and other passages in the Bible. Obviously these pointers have to be weighed up in the light of the communication situation. The **key symbols** will now be discussed.

The child: the passage itself gives us clear indications that the child is Christ - he is male and will rule all the nations and is now at the throne of God. From the next episode in Revelation, we find a clear reference to the fact that the dragon was overcome by 'the blood of the Lamb' (12:11). From the background of the Old Testament, this vision reminds one strongly of the image given in Gen 3:15 of enmity between the woman and the serpent and the promise of the woman's offspring that will crush the serpent's head. The reference to the son 'who will rule all the nations with an iron sceptre' is taken from Ps 2:7 and has traditionally been seen as Messianic. It is also used for the rule of Jesus in Rev 19:15 and the authority that the faithful will share with Christ one day. The centrality of Christ in the destiny of the world is clearly brought out throughout the whole New Testament.

The dragon: the passage itself shows that the dragon is a major opponent of Christ. The next episode discloses the identity of the dragon in no uncertain terms as 'that ancient serpent called the devil, or Satan...'(12:9). The dragon is therefore described in the same terms as the serpent in Gen 3, and refers to the devil. From the New Testament, in particular the Gospels, one clearly discovers the devil as the furious enemy of Christ. He tried to have Jesus killed as a baby, tempted him and was involved in the crucifixion (Lk 22:3).

The woman: the passage itself shows that the woman was going to give birth to Christ and that she stays on earth after Christ's ascension. From another passage in Revelation, two episodes further (12:13-17), we see Satan aiming all his fury against the woman and her offspring as 'those who obey God's commandments and hold to the testimony of Jesus'. The woman in chapter 12 is in clear contrast to the great prostitute of chapters 17-18. When one interprets the role of the woman against the background of Gen 3:15, it becomes clear that she represents those from the Old Testament who expected the birth of the Messiah, and those who after his birth followed him. In other words, the believing community in the Old Testament and the church in the New Testament. The importance of the role of the church in the New Testament supports this interpretation.

In finding the meaning of these symbols and indeed of the whole episode, it is important not to be bogged down by the detail of the symbols but to discover the main concepts which they represent and the central idea of the message communicated by their interaction. For example, from our above discussion it became clear that the woman represents the believers in the Old and New Testament. The meaning of the details of the woman symbol, eg 'clothed with the sun', 'with the moon under her feet' and 'a crown of twelve stars on her head' is not as clear. Because these details serve to highlight the main concept of the symbol, it does not make a real difference to the central meaning whether one interprets the twelve stars as referring to the twelve tribes of Israel or as a symbol of the fact that the woman is victorious. Both these possibilities are in any case included in the vision as the faithful from the OT came mainly from the twelve tribes of Israel and the woman was certainly victorious, or else Christ would not have been born.

Our example is no exception in the use of symbolism from the Old Testament, as there are numerous examples of this in Revelation. For example, of the description of the Son of Man in Rev 1 (Dan 7:9ff; 10:5; 6; Ezek 1:7, 26ff; 43:2), the throne set in heaven in Rev 4 (Is 6:1; Ezek 1:26,28) and the two witnesses of Rev 11 (Zech 4:2ff). Hendriksen (1967:61) gives a whole list of passages which, 'at least as far as their form is concerned, are patterned after and rooted in what is found in the OT'. One can assume that the original recipients of Revelation were familiar with the symbolism that comes from the Old Testament. This is a great help for us in interpreting Revelation as we share this familiarity with the Old Testament.

However, in each case where symbolism is used, we need to make sure that we understand the symbolism in its particular context. When symbolism from the Old Testament is used it should be remembered that the author of Revelation employs it in a particular context with a particular message that can only be established from the passage itself. This is also true for a symbol used in more than one place in Revelation.

Step 3.4: Establish the meaning structure
With this step, the findings of the previous steps have to be brought together to find the message of the passage. Therefore, it is important not to summarise the narrative, but to find what it communicates, namely the meaning of the symbolism of all the complete pictures.

The structure proves very helpful in finding the message of the passage. We will now summarise the message of each one of the different blocks in this chiastic structure. This can only be done in the light of the findings of step 3.3 (explain words and phrases).

Block A:	Christ was going to be born from the faithful of the OT according to the promise of Gen 3:15.
Block B:	Throughout history Satan tried to hinder Christ's birth and to destroy him.
Block C:	Christ was born.
Block B*:	Christ has all authority as he shares God's authority.
Block A*:	The church is looked after by God for the whole period until Christ comes again.

Step 3.5: Conclude and summarise the message
The relationship between the different meaning blocks must now be taken into consideration and also the message that this must have had for the original recipients. This is done as follows:

The birth (incarnation) of Christ was promised to the believers of the OT. Throughout history Satan tried to prevent this and to destroy Christ when he was born. His birth did take place and he has all authority as he shares God's authority. For the believer it means that he can feel encouraged, as Christ has the real authority and looks after his church until he comes again.

Let us reflect, for a moment, on the method of exegesis. The method that we followed actually has elements from both the methods of dramatic history and exposition. It is narrative as far as the analysis of the plot structure is concerned. However, as far as the meaning of the symbols and their interaction is concerned, they represent a message and therefore the message of each block could be summarised in a similar way to exposition. It is different from dramatic history, where one has to draw conclusions from the behaviour of people and through that arrive at the message as the participants themselves do not symbolise a meaning.

This illustrates that it will always be necessary to fine-tune one's method of exegesis according to the specific characteristics of a particular passage. In order to do so, the following requirements have to be met:

- Have a good understanding of the principles and methods of the exegesis of exposition and exhortation, poetry and narrative (dramatic history);

- Have a good understanding of the characteristics of the specific genre that a passage is written in.

30.4 The broader biblical framework

The message of Revelation is not about the prediction of specific events, but about God's rule (through Christ) of the church and of the world. We therefore find an exciting message that is in line with the message of the rest of the Bible. This is the ultimate test of one's exegesis of Revelation: Is the message consistent with that of the rest of the Bible?

30.5 Hermeneutics

The message of Revelation is not only consistent with the rest of the Bible, but it also makes a number of significant contributions to the message of Scripture, not least in giving us a helpful philosophy with which to view and interpret history. One thinks, for example, of the three enemies of the church that are introduced in ch 12-14. Satan makes use of the help of antichristian governments and political powers, false religion and philosophies, and seductive lifestyle. As one studies the histories of the church and of countries, all three of these forces are found in interaction.

We do not only find a philosophy of history in Revelation, but also a framework for a better understanding of individual events. The same calamity could serve for some people as a trial (seals of ch 4-7), for others as a warning (trumpets of ch 8-11), and still for others as judgment (bowls of ch 15-16). Therefore, it helps the Christian to make sense of the world, so that he can faithfully and confidently serve Christ within it. We will not always be able to accurately interpret individual events, but we are given an understanding of God's purposes in history. Above all we have comfort and challenge of knowing that Christ is in charge.

With the wonderful philosophy of history that Revelation presents, it is most exciting to apply it to current events in the church and in the world. For example, in so many cases in history, it is very easy to see how evil governments are supported by false religion (and philosophy) to justify their actions. These two are often accompanied by an immoral and seductive lifestyle. It would be very exciting if more Christians were able to see world events from this perspective and indeed read the newspaper and watch the news with their Bibles next to them.

APPENDICES

APPENDIX A

The different types of relationships

Appendix to chapter eleven

Objectives

1. To know what type of relationships can be expressed in language
2. To be able to identify the relationships between and within units of language

Contents

STUDY TIP

A list of almost all relationships that can be found, is given in this appendix. It can serve to help with steps 3.2, 3.3 and 3.4 where relationships have to be established.

The same type of semantic relationships found between the main parts of a single sentence, can be found in all structural levels of language. In other words, the same type of relationships can apply between clauses, sentences, paragraphs, sections and even chapters. For example, reason could be expressed within a single sentence: 'Because it rained hard, he could not come.' That same relation can also be expressed between the two sentences of a paragraph: 'It rained hard. He could not come.'

In some cases, sentences do not relate as full sentences to one another, but one relates to a word in the other one, eg 'John kicks the ball. The ball is red.' The second sentence relates to the first one as a description of one of its elements, namely the 'ball'.

In other cases, groups of sentences could relate to another sentence or group of sentences: 'John kicked the ball. He kicked it hard. He wanted to score a goal.' The first two sentences relate together. The second one describes how the event of the first one was done. The third one relates to the first two, in that it gives the purpose (to score a goal) for them. It could be indicated as follows:

John kicks the ball.
He kicked it hard.
He wanted to score a goal.

How should one establish the relationships between sentences or linguistic elements that are related? The surface structure should be taken into consideration and sometimes it provides real clues (eg 'because' in the example 'because it rained hard, he could not come'). In other cases the surface structure is not clear, eg in the case of the two sentences: 'It rained hard. He could not come.' This is made even more complex by the fact that one form of surface structure can express different relationships, and one relation can be expressed by different surface structures.

The key is that in addition to the surface structure, the main evidence is to be found in the content of the related units. This content is always determined by the context, and therefore, it has to be seen in the context of the paragraph that in turn should be seen in the light of the context of the whole document (step 2 of exegesis) and the communication situation (step 1 of exegesis).

The relationships used on all levels of language can be defined and grouped in different ways and are sometimes known by different terms. In this chapter the relationships will be grouped and discussed in such a manner as to make it as easy as possible to understand and establish in the text. Callow (1989) has largely been followed in these groupings (although not always and sometimes by different terms).

All semantic relationships can be divided into three broad categories: those with time in focus, those with causality as basis and those that are descriptive.

The first two categories of relationships, time and causality, carry the message forward. The descriptive category dwells for a moment on a thought and expands or emphasises it (Callow 1989:136, 149). The first two could be compared to a road on which you drive from one place to another along the line of either time or causality. The descriptive relationships then are like the filling stations, restaurants and picnic areas along the road.

The relationships can be between elements with two events in focus, with an event and attribute in focus or with two attributes in focus.

Between events: The boy eats because his mum told him to do so
Between event and attribute: He plays while the dog is wet
Between attributes: She is clean while he is dirty

Any number of events or attributes could be involved, eg two reasons could be given for a specific event:

Because it rained hard and he was tired, he did not go for a walk.

In the following description of different types of relationships, reference will be made to only one element (with an event or attribute in focus) that is related to one other element (with either an event or attribute in focus). This is done with the understanding that multiple events or attributes could actually be related simultaneously (as in the last example). Each event or attribute involved in a relationship will be called an 'element', so as to avoid referring to 'an element with an event (attribute) in focus' every time.

In step 3.2, mark the significant meaning indicators, we have to establish the relationships between different elements. However, at this stage it does not have to be done for each relation, but only for those between the syntactic units (see 11.7). When it is very difficult to find out what the relationship is, it could be left as all the relationships will be established in the end under step 3.5. There are three reasons why one may not be able to actually make a final decision at this stage:

Firstly, it may be that a sentence, or part of it, contains events that are written as nouns. This could lead to a further number of relationships within that specific part, eg the phrase 'baptism of repentance' that we looked at under 7.2. It can be recast as 'turn away from your sins and be baptised', in which case it will be necessary to find out what the relationships are between 'turn away from your sins' and 'and be baptised'. This we will only be able to do after the following step of text analysis, step 3.3 (explain difficult words and phrases), has been completed.

Secondly, the nature of the relationships may be obscured by the language of the literal translation on which we are working. This will be found frequently, especially with the New Testament epistles. The reason being that the Greek words that are used to connect sentence, clauses and phrases are not always that easy to translate because of the variety of relationships that could be expressed by the same word. Remember that we have said earlier in this part that in order to establish the relationships we have to take the content of the related units in consideration in addition to the surface structure. In many cases it is only when the whole structure of the paragraph is established under step 3.4 that a decision could be made about the semantic relationships.

Thirdly, it must be remembered that the meaning of a paragraph is also determined by its structure. For example, in a chiastic or parallel structure the repetition could be to explain or give the reason for the first statements. Only through a careful analysis of the structure will one be able to discover that.

1. Relationships with time as basis

In relationships with time in focus, elements are related to one another within the framework of time. It is not that the time of a specific event is given, (that will fall into the category of description), but that the elements are co-ordinately related to one another in the framework of time.

Callow (1989:137) points out that causal relationships are actually also related to one another in time. The other way around the relationships of time are also related causally. This is because in our overall view of our world we see all the events and attributes in it as being related in time and cause. All events and attributes in the world could be ranked on a time scale where every one takes place or exists before, after or simultaneously with others. At the same time, all events and attributes are caused by preceding ones and in turn cause others that follow them.

Nevertheless, in our minds we distinguish between the relationhips of time and causality. In some cases we are interested in the chronological relationship, while the causal relationship is less important (if present in the relation between the specific related units). In other cases we are interested in the causal relationship while the chronological relationship is very far in the background. It depends which one is foremost in the communication.

Relationships with time in focus can express the following:

1.1 Simultaneity

This is when one element happens at the same time as the other, eg

While John kicked the ball, his sister baked a cake.

1.2 Sequence

This is when one element has happened before the other one, eg

John kicked the ball after he had done his homework.

2. Relationships with causality as basis

As with all types of relationships, each one of those with causality as basis could be expressed by a great number of different surface structures and in any order.

In some cases where causality is the basis, it is not in focus. In such cases other relationships are in the foreground. Nevertheless, for the sake of simplicity such relationships will also be grouped in this category of causality.

Relationships with causality as basis (not necessarily in focus) can express the following:

2.1 Reason

In this case, one element provides the reason for the other one. However, the element that causes the other one to take place, had no intention of doing so, eg

It rained and therefore John could not play football.

The fact that it rained caused John to not be able to play football. In this example, the first element is the reason for the second (the result) to take place. However, it was not by any intention to cause John not to play football, that it rained.

2.2 Means

In this case, one element also provides the reason for the other one. The difference is that the one (the means) that causes the other one to take place intended to do so, eg

Because his father encouraged him, John played football.

The fact that his father encouraged him, caused John to play football. In this example the first element thus is the means for the second (the result) to take place. The fact that John played football was the result of his father's encouragement (the means).

2.3 Purpose

In this case, one element expresses the purpose for the other one to take place. The purpose is not stated as fulfilled, eg

John bought himself a pair of boots **so that he could play football**.

The fact that he intended to play football, caused John to buy himself a pair of boots. In this example the second element thus presents the purpose that led to the first one to take place. The first one in turn is the means that may make it possible for the second one to take place.

In the element that expresses the purpose, there is always the possibility that it could not be successfully accomplished. If that factor of uncertainty is not present, then the type of relation changes. If we were to take this same example and remove the element of uncertainty, then it does not express purpose any more, eg 'John bought himself a pair of boots so that (with the result that) he played football.' In this example, the fact that he bought the boots is the means for the result that he played football.

2.4 Condition "If"

In this case a causative relation is present, but with the factor of envisaging added.

Communication sometimes involves envisaging, that is, referring to an event or state that has not yet happened at the moment of communication, but that could still happen. An example is referring to an event in the future. It has not yet happened, but it may happen, eg 'John will kick the ball.'

In the case of a relation where condition is expressed, the fulfilling of the one envisaged relation is the condition for the other envisaged relation to take place. It means that the one event envisaged will only take place if the other one takes place, as there is a causative relation between the two, eg

(only) **If John gets his boots in time**, he will play football.

In this example there is a link of causality between the two events. It is only if John gets his boots in time that he will play football.

The relationships of causality underlying a conditional relation could be that of reason, means or purpose:

Reason:
If it rains John will not play football.
Means:
If John's father encourages him, he will play football.
Purpose:
If John buys himself a pair of boots, he might play football.

2.5 Contra-expectation "Although"

In this case, one would normally envisage that one element would cause a specific other element to take place. However, not the expected response takes place, but one contrary to expectation. In English the word 'although' is frequently used to express this relationship, eg

Although John was injured, **he played football**.

In this example one would have expected John not to play football because of his injury. However, contrary to what one would have envisaged, he did play football.

2.6 Alternation

In this case it would be envisaged that either one or the other element occurs. The causal relation between the two elements is that both cannot occur, but that if one occurs the other one will not, eg

John plays either football or base ball.

The factor of envisaging is present because it is not known which one he does. At the same time the causal relation between the elements is that if he does one, he doesn't do the other.

2.7 Conclusion

In this case, one element is known to be true and the other one is the conclusion that the communicator makes on the basis of the first one. The one that is known to be true forms the grounds for the conclusion of that stated in the other one, eg

John must like football, he plays regularly.

In this example, it is known that John plays football regularly. From that grounds it is deduced that he likes football. The causal relation functions in the sense that the communicator draws a logical conclusion from the one relation that is known to be true.

3. Descriptive relationships

With the previous two main groupings of relationships, time and causality, we find that the message is moved forward, either with the focus on time or on causality. The descriptive relationships are quite different. Their purpose is not to carry the message forward, but to expand on it or in some other way make sure that the communication is understood clearly. Usually the framework of any message will be based on relationships of time or causality and the descriptive relationships will be interwoven. The exception is where bare facts are related without causative and time relationships.

Relationships with description in focus can express the following:

3.1 Specification

In this case, the time, place, manner and/or circumstance of an element is specified, eg 'John will play in the match **tomorrow**' (specifying time). The specification of things can also take place, eg 'John kicks the **red** ball' (specifying ball).

This same relation can also exist between two sentence units where one provides more information about an aspect of the other one. That can happen by repeating the content of the first, and then adding some additional information:

John will play in the match. He will play tomorrow.

In this case the second element provides the time that the first one takes place.

The content of the first can also be assumed and then some additional information added:

John will play in the match. It will be tomorrow.

The place could be specified:

John will play in **London**.

The manner could be specified:

John played **well**.

The circumstances could be specified:

John played **while it was raining**.

3.2 Comparison

In comparative relationships, a thing or event is described by comparing it with another one, eg

John kicks the ball harder than Jack.

In this example the event of how John kicks the ball is compared to how Jack does it. It actually describes how John kicks the ball, namely harder than Jack. An example of a comparison in which a thing is described, is the following:

This ball is heavier than the other one.

In the various types of illustrations a comparison is also involved, as the illustration forms the basis for the comparison. In the following example my hunger is compared to that of a horse:

I was as hungry as a horse.

3.3 Contrast

Contrasts are comparisons, but the point of comparison is connected to a negation, eg

This ball is heavy, but that one is light.

One ball is compared to the other one, but they are not compared as sharing the same point of comparison, namely their degree of heaviness (as in the example of 14.3.2). They are compared from a position where their weights are contrasted, heavy and light.

3.4 Equivalence

In equivalence relationships, one element says virtually the same as the previous one, but in a different way, eg

John played a good game. He played well.

In the strictest sense of the word, we do not have description here, but repetition of the same meaning. It could serve different purposes, like emphasising the point, raising the tension, slowing down the tempo, etc.

3.5 Classification

In a relation of classification, the elements stand in a generic-specific or in a specific-generic relation.

In a generic-specific relation the general statement that includes every thing that follows, is mentioned first and the specific one(s) that could be included in the first one, is mentioned afterwards:

John made all the preparations for the match: he bought a new pair of boots, exercised regularly and worked on his motivation.

In a specific-generic relation the specific element(s) is mentioned first and the general one is mentioned last:

John kicked accurately, defended well, and scored two goals: he played well.

Key concepts in the Gospels

Appendix to chapter twenty seven

A short discussion of some of the key concepts found in the Gospels will now follow.

MESSIAH

This is a Hebrew word which means "the anointed one", the Greek equivalent is 'Christ'.

1. Usage in the Old Testament

In the Old Testament, this word was used to describe someone called to a godly ministry. It is used for the nation of Israel (Hab 3:13), the king of Israel (1 Sam 24:10, 2 Sam 1:14, 1 Sam 9:16, 2 Sam 19:21, Ps 2:2), perhaps for prophets (1 Kgs 19:16), for priests (Lev 4:3) and for a Gentile king who God used for a specific task (Is 45:1).

Over a period of time this term obtained a special meaning and was used for the ideal King that God would anoint to free his people and govern them justly.

The Jews started believing that an earthly kingship would introduce future salvation for them.

For the people of Israel, this produced a Messiah expectation which probably originated in 2 Sam 7:16. This expectation was further strengthened by passages such as Is 9:1-7, Ps 89 and Zech 9:9.

The inter-testamental period literature eg Apocalypse of Ezra, Baruch, Psalms of Solomon, etc does not have a uniform idea about who the Messiah is.

2. Usage in the New Testament

In the New Testament, the idea of a coming Messiah is linked to the coming of the Kingdom.

The Jewish expectation, however, was very nationalistic and Davidic - linking the Messiah strongly to the house of David.

Throughout the Gospels, Jesus does not accept or reject the title 'Son of David' from others but he strongly rejected the idea of a political kingship and a sonship/brotherhood which was natural and physical - his Kingdom is not of this world.

Jesus knew that he was the Messiah. Evidence of this is found in Lk 2:49 where Jesus calls the temple his father's house, in Lk 4:18-21 (cf Is 61:1-2) where Jesus announces that Scripture is fulfilled and in Mt 16:16 when Jesus acknowledges Peter's Messiah confession. The temptation was also an attack on the Messiahship of Jesus (Lk 4:1-13). Other references can be found in Lk 19:38 (cf Zech 9:9) and Mk 14:61. Jesus was hesitant to accept this title because he knew that he had to suffer (Mt 20:28).

THE SUFFERING SERVANT

1. Usage in the Old Testament

References to the suffering servant are found in Is 42:1-4; 49:1-7; 50:4-11 and 52:13-53:12. In the book of Isaiah, this term is used to refer to a whole group (people of Israel) as in Is 49:3, a remnant of God's people (Is 10:20-23) and an individual (Jesus) who is then also a representative of the first two.

The suffering servant completes his work through total obedience which involves suffering.

2. Usage in the New Testament

2.1 Jesus referring to his suffering: Mk 8:31; 9:31; 10:33,38; 14:8; Lk 12:50; 22:37 cf Is 53:12. Heb 5:8 also confirms the suffering aspect of Jesus' ministry.

2.2 Referring to his representative work

Jesus is the servant of all (Mt 20:26-28) and he suffers (death) for many in order to re-establish a covenant - see Mk 10:45; 14:24; Lk 22:20; Mt 26:28; Heb 2:14-18.

3.Conclusion

Judaism did connect the suffering servant (Ebed Yahweh) with the Messiah, but not that it would be a voluntary atonement for others.

By suffering for many and by restoring a New Covenant, Jesus takes the task of the suffering servant but not the title.

SON OF GOD

This term was known in ancient oriental religions and especially used for kings.

1. Usage in the Old Testament

It was used for the nation (Hos 11:1; Ex 4:22), the king (2 Sam 7:14; Ps 89:26) and the Messiah (Ps 2:7). The Old Testament and Jewish concept was of someone elected to participate in divine work through carrying out a particular commission in strict obedience to the God who elects. Originally, the reference in Ps 2:7 was for the king of Israel, but in the time of Jesus it was interpreted as Messianic, eg Mt 16:16.

2. Usage in the New Testament

In the Gospels, the title is used by Jesus and others.

2.1 Others

In the following verses the term Son of God is closely linked with the Messiah, Mk 3:11; 5:7; 14:61; 15:39; Mt 4:3,6.

2.2 Jesus

Jesus is conscious of his unique relationship with God as his Father, especially emphasised in John's Gospel - Jn 1:18; 10:15,30,38; 12:50 (always 'my' or 'your' Father, but only once 'our' Father - Lk 11:2. See also Mk 14:36; Lk 2:49; 10:22

SON OF MAN

Jesus' most common title for himself, used 81 times in the Gospels and never used by anyone else. He even replaces the Messiah title with 'Son of Man' - Mk 8:29,31; 14:61-62. It seems that the early church did not use this title as a Messianic one (except Acts 7:56). Mark especially understands the significance that Jesus attaches to this title.

1. Usage in the Old Testament

It was used with the meaning of man as a human - Ezekiel and Ps 8:4. This however is not Jesus' use of the term.

Over against this is the use of the term in Dan 7:13,14 in connection with the nation of God - the Son of Man is head and representative of the nation, an everlasting kingdom, the suffering of the nation (people) of God (Dan 7:21,22,25) and judgment that will free God's people.

This person described in Daniel could be seen as a Messianic figure (described in the parables of Enoch in the Apocrypha).

2. Usage in the New Testament

In the synoptics, the term is used in connection with the earthly task of Jesus where he has the power to forgive sins (Mt 9:6; Mk 2:10; Lk 5:24) and where he is Lord of the Sabbath (Mt 12:8; Mk 2:28; Lk 6:5). The term also refers to the suffering and resurrection of Jesus (Mt 16:27; 17:12,22-23; 20:18; Mk 8:31; 9:12,31; 10:33,45; Lk 9:22,44; 18:31) and to his second coming (Mt 24:30; 26:64; Mk 8:38; 13:26; 14:62).

3. Conclusion

- The title 'Son of Man' was probably known but was not a popular name for the Messiah
- Jesus knew of the wrong Messianic expectations and so discouraged people from making him known as such
- The real meaning of the Messiah became known through the title 'Son of Man' - it speaks of glory (Dan 7:13 cf Rev 1:13; 14:14) but also of suffering (Is 53).
- The titles 'Suffering Servant' and 'Son of Man' existed in Judaism but Jesus combined these two concepts.

THE KINGDOM OF GOD

1. Characteristics of the kingdom (New Testament)

1.1 Theocentric

This means that God is in the centre - God's kingdom starts through himself, is built and sustained by him. God's kingdom is a gift to believers (Lk 12:32) and we must accept the kingdom as children (Mk 10:15) and through repentance (Mk 1:15).

1.2 Dynamic

The kingdom is not just a territorial concept, but one meaning "reign" or "rule" (Mt 3:2; 4:17; Lk 21:31; Mk 1:15). The coming of the kingdom causes action (Mt 1; Lk 2; Mt 4:3-11; Mk 1:24; Mt 12:29; Lk 10:18), and is in the person of Jesus (Mt 13:2; 18:23; 21:33; 22:1; 25:14) and therefore also through the Messiah. God's kingdom is one of peace (Mt 26:29; Lk 14:15), order (Mk 5.19; Lk 11:11) and a certain attitude (Lk 9:62; Mk 7:7-8; 12:34). If we choose to enter this kingdom of God, we have to make certain choices to live by new standards and principles.

1.3 Time element
God's kingdom is relevant to the present time, to the here and now (Mk 1:15; Lk 4:18-21; 11:20; 10:9; 16:16; 17:21; Mt 21:31). But it also has a strong future element. The coming of the kingdom of God in Christ, is the beginning of the end and John the Baptist tells of a future judgment (Mt 3:7-12) which will be carried out by Jesus as the Son of Man (Jn 5:27). The teaching and preaching of Jesus also emphasises these elements (Mt 6:10; 7:21; 8:11,12; 13:43,49; 16:28; 19:29; 25:34; 26:29; Mk 9:1; Lk 20:36).

2. Differences between the present and future kingdom

2.1 Present - has a gradual development
Future - has a catastrophic element

2.2 Present - filters through in the lives of people - not always visible (Lk 17:20-21)
Future - will come with visible manifestation

2.3 Present - it is not perfect
Future - it will be totally perfect

The main reason why many of the Jews could/would not accept Jesus was that they expected an earthly kingdom which would be for Israel only - a kingdom where they would be free from all oppression, sickness, poverty, etc.

'THE SECRET OF BELONGING TO THE KINGDOM LIES IN BELONGING TO HIM'

Answers to exercises

Suggested answers are provided only where the answers are not contained in the chapter.

CHAPTER FIVE

2. There are many differences but some of the obvious ones are that the GNB has shorter sentences, uses words that are easier to understand as well as clearer grammar.

3.

NIV	Living Bible
She who is in Babylon	The church here in Rome
chosen together with you	she is your sister in the Lord

CHAPTER SEVEN

1 and 2. There are many examples that can be found in the Bible. If you are uncertain about the answer to these questions, return again to the content of this chapter.

CHAPTER EIGHT

1. Information on the communication situation of Philemon:
Paul is a prisoner (v1)
Timothy is with him (v1)
The letter is to Philemon who Paul sees as a friend and fellow-worker (v1)
The letter is also addressed to Apphia and a 'fellow-soldier', Archippus and the church which meets in Philemon's house (v2)
Although it has a wider audience, Paul specifically addresses Philemon from verse 4 and onwards
Paul hopes to visit Philemon soon (v22)
Epaphras is a fellow-prisoner (v23)
There are other fellow-workers with Paul, namely Mark, Aristarchus, Demas and Luke (v25)

2. Information in other Bible books can be found as follows:
Timothy: Paul's letters to Timothy and references to him in his other letters; Acts 16:1 and further references in Acts.
Archippus: Col 4:17
Epaphras: Col 1:7, 4:3,12
Aristarchus: Col 4:10
Mark: Col 4:10, Acts 12:25, 15:38-39
Demas: Col 4:14, 2Tim 4:10
Luke: Col 4:14, Gospel of Luke, Acts 16:10-17, 20:5-21:18, 27:1-28

3. Purpose of the letter and problems addressed:
Onesimus was a slave in the service of Philemon. It appears he had stolen from Philemon and ran away (v18). On the basis of Philemon's love for others (v5,7), Paul asks Philemon to accept Onesimus back as a brother (v16) because he has now become a Christian (v10) and has served Paul (v11). Moreover, Paul wants reconciliation between Onesimus and Philemon (v14,15) and for this reason is sending Onesimus back to Philemon (12).

CHAPTER TEN

2. An example follows of how Col 3:5-11 can be written out in smaller units :

1 5] Put to death, therefore,
2 whatever belongs to your earthly nature:

3 sexual immorality,
4 impurity,
5 lust,
6 evil desires
7 and greed,
8 which is idolatry.
9 6] Because of these, the wrath of God is coming.
10 7] You used to walk in these ways,
11 in the life you once lived.
12 8] But now you must rid yourselves
13 of all such things as these:
14 anger,
15 rage,
16 malice,
17 slander,
18 and filthy language from your lips.
19 9] Do not lie to each other,
20 since you have taken off your old self with its practices
21 10] and have put on the new self,
22 which is being renewed in knowledge
23 in the image of its Creator.
24 11] Here there is no Greek or Jew,
25 circumcised or uncircumcised,
26 barbarian,
27 Scythian,
28 slave or free,
29 but Christ is all, and is in all.

CHAPTER ELEVEN

1. Meaning indicators of Col 3:5-11 marked. The marking on the passage is first shown and then discussed:

1 5] Put to death, therefore,
++++++++
2 whatever belongs to your earthly nature:
vvvvvvvvvvvvv ^ vvvvvvvvv
3 sexual immorality,
>>>>>>>>>>>>>>
4 impurity,
>>>>>>
5 lust,
>>>
6 evil desires
>>>>>>>>
7 and greed,
<<<<
8 which is idolatry.
<<<<
9 6] Because of these, the wrath of God is coming.
vvv ≡

10 7] You used to walk in these ways,
∧ vvvvvv
11 in the life you once lived.
/// ∧ /////////////
12 8] But now you must rid yourselves
∧ ++++++++
13 of all such things as these:
vvvvvvvvvvvvv
14 anger,
•
15 rage,
•
16 malice,
⊂
17 slander,
⊂
18 and filthy language from your lips.
⊆⊆⊆⊆⊆⊆⊆ ∧
19 9] Do not lie to each other,
⊆
20 since you have taken off your old self with its practices
∧ ≈≈≈≈≈≈ ∧ //////// /// vvvvv
21 10] and have put on the new self,
≈≈≈≈ xxxxx
22 which is being renewed in knowledge
xxxx
23 in the image of its Creator.
× ====
24 11] Here there is no Greek or Jew,
A B
25 circumcised or uncircumcised,
B A
26 barbarian,
C
27 Scythian,
C
28 slave or free,
D E
29 but Christ is all, and is in all.
=== ⊕ ⊕

Discussion:
you: Paul uses only 'you' and not 'us' in this paragraph
God: Two references to God the Father: 'God' in L9 and 'Creator' in L23
Christ: one reference to Christ at the end of the paragraph (L29)
put to death (L1): this has the same meaning as 'rid yourselves' in L12. Both are commands and both mean to put an end to some activity
sexual immorality (L3): refers to sexual sins together with 'impurity', 'lust' and 'evil desires'. The last two sins have the emphasis on desires to sin
all (L29): the same word but with different meanings
taken off (L20): contrasted with 'put on' (L21)

life once lived (L11): the same meaning as 'old self' (L20). Both these references are to the sinful existence or character that characterised their behaviour before they became Christians. In contrast to that God gave them a new character or existence (new self) when they became Christians
anger (L14): very similar in meaning to 'rage'
malice (L16): just like 'slander' directed against others
filthy language (L18): related to 'lie' in referring to verbal sins
new self (L21): also referred to in L22 and L23. Used in contrast to the concept expressed by 'earthly nature' in its various forms in this paragraph
whatever belongs to your earthly nature (L2): also found in L9, L10, L13, L20. It refers to sins. The specific sins in each case will depend on where it is found in the paragraph
greed (L7): referred to in L8
Greek (L24): used with 'Jew' in L24 and then repeated in L25 in reverse order where 'circumcised' refers to Jew and 'uncircumcised' to Greek
barbarian (L26): used with 'Scythian' in L27. Scythians represented the ultimate in being a barbarian
slave (L28): used with 'free' with which it is contrasted

CHAPTER TWELVE

Meanings of the words and phrases of Col 3:5-11 explained:
Numbers in square brackets are references to Louw and Nida (1988)
put to death: get rid of completely
therefore: because of what has been said in the previous paragraph
whatever belongs to your earthly nature: activities that you do because of the influence of your sinful nature
sexual immorality: to engage in any kind of unlawful (sinful) sexual intercourse [88.271]
impurity: state of moral impurity, especially in relationship to sexual sin [88.261]
lust: sinful sexual desires and passion [25.30]
evil desires: sinful sexual desires [25.20]
Explanation: This could refer to sinful desires in general or if read together with the previous three sins, it can refer to sinful sexual desires. If it refers to sexual desires, it is very similar in meaning to 'lust'.
and greed: strong desire to possess more things than other people have, irrespective of need [25.22]
which is idolatry: to be greedy is just like serving idols
because of these: because of these sins (as just listed)
the wrath of God is coming: God is going to punish (those who do these sins)
you used to walk in these ways: you used to do these sins (those just listed)
in the life you once lived: when your lives were characterised by this kind of behaviour (when you used to act in that manner)
but now you must rid yourselves of: but in contrast (to the old lifestyle) get rid of
all such things as these: all activities like the following
anger: to be angry with anyone [88.173]
rage: to have passionate outbursts of anger [88.178]
malice: to have hateful feelings against others [88.199]
slander: to speak against someone in such a way as to harm or injure his or her reputation [33.400]
and filthy language from your lips: speaking in an obscene, shameful way [33.33]
do not lie to each other: do not tell lies to each other
since you have taken off your old self: because you have stopped having an old character (old way of living)

with its practices: with the sins that accompanied it
and have put on the new self: and have a new character (a new way of living)
which is being renewed: this new character (person) is constantly caused by God to act more and more (in the image of its Creator)
in knowledge: in order to cause you to know him completely (this should be read at the end of the sentence as it gives the result of the new character that is constantly caused to act more and more as God wants it to act)
in the image of its Creator: as God does who created you with this new character
Here there is no: because of this new creation (new character) it does not matter whether a person is (it is not important whether)
Greek or Jew: a Gentile or a Jew
circumcised or uncircumcised: a Jew or a non-Jew
barbarian: a person who speaks a strange language
Scythian: an uncivilised person
Explanation: Scythians were originally from what is today the south of the Commonwealth of Independent States (old USSR). The historian Josephus said of them that they were little better than wild beasts.
slave or free: a slave or a free person
but Christ is all: Christ is all that matters
and is in all: and he is in all (those who are created by God with a new character)

CHAPTER THIRTEEN (see next page)

CHAPTER FOURTEEN

The Colossian Christians must not commit sexual sins, be greedy, become angry, have hateful feelings against others, speak against others to harm their reputation, speak in an obscene way, or lie to one another. They don't have their old character anymore. Should they persist in sin, God will punish them. God gave them a new character and God is constantly causing them to act as he does. By doing so (acting as he is acting) they come to know God better. People get the new character, not because of their human status, but because of their relationship with God through Christ.

Discussion:

Paul is very specific in his exhortations that they should not sin - he mentions specific sins that they need to watch out for. With that, he is not saying that these are the only sins that they need to watch out for, but we can assume that these sins were very specific temptations for the Colossians. Perhaps he had heard that some of them were actually involved in these sins.

The emphasis on the fact that they should make sure that they do not sin, is in line with the description of spirituality in 3:1-4. This is in contrast to the view of the gnostics for whom it was not important to stop sinning, but whose aim was to live 'spiritual lives' that would free them from matter.

Paul stresses the fact that God did something in the lives of the Colossians in the past - they have left their old lives (characters) behind and have been given new lives. This stresses the fact that God made them new.

The fact that there are not differences between Christians from different backgrounds comes out very clearly at the end of the paragraph. The relationship with Christ is all that matters. The centrality and supremacy of Christ is highlighted.

CHAPTER THIRTEEN

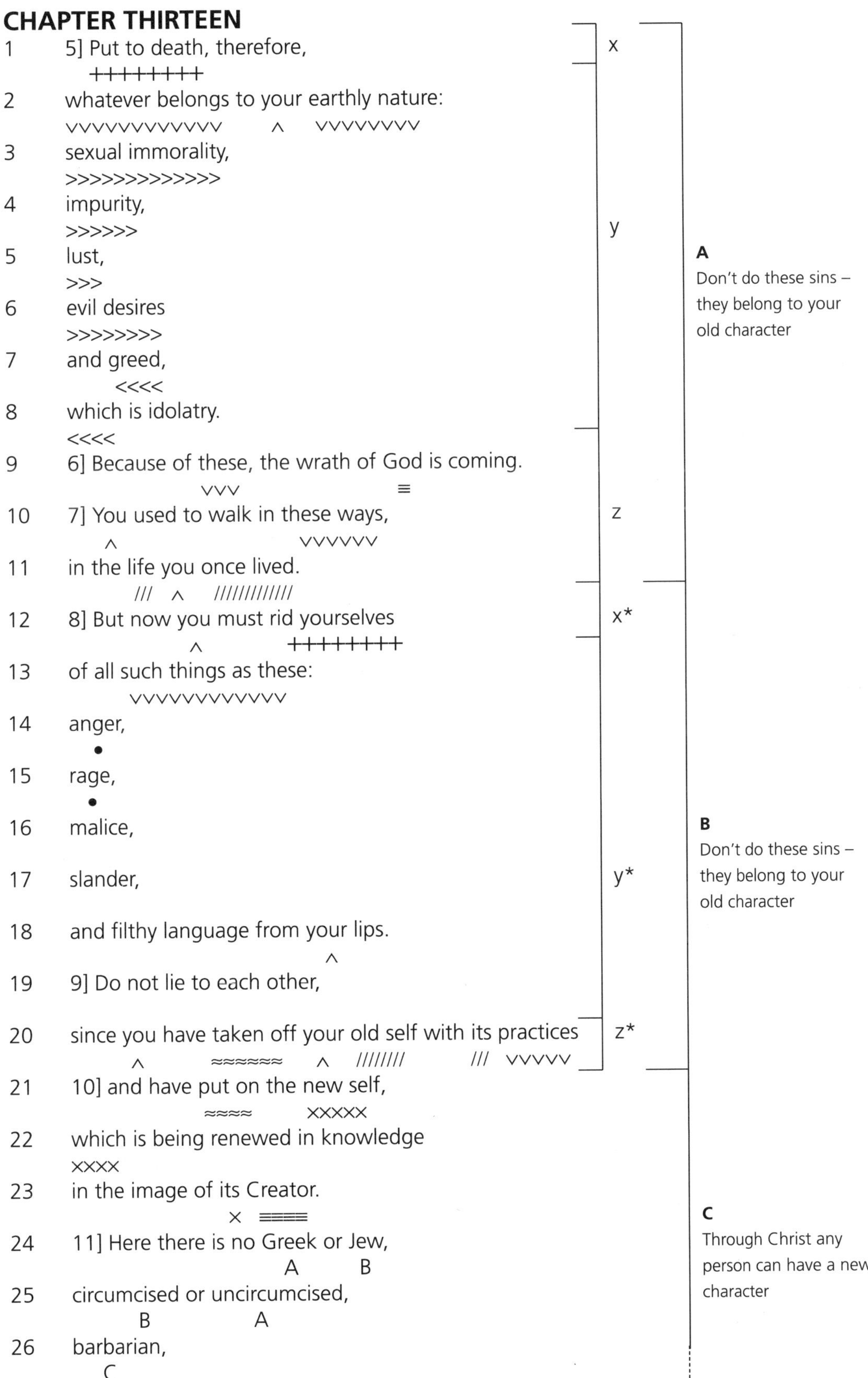

1 5] Put to death, therefore,
++++++++
2 whatever belongs to your earthly nature:
vvvvvvvvvvvvv ^ vvvvvvvvv
3 sexual immorality,
>>>>>>>>>>>>>
4 impurity,
>>>>>>
5 lust,
>>>
6 evil desires
>>>>>>>>
7 and greed,
<<<<
8 which is idolatry.
<<<<
9 6] Because of these, the wrath of God is coming.
vvv ≡
10 7] You used to walk in these ways,
^ vvvvvv
11 in the life you once lived.
/// ^ /////////////
12 8] But now you must rid yourselves
^ ++++++++
13 of all such things as these:
vvvvvvvvvvvvv
14 anger,
•
15 rage,
•
16 malice,
17 slander,
18 and filthy language from your lips.
^
19 9] Do not lie to each other,
20 since you have taken off your old self with its practices
^ ≈≈≈≈≈≈ ^ //////// /// vvvvv
21 10] and have put on the new self,
≈≈≈≈ xxxxx
22 which is being renewed in knowledge
xxxx
23 in the image of its Creator.
× ≡≡≡≡
24 11] Here there is no Greek or Jew,
A B
25 circumcised or uncircumcised,
B A
26 barbarian,
C

27 Scythian,
C
28 slave or free,
D E
29 but Christ is all, and is in all.
=== ⊕ ⊕

The paragraph consists of three main parts of which the first two are very similar in meaning and structure:

A & B: Start with an exhortation to get rid of (x) a number of sins (y). These sins used to characterise their old way of living (z).

C: In contrast to the old way of living they now have a new way of living (character) that was created by God. This new character is given to anyone, independent of his human status, because of Christ.

Discussion:
The decision about the structure of this paragraph is greatly determined by the pattern of repetition with the x, y and z motives repeated in the same sequence (parallelism) in parts A and B. In the first two parts the emphasis is on the exhortation to get rid of certain sins in their lives. They need to do so because God will punish people who don't (A) and these sins characterised their old character (A & B).

The third part (C) latches on to the motive of the old character by referring to the contrasting new character that they have. As far as the new character is concerned, it makes a few statements:

- God gave the Colossian believers their new characters
- God is constantly causing them to act more and more as he (God) acts
- By acting more and more as God wants them to, they come to know God better
- People get the new character not because of their human status but because of their relationship with Christ

CHAPTER FIFTEEN

1. Some other passages in the Bible which have a similar message as the one found in Col 3:5-11 are the following:

Eph 4:22-5:7, Rom 6:1-14, Jas1:19-21, 1 Pet 2:1, 2 Cor 5:17

CHAPTER SEVENTEEN

1. Similar parallelism is found in Ps 147 in all the verses and between all three the lines of verse 8.

2. Contrasting parallelism is found in the following verses of Prov 14-15:
Prov 14: 1-6, 8, 9, 11, 12, 15, 16, 18, 20-25, 28-32, 34, 35.
Prov 15: 1, 2, 4-9, 13-22, 25-29, 32.

3. For the metaphor, 'But you are a shield around me, O LORD'.
- the topic is — what God does for me
- the illustration is — a shield
- the point of similarity is — protection in danger

Non-figurative equivalent: God protects me in danger

For the metaphor, 'the tongue also is a fire'
- the topic is — what we say
- the illustration is — a fire
- the point of similarity is — destructive

Non-figurative equivalent: what we say can be destructive

For the metaphor, '"I am the gate"'.
- the topic is — what Jesus does
- the illustration is — a gate
- the point of similarity is — providing a way

Non-figurative equivalent: Jesus is the means to salvation

4. For the simile, 'we all, like sheep, have gone astray'.
- the topic is — disobedience of people
- the illustration is — sheep
- the point of similarity is — going own way

Non-figurative equivalent: we all disobeyed God in our own way

For the simile, 'he was led like a lamb to the slaughter'
- the topic is — how Jesus was killed
- the illustration is — lamb
- the point of similarity is — not resisting

Non-figurative equivalent: Jesus was killed without any resistance from his side

For the simile, 'I will bring them together like sheep in a pen, like a flock in its pasture'
- the topic is — what God does for the remnant of Israel
- the illustration is — sheep
- the point of similarity is — cared for

Non-figurative equivalent: God cares for the remnant of Israel

5. The hyperboles mean the following:
Acts 19:27: The meaning is that Artemis is widely worshipped in the known world.
Num 13:27: The meaning is that the land is very fruitful.

6. Wisdom is personified as a noble woman.

7. The simile in the first two lines appeals to our senses as we can visualise the grass and the flowers. On the emotive level, the comparison of our own lives with grass and flowers helps us to realise how fleeting life can be.

CHAPTER NINETEEN

1. Events are mentioned in sequence (time line/chronological framework).
Non-prescriptive (no specific instructions are given to the reader).

2. All three examples are part of the narrative discourse type.
4a. Parable
4b. Dramatic History
4c. Apocalyptic text
4d. Allegorical parable (Amaziah is compared with the thistle and thus with insignificance and weakness; his request identified with the thistle's request and thus with arrogance; Jehoash with a cedar and thus with power, etc. It makes one point, namely 'don't over estimate your significance and power'.
5. Because the genre makes a significant contribution to our exegetical approach and understanding of a passage. A wrong identification of the genre can lead to a wrong understanding of the message.
6. Because the author wants to arouse and keep the reader's interest.
7. See figure 19.3
8. It highlights what events the author has selected and what he considers the most significant elements in the story. Thus he provides clues to help us understand his purpose better.
9. No
10. **setting:** 'As Peter travelled about the country, he went to visit the saints in Lydda'
problem: 'a paralytic who had been bedridden for eight years'
resolution: 'Immediately Aeneas got up'
outcome: 'All those who lived in Lydda and Sharon saw him and turned to the Lord'
The writer emphasises his purpose by selecting and writing about a specific outcome to the solution of the problem. Thus we may summarise his purpose as follows: Just as people in Lydda and Sharon believed in Christ when they saw this miracle so should the reader believe on the basis of my account of it.
11. It means that there are no direct and specific instructions addressed to the reader.
12. (1) It is non-prescriptive.
(2) There is no direct, personal relationship between the writer and the original receiver.
(3) The writer does not directly and specifically address the reader.
(4) Dramatic history is generally about people and events of the past.
13. He or she has to decide or conclude what the story teaches. This means that the **mental process of conclusion** is required.
14. Episode
15.
- The episode can be conceptualised 'After Peter prays, Aeneas is healed'.
- Its place and purpose in the overall structure: It is the beginning of a new thought block in Acts focusing on the activities of Peter and in particular setting the stage for his dealings with the Gentiles. It is an episode which fits into the plan-execution framework of Acts as the plan set out in 1:8 'be my witnesses' is being fulfilled through Peter's witness.
- The previous verse (31) is one of the major summary statements indicating a break in the flow of thought.
- There is a change of location from Jerusalem to Lydda marking the beginning of the episode.
- There is a shift of location from Lydda to Joppa marking the break between this and the next episode.
- Paul leaves the scene and Peter is now the main character.
- The episode goes through the complete problem-resolution cycle.

Bibliography

Aharoni, Y. & Avi-Yonah, M. 1968. **The Macmillan Bible Atlas** Revised Edition. New York: Macmillan.

Bailey, Kenneth, E. 1976. **Poet and peasant**. Grand Rapids, Michigan: William B. Eerdmans Publishing Company.

Bailey, Kenneth, E. 1980. **Through peasant eyes**. Grand Rapids, Michigan: William B. Eerdmans Publishing Company.

Barnwell, K. 1980. **Introduction to semantics and translation**. Horsleys Green: Summer Institute of Linguistics.

Barnwell, K. 1984. **Introduction to semantics and translation**. SIL: High Wycombe.

Barnwell, K. 1986. **Bible translation - An introductory course in translation principles**. Dallas: Summer Institute of Linguistics.

Barr, J. 1969. **The semantics of biblical language**. Oxford: Oxford University Press.

Beasley-Murray, G.R. 1974. **The book of Revelation**. London: Oliphants.

Beekman, J. & Callow J. 1978. **Translating the word of God**, (Fourth edition). Grand Rapids: Zondervan.

Beekman, J. & Callow, J. 1989. **Translating the word of God**. Michigan: Zondervan Bible Publishers.

Beekman, J., Callow, J. & Kopesec, M. 1981. **The semantic structure of written communication**. Dallas: Summer Institute of Linguistics.

Bliese, L.F. 1990. **Structural marked peak in Psalms 1-24** in OPTAT (Occasional Papers in Translation and Textlinguistics). Vol 4, Number 4, 265 -321.

Blood, D.L. & Blood, D.E. 1979. **Notes on translation no. 74 overview of Acts**. Dallas: Summer Institute of Linguistics.

Bruce, F.F. 1982. **New Testament History**. Basingstoke: Pickering & Inglis.

Bruce, F.F. 1988. **The book of the Acts** (Revised Edition). Grand Rapids: Eerdmans.

Burden, J.J. 1986. **"Poetic text" in Words from Afar (eds)**. Deist F & Voster W, Tafelberg: Cape Town.

Caird, G.B. 1988. **The language and imagery of the Bible**. London: Duckworth.

Callow, K. 1974. **Discourse considerations in translating the word of God**. Grand Rapids: Zondervan.

Callow, K. 1989. **Man and message**. Notes to students.

Carson, D. A. 1989. **Exegetical fallacies**. Grand Rapids: Baker Book House.

Collins Cobuild Essential English dictionary. 1989. London and Glasgow: Collins

Cotterell, P. & Turner, M. 1989. **Linguistics & biblical interpretation**. London: SPCK.

Craigie, P.C. 1986. **Word biblical commentary no. 19**. London: Word Publishing.

Cundall, A.E. & Morris, L. 1968, **Judges and Ruth**, Tyndale Old Testament Commentaries. Leicester: Inter Varsity Press.

De Waard, J. & Smalley, W. A. 1979. **A translator's handbook on the book of Amos**. New York: United Bible Societies.

Drane, J. 1994. **Evangelism for a New Age - Creating churches for the next century**. London: Marshall Pickering.

Drane, J. 1986. **Introducing the New Testament**. Oxford, Batavia, Sydney: Lion Publishing.

Du Toit, A.B. 1992. Chapter one. **The Pauline letters - Orientational Remarks** in Guide to the New Testament. Volume 5 The Pauline Letters: Introduction and Theology. Pretoria: N.G.Kerkboekhandel (Edms) Bpk.

Dumbrell, W. 1988, **The faith of Israel**. Leicester: Apollos.

Fee, G.D. & Stuart, D. 1988. **How to read the Bible for all its worth**. London: Scripture Union.

Fee, G.D. 1991. **Gospel and Spirit - Issues in New Testament hermeneutics**. Massachusetts: Hendrickson

Gooding, D. 1987. **According to Luke - a new exposition of the Third Gospel**. Leicester, England: Inter-Varsity Press.

Gooding, D. 1990. **True to the faith - A fresh approach to the Acts of the Apostles**. London: Hodder & Stoughton.

Graber, P.L. 1990. **A textlinguistic approach to understanding Psalm 88** in OPTAT (Occasional Papers in Translation and Textlinguistics). Vol 4, Number 4, 322-339.

Graber, P.L. 1990. **The structural meaning of Psalm 113** in OPTAT (Occasional Papers in Translation and Textlinguistics). Vol 4, Number 4, 340-352.

Harris, H. 1990. The Tubingen School. **A historical and theological investigation of the school of F.C. Baur**. Leicester: Apollos (pub).

Harrison, R.K. 1969. **Introduction to the Old Testament**. Grand Rapids: Eerdmans.

Harrison, R.K. 1970. **Old Testament Times**. (reprinted 1982) Michigan: Eerdmans.

Heim, Knut M. 1993. **Coreferentiality structure and context in Proverbs 10:1-5**. Journal of Translation and Textlinguistics, vol 6, no 3, pp 183-209.

Hendriksen, W. 1976. **More than conquerors**. Grand Rapids: Baker Book House.

(The) International Standard Bible Encyclopedia (Fully revised edition). Grand Rapids: Eerdmans.

Kaiser, W.C. Jr. 1981. **Toward an exegetical theology**. Grand Rapids: Baker Book House.

Kaiser, W.C. 1993. **The journey isn't over**. Michigan: Baker Book House.

Loader, J.A. 1979. **Polar structures in the book of Qoholet**. Berlin, New York: Walter de Gruyter.

Loader, J.A. 1986. **Ecclesiastes - A practical commentary**. Grand Rapids: William B. Eerdmans.

Louw, J.P. 1982. **Semantics of New Testament Greek**. Philadelphia: Fortress Press.

Louw, J.P. 1985. **What dictionaries are like, in lexicography and translation**. Edited by J.P. Louw. Cape Town: Bible Society of South Africa. p. 53-81.

Louw, J.P. 1987. **A semantic discourse analysis of Romans**. Pretoria: University of Pretoria. Vol 2.

Louw, J.P. & Nida, E.A. (Ed). 1988. **Greek-English Lexicon of the New Testament**. **Based on Semantic domains.** New York: United Bible Societies. Vol. 1&2.

New Bible dictionary. 1988. Leicester: Inter-varsity Press.

New dictionary of theology. 1988. Leicester: Inter Varsity Press.

New international version Study Bible. 1985. London: Hodder and Stoughton.

Newman, B.M. & Nida, E.A. 1972. **A translator's handbook on the Acts of the apostles**. New York: United Bible Societies.

Nida, E.A. & Taber, C.R. 1974. **The theory and practice of translation**. Leiden: Brill.

Nida, E.A., Louw, J.P., Snyman, A.H. & Cronje, J.v.W. 1983. **Style and discourse**. Cape Town: Bible Society of South Africa.

Parker, J.I. et al. 1982. **The World of the New Testament**. Alton: Window Books.

Peacock, H.F. 1992. **A translator's guide to selections from the first five books of the Old Testament**. London, New York, Stuttgart: United Bible Societies.

Ridderbos, H. 1975. **Paul An outline of his theology** Grand Rapids: William B. Eerdmans Publishing Company.

(The) Shepherd scale: Separating the sheep from the goats, by R.L. Basset, R.D. Sadler, E.E. Kobischen, D.M. Skiff, I.J. Merrill, B.J. Atwater and P.W. Livermore. 1981. Journal of Psychology and Theology, Vol. 9, 335-351.

Stek, J. 1884. **Introduction to Psalms in the NIV Study Bible**. Michigan: Zondervan Bible Publishers.

Stott, J.R.W. 1990. **The message of Acts**. Leicester: Inter Varsity Press.

Taylor, R. 1987. **The Prisoner and other stories**. MARC Europe.

Van Leeuwen, Raymond C. 1988. **Context and meaning in Proverbs 25-27**. Georgia: Scholars Press Atlanta.

Von Rad, G. 1984. **Genesis**. London: SCM Press.

Wendland, Ernst R. 1990. 7X7(X7) **A structural and thematic outline of John's apocalypse** in OPTAT (Occasional Papers in Translation and Textlinguistics). Vol 4, Number 4, 1990, 371-387.

Whybray, R.N. 1994. **The composition of the book of Proverbs**. Sheffield: JSOT Press.

Whybray, R.N. 1995. **The book of Proverbs—A survey of modern study**. Leiden, New York, Koln: E.J.Brill

Wolvaardt, B.P. 1984. **'n Toets vir die meting van geloofsbetrokkenheid**. Unpublished doctoral thesis. University of South Africa.